Intern with Visual FoxPro® 6.0

Rick Strahl

Hentzenwerke Publishing

Published by:
Hentzenwerke Publishing
980 East Circle Drive
Whitefish Bay, WI 53217

Hentzenwerke Publishing books are available through booksellers and directly from the
publisher. Contact Hentzenwerke Publishing at:
414.332.9876
414.332.9463 (fax) or
www.hentzenwerke.com

Internet Applications with Visual FoxPro 6.0
By Rick Strahl
        Technical Editor: Gary DeWitt
        Copy Editor: Jeana Randell

ISBN: 0-96550-939-7

Manufactured in the United States of America

I want to dedicate this book to the Microsoft Visual FoxPro team for all their efforts in building and maintaining such a powerful development tool. Even in the face of adversity, this product continues to kick butt, allowing developers like myself to build amazing applications with ease without sacrificing power. I, like many of you, I suspect, have benefited tremendously from the power of this product, and I want to thank the team for continuing to pour their creative resources into this tool. Thanks, guys (and gals)!

And don't ever let a Dilbert-head tell you that it can't be done with the Fox!!!

Table of Contents

CHAPTER 5: FoxISAPI   107

Chapter 8: Remote Data Service   271

SECTION 4—Enterprise Development   299

Chapter 9: Visual FoxPro and COM   301

Chapter 11: The Development Process   359

Chapter 12: Loose Ends   375

Acknowledgements

Writing a book always seems to be more work when you're actually doing it, than before or after the job's in process. I'd like to thank the following people who have helped make the work easier and worthwhile:

Most importantly I want to thank Whil Hentzen and Hentzenwerke for putting out the book and the entire Visual FoxPro series. Good books that deal with specific topics for a particular tool are rare, and this series captures the essence of very specific technical books well. Gotta thank Whil for seeing the wisdom in that. I also want to thank Jeana Randell and Gary DeWitt for an excellent job editing the book.

Steven Black also made an 'unofficial' editing appearance, and I thank him for his thoughtful comments on the scalability chapters. Ken Levy got me out of a bind on a few topics and bugs with Internet Explorer. He also helped with the short XML section of the book and provided valuable feedback on various ideas I had during the course of writing. Randy Brown I have to thank for frequent heads-up on what's supposed to work and what doesn't. And of course, Calvin Hsia for making me figure out my own COM coding issues (just kidding). Thanks to Markus Egger for, well, being Markus—his feedback has been very valuable on a variety of coding issues. Rod Paddock also was kind enough to provide a short review of Cold Fusion for this book. I also want to thank Randy Pearson for his support over the years and of course for his CodeBlock tool, without which a number of things I've been doing would not have been possible.

Finally, I want to thank some of my friends who've been wondering what the heck I've been doing 'inside' the house so much: Morgan V.I.G.G.E.R.S. who has fallen and can't reach his adrenaline drug—glad you caught it good this year on your weekend schedule. Tim and Layne, who probably can't wait to come back to Maui—the sharks don't bite, Layne! Mike White, who'll pace a hole in the ground waiting for the swell to come up at Davenport—start investing in the Ho'okipa fund for next year! C.K. from the Warehouse (when are you getting your butt over here?) for providing the gear when it breaks. It may be a good thing when it does—some work actually gets done while bones and epoxy heal. Glenn Phillips and Dan Bubb at Gorge Net and Solution Engineering in Hood River for putting up with my server. Andy 'Andyboy' Anderson for the celebrity impersonation phone calls at 2 a.m. Mom and even Dad, because I have to. And last but not least, the 10:30 p.m. reruns of *Seinfeld* for keeping me straight on what's really important.

Mahalo to all of you!

Foreword

In the last couple of years, there has been a tremendous increase in the number of Visual FoxPro developers building Web applications. One of the people we have to thank for this is Rick Strahl. Rick has been at the forefront of marrying Visual FoxPro to the Web. His articles and conference talks, as well as his West-Wind Web Connection, have been invaluable in making Web development easier for Visual FoxPro developers.

West-Wind Web Connection has proven to be a powerful and easy-to-use tool for building Web applications with Visual FoxPro. It has been used by several of the finalists in the Best Web Site category of the Visual FoxPro Excellence Awards (both this year and last year), as well as the Surplus Direct site, our extremely popular Visual FoxPro Web site case study, which was developed and documented by Rick.

I can think of no one more qualified to write this book than Rick. He knows Web technologies inside and out and knows how to apply them to Visual FoxPro (and vice versa). He has proven time and again that he not only knows how to do this stuff for real, but he also knows how to explain to others how to do it. That is a very valuable combination.

I hope you enjoy this book and that it helps you build better and more powerful Web applications with Visual FoxPro.

Robert Green
Visual FoxPro Product Manager
Microsoft Corp.

Section 1
Internet Technologies

The Internet has tremendously affected the way we build applications and how we think about information in general. We've seen an incredible boom in information being published on the Web, and database application development is a key feature in this connected world.

The first section of this book introduces Internet technologies and terminology, and tells you what you need to get started. The technology that drives the Internet is very exciting but also somewhat overwhelming at first, because of the many related and distributed pieces that make it work. These first chapters are meant to ease you into the distributed mindset if you are new to Internet development. These chapters review the basic concepts of why you might write an Internet-enabled application as opposed to a standalone application.

Chapter 1 introduces the author and the layout of the book, followed by an overview of why Internet technologies are important for developers as well as for application functionality. Chapter 2 dives straight into an overview of how the Internet works by providing information flow and a few examples that describe how data moves from the client to the server and back. The discussion starts with a basic overview and then drills into the details, so even if you have done previous Internet development you might find some useful ideas here. This chapter also briefly discusses issues such as scalability and server-based environments to get you thinking along these lines right from the start of your development efforts. (These issues are followed up in Section 3 of the book, which includes an in-depth discussion of scalability.) Chapter 3 takes you through the software requirements and configuration of Internet Information Server.

Once you've worked through Section 1, you'll have the background to tackle the actual development tools to start building Internet applications.

Chapter 1
Introduction

Welcome to *Internet Applications with Visual FoxPro*. If this is your first experience with Web development, read on to find out what you'll learn. If you're a seasoned Web developer, be ready to find out a few new tricks and tips, and explore some advanced issues of Web development with Visual FoxPro that you might not have thought about.

This book follows a logical format for making it easy to learn with, as well as providing a reference that you can use to look up specific issues by topic after you've read through individual chapters. This introduction discusses how the book is laid out and identifies the high-level topics. It also lets you know what you should be familiar with before diving in. Finally, this chapter introduces some of the motivations behind Web development, and some thoughts on the advantages and disadvantages that come with this new development platform.

Who should read this book

This book is geared toward the very specific topic of building Web applications with Visual FoxPro. As such, it makes a few assumptions about the reader's understanding of Visual FoxPro. This book is an intermediate text in terms of knowledge expected of Visual FoxPro. I won't spend a lot of time discussing FoxPro commands or structures unless there's some special or unconventional use for them in the context of the discussion. I will discuss advanced topics, especially in Section 4, *Enterprise Development*, but these topics are mostly isolated or are introduced when the prerequisite topics have been discussed in the prior text.

This book begins with the assumption that the reader has never built an Internet application, so you *will* find detailed discussions of the technologies and how they tie together the client and server sides of the Internet platform. We'll start with the very basics and work up into the more advanced topics. You'll see basic examples that demonstrate how each tool applies to Visual FoxPro and more complex scenarios that show how this stuff applies to real-world application development.

 And yes, there will be lots of code shown in short snippets. Extensive examples or tool code might be referenced to code available from the Developer's Download Files at www.hentzenwerke.com, but I've tried to keep most of the relevant code inside the text to keep you in the context of the discussion. Paragraphs marked with this "web" icon indicate that you can download the referenced application or tool from www.hentzenwerke.com. Future updates of these tools will be available from my Web site, www.west-wind.com.

How this book works

This book is laid out in sections that group together various related topics. Each section includes a short introduction and general terminology that you should understand before looking at the specific technologies covered in the individual chapters.

The chapters discuss in detail the Internet technology or tool and how to apply it to Visual FoxPro. I start with simple examples that show the mechanics and then, wherever possible, advance into short sample applications that demonstrate the technology and how it applies in the context of an application.

Most chapters also contain notes (marked with this icon) about what to watch out for. Much of Internet technology in use today is far from perfect and there are a number of gotchas that you need to be aware of. I've tried to point out as many of these as possible to save you time when building your own applications.

Tips—marked with this "information" icon—include ideas for shortcuts, or alternate ways of accomplishing tasks that can make your life easier or save time. Finally, each chapter contains a short summary and a list of Pros and Cons that highlight what works and what doesn't.

Each section closes by reviewing the individual tools and technologies, and making suggestions about which work best in a given scenario. These are only suggestions, of course, but they should give you a good starting point to understand what to look for when choosing your tool for a particular application.

What we'll cover

Internet and Web development is a large topic, and this book crams a lot of information into its pages. I hope you will find useful some of my experiences that are summed up in these pages so they will save you time on your way to building your own Web applications.

In this book I focus on the development technologies available to Visual FoxPro developers. Chapter 2, which discusses Internet application technologies, briefly touches on some other avenues such as Java, ActiveX controls and writing straight CGI or ISAPI code. But other than that, the discussion centers around Visual FoxPro-driven designs.

There's detailed discussion of server-side technology using scripting with Active Server Pages, and Visual FoxPro server-driven development with FoxISAPI. Whether you're building pure server-driven applications that only work with plain HTML, or distributed applications that mix both client- and server-side tools, the server side will most likely be part of any Web solution that you build.

Server-side applications continue to be the mainstay of Web application development, but client-side development is becoming more popular. In client-side development, applications running on the individual users' machines communicate with servers using the Internet as the network. In this section I'll show you some of the fat and medium client technologies that make it possible to build applications that may not use HTML at all for Web development. You'll see examples of a Visual FoxPro client application talking to a Visual FoxPro server application over the Internet using HTTP, as well as technologies such as RDS running queries over the Web from Visual FoxPro client applications. We'll also look at how COM will extend its reach to the Internet to make it possible to activate objects on the server over HTTP.

The final section of the book deals with building large-scale Web applications and some of the issues of making Visual FoxPro work well in this environment. The focus here is on server development and how to build applications that can withstand the pounding of a popular commercial Web site. Building these types of applications requires a different mindset and a thorough understanding of how Visual FoxPro works with the Component Object Model

(COM). You'll find out about Visual FoxPro 6.0's new Apartment Model Threading and how you can work with Microsoft Transaction Server. You'll also find out about some limitations you'll face with Visual FoxPro and some ways to work around them.

This section also deals with performance tuning, server and application configuration, application and data performance, choice of data engine (Fox or SQL database), testing for load, and balancing load in truly large-scale applications that require multiple machines to run. In this section you'll also find information on the development process for commercial Web applications, which involves dealing with teams of people with very different skill sets. Discussions include topics such as integrating code and HTML and graphics, as well as dealing with source control and the actual administration process involved in getting applications online without causing significant downtime.

What you need to work through the book

Because this is a Visual FoxPro book, first you need a copy of Visual FoxPro 6.0. Most of the code presented here will work with version 5.0, but the code shown is tested and built with version 6.0, and no guarantee is made that it will work elsewhere.

This is a book about Web development, so there are a few things beyond Visual FoxPro required. I'm going to focus on Microsoft technology—here's a list of the major tools that I'm using while putting this book together:

- Windows NT 4.0 Server with the NT Option Pack installed
- Internet Information Server 4.0 (IIS)
- Internet Explorer 4.0 (IE)
- ActiveX Data Objects 2.0 and Remote Data Service 1.5

I also recommend you get hold of a copy of Visual InterDev 6.0 or Visual Studio. While not required, it is definitely *the* tool for working with Active Server Pages applications, which are discussed in Chapter 4.

I'm running all of my development and deployment on NT Server. You can use Personal Web Server on NT Workstation and Windows 95 as well. However, note that Chapter 3 addresses features specific to the IIS version. I would recommend you stay away from Windows 95/98 as even a development platform for Web development. It works, but the PWS95 Web server is rather unstable, unpredictable and very unconfigurable under Win95/98. If you're planning to build serious Web applications, now is a good time to consider moving to NT for your development environment. Don't even think about running a live Web server for deployment under Windows 95. Besides the legal licensing issues, this is not a stable environment to host a live application.

This is a book about Microsoft technologies. Although a number of the tools will work with other Web servers, it's beyond the scope of this book to point out which and why. This doesn't necessarily mean that you need Microsoft tools on the client (IE in particular), but it does mean that you should have a Microsoft server. In regards to interface display, the text points out which technologies are specific to IE and which can be viewed with any browser.

What you should know about me

My company has been building Web applications and tools for over three years now, and I've used all of the tools in this book in real applications. Some work better than others, and I'll try to point out what didn't work well and why. Some of these observations are subjective and based on my own preferences. I'll discuss those in the deliberately subjective chapter and section wrap-ups.

You also have to understand that I'm primarily using a tool for Web development that is not going to be covered in this book. My company's West Wind Web Connection is what I use on my site and what I've used for most of the large-scale Web applications I have built over the years. Some of the techniques discussed in this book come directly from Web Connection's libraries or support tools. The application we'll look at in Chapter 10 uses Web Connection, but the topics presented will be just as relevant to Active Server Pages or FoxISAPI. While Web Connection is one of the most widely used tools for Fox Web development in the Fox community, I didn't think it appropriate to include coverage in this book because of my obvious bias. If you want to find out more, go to my Web site at www.west-wind.com and check it out there. The same goes for other third-party tools that are not covered here.

That said, keep in mind that I do use most of the other technologies either in parts of my Web Connection applications, or in some cases for full sites I have developed. But I have a definite preference when it comes to the type of back-end tool that I want to use. As you read some of the notes, sidebars, and especially the Pros and Cons sections, keep this in mind and interpret it accordingly.

Is the Web in your future?

Building applications that are integrated with Internet technology and can connect databases to Web sites is likely becoming an important aspect of your software development future, if it hasn't become so already. We're just at the beginning of the move toward *Active* Web content, and while we'll surely see improvements in the tools available down the line, applications built with Visual FoxPro can provide extraordinary power, versatility and speed using standard PC hardware to drive high-powered Web sites today.

Commercial Internet development is exploding

People are flocking to the Internet and the World Wide Web by the millions. Because of both the hype and the actual traffic, the Internet is an exploding market as businesses are trying to integrate it into their existing business strategies. Electronic commerce is just starting to shed its infancy jitters to become a major market force for businesses. Consumer confidence in security and general reliability in Internet merchants is finally reaching acceptable and rapidly growing levels. Only a year ago it was rare to find people buying stuff online; now sites such as Amazon.com, online music stores and other electronics shops are commonly used to purchase online. Forecasts for electronic commerce have the market more than doubling for the next few years, and if the current growth is any indication, these forecasts are going to turn out on the very conservative side.

But it's not just large-scale commerce on the Web—even small businesses can hook into the Internet as a tool for doing business as well as promoting business. Just about any traditional business can benefit from being online and providing information about the services and products available. And the best part is that they can afford to do it! While getting online is not free, it can be accomplished relatively cheaply. Renting space on an ISP's Web server and running basic data applications can cost under $200 a month for small, low-bandwidth applications, which is cheap enough for even small Mom and Pop shops. Bigger applications that consume lots of bandwidth and require full-scale development obviously can get expensive to build and maintain, but this is no different from any other custom-built solution. Developers have plenty of opportunities to build packaged, vertical Web solutions for businesses to bring down the high cost of custom development.

Beyond the commercial Web sites for public consumption is the even bigger need for companies to build internal, *intranet* applications that can take advantage of Internet technology. Intranet development is becoming popular also because of the potentially lowered administration costs of server-centric, three-tier development that is common for Internet applications. Intranet development focuses on the same technologies used for public Internet applications, but is applied in a more controlled environment: either over a local network, or over a closed-off section of the Internet that's guarded by security measures to keep out external visitors (often called an *extranet*). Intranet applications often have more flexibility in what tools or which browser can be used because the company can dictate the rules by policy. In addition, intranet applications often have more bandwidth available because they frequently run on the same network that is used for file access or other standard network applications. The big payoff for intranet applications comes in distributing applications quickly to the entire company, and maintaining them centrally where updates are managed in one place instead of on everybody's desktop.

The move to develop the active Web

With this growth in demand comes the need to build these applications for the Internet, or extend existing ones. There is tremendous demand for developers who can build the dynamic content necessary for truly useful, distributed business applications that can run over the open Internet or the local intranet. *Active* database applications are in high demand.

Database applications are the key to building active Internet applications. Until recently, static content via plain HTML pages has been standard fare on the World Wide Web. However, for conveying lots of information, the static HTML concept falls apart quickly and becomes a maintenance nightmare. The true potential of the Web lies in giving users access to data that is always up to date, and allowing them to see only what they choose to look at by filtering and querying the data to display only small, appropriately sized chunks at a time.

Hey, that sounds exactly like what you've been doing for years in stand-alone applications! You're right—the basics of writing applications do not change with the Web. Only the presentation and plumbing changes. The bottom line: Although the Web is a very different development platform, the core knowledge for building intelligent applications doesn't change. Good design continues to be the most important aspect of development, and if you've built smart applications that separate the user interface (UI) from the business logic, the move to the Internet and distributed applications and servers should be smooth. Learning the basic Web technology is not that difficult, especially if you take some time to dive right in with some of the tools to get a little hands-on experience. You'll be surprised how much you can accomplish rather quickly without understanding every aspect of the technology beforehand. I found the most important thing is to have an open mind and not try too hard to mimic behavior of an existing GUI application onto the Web. Some things are simply easier to implement on the Web, while others are next to impossible if you stick to the traditional GUI-based application mindset. The Web is all about simplified interfaces in exchange for a distributed platform—take advantage of it!

Why build a Web application?

By now you're probably asking, "Why is he telling me all of this?" After all, you probably bought this book because you're sold on Internet technology or at least on finding out more about it, right? Well, I think it's crucial to understand why the Web is with us today and why it is an important environment for us as developers. Most importantly, the technology brought on by the Internet explosion is taking us a few huge steps toward building distributed applications that can increase the reach of your applications to a global scale if you choose. But at the same time, it's taking us a few steps back in terms of the development process, which gets a bit more complex and takes away some of the flexibility you may be used to from building Windows GUI applications. I'll start by pointing out some of the strengths and weaknesses of Web-based application development.

Advantages of building Web applications

There are certainly many pros to Web development. Following are the most important ones as they relate to database application development.

Distribute widely, administer centrally

The Internet's most appealing aspect can be summed up in a single word: Reach. With the Internet it's possible to build truly distributed applications. And for the first time it's possible to do it economically, even for small businesses that in the past may not have had a chance to provide widespread public access. In the past, building distributed applications was reserved for large corporations that could afford proprietary networks and WANs or large phone banks to connect users from spread-out locations. The Internet has become the great equalizer, and it's now possible for most small businesses to put up a Web site that provides even database connectivity at a reasonable cost.

Companies are also building applications that utilize the Internet as a giant network. Although HTML is the biggest focus, distributed applications that transmit raw data or communicate between a client application and server are making the Internet the ultimate client/server network.

The Internet provides the following:

- **Easy access from any network connection**
  Web applications are accessible from any network connection using TCP/IP. As long as the network is not locked off intentionally with security measures, you can access the same application from anywhere within your company or even from the outside when you're on the road. Global connectivity is no more complicated than connecting your neighbor across the hall. Enormous reach at reasonable cost.

- **Applications maintained in one place**
  Although the application can be run from any network connection, the server is centrally located and maintained. The application can be updated in one place, and all clients automatically see the update next time the application runs. The application also does not need to be installed on the client in any way—no making sure all the DLLs are available, nor does the client run an EXE file directly over the network. No more making sure the guy on the 20th floor who went home early for the weekend and locked his office is out of the App before you can update the EXE). All the "thin client" needs is a compatible Web browser.

   Keep in mind that if you start mixing a thin client-server solution with fat client (running a full VFP or VB application on the user's machine) or medium client (running ActiveX controls or Java applets) you are negating some of the low-maintenance benefits. The more client-side code you introduce, the more maintenance is required. However, most distributed fat or medium client applications tend to rely heavily on business logic on the server, so the clients tend to be more stable in terms of updates.

- **Clear separation of client and server**
  The Web provides a typical client/server n-tier implementation where the client has no direct access to the server's functionality but converses with the server via transactions. Since most or all processing happens on the server only the result returns to the client, helping to maximize limited network bandwidth.

   Visual FoxPro can act as a server in this type of client/server environment. The Web and Web server act as the middleware that connects the client to the server, with VFP responding to the request made by the Web server.

Universal client interface
The Web browser has quickly become the killer application that comes around and changes the computing environment. The cross-platform aspects of Web applications bring the following advantages:

- **Cross-platform functionality**
  Cross-platform issues have been short-changed by software developers for a long time. Browsers are perhaps the first tools that truly bring the various operating systems and environments together and allow them to run the same applications. While HTML and even the newer DHTML and XML standards are a far cry from the power you get with typical Windows applications, it is now possible to build true cross-platform applications.

  But there is a price to pay: much reduced user interface flexibility if you want to build applications that truly conform to the lowest-common-denominator browser support.

> *Cross-platform issues apply mainly to server-driven HTML applications. The more focus that is on the server, the more likely your cross-platform compatibility. Adding browser-specific features or platform-specific objects such as ActiveX controls immediately reduces your cross-platform range, which may or may not be a problem. Java is also supposed to provide application-level cross-platform support, but to date the differences between platforms make this more a dream than reality.*

- **Develop on your platform of choice and run on any platform**
  Another big advantage of a server-based Web application is that you can build it under 32-bit Windows using Visual FoxPro (or whatever tool you'd like to use) and expect users on Unix, Mac or Windows 3.x boxes to run the app as-is. Browsers make it possible to use whatever tool or platform you're comfortable with to build back-end applications and still provide the cross-platform capability to client apps. No extra development is required, other than making sure you create compliant output that's supported on each browser.

- **Interoperability**
  The hyperlinked nature of the Web makes it possible to link together applications that are built with different tools—a Windows application might call a Unix server to complete some of the support tasks, or simply spread the load onto another server in another department. In addition, Internet protocols are used more and more to handle transaction-based operations. For example, a commerce store might talk to a bank server application over an HTTP link to validate credit card information when a user buys a product online. The Internet makes this type of application feasible for intra-company and even business-to-business communications.

- **Support for multiple content types**
  Web browsers are built with extension in mind. They can easily display different content types, so it's a snap to display static text as well as graphics and other multimedia content in the same page. Browsers also have the ability to read a *content type* to determine what type of document they are displaying. For example, you can use the browser to display an HTML document, a Word document, an Adobe Acrobat (PDF) document, or a static image. The browser determines which content type is requested and then either displays the content natively or uses extension technologies such as plug-ins, ActiveX controls or document extensions to host the content. This open architecture makes the browser flexible to new functionality introduced by third-party vendors, as well as new technologies that haven't been dreamt up yet.

The application development platform of the future

For better or for worse, the Web is here to stay, and it will continue to intrude into our development process. The quick acceptance of the Web interface is driving changes in software design that are moving more and more technology toward a Web-centric interface. Most mainstream software now includes support for Web views and output options to generate HTML. Applications like Office 2000 freely mix traditional Windows-based interfaces with new HTML interfaces and live online views that get data from the Web. This kind of integration likely will accelerate in mainstream and custom applications to take advantage of the rich text interface provided by the Web, and will blur the interface differences between data retrieved from the local machine and the Internet.

I'm betting that within the next year we'll see most development tools merging their interface technologies into a common HTML- or DHTML-based engine that provides a common interface accessible from multiple development tools. The common interface will then be able to run both local applications and those that must run on the Web.

Limitations to building Web applications

There are many benefits to building an application that runs over the Web. But it's also extremely important to understand the limitations that you face when building these types of applications. If you've never looked at Web development before, you might be scared off by the complexity that you initially face in terms of different technologies and terminology. Don't let that happen to you—it's easy to get past the techno-babble, and I'll take you through most of what you need to know in the next chapter.

But it's important to know beforehand where the limitations are, so you can prepare yourself and know not to waste time on things that are either impossible or difficult to accomplish. The problems are not of the "do or die" kind—they are not insurmountable, but they do require rethinking application development to some extent.

Configuration issues

Probably the most confusing aspect of Internet application development is the sheer variety of tools you need to work with in order to create an application. In stand-alone development, you typically use a single tool like Visual FoxPro to build end-to-end solutions. You use the class designer to build your business objects, the form designer for your user interface, the report writer for creating reports, and the entire IDE to build, test, debug and finally deploy the application.

Web development is definitely more involved than that! Here you are dealing with multiple, totally separate environments: a Web server, a Web browser, potentially some middleware connector application (ISAPI or CGI "connectors"—more on that in the next chapter), script code and a development environment like Visual FoxPro. If you're building applications that mix client- and server-side code, you have to deal with creating test environments locally that can simulate the network environment. You might be running multiple copies of Visual FoxPro simultaneously—one to run the client code and one to run the server code, for example. Or you might use a browser to test the application that you built using HTML pages designed in FrontPage, calling components inside a Visual FoxPro COM component. Then there are the complexities involved with Microsoft's Component Object Model (COM) and configuring the components you build to work properly as Web components. Add to that configuration issues: security rights for the Web server; network configuration to make machines safely accessible over the network; and managing HTML pages in addition to code.

It's actually not as bad as it sounds, but the reality is that when you're building distributed applications you'll likely be working with four or five development-related tools all at once, switching back and forth between them continuously. And without a doubt you need to have at least a basic understanding of how the components fit together in order to make all these different technologies work together. The promise of component-based software is starting to materialize with the Web, but as of now, it's not necessarily easy to make the components and the operating systems 'play nice' together.

Interface limitations of HTML

If you believe the computer and development magazines, the Web and HTML are the nirvana of application development that will solve all your problems. Yeah, right! Although new distributed technologies that might move us away from HTML are emerging, the majority of the focus on the Internet continues to be in HTML-based applications.

The tools that are available today are downright primitive when compared to full visual development tools, and Web applications reflect this in rather simplistic interfaces that are used to present forms and interact with the user. The tools are getting better, and Visual Studio 6.0 vastly improves your ability to work in a more centralized environment for more of the development process. But even so, the development environment remains primitive.

There are several reasons for HTML's inability to provide the same kind of functionality that a typical stand-alone application can deliver:

- **No data access from client**
  The browser has no direct access to the data, which is maintained and accessed by the server. Data access is transaction–based, and any updates based on data retrieved from the server typically require reloading of the HTML documents containing the form data. This is a very important point: Without direct data access, any lookup—including field validations—requires a trip back to the server and reloading the HTML with the updated data or error message from the server. This means that much of what goes into an 'event-driven' database application interface goes out the window. Typical HTML interfaces are form-based, where validation occurs after the user has entered all the data. For true public Web applications, there appears to be no change in sight for this situation and it's something you have to design for.

  Technologies like Remote Data Service (RDS) make it possible to access data directly from a Web page, but this implementation moves away from a thin client environment and can require extensive scripting code on the client side to drive the HTML. Even with the ability to access data over the Web, there are still bandwidth and speed issues to overcome. Accessing data over the wire can be very slow, especially at modem speeds. Most of these technologies are also browser-specific and therefore limit your reach for public applications (for example, RDS works only with IE).

  This has several important effects on application design. First, your user interface cannot be as flexible as a GUI app. For example, a typical application will let the user select from a full list of customers and make sub-selections that might fill multiple combo boxes with the relevant data. Further selections repopulate fields relevant to the choices made by the user. This might work well for local applications, but for a Web application, pulling this data down (in the case of RDS) or entirely refreshing the page with an update from the server would be too slow and resource-intensive. Along the same lines, field validations are often handled on the field level. If these validations include data lookups, you might not be able to do them on the client side at all; instead you might have to delegate this task to the form submission, which sends the data to the server.

- **Limited object model/scripting**
  Although both Microsoft and Netscape provide enhanced DHTML form interfaces to their browsers via JavaScript (Internet Explorer also supports VBScript), the object model of these scripting engines is extremely limited compared to full-blown visual tools and lacks direct data access. Worst of all, there are compatibility problems between the leading two browsers that make it next to impossible to use the high-end code for each browser to make it run on the other. It can be done, but it requires lots of conditional, bracketed code.

  Internet Explorer provides a rich scripting model that allows control over the entire browser interface and HTML page elements. It also allows control of ActiveX controls and Java applets to make it possible to drive data access over the Web, for example. Still, the functionality that the scripting languages provide is fairly minimal, especially when compared to a rich, object-oriented, data-manipulation language like Visual FoxPro.

- **No easy way to print output**
  The Web browser is taking over our computers and is bringing us a wonderfully distributed world view. Unfortunately, there's one serious problem with browsers: There's no decent way to print anything from the browser directly. Sure, there's a Print option, but try that with a long table that goes on for five or more pages. While information presented in the browser may look beautiful, printing it may not look so nice. One fundamental reason is that HTML has no concept of a page break, so long pages are broken arbitrarily.

  HTML does not map very well to output generated by the report generator. There are some third-party workarounds such as using Adobe Acrobat to print output and then viewing the output in a reader or ActiveX control. I'll show how to accomplish this in Chapter 5. But none are natively supported, and once you start using them you give up some of the cross-platform flexibility.

- **Mostly non-visual development**
  For the most part, Web-based application development is nonvisual. You can use visual HTML editors like FrontPage, Visual InterDev, or Homesite to build the HTML pages you display on browsers. But the actual application code you write is usually transaction-based, involving mostly straight database code (queries, validations, inserts, and so on) and either generating the HTML via code or loading HTML pages from disk to evaluate embedded logic in scripts. Even when using Visual FoxPro, you aren't likely to use the screen builder or report writer to generate your output because these tools don't map well to the HTML output mechanism. HTML code is typically created via template or script pages that evaluate code, or via straight-line output that generates HTML from code.

Server-based programming model

When building a Web application, you're typically building a server-based application. If there's database access involved, you're definitely working at least partially on the server. This means that all of a sudden you need to think a lot more about load, performance and concurrency than you had to in stand-alone applications. Incoming requests must be processed and passed back with a response in a timely fashion or blocking will occur to tie up resources and processor time.

Another state of mind

In addition, server programming introduces the concept of stateless requests, which means that users hit each server request without maintaining context or identity between requests. In other words, the current request knows nothing about the previous request that occurred a few seconds back. This means that you can't expect to keep tables open between requests and expect the record pointer to still be set on the same record as before—another user could have hit your server and processed a request since your last request. This has implications for things like tracking users through a site or session, dealing with locking issues for databases and generally reestablishing some sort of base environment on each server request.

Take a load off

Once you've built an application that's enjoying success and growth, you'll probably run into issues of scalability. Application servers need to properly balance incoming traffic against the available hardware and software running to handle that load. This involves fine-tuning applications for performance and CPU load, understanding where load points are and how to maximize the hardware and software. You might also need to look into scaling applications to multiple machines in order to take the load. As you might expect, these are not trivial tasks. Unfortunately, there isn't a lot of information available on these types of topics. We'll look at a number of these issues and how they apply to Visual FoxPro in Chapter 10.

Security is not optional

When dealing with server applications, security is important, especially if you're building public access applications. Making sure that nobody snoops the data as it travels over the Web is a big issue to deal with. There are also issues like spoofing and hammering a site—can't you just see your competitor overloading your site with bogus requests so that no other users can get on? Or better yet, that they would send you data that will eventually overload your hard drive or data capacity?

Regardless of the limitations, it's possible to build sophisticated applications that utilize the Web, and we'll look at the technologies in detail starting in the next chapter. So, kick up your feet and read on...

Chapter 2
Internet Application
Technologies

The first thing that you'll notice when starting to build Web applications is new terminology. Building Internet applications is more involved than building stand-alone applications because you have to deal with multiple environments simultaneously. With this additional complexity comes terminology. The bad news is that you have to become familiar with lots of three- and four-letter acronyms; the good news is that most of these technologies are easy to work with once you have a broad view of how they fit together. This chapter provides this broad overview. It talks about the technologies and information flow for distributed and Web applications, and discusses a number of the terms you need to know.

When you look back a few years, it's quite amazing to think how quickly Internet technology has taken over the network and network application environments. Four years ago, relatively few PC-based networks were running the TCP/IP protocol, which is the base network protocol used by all high-level Internet protocols. Today, other network protocols have been pushed to the sidelines or now run on top of TCP/IP. You probably use Internet protocols like Hyper Text Transfer Protocol (HTTP) , File Transfer Protocol (FTP) , and Simple Mail Transfer Protocol (SMTP) throughout your workday without giving them much thought.

Open standards open doors to the world

One major reason why TCP/IP has taken over is that it provides an open and standards-based protocol governed by a standards body rather than by a single company or vendor. The protocol can be freely implemented by any operating system or network solution provider, which makes it accessible from just about any machine that needs to communicate over a network. This common network protocol is a crucial requirement to allow for ubiquitous access from anywhere, and a key reason that the Internet has grown in popularity so quickly.

TCP/IP was around for a long time before the Internet started taking off. But the combination of an open network architecture, along with higher-level and equally open protocols and application implementations of these protocols, brought TCP/IP into the PC mainstream. In particular, the HTTP protocol used for accessing the World Wide Web and the first implementation of a graphic Web browser triggered the focus toward the TCP/IP-centric world of the Internet and its supporting technologies.

The success of TCP/IP is based on the openness of the standards as well as the relative simplicity of the protocols implemented on top of it. Most of the popular protocols like HTTP, FTP and SMTP are text-based and are fairly easy to implement even at the application level— simple protocols make for wide adaptation because more products can support the standards. Simple protocols also make for flexibility—if it's easy to access information at the protocol level, programmers have control over changing the way data is sent or communicated over the given protocol. You'll see some examples of this once we start talking about building Web applications and modifying the Request headers when returning results to the browser, in order to tell the browser to display the information in a certain way.

Of clients and servers

Most Internet technology works based on client and server relationships. A *client* is a consumer of services or content provided by a *server*. Typical Internet server applications have multiple simultaneous clients that request data from servers. The servers respond by sending information back to the client, which uses this information. The most familiar scenario is a Web browser requesting data from the Web server and then displaying the returned information. The server functionality is hidden from the browser, which doesn't know or care how the Web server provides the information. The Web server might provide the information as a simple HTML file loaded from disk, or it might ask a dynamic back-end application to create a data-driven table for display. The browser requests, while the Web server responds and supplies the content.

This simple concept gets skewed a bit by the fact that machines or even applications can be both servers and clients at the same time. For example, a Web server responds to a dynamic request that requires it to call another application to perform the actual processing. A common example is the Web server making a request to SQL Server to retrieve some data. In this case the Web server is a *server* to the Web browser but also a *client* to SQL Server, which is the server providing the database data results for the Web server.

As you can see, the client/server concept is often applied to more than physical machine boundaries, and deals with logical aspects of an application and the relationships between the interacting components. Let's take a closer look at the server and client definitions to put these concepts into perspective as they apply to the development process.

Servers

For database applications, most of the application logic continues to reside on the server. Pure server-side applications running HTML-based interfaces are by far the most common Internet applications running today. When you visit a Web site that displays dynamic data brought back by criteria you supply, or when you fill out a form that captures your contact or registration information, you're running a server-side application that generates all the application and HTML on the server. The client side acts only as a terminal to display and navigate the data. Focus is on the server because the database almost always resides on the server. In most cases, clients don't have direct access to the database, both for performance and security reasons.

There are different approaches to servers, from direct client access to a server over a TCP/IP socket connection, to the more common Web-based interfaces that use Web-based processing engines to access back-end applications that can create dynamic output. Servers are workhorses—they are asked to perform tasks and return results as follows:

- A browser asks a Web server to provide HTML.
- An application calls a COM object to retrieve a result.
- A Java applet talks to a server-side Java application to download some data.
- An e-mail client makes a request to download all messages from a mail server or asks it to send messages.

In all of these examples, the server is asked to perform a task and often returns a result to a client.

This book discusses high-level server tools, which continue to be the most popular and most scalable solutions both in terms of load and accessibility. In particular we'll look at server-side Web back-end solutions that allow you to create HTML/HTTP applications with Microsoft Active Server Pages (ASP) and FoxISAPI. With these tools, code runs on the server to build HTML that gets sent back to the browser for display. The tools allow flexibility in output creation and can be extended by using custom Visual FoxPro code to build business logic and handle database access. Here, everything happens on the server: business logic, database access, and generation of the display logic as HTML. The browser merely acts as reader for the information sent back by the Web server (that's not entirely true—you can write scripting code and use Java and ActiveX, but for the sake of discussion here we're dealing with server technology). I call these *high-level tools* because they work through the Web server rather than allowing the client to directly access the application using a standard protocol: HTTP. The Web server takes the request and routes it to the appropriate back-end application, which provides the actual application logic.

Contrasting with high-level Web server applications are low-level servers, which are directly accessed and use straight network connections. For example, a Java Applet or ActiveX control running on a browser might access a Java application over a direct TCP/IP socket connection. In this scenario, the client directly accesses the back-end application by programming a network connection directly, rather than talking to an intermediary like the Web server. Although this can provide better performance, it also involves a lot more work because you have to come up with your own protocols instead of using existing, proven ones such as HTTP and the formatting provided by the Web server. Client and server share responsibility in this scenario, but even well-designed applications will likely leave most of the hard-core business logic on the server, with the client side code providing the front-end user interface services.

Some technologies, such as Microsoft Remote Data Service (RDS) use both client-side logic and server-side components. With this technology the code is written on the client, but the actual data operations are *marshaled* over the Web and actually performed on the server. Marshalling means taking requests on one end of a connection and then passing the request to the other end, which does the actual work. The server returns the result and the client can then use the result data. The point here is that the technology spreads some logic to both ends of the connection. Most tools in this category implement the low-level server and then wrap the logic into a simpler interface (RDS uses an ActiveX control) that can be directly used on the client side in the Web browser or a stand-alone application. Microsoft is implementing several technologies along these lines.

Finally, there's a drive to make it possible to instantiate objects over the Internet just as you can with local COM objects on your computer. Of particular interest is Distributed COM (DCOM) over HTTP, which makes it possible to efficiently access COM objects over a regular HTTP connection. Java also implements this sort of connectivity using a standard protocol called Remote Method Invocation (RMI) over CORBA (a non-Microsoft object model implementation similar to COM).

Server contexts

When discussing servers, it's crucial to understand in which context a client/server relationship exists. As pointed out above, servers can exist in two entirely different contexts:

- **Physical (Machine)**

  For an application user who accesses a Web server via a browser, the local browser is the client and the remote Web server is the server. There's a clear separation between the client and the server by way of the separate machines that handle the client and server chores.

- **Logical (Application)**

  Client and server applications can exist on the same machine. One application can make requests to another to retrieve information.

This book focuses extensively on logical client/server relationships between applications. The transfer mechanism most prominently addressed is Microsoft's Component Object Model (COM). Note that an application server can be physically deployed on either a local or remote machine. A good example is a COM object that you can access via DCOM.. The COM object is an application server, but it can also be called from a remote client that accesses the server over a network.

Physical connections between machines are essentially hidden by network protocols. You can access an application either locally or across the wire with very few changes in the way the tools are used. All that changes is the network address. This applies both to physical network access (such as browsing a Web page) as well as the lower level, direct access using COM or custom created clients and servers. With all of these, the network abstracts the fact that the application might be talking to a local application or one that's running across the globe in Singapore.

Server states

Server programming tends to be a little different from standard application programming. Stand-alone applications deal extensively with responding to events that occur when the user performs certain operations. In server programming, this event-driven model is replaced by a transaction-based model in which requests are treated as self-contained requests to the server that are completed and returned to the client.

Think of a server as a typical non-visual class in Visual FoxPro. The class has methods that you call and that have return values of some sort of result data or content (I use the term *content* here for returning document data that gets embedded in the output stream). Servers are very similar to this scenario, and in fact this is how you built COM servers in Visual FoxPro. But because of the way the distributed architecture works, servers can be either stateless or stateful:

- **Stateless**

  A *stateless* server does not retain any context for the client. The server does not know what action the previous request performed and does not make any assumptions about the current environment. The client typically must provide some mechanism for the server to establish state as part of the request on the server. For example, a client requests a record object from a server and passes in a primary key (PK) to let the server know which record to retrieve. Based on the PK, the server can establish the state required to retrieve the record. In a stateless server, the PK would be required even for an operation like MoveToNextRecord() because the server doesn't explicitly know what record the previously retrieved record was. So the required parameter to MoveToNextRecord() is the primary key of the current record, and the server then uses that record as its starting point. The concept behind a stateless server is to connect to the server, let it establish context, get your data and then disconnect—losing state at that time. For this reason, stateless servers are often referred to as *connectionless servers*.

- **Stateful**
  Servers that can retain state between requests are appropriately called *stateful*. Each client that uses a stateful server gets a persistent connection to the server, and the client and server both can make assumptions about the values set on the server. If you set a property on a stateful server, the property will still be set in the next request. An example of a stateful server is a Visual FoxPro application creating an instance of Word to create a form letter. Each call to the Word COM object causes the document to be filled or manipulated. Because the document sticks around for the lifetime of the object and the user holds a unique copy of the object, the server is considered stateful. The continued existence of the changing document is the server's state.

Most Internet solutions call for stateless servers because they provide much better scalability than stateful servers for large numbers of connected users. The reason for this is simple: Keeping state requires each user to have his own copy of an object with its own private address space. If you have 5000 simultaneous users of your Web site, a stateful server would use 5000 instances of an object or, at the very least, 5000 copies of the unique data for that server. As you can imagine, this places a huge load on the server's resources. It's also inefficient because only 10 or 20 users might actually be using the server at any given time.

With stateless servers, resources are recycled. Rather than having 5000 objects you might have only 10 or 20 that are cycled to service the immediate incoming requests. This is known as *resource management* or, in more technical terms, as a *pool manager*. Pool managers are implemented at all levels:

- Web servers use HTTP connection pooling to provide services to large numbers of users without giving each user a dedicated connection.
- ODBC uses connection pooling to handle multiple connections to the same data source without having to reconnect each time.
- *Microsoft Transaction Server* (MTS) implements a resource management feature called *Just In Time Activation* that pools server resources by unloading and reloading servers as needed. (A future version of MTS will provide a real pool manager for pooling references to stateless objects.)
- FoxISAPI includes a built-in pool manager to manage multiple, simultaneous Visual FoxPro COM objects for back-end operation. With a pool manager, a few objects can service thousands of simultaneous clients.

Clients

Although distributed architecture places a heavy emphasis on server-side processing, the client side also has a lot to contribute. Client-side code can work in combination with server-side code, which is happening more and more now with the richer Dynamic HTML object models becoming available in the HTML 4 and 5 and XML standards. Still, client-side code suffers from the lack of direct access to the database and typically just sits on the Web server. Without data access, the client side is fairly limited in what it can do beyond providing a "smart" user interface. It is possible to access data directly over the Web, but only at the cost of building applications that move more code (both application and system) to the client. In many cases, they also become platform specific, as is the case with most of Microsoft's client-side technologies like Dynamic HTML and RDS that only work in Internet Explorer 4.0 or later on Windows platforms.

Client-side technology makes a lot of sense if you are not focused entirely on building solutions that have to run on every conceivable platform. In fact, by using the Internet protocols discussed earlier in this chapter, you can build extremely powerful applications that take advantage of the distributed platform without getting shoehorned into a limited, HTML-only implementation. By implementing more code on the client side, you make the client more flexible. But at the same time the solution becomes less cross-platform-capable and requires more administration because the proper software needs to be installed on the client's machine.

At the highest level there's the Web browser as the client to the Web server. The browser has become the "Universal Client" interface. For better or for worse, the focus is now on getting everything to run inside a browser. Today you can view your daily Web HTML, graphics and multimedia in the browser as well as word processing, spreadsheets, graphics and presentation documents. Even full-blown applications built with Visual FoxPro using the new 6.0 Active Documents can run inside the browser as a type of specialty document. Keep in mind that that these Active Documents are not real Web applications, but simply local applications hosted in the browser running against local data in most cases. The applications make no provision for communicating with the server—it is simply a specialized viewer. In the case of VFP, it's a viewer for a local Visual FoxPro application.

Yet HTML and graphics continue to be the most common use for the browser, with many an interface forced into this rather limiting display environment. What makes the browser so powerful is its ability to mix content of different types in one place and to allow hosting of additional functionality in form of Java applets, ActiveX controls, plug-ins and embedded documents. The browser is simply a host container, and if a new technology comes along, viewers can be snapped onto the existing interface to make that content available in the browser as well.

The next step toward dynamic content is direct browser integration of scripting languages such as JavaScript and VBScript, and object model support for *Cascading Style Sheets* (CSS) that expose each object in the HTML document and make it scriptable. These scripting languages make it possible to build simple logic that deals with the user interface displayed in the browser. Scripting languages by themselves are useful but quite limited because they don't support direct access to the server and data. For this reason the browser model is extended through Java applets and ActiveX components that can be controlled by the scripting language. Applets and controls can either be applications in their own right or interact with the browser environment by letting themselves be controlled by scripts. The combination of scripting plus applets and components is a powerful one that has not been fully realized to date. However, significant moves are being made in that direction, especially in relation to doing direct database connectivity over the Web. The middle layer of components is responsible for abstracting the low-level interface with the server, making it possible to use HTTP as a data transfer mechanism. Applets and components are useful in more than just browsers. For example, ActiveX controls run most Windows-based applications. Furthermore, applets can be hosted inside a browser hosted in an application, which provides the full browser functionality directly to client applications including the ability to control the browser and the HTML document object inside of it through code. It's possible to build VFP code that entirely controls actions that occur inside of the browser (see Chapter 6). As you can see, these technologies have reach beyond the limited pure browser interface.

Finally, clients can run plain Windows applications built with high-level tools like Visual FoxPro. For example, it's possible for Visual FoxPro to act as a browser by using HTTP directly from within a VFP application. Rather than being limited to non-interactive HTML interfaces, you could have forms that fire validation events against locally cached data and send updates to the server. You can use HTTP protocols directly as you'll see in Chapter 7. Or you can use higher level technologies like Microsoft Remote Data Service, which allows you to talk to server-side data server objects from a VFP client app. With the RDS control, you essentially are allowed to run SQL statements over the Web. This type of setup allows the greatest flexibility because you get the power of a full-fledged GUI application as well as the ability to take advantage of the distributed network. But with this approach you also get away from some of the administration benefits because you must create GUI applications that need to be updated on every desktop that runs them. Compared to the browser-only requirement of pure HTML applications, this makes for much greater maintenance overhead. These solutions also often are platform specific because they take advantage of the operating system on which they run. Java promises a way to build client applications that can run on any platform, but the reality of creating powerful, cross-platform Java applications is one of very difficult and limiting implementations, which shows in the lack of many cross-platform Java applications to date. So much hype, yet so few actual applications run Java today. However, don't count on that being true in the future as Java tools get better and the technology matures and speeds up.

On a lower level, clients can talk to custom servers across the Internet. As with stand-alone applications, it's possible to build ActiveX controls and Java applets that talk to custom servers on the server side to retrieve information. In this scenario, your own custom ActiveX or Java code acts as the middleware that uses lower-level Internet protocols to abstract complex operations such as data transfers, resulting in a simple familiar interface using object syntax and SQL commands. This approach is very powerful, but also more complex because the client/server communication and protocols need to be handled by your own code.

Clients on a diet

There's been a lot of discussion in the press about *thin clients* and *fat clients*. These terms relate to the amount of code that runs on the client side of the client/server connection and the amount of hardware resources needed to run the application. Here is a breakdown of the terminology:

- **Thin Client**

  Thin-client technology suggests that all or most of the application logic resides on the server and that the client runs little or no custom-written software. Hardware requirements should be minimal and software requirements should use standard software such as a Web browser or terminal program. A Web browser running a pure HTML application driven by server-side code, possibly assisted by some browser scripting code, is considered a thin-client solution.

- **Fat Client**

  Fat-client solutions are typically used to describe stand-alone, traditional, file-based or two-tier client/server systems where a rich GUI application talks to a SQL Server or other server back end. In most of these applications, the logic resides mostly on the client, which uses the server for special purposes but not as the primary application server. Fat-client solutions tend to require lots of resources on the client machine—typically a full installation of an application written in languages such as Visual FoxPro. The "fat" term comes from these resource requirements and the amount of code residing on the client.

- **Medium Client**

  Recently there's been a distinct shift toward medium-client solutions that focus on taking advantage of the horsepower and operating system that the client provides, while still leaving the heavy processing and logic on the server. Medium-client applications might focus on using system tools like ActiveX controls and DHTML to enhance the user's experience as well as providing much of the interface logic on the client. These apps typically have a three-tier architecture where the client side is responsible for controlling the server side as well as handling much of the user interface. What really separates medium client from fat client is that medium client focuses on standard technologies and leaves all heavy processing tasks to the server. In particular, most of Microsoft's new technologies like RDS fall into this category because they require significant resources and the ability to script the components on the client.

The lines between these three modi operandi are not always clear, but each mode has its advantages. Fat-client technology is definitely on its way out because there's a big drive under way to minimize the administrative headaches involved with maintaining and administering installed applications. Thin-client solutions have been around for a long time in the form of terminal apps; with the Web, many people have been introduced to a new kind of terminal app hosted in a slightly smarter and much prettier terminal application called a Web browser. For Web apps, thin client is by far the most popular implementation because it allows access to anyone who has a browser, from a little notepad computer to a 20-processor HP Unix server in the glass box in the IT department. Medium client walks the middle ground and is becoming much more popular for intranet applications where the hardware and software can be standardized and forced to conform to the application requirements. Still, fat-client applications will be around for a long time to come. I don't think stand-alone, monolithic applications are going away any time soon—not as long as users ask for new features, more speed and convenience in their computer applications.

HTTP makes clients and servers go 'round

Between the client and the server sits the Internet with its TCP/IP architecture and the increasingly universal HTTP. Because of the popularity of the Web, HTTP has become the most prominent of the Internet protocols. HTTP has traditionally been a *connectionless protocol*, which means that each time you make a request over HTTP the server establishes a connection, performs the request, and then releases the connection. This architecture makes it possible to handle large numbers of simultaneous clients because users are connected only while they process a request. HTTP is also optimized for this type of on-again, off-again connection by caching connection information and DNS information to speed transfers over the Web. Recent changes in HTTP 1.1 support automatic keep-alive connections, where the server tries to maintain connections as long as resources allow in order to optimize performance by not requiring reconnects for every request. These improvements provide better performance under most circumstances, but can be a burden for servers carrying large volumes of user connection loads.

When you think of HTTP, don't think that it's only for serving HTML content. You can provide any kind of content over HTTP. Not only does it handle ordinary Web traffic like documents and multimedia content, but it can also serve raw data such as query results. It is also emerging as a transport mechanism to allow communication of components over the wire. Several key Microsoft technologies are already working over HTTP: DCOM can now be marshaled over HTTP, and RDS uses packaged data streams over HTTP to handle the communication between the client and server for a SQL-based data object.

The reason HTTP is popular for these types of solutions is that it's optimized for connectionless communications, unlike straight TCP/IP connections, which can take a long time to establish over the Internet especially if not listed in Domain Naming Service (DNS) tables. For example, connecting over TCP/IP to a standard back-end application like SQL Server can take an excruciating amount of time (several minutes), where the same mechanism can be relatively quick over HTTP. HTTP connections are much quicker to connect and automatically take advantage of caching mechanisms built into the Domain Naming Service. In addition, HTTP implementations provide the wrapping and security layer necessary to prevent unauthorized access to data or applications directly over the Internet. It might be okay to access a SQL server directly from the company LAN, but over the Internet the sheer volume and possible security issues call for tighter control than direct access allows through an intermediate application or system layer.

Many companies have also discovered that HTTP is a great mechanism for building custom solutions with intelligence both on the client and server without having to build complex, low-level servers and clients. HTTP is a text-based protocol and thus it's rather easy to work with both on the client and server—I'll show some examples of this in Chapter 7. HTTP-based applications can take advantage of the infrastructure that might already be in place from an HTML-based Web application by simulating a browser. Fat or medium clients can access the same Web server used for HTML apps to retrieve data directly or communicate with the server using the same implementation details as HTML-based applications, but without generating HTML and instead returning data (text or binary) or commands. You can transfer data or simply tell the server to retrieve information and return it as data to be used in the application. This can take the simple form of a command-based approach where the client

tells the server to perform tasks, or to the other extreme of full-fledged, two-way
communication that involves data transfers along the way.

From Web browser to Web server

Now let's take a closer look at how the active architecture binds together the client and the
server in a typical Web application. **Figure 2.1** shows the relationship between the client and
server sides. Note how they are separated by a dotted line representing the physical machine
boundary that is crossed only by the HTTP protocol. HTTP is the primary mechanism for
transporting requests and data across this boundary.

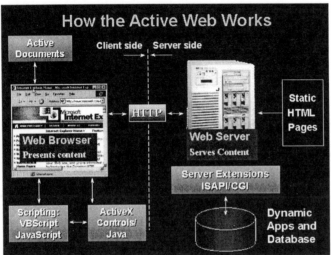

Figure 2.1. The relationship between the client and server sides of a Web application.

Let's take a look at how a request travels from client to server, and refer to Figure 2.1 for
additional flow:

- **The browser provides the active interface.**
  The browser is essentially a terminal program on steroids, responsible for displaying
  content that the server provides.

- **The browser uses scripting and components to extend functionality.**
  Browsers support scripting for building logic to handle the user interface. Components can
  extend the browser's functionality and can consist of ActiveX controls, plug-ins and Java
  applets that are parameterized and embedded within an HTML document. Components
  can be controlled by using scripting languages.

- **Active Documents embed applications.**
  Active Documents are a special type of document available only for Internet Explorer that
  make it possible to run standard GUI applications inside the Web browser. It's possible to

view Office apps directly in the browser. Visual FoxPro 6.0 also supports creation of Active Document applications that allow a VFP app to run inside the browser virtually unchanged. Keep in mind that this technology is merely a packaging solution: The app runs on the local machine as a fat client without any support for data connectivity over the Web. It's no different than a local VFP application except it's *hosted* in the browser.

- **HTTP is the client-to-server transfer mechanism.**
  The HTTP protocol is used to send requests from client to server and result content back to the client. This diagram shows the most common implementation, where HTTP is the only avenue of getting to the back end. Rather than talking directly to the data, the browser always talks to the intermediary of the Web server over HTTP.

- **The Web server provides connectivity to content, data and application services.**
  Web servers are responsible for handling the HTTP requests from browser clients. Based on the URL information provided by the client, the Web server decides what type of content to send back to the browser. Requests made to the server can ask for static content, which is simply pulled from disk and sent back to the client. Alternatively, the server can be asked for dynamic data, in which case the server passes on the request information to server extensions.

- **The Internet Server API (ISAPI) and Common Gateway Interface (CGI) are used for server-side extensions.**
  The Web server by itself is not terribly smart when it comes to providing dynamic data. Dynamic requests are instead passed on to server extensions that do the dirty work of actually creating the dynamic output that goes back to the browser. The server extensions, or "scripts" as they are often called, can then decide how to create the dynamic output. ISAPI and CGI are standard extension protocols that establish how the Web server makes requested information available to the applications that want to build dynamic data. The protocols consist of formatting for incoming request data and formatting for creating the output that is sent back to the Web server. Note that just about all server-side tools use either ISAPI or CGI, including scripting engines like ASP and Cold Fusion, which hide the ISAPI/CGI scripts by using script mappings to give the impression of "scripted pages." Behind those scripts sits an ISAPI/CGI engine that actually communicates with the Web server.

- **Visual FoxPro communicates with ISAPI.**
  Because ISAPI and CGI tend to be low-level interfaces that are coded in C++ or other low-level languages, these extensions are frequently used to build middleware software pieces. They call on external tools such as Visual FoxPro or Visual Basic, or internally implement a scripting engine like Active Server. FoxISAPI and Active Server Pages, both of which are discussed in this book, are implemented as ISAPI extensions. Tools like Web Connection, Cold Fusion, and some of the FrontPage extensions are also implemented as ISAPI and/or CGI extensions that abstract the low-level HTTP logistics.

- **COM is the messaging mechanism.**
  With Microsoft technologies, the mechanism for connecting back-end applications tends to be COM. The connector scripts act as COM clients that call COM objects by passing parameters and retrieving return values. Using this mechanism it's possible to call a Visual FoxPro Automation server directly from a Web page and return Web content to the server.

Typical HTML-based Web applications follow these steps:
1. The user clicks a link or HTML form button in the Web browser.
2. The browser sends a request over the wire to the Web server via HTTP.
3. The Web server decodes the URL that the browser sent as part of its request, along with any additional information that the browser provides. Typically this will be HTML form variables or *Extra Headers* that tell the server to perform certain actions based on the request.
4. The server is now responsible for deciding what to do with the request. If it's a static document (HTML, graphic or other file content type) it simply pulls the file from disk and sends it back to the client. If it's a request for an extension, the server loads the extension, if not already loaded, and passes control to the extension.
5. The extension can process the request directly—it is possible to write ISAPI or CGI extensions in C if you have the need for speed or the patience to debug system level software. More commonly, the extension passes control to a back-end application, which could be a scripting engine like Active Server Pages or a back-end application called via COM, as is the case with FoxISAPI.
6. Once the back end application gets control, it is free to perform business logic, including providing access to databases and business objects. If you're using Visual FoxPro code directly with FoxISAPI, you're free to use any FoxPro code as long as no modal user interface code is run. When complete, the application returns a result (typically a string) to the ISAPI extension. Although Active Server Pages appears to be part of the IIS Web server, it really is also an ISAPI extension that implements a scripting engine. The ISAPI extension calls the engine, which calls a rich language library that allows access to both internal and external COM objects. The result is the same: The script essentially creates HTML output that's sent back to the Web server by the ISAPI extension.
7. Once the Web server receives the result from the extension, it passes that result over the HTTP link back to the browser.
8. The browser displays the content.
9. If the content contains scripting code, that code fires once the page has loaded on the client.
10. If using Dynamic HTML, code can continue to run once the page has finished loading, allowing access to all user interface elements of the HTML document.
11. If the HTML document also contains references to ActiveX controls or Java applets, these are either loaded from the local machine, if available, or automatically downloaded (with a prompt) from the Web via a CODEBASE tag in the document. The HTML document contains only an embedded *reference* to the object rather than the actual document. Based on the reference, the browser knows what to load or download.
12. Once loaded, the controls and applets can also be controlled by script code or events that fire in the control.

13. If the page loaded was an Active Document, the application in question is started and hosted inside the browser. The application partially takes over the browser's UI, with the client area being the "desktop" for the application and the menu bar allowing access for extension by the client application.

In this scenario, all data is accessed by going from the browser through HTTP to the Web server, through an ISAPI extension to a back-end application, which finally gets the data and sends back a result to the client in the form of HTML. This is the typical scenario that you see in today's dynamic, data-driven Web sites. While this process seems complex and potentially slow, it is a proven mechanism for providing access to data in online Web applications.

You can bypass this long way using custom client and server implementations or by using special data components, but it will sidestep standard protocols and typically involve getting your hands dirty in low-level server programming, which is exactly what the high-level HTTP protocol aims to eliminate. The key is that the "custom" part of this cycle is the code you create in the COM component that responds to a Web request. This code is not difficult to write, but it is different in that you retrieve your inputs from specialized objects and generate output as HTML or raw HTTP content. The rest of the process is wrapped up in the HTTP protocol and you don't have to worry about it how it works.

A closer look at the server side
When dealing with Visual FoxPro servers on the back end, the Web server needs to hand off control from its own internal processing to the Visual FoxPro back-end application. **Figure 2.2** illustrates how this process works on the server.

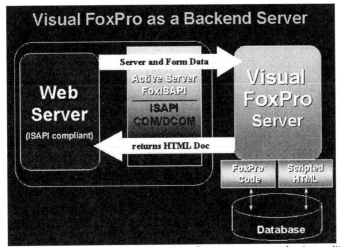

Figure 2.2. *Internet Information Server communicates with a back-end application using ISAPI. When using VFP, the mechanism to reach VFP is COM. The VFP server is called and VFP responds by supplying either HTML/HTTP output directly or by providing business logic processing to a script page.*

ISAPI, the high-performance extension interface

The Web server receives the request from the browser. If the server is Internet Information Server (IIS) or another Microsoft or ISAPI-compliant server, it will pass the request to an ISAPI extension. ISAPI extensions are:

- **High-performance system-level libraries**
  ISAPI extensions are Win32 DLLs written in C++ or another low-level language. They tend to provide system-level code that handles the logistics of passing control to other back-end applications like Visual FoxPro or a script engine like Active Server Pages. However, ISAPI extensions can also be used to build application-level logic if you're willing to build applications in C++ and debug them in a hostile DLL environment hosted inside the Web server.

- **Hosted persistently inside the Web server's process**
  ISAPI extensions load into the Web server's address space and remain there. They essentially become part of the Web server itself. Once loaded, ISAPI extensions cannot be unloaded except by shutting down the Web server or an individual Virtual Application (more on that in the next chapter). This is the opposite of CGI, which creates a new process for each incoming request, runs the request and then unloads the process. This is much less efficient than a preloaded ISAPI extension. IIS also provides a configurable ceiling for how many ISAPI threads the process can create. This is to limit the amount of resources that are allocated to processing ISAPI requests to prevent overloading the Web server when traffic gets heavy.

- **Multithreaded**
  ISAPI extensions are multithreaded, which means they can process multiple requests at the same time. The same DLL can service multiple clients efficiently because the extension is already loaded in memory. But multithreading also makes programming ISAPI a tricky proposition because all code written must be thread-safe to avoid simultaneous access to common global data from different threads. One thing to keep in mind is that although the ISAPI extension is multithreaded, back-end applications that interact with ISAPI extensions may not be. For example, Visual FoxPro and Visual Basic are not multithreaded, so when servers built with these tools are called from ISAPI extensions directly, a simulation of multithreading must be implemented.

Remember that you're not likely to write ISAPI extensions yourself, but rather you'll interact with them indirectly through a back-end application or scripting engine.

Calling all Visual FoxPro servers

So how do you actually get control to your Visual FoxPro code from the Web server? There are a number of ways, but in this book I'll look at two approaches:

- **Scripting engine**
  ISAPI extensions can be used to implement a scripting engine that makes it possible to use simple text-based documents to mix code and HTML in the same page. Microsoft Active

Server Pages and Cold Fusion are examples of engines that implement scripting engines on top of ISAPI extensions. (Cold Fusion is actually implemented in ISAPI, NSAPI and plain CGI.) The scripting engine makes it possible to access databases via ODBC directly from the scripting code, or allows extension of the scripting code by calling COM objects. You can access Visual FoxPro data directly with ODBC or choose to access business logic contained in Visual FoxPro COM objects that are loaded and called from a script page. Scripting engines work by assigning a script map to an ISAPI DLL that causes the specified extension (like .ASP) to be routed to an ISAPI DLL (like ASP.dll) that implements the scripting engine. Based on the URL, the ISAPI DLL can figure out where the page is located and then parse and evaluate the scripting code in the page.

- **ISAPI → back-end application communication**
  Another, more traditional mechanism is an ISAPI extension calling a back-end application directly. Examples of this mechanism are FoxISAPI and third-party tools like Web Connection, FoxWeb and X-Works. Here the Web server simply packages all the request information available and sends it to the back-end application. The actual mechanics of how this is accomplished differ from using COM to instantiate and call servers, to using DDE, or using a file-based polling mechanism to send and receive the request information and result content. Either way, the Web server passes request information (HTML Form variables, server status, browser information, and so on) to the back end, which returns a result in the form of an HTTP response or a specific result value. There are two advantages to using this implementation: Direct access means better performance and full control of input and output. If FoxPro is your back-end server you can take advantage of the FoxPro language and data access directly. You can also bring up forms for HTML rendering and even implement a scripting engine inside the Visual FoxPro code. I'll show some of these techniques in Chapter 5.

Whether you call your Visual FoxPro servers from scripts or using the direct back-end server approach, once your code gets control, all of Visual FoxPro's power is available to you to perform complex operations. You can access existing business objects and classes and use the VFP data engine, which continues to be the fastest, most flexible way to access data.

Microsoft's Component Object Model— The glue tying Windows to the Web

In case you haven't noticed, COM is Microsoft's religion. Everything coming out of Microsoft these days is implemented using COM interfaces. This is great for developers because the technologies are inherently accessible from any environment that can be a COM client. COM is a mechanism for abstracting objects and binary code with logical interfaces. Interfaces decouple the binary code from the rules of the interface—the calling conventions. This makes it possible for otherwise binary-incompatible applications to share functionality. For example, you can't call FoxPro code directly from a Visual Basic application. But if you create a COM object out of your Visual FoxPro class, that object is now available to be called by the VB application, or Visual Basic for Applications in Word or Excel, or Delphi or Visual C++.

COM is built around the concept of creating components and building applications in logical pieces that communicate with each other, rather than creating one big monolithic executable. This is important on the Web in particular because it allows you to build components in disparate development environments and then integrate them into a single application via COM. This pushes the concept of using the best tool for the job rather than doing everything with the same tool. COM makes the implementation phase easy by providing full-featured development environments like Visual FoxPro or Visual Basic to build COM objects, with minimal changes from traditional code models.

Microsoft is actively pushing COM by exposing most of its new technologies through COM to allow universal access from any COM-capable client, including support for invoking objects across the network. There are system services like Active Directory (for managing system resources such as the directory and security structures, IIS Web server administration, and so on) and ActiveX Data Objects (ADO), which is a system data access engine. Then there are ActiveX controls, which are simply a set of specialized COM interfaces. Even business productivity applications like Word and Excel are COM servers that can be accessed from other applications and scripted through them. Microsoft's Web browser also exposes a rich COM object model that allows browser functionality to be integrated directly into applications. Expect this trend to continue: Windows 98 and Windows 2000 (NT 5.0) will expose almost every aspect of the Windows operating system via COM interfaces that can be scripted with the Windows Scripting Host, a new batch language (using VBScript or JavaScript) that allows access to system objects.

COM is extremely important in Microsoft's Internet strategy because the extensibility of Microsoft tools is built around it. This includes server engines like Active Server Pages and FoxISAPI, which can be extended by calling COM objects. As you've seen in the previous section, COM can be used to hook Web back-end applications directly out of the ISAPI layer. COM is also used for extending Active Server Pages with system functionality. COM is used as the binding mechanism for RDS, which consists of a client-hosted ActiveX control and a server-hosted COM object marshaled over HTTP. The two objects communicate using COM over HTTP. In short, COM is everywhere when you work with Microsoft Internet technology.

COM and Visual FoxPro

The good news is that COM integration with Visual FoxPro is easy and almost transparent if you're already familiar with Visual FoxPro. Visual FoxPro can be both a COM client and server. COM client support has been in Visual FoxPro since version 3.0 and includes both the ability to call COM servers like Word or Excel from an application as well as the ability to host ActiveX controls. Creating COM objects makes it possible for Visual FoxPro classes to expose any PUBLIC methods and properties to COM client applications.

To create a COM object in VFP, you simply need to know how to create a class and add a special OLEPUBLIC keyword to the class definition (or check the OLEPUBLIC flag in the Class Info dialog):

```
DEFINE CLASS SimpleServer as Custom OLEPUBLIC

FUNCTION HelloWorld
LPARAMETER lcName
RETURN "Hello " + lcName + "! The time is: " + TIME()

ENDDEFINE
```

Compiling this little class definition into an EXE or COM DLL will cause Visual FoxPro to create a COM object that can be called from any COM client. To call your COM object in VFP you can do this from the command window:

```
loServer = CreateObject("SimpleServer.Simple")
? loServer.HelloWorld("Rick")
```

Not so useful, since you could also call the class directly. But you can also call your COM object from a Visual Basic application:

```
SET loServer = CreateObject("SimpleServer.Simple")
lcHello = loServer.HelloWorld("Rick")
```

If you're ready to take the object onto the Web, you can call it from an Active Server Page (if you plan to use ASP make sure to compile the server to a DLL):

```
<HTML>
<% SET loServer = CreateObject("SimpleServer.Simple") %>
<%= loServer.HelloWorld("Rick") %>
</HTML>
```

As you can see, COM servers are simple to implement from the Visual FoxPro perspective. Calling these servers from other applications is also very straightforward and not all that different from the way you call the same object in Visual FoxPro natively.

The basics of COM are easy to deal with in Visual FoxPro. Complexities come into play when you start building applications that call your servers in high-volume environments. Any server application that expects high volumes will have to deal with load balancing and issues of making sure that the resources on the server are used efficiently. Technologies like Microsoft Transaction Server and Microsoft Message Queue become important in balancing resource use and handling server availability for creating applications that are scalable and provide reliable service. Because Visual FoxPro can build only single-threaded servers, there are some special issues involved in scaling Visual FoxPro COM objects. I'll introduce some of these issues in Chapter 4, and discuss them in more detail in Chapters 9 and 10.

What else do you need to know?

This chapter has gone over the terminology and reviewed the data flow between client and server. I've touched on what I think are the most important aspects that you should be familiar with before diving into the individual technologies and getting your hands dirty with code. The terminology can be a little overwhelming at first, but after reading through this chapter you should feel confident when you see certain terms come up again in the context of the discussion.

There is much more to discuss in terms of technology. I consciously deferred discussion of specific technologies that are more implementation-specific to the appropriate chapters. You will find out about ADO in the next chapter, and about RDS in Chapter 8. These technologies are important, but they are not essential to the infrastructure and can be better covered in the context of actually being used. I'll also expand on using COM with Visual FoxPro as we get into building COM objects.

This chapter has dealt with the infrastructure. The next chapter will take you through the configuration issues of setting up your server and development environment.

Chapter 3
Setting Up

Getting started is always a hard thing. But Windows NT makes it relatively easy to get a Web server up and running simply by installing the operating system. In this short chapter I'll look at what you need to run a Web server and some of the services that it provides. I'll also take you through some configuration options of Internet Information Server and how they affect the operations of the Web server.

The last two chapters have given you an overview of some of the technologies involved in building Internet applications. At first glance it seems as if you're dealing with a truly complex environment that would be difficult to set up. The good news is that it's rather straightforward, especially if you're using Windows NT Server with the NT Option Pack (or Windows 2000 Server or higher). Windows NT can provide you with everything you need. To get started, you need the following:

- A fast Pentium box (200Mhz+ and 64M+ memory)
- Windows NT
- Web server (IIS 4.0)
- Server-side Web development tool (ASP or FoxISAPI, etc.)
- Web browser

Web development is resource intensive, so I highly recommend doing development on a beefy machine. Get a fast processor. Web apps will run on slower processors, but they'll run slowly. There's nothing worse than waiting for your disk light to spin while you're waiting for the Web browser to render the current page. Or, worse: waiting for Visual InterDev to start "running an application"—it's slow even on a blazing machine. One thing you don't want is an application that's slowed down by an aging CPU. While developing, you'll be using a lot of resource-intensive applications simultaneously, so make sure you have lots of memory—I recommend at least 128M for a development machine. A large, fast hard disk is also recommended, because installing Visual Studio in full can chew up close to 1 gigabyte (a typical install is still 300-400M).

I highly recommend using Windows NT for your development machine. You can use Windows 95/98 and add the Personal Web Server for Windows 95/98, but it isn't terribly stable and can't be interactively configured. Other Web servers like Apache and Website also run under Windows 95, but they aren't as stable under these platforms, either. Windows 95/98 Web servers are generally slow, and this platform might not be a good choice for running lots of resource-intensive development applications simultaneously. Finally, Windows 95/98 is not licensed to allow access by more than 10 simultaneous users, which means it can't legally be used by Web applications other than those under development. For this reason, all online servers—including those running Website or Apache—must use Windows NT (okay, or Unix, Linux, and so forth).

Windows NT—Platform of choice for Web applications

Windows NT provides all you need to get a Web server up and running out of the box. You can install Windows NT 4.0, Service Pack 3 or later, and the Windows NT Option Pack. Once installed, your NT machine is a Web server (on NT Workstation you have to install Personal Web Server, or PWS, by checking an option from the setup program).

Windows NT comes with IIS (on NT Server) and PWS (on Workstation). These servers are identical in functionality, but differ in their administrative interfaces. Personal Web Server has a few advanced features disabled, but essentially the same system service power as IIS.

> ### Windows NT Workstation and Personal Web Server 4.0
> *During installation of NT Workstation, the Web server setup does not automatically install the Microsoft Management Console. When you run setup, make sure you opt to install the Management Console, since it provides the administration interface to the Web server. Without it, the Web Configuration Wizard is all that's available, and it provides only a small subset of functionality. In order to properly configure Personal Web Server, the Management Console is required. You can install it by re-running the PWS setup program.*

Once NT is installed, you should be able to access your Web server on the local machine by firing up your browser and typing `http://localhost/`. This will bring up the default IIS home page that the IIS setup program installed.

This demonstrates that everything can run on a single machine. A machine configured with a Web server can be Web server and Web client at the same time. This means that you can—and usually will—develop your applications locally and then deploy them on a production server once you get it running and debugged locally.

Windows NT is the platform of choice, not only for its Web support as part of the operating system, but also because of stability, which is critical when building applications that take advantage of NT's architecture to provide a distributed environment. As pointed out in the previous chapter, Internet technologies rely heavily on interdependencies of multiple technologies.

Windows NT also provides the key piece required for Web development: the Web server.

Internet Information Server

Web servers are relatively simple applications on the surface—it's their job to take incoming TCP/IP requests from clients and route them to the appropriate files or services via the HTTP protocol. Web servers use HTTP to communicate with the client, which typically is a Web browser but can be any type of application that can communicate via HTTP. In Chapter 7, you'll see some examples of Visual FoxPro as a Web client instead of a browser.

The Web server is configurable to tune performance and adjust the layout of your Web site. A Web server presents its interface in much the same way as a file system. It's based on the same metaphor of folders starting at a root directory with subdirectories (also known as virtual directories) that sit below the root directory. Unlike a file system, a Web server is based on virtual directories—logical directories that are mapped to specific physical directories on the machine. So the root directory, or "/", is mapped to something like `c:\inetput\wwwroot` by default. You can change the root directory to any location that you chose in the IIS Management Console, which you can open from the Start menu's Internet Information Server group. The Console form in **Figure 3.1** displays your Web site's directory structure.

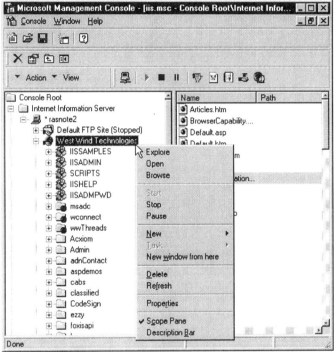

Figure 3.1. *The Microsoft Management Console displays your Web site's directory structure. The root is the Web site—in this case West Wind Technologies.*

The console displays a hierarchical view of the Web site, with the Web site at the top level. You can have multiple Web sites on a single machine, with each Web site tied to a separate IP address on your server. To configure multiple IP addresses, use the Network Control Panel applet and the TCP/IP Driver Properties dialog. Once you've configured multiple IP addresses, you can create a new Web site and tie it to this IP address.

Below the Web server root are virtual applications, virtual directories and subdirectories. Figure 3.1 displays these with different icons: The package icon is a virtual application, which means it is configured to run in its own memory space and has several ASP-specific options enabled (I'll discuss this in more detail in Chapter 4).

Virtual directories are specially configured. They can live anywhere and are mapped to be visible underneath the Web server root. For example, if the Web root is installed to point at a physical path of c:\inetpub\wwwroot\, you can create a virtual directory that points at c:\http\MyVirtual and name it MyVirtual. Although the physical path is not below the Web root path, you can reference the virtual directory through the Web as
`http://localhost/MyVirtual/`.

Any directories below the Web root directory that are not specially marked as virtual directories inherit all settings from the Web root. These directories are accessible just like virtual directories. In terms of IIS, plain subdirectories belong to the virtual directory or the root that they reside under. Each virtual directory defines its own application, and any plain subdirectories below the virtual directory belong to it and inherit rights from the virtual directory.

All directories can be configured with a complex Properties dialog. **Figure 3.2** shows the Home Directory tab of this multi-page dialog. The Home Directory tab is the most important because it's used to configure every virtual directory, including the Web root and virtual application paths.

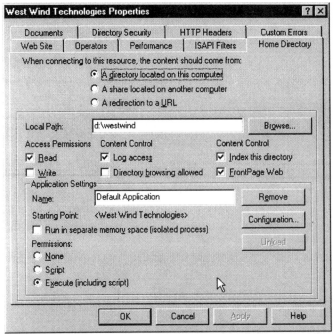

Figure 3.2. The property sheet for a virtual directory allows you to configure where the virtual directory points and how that directory and any below it can be accessed. Directories using ASP or ISAPI applications must have script access (ASP and other script engines) or Execute access (ISAPI (.dll) or CGI (.exe)).

The most important item on the Home Directory tab is the Local Path field, which tells the server to which physical DOS path to map the virtual directory. In Figure 3.2, my home directory is d:\westwind and all my virtual directories tend to sit below that directory. Note that I have this directory set up to allow Execute access, which makes it possible for me to run ISAPI and CGI extensions from that directory and any below it. ISAPI/CGI requires Execute rights, while ASP and any other script extension can get by with script rights. This maps directly to NT user rights for the IUSR_Machinename account on that machine. The rights are set as RX (Read/Execute) if you look up the permissions created in that directory.

> ### Be careful with Execute rights
> *Execute rights in directories that hold downloadable files can be a problem.*
> *For example, if you have some self-extracting ZIP files with EXE extensions*
> *in a directory that is marked for Execute rights, the Unzip utility will actually start to*
> *run on the server, thinking the EXE file is a CGI executable. Because the Zip utility*
> *has a user interface that asks the user for input, the program will simply hang*
> *invisibly (you can see this in Task Manager, but won't see it on the desktop). If a*
> *few people do this, you'll run out of resources quickly.*
>
> *Make sure that any directory that contains executable/binary files has Execute*
> *rights disabled. Execute rights must be set only for direct ISAPI (.dll) and CGI*
> *(.exe) executables. Active Server Pages and other script engines like Cold Fusion*
> *and Web Connection require only script access.*

Understand that a virtual directory propagates its settings down the directory tree. If I set up a virtual directory named /demos, all directories below it (such as /demos/examples/) automatically inherit the rights from the parent, unless the directory in question is a virtual directory itself.

When you set up a new Web application it's usually a good idea to create a new virtual directory for it. This ensures that changes at a higher level of the Web site won't adversely affect the settings you're expecting for your application.

So far I've shown you all you need to get started. The IIS defaults are reasonable, and even the basics I outlined so far don't need to be changed. Following are more detailed settings that you might be interested in as you get into development.

Configuration of the site

When you install Windows NT, the Web server configures itself for basic operation and is ready to run. As soon as NT is installed, `http://localhost/` has you on your way. Take a look around the Web server's property sheet as shown in **Figure 3.3**.

The Web Site tab gives you the opportunity to name your Web site and assign it to an IP address and TCP port. In general, HTTP servers all work on port 80, so it's unlikely you'll change this setting. You can use a different port if you choose, but your clients must explicitly specify that port (http://localhost:125, for example). Because your machine can have multiple IP addresses, there's an option to change the IP address to a specific one. The default (All Unassigned) simply means to use the primary IP address assigned to the network adapter. If you've added additional virtual IP addresses, you can use the drop-down list to map to a specific address. Also, note that if you're online with an ISP you might see your dynamic IP address assigned by the ISP. What's cool is that by assigning the server to this IP address you can make your server accessible to anyone over the Internet—as long as they know that IP address. It's a good way to demo applications if you don't host your own server on the Internet.

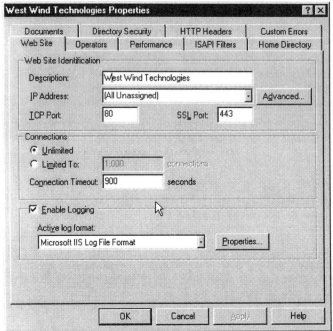

Figure 3.3. The Web Site tab displays basic information and allows you to configure the server to handle client connections.

Connection Timeout is an important setting that determines how long IIS tries to hang on to a client connection. This means if you run a request that takes more than 900 seconds, an error will occur in the client browser. The timeout controls how IIS manages a TCP/IP connection. IIS 4.0 uses HTTP 1.1, which uses keep-alive connections. The timeout also deals with how long IIS will try to maintain the connection to the HTTP client/browser, even if it goes idle. This can improve performance because the client doesn't need to reconnect to the TCP/IP port on the server, but it also uses resources on the server and ties up a connection. The longer the timeout, the more connections are likely to be open at any given time. Therefore, you want to make this timeout as short as you can. It should be slightly longer than the longest request you intend to run—and I sure hope you don't plan to have requests that run for 15 minutes!

The Documents tab lets you configure which pages are considered "default" documents, so a URL like http://localhost/ automatically goes to a default page like Default.asp. When IIS receives a URL without an explicit file link, it looks for the default file list to display a page as if the filename were typed into the URL. If not found, it displays an error stating that directory browse access was denied. You can configure a virtual directory to allow directory browsing on the Home Directory tab, as shown in Figure 3.2.

Another important page is the Security tab. Select the Allow Anonymous Access option and you should see a dialog like the one shown in **Figure 3.4**. IIS uses a special account called IUSR_MachineName (where *MachineName* is the name of your machine) to identify anonymous Web users. This account is created by default when IIS is installed, and it creates a random password for this account. You can change this user and password to a specific user's account on your machine by clicking the Edit button in the Allow Anonymous Access section.If you want to force everyone to log in before they access the site, disable the Anonymous user account, in which case every user will receive the Login dialog box.

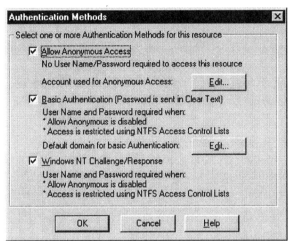

Figure 3.4. *Select all security options on the Application Methods dialog to take advantage of NT security at the directory and application levels.*

Web applications that want to tie into NT security can do so using a mechanism provided by HTTP called *Basic Authentication.* This process allows a Web application to ask the user for a username and password, which brings up a login dialog in the browser. Once the user types in this information, the information is sent back to the server, which can retrieve the username if the user logged in successfully. This is extremely useful for administration tasks on a Web site, but it can also be used as a security mechanism to track users through a site. Basic authentication is not secure! The username and password are sent over the wire with only minor (non-secret) encryption, which makes it possible to hijack the password with a network protocol analyzer. To avoid this problem, you can use Secure Socket Layer (SSL or HTTPS) encryption on any links that asks for a password.

The Windows NT Challenge Response option deals with file-level access control. You can control access rights to Web-accessed files simply by setting file-access rights in Explorer. You can add and delete users and groups as needed, and the Web server will forward access requests with the login box to the browser. Unlike basic authentication, NT Challenge Response is secure. For any file to which you want to limit anonymous Web access, make sure you remove the IUSR_xxxx account from the Access Control List (Explorer's Permissions dialog).

SSL and secure certificates

To serve information securely so it can't be picked up off the wire with a protocol analyzer, run requests in secure SSL mode. SSL is an encryption mechanism that encrypts and decrypts data as it travels over the network, making it impossible to capture usable data off the wire.

You can set up HTTPS operation (which uses SSL) by installing a secure certificate on the Web server. Third-party Certificate Authorities (CA) like Verisign (www.verisign.com/) offer certificates that cost $350 to establish and $250 a year to renew. Prices vary depending on the CA. You use the key manager to create a key request, which is simply a text file. You then go to the certificate authority's signup page, which will ask for the key request as input. Based on the key request, the CA will issue you a completed certificate—another text file—that you can install on your server.

Once the certificate is installed, you can use HTTPS requests on your server. SSL requests run through a different TCP/IP port—443—which is configurable as shown in Figure 3.2. Using secure pages is as simple as changing any URL's protocol to HTTPS:// instead of HTTP://.

Active Server application options

Every virtual directory you create also has options that determine the behavior of Active Server Pages for the application. These settings are crucial if you use Active Server Pages because they can improve performance considerably. **Figure 3.5** shows the Application Configuration dialog, which you can access from the console's Home Directory tab by clicking the Configuration button.

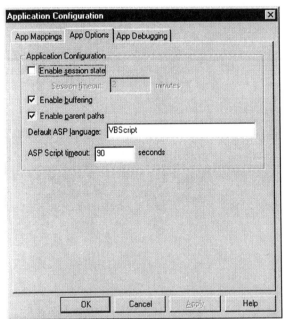

Figure 3.5. The Application options allow you to configure various ASP settings. The settings can affect performance, so any features not used by applications should be turned off.

If you're using ASP and you don't use the Session object in your applications, turn off the "Enable session state" option. This option is resource intensive and creates an HTTP cookie on every page hit, which wastes bandwidth in addition to requiring server resources.

Buffering affects output from an ASP page. When buffering is not enabled, ASP uses an internal buffer to hold small chunks of output and send the output when ready. In most cases it uses the underlying ISAPI WriteClient() function to send output to the output stream. When buffering is enabled, all page output is first collected in memory and then sent to the output stream all at once. In most cases, buffered pages run faster than continually writing out the data in small chunks. In addition, buffering allows you to manipulate the page headers after some data has been sent to the page. If you're modifying HTTP headers, you must have buffering enabled, either through the server option or by setting the Response.Buffer property in the first line of ASP code. In general I set buffering on.

Explore the dialogs
A number of additional options are available to customize your server. For example, you can customize error messages, assign administration users to the site, allow and deny access to specific IP address blocks, and add and remove ISAPI filters. The interface is nice because it exposes a lot of functionality—a huge improvement over IIS 3.0. But it comes at the cost of complexity: Finding the option you want can require several trips through these dialogs.

IIS admin objects—do it programmatically
IIS keeps its administration information in a special Metabase file. The Microsoft Management Console exposes most of the common settings, but a large number of additional keys are available that are not configurable through the user interface. The IIS Resource Kit includes a utility called Metabrowse that allows browsing the metabase and setting specific keys in it.

The metabase also can be administered through Active Directory and the IIS Admin objects. The interface is COM based and can be run from VFP or even through an Active Server Page. Here is the VFP code for creating and configuring a virtual directory:

```
o=createobject("iisNamespace")

oServer = o.GetObject("IISWebServer","LOCALHOST/W3SVC")
? oServer.ASPAllowOutOfProcComponents
oServer.ASPAllowOutOfProcComponents = .T.

oServer.SetInfo()    && Save Settings

*** Get Virtual directory information
oVirtual = o.GetObject("IISWebVirtualDir","LOCALHOST/W3SVC/1/ROOT/wconnect")

? oVirtual.Path
? oVirtual.AccessExecute
? oVirtual.AccessRead
```

```
*** Create a new virtual directory and configure
oVirtual = o.GetObject("IISWebVirtualDir","LOCALHOST/W3SVC/1/ROOT")
oNewVirtual = oVirtual.Create("IISWebVirtualDir","Test")
oNewVirtual.Path = "c:\http\Test"
oNewVirtual.AccessRead = .T.
oNewVirtual.AccessScript = .T.

oNewVirtual.SetInfo()
```

Using the Admin objects is easy enough, but it's more difficult to find out which key names and object types to access. The Metabrowse mentioned above can make it easier to figure out keys. ADSI will be integrated with Active Directory in Windows 2000 (NT 5), and that operating system will allow you to browse any Active Directory trees and nodes as part of the operating system.

Because the ADSI is COM based, you can also run code like this directly from Visual Basic, an ASP page and the Windows Scripting host. With this interface you can create virtual directories and script maps, and add filters programmatically. If you need to build installation programs that require setting IIS configuration information, this is your ticket to ride.

Starting out

The basic configuration to get started with Web development is straightforward. If you use NT Server with IIS, the Web server is ready to use as soon as you finish installing the operating system. Take the time to create a new base Web site in a new location to display company data. If you're just getting started, play with adding virtual directories and accessing pages on the Web server. Take the time to think about how to lay out your Web site—put images in separate directories and layer your site so all the information doesn't end up in a single directory. It might seem like overkill when you start out with directories of just one file, but as you get going you'll find that pages explode very quickly and become unmanageable.

Finally, try to look past the initial complexity of options available to you. This is probably the number one complaint I hear from people: too many choices and an overload of options that you might not understand at first. Don't worry—it's not that difficult, but there is a lot of information to absorb. As you read on, stick to the book and it will guide you through the technologies one at a time, giving you a chance to understand each step as a piece of the complex puzzle that is Internet development.

The next section will let you get your hands dirty with some code.

Section 2
Server-Side Development

Server-based Web applications continue to dominate the Internet application landscape. Pure Web applications that are driven entirely from a Web server are probably your main use of Internet applications. Every time you hit a Web site with your browser to look up information—from shopping at an online store for computer hardware, books or CDs, to looking up the shipping status of a UPS tracking number—you run an application on a remote server, which provides the logic and interface display through server-generated HTML.

Server-side Web development is the cornerpiece of most Internet technology that is arriving today. While Section 2 deals specifically with building pure server-side Web applications, the very same Web server backbone can also service rich client/server applications that use HTTP as the message protocol. You can apply the technologies learned in this chapter to Section 3, Client-Side Development. The beauty is that the exact same technology and concepts can be applied.

This section describes two specific server-side Microsoft development technologies, which you can use with Visual FoxPro. Active Server Pages is Microsoft's prominent server-side tool for building script-based applications that mix HTML with a scripting language to build dynamic content. Active Server Pages can provide direct data access via OLE DB and ODBC and also provide the ability to create and call COM objects from within the script code. COM calls allow you to take advantage of Visual FoxPro's ability to build COM components, which can then be accessed directly from the scripted ASP pages.

FoxISAPI is based on a more traditional approach of building a Web application—calling a back-end server process that responds to Web requests. FoxISAPI provides a much more Fox-centric development approach than ASP by requiring a Fox application to handle requests directly. Chapter 5 introduces a framework that makes this process straightforward and even provides the tools to implement much of the same functionality that ASP provides from within the Fox code. FoxISAPI also makes use of COM to interface Visual FoxPro servers with the Web server via the ISAPI interface—this fact makes FoxISAPI a little more complex to get started with.

Both chapters in Section 2 contain Web development information that is useful beyond the individual tool, so even if you don't use one or the other you might want to look at the chapter for alternative Web development techniques.

Chapter 4
Active Server Pages

Microsoft's premier push to server-side Web development has been with Active Server Pages (ASP). This technology is an accessible scripting language added to HTML documents and a powerful, component-based object model that allows advanced functionality and extension through COM.

ASP support automatically installs with the IIS Web server. The beauty of ASP is its initial simplicity, both for creating dynamic content quickly and the ability to easily deploy the content online without further configuration. Beyond the basics, however, ASP requires a good understanding of COM and how NT works under the hood. Extending functionality through external components can be complex.

This chapter starts out with a technology overview of how ASP is implemented, followed by an introduction to the scripting model. Then I'll examine basic database connectivity using ADO to hook up to the TasTrade sample application. The next steps will integrate Visual FoxPro COM objects with Active Server Pages—from a few simple examples to some specific issues that you need to deal with to effectively run your VFP COM components through ASP.

Scripting people in a component world

Building complex Web applications is no trivial task. Many different technologies must be integrated to provide a solid back-end Web development environment. Getting all the components to work together is a difficult task. Microsoft has done a good job of addressing many of these integration issues with the release of Active Server Pages as part of Internet Information Server (IIS).

ASP is a scripting engine, but Microsoft is not the first company to release a scripting engine for Web development. Tools like Cold Fusion had introduced the ability to build scripted HTML pages that mix both HTML and program logic a few years before Microsoft got into the act with ASP. But Microsoft has legitimized the concept of server-side scripting by directly integrating the Active Server Scripting engine into IIS—when you install IIS 4.0, the scripting engine and ASP pages are automatically available for your use. Because Microsoft is behind this standard and ASP uses all the standard Microsoft technologies—VBA (VBScript is a subset of VBA) and COM—ASP has quickly become an accepted standard for building Web applications. One of the main reasons for the quick acceptance of ASP is the ability to utilize code and knowledge from non-Web environments in the ASP environment without having to make many changes.

The scripting engine allows mixing HTML and code on the same page. The language engine gives ASP its power by supporting both VBScript and JScript natively. Other languages can be plugged into the COM-based scripting engine by third parties. While both VBScript and JScript are stripped-down versions of full development languages, both make it possible to extend the basic language by calling external COM objects. Since Microsoft is exposing just about everything via COM these days, most of Windows is already available to scripting through ASP. A good example is ActiveX Data Objects (ADO), which is Microsoft's latest and preferred data access mechanism, and the most commonly used mechanism with Active Server Pages. Because ADO is built with COM interfaces, it is accessible from ASP, just as it is from Visual FoxPro or Visual Basic.

The power of ASP doesn't stop with system-provided components. You can, of course, build your own components to extend the functionality of ASP. You can create a COM object with Visual FoxPro, VB or VC++ using your own program logic and call that object directly from an Active Server Page using the CreateObject syntax familiar in Visual FoxPro. There is tremendous power in this. Microsoft doesn't need to support every possible feature of the operating system, because the model is fully extensible through COM. You only add what you need. The component model has finally arrived!

Microsoft is also pushing tools to make development of ASP applications easier. Visual InterDev (VID) is targeted squarely at ASP developers with an amazing array of tools, wizards and widgets to make it easier for developers to get into the Web. Personally, I'm not sold on Visual InterDev—there's too much clutter and the tools are not very well integrated. It's also very slow because everything is connected to a virtual Web, and startup to run individual pages can take upwards of 30 seconds—productivity really suffers with this kind of delay. Your mileage may vary, but I find that I'm much more productive working directly with script code and HTML, rather than letting wizards do it for me and later having to figure out the wizard's code. While I do use VID, I tend to use the editor and the data viewer but not much else. Since VID is a big enough product to require a whole book on its own, I won't talk about its features here, but instead I'll focus on the core ASP technology. I leave the choice of tools up to you, whether it's something as simple as Visual Notepad, or a full-featured package like Visual InterDev, or a fancy graphic page designer like Microsoft FrontPage. Here I'll use Visual InterDev for code editing and FrontPage for pages that require more visual design aspects. I'll point out which one I'm using—and why—when appropriate.

How it works

The Active Server Pages engine is implemented as a *script mapped* ISAPI server extension. The driving engine—ASP.dll—is an *ISAPI extension* that is called whenever someone accesses a page with an .ASP extension. A script map in the server's metabase (or registry settings on IIS 3.0) causes the ASP script to be redirected to this DLL. Script maps are meant to give the impression that the developer or user is "executing" the .ASP page directly, but in reality ASP.dll is invoked for each .ASP file. ASP.dll hosts the VBScript or JScript interpreter and HTML parser, which in turn parses the ASP pages, expanding any code inside the page and converting it to HTTP-compliant output to return to the Web server. **Figure 4.1** shows how the architecture is put together.

The script code can use any feature that the scripting language supports. One important feature of the engine is its ability to support COM objects. ASP starts up with several built-in COM objects that are always available to you in your ASP pages. The Request and Response objects handle retrieving input and sending output for the active Web page. The Server object provides an interface to system services, the most important of which is the ability to launch COM objects. The Session and Application objects provide state management to allow creation of persistent data that has a lifetime of the application or of a user's session, respectively.

Figure 4.1 also shows ActiveX Data Objects. Although ADO is not an intrinsic component of ASP that must be explicitly created with Server.CreateObject(), it is so closely related to ASP that it should be listed here. ADO is used to access any system data source (system DSN or OLE DB provider) on your system through familiar SQL connection and execution syntax. Finally, you can load any COM object available on the local system. But there are some limitations: The object must support the IDispatch interface and late binding in order to be used by ASP, but that's hardly a limitation since most objects support the dual interface standard. All COM objects built with Visual FoxPro or Visual Basic support this interface.

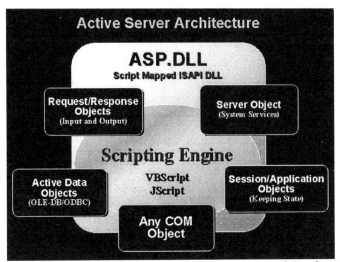

Figure 4.1. *The Active Server Architecture consists of an ISAPI extension that hosts a capable scripting engine. Among other things, the scripting engine has the ability to load COM objects to extend Active Server Pages into the system and into your own custom components.*

Notice that the ISAPI DLL is the actual host of the scripting engine. ASP.dll is hosted in the IIS process and the scripting engine, and any in-process COM objects launched from it also run inside this process. This is an important fact—since components run inside IIS, they have the potential to crash or hang the Web server on failure. Moreover, component development can be very tricky because components running inside IIS can be difficult or impossible to debug at runtime.

In order to "run" ASP pages, you need to make sure that your Web directories that access ASP pages are set up to allow script execution. You can find this option in the IIS Administration utility under the virtual directory options. **Figure 4.2** shows the IIS Management Console with the properties for a virtual directory pulled up. Notice the Script Permissions—if you also run any ISAPI DLLs or CGI EXEs in this directory, check the Execute flag instead of Script.

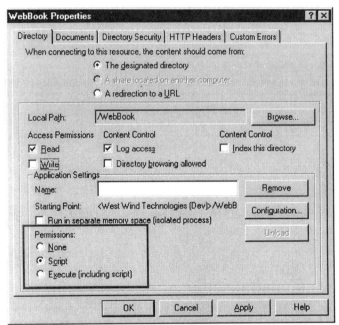

Figure 4.2. Make sure you configure your server either globally or at the virtual directory level for script execution. ASP requires either script or execute rights to run scripts. Otherwise you'll get an Access Denied error.

Also notice the "Run in separate memory space" checkbox. When checked, you set up your virtual directory as a separate Microsoft Transaction Server-hosted application that runs independently of the "global" Web server's COM environment. This means that if you have ill-behaved code, especially badly behaved COM objects, it doesn't affect the rest of the Web server, except for this virtual directory and the application associated with it. If a COM component crashes, it might take down the virtual application, but it won't crash the server. Another useful feature of a separate application is the ability to unload it independently of the Web server; you can do so with the Unload button shown in Figure 4.2. The button is disabled here because the application has not yet been started. Once you hit any ASP page in the virtual directory, this button becomes enabled and allows you to "reset" the application. This feature is very useful for unloading COM objects loaded from ASP pages because COM objects cannot be unloaded in any other way—other than shutting down the IIS Web service. I'll discuss this in more detail later when we talk about COM access.

Scripting for the masses

In this text I'm using VBScript because it is the more popular server-side scripting language, while JavaScript/JScript is the more common client-side language. Keep in mind that if you prefer JScript you can use it instead of VBScript. In fact, you can use both languages in the same ASP document by explicitly providing the LANGUAGE tag for script code:

```
<SCRIPT RUNAT="SERVER" LANGUAGE="JScript">
Function MyCode
  var MyCode = "Hello World JS";
  Return MyCode;
End Function
</SCRIPT>
<SCRIPT RUNAT="SERVER" LANGUAGE="VBScript">
Function MyCodeVB
  MyCodeVB = "Hello World VB"
End Function
</SCRIPT>
```

Because ASP is a server-side development tool, you can use it to build browser-independent output. Although you can use Microsoft-specific VBScript in your scripting pages, the output you generate will run on any Web browser assuming you return compliant HTML. The output you generate can be anything at all, from HTML or plain text to binary data or XML. ASP by itself doesn't generate any output for you—rather, you use the document itself as the output mechanism. Anything that isn't delimited as code is output as is. Embedded script tags are evaluated or executed from the top of the page down and expanded into the HTML base document, replacing the original script tags. In addition, output can also be generated from within scripted code using the Response object. Think of an ASP document like a VFP TextMerge document where TEXT/ENDTEXT and << >> merge expressions are delimited with <% %> tags instead.

An ASP document can contain HTML text, script code, or both HTML and script code. Because ASP pages are script maps, they always run through the ISAPI extension that must parse the ASP document for script tags. For this reason, an ASP document that contains only HTML will run slower than a plain HTML document loaded directly from disk.

Script code you write inside scripted pages is delimited from the rest of the document with special script tags. There are two kinds of script tags: *output expressions* and *code blocks*. They can be used in three different ways:

- **Output expressions**
  Single expressions can consist of fields from a database, any single function, or object method calls that return a single value that is to be embedded into the HTML document. Embedded expressions use the <%= %> tags and look like this:

  ```
  The time is: <%= now %>
  <%= oRS("DataBaseField") %>
  <%= oObject.Method("Parameter") %>
  ```

  These expressions cause output to be embedded directly into the HTML document. In other words, the expression is replaced with the result value of the expression. Note that VBScript automatically converts all types to strings—if you need special output formatting, you need to use the various VBScript Format functions (like FormatDateTime, FormatNumber, and so on).

- **Code blocks**

  Basically any code that's not an expression must be in command format. This includes any VBScript command or control statements. Unlike expression tags, command blocks don't output any text—if you need to do any output from within the code, you have to use the Response object as shown in the snippet below. Code can be either in entire blocks or multiple commands in a row. All command and code blocks use <% %> tags:

  ```
  <%
  For x = 1 to 10
     '*** Send string to output document
     Response.Write("Pass Number: " & x & "<br>")
  Next x
  %>
  ```

- **Single-line commands and control structures**

  Realistically, single-line command structures are no different from code blocks, but they illustrate the dynamic nature of the ASP scripting model. Consider command structures such as IF and FOR that have code or text between the control statements. For example:

  ```
  <% If rs("Sex") = "Yes" Then %>
     <b>Please!</b>
  <% Else %>
     <b>Put a lock on it</b>
  <% End If %>
  ```

  VBScript command structures can be broken up with HTML between the individual control structure statements. You can also have code following the first snippet before the closing script tag. If you were to rewrite the command block from the previous section, you'd end up with:

  ```
  <% For x = 1 to 10
     lcString = "String" & x %>
     Pass Number: <%= lcString %> <br>
  <% Next x %>
  ```

  The ability to embed code simply by delimiting the code from the HTML text is a powerful tool for creating applications that are easily deployed. Because the code is contained in the HTML—a text document—updating code online is as simple as updating a file. On the downside, code mixed with HTML makes for a very messy coding environment—finding code might not be straightforward because it may be lodged between some HTML display logic.

Objects galore

In order to do anything interesting with Active Server Pages, you need to look at the available objects. Most tools and functionality provided by ASP are brought to you through objects. The base engine exposes a number of useful objects that can be easily accessed by your scripting code. **Table 1** is a list of the available built-in objects.

Table 1. Built-in ASP objects.

Object	What it does
Request	Handles all input from HTML forms, the Web server and the browser. The Request object is responsible for providing the information you need to create queries or act on requests. The Request object provides a number of collection objects you can access, which include Form, QueryString, ServerVariables and cookies.
Response	This object is the counterpart to the Request object that is responsible for dynamic output. The basic method is Response.Write(), which allows dynamic creation of text output to an HTML document that gets sent back to the server and then the browser. With this object you can control direct output as well as the HTTP header, including cookies and special features such as redirection and authentication.
ADO	The ActiveX Data Object is an external object that you can use to access any ODBC or OLE DB data source. This object must be explicitly created with SERVER.CREATEOBJECT("ADODB.Connection") and/or ADODB.RecordSet.
Server	The Server object provides an interface to system services. The most important aspect of the Server object is its ability to instantiate external COM objects including Visual FoxPro Automation servers.
Session/Application	These two powerful objects allow you to manage state between individual requests. By its nature, HTTP requests are stateless, meaning the current request knows nothing about the previous request unless you pass the relevant data to it. These objects allow attachment of external property values to dynamic objects so you can create persistent variables that are available for the duration of a user's connection or an approximation of "global" variables via the Application object.

All input comes from the Request object

The Request object is used extensively in this chapter to retrieve input from users of the Web application. The Request object brings back information from HTML forms that the user entered using a POST request, as well as information about the ServerVariables—information that the Web server makes available about itself, the Web browser and the current request that's running. For example, we can use the request object to retrieve some user input. Take the following HTML form:

```
<HTML>
<form action=" RequestDemo1.asp" method="POST">
Enter your name: <input type="TEXT" value="" name="txtName"><br>
Enter your company: <input type="TEXT" value="" name="txtCompany"><br>
<input type="SUBMIT" value="Send">
</HTML>
```

This request submits a name and company to the Web server and the RequestDemo1.asp. On the server, the RequestDemo1.asp page and then does the following:

```
<HTML>
<%
 lcName = Form("txtName")
 lcCompany = Form("txtCompany")
%>
```

```
Thank you, <%= lcName %> <p>
You're calling from the following IP address:
<%= Request.ServerVariables("REMOTE_HOST") and your browser is:
<%= Request.ServerVariables("HTTP_USER_AGENT")

</HTML>
```

This simple code demonstrates the use of the Request object to retrieve form variables and server variables. Note that you can assign anything retrieved to a variable and use that variable in the remainder of your page. The entire page is essentially treated as one running program that also happens to contain some static HTML text. I assigned the name and company to variables, but this is not strictly necessary. Just like the Request.ServerVariables() method calls that are directly embedded in the code, you could use the Form object directly and output the result using the expression evaluator <%= %>.

At this point you might be wondering which server variables are available. **Table 2** shows a few commonly used ones—for a complete list, see the MSDN documentation for the ServerVariables collection.

Table 2. ASP server variables.

Server Variable	What it does
HTTP_REFERER	The link that called the current page. Not available (blank) when typing in the URL.
HTTP_USER_AGENT	Browser identification string. Useful for deciding what type of browser-specific output to generate.
REMOTE_ADDRESS	The remote user's IP address. Note that it's possible for users coming through proxy servers to have the same IP address. Don't assume this value is unique and can be used as a key!
REMOTE_USER	The user name of a user who has successfully logged on with a username and password via Basic Authentication or by NT Passthrough security.
SERVER_NAME	The name of the server as it appears on the URL. Useful for dynamically building URL strings.
SERVER_PROTOCOL	The protocol (HTTP, HTTPS, FTP) used to access this URL.
URL	The relative URL on this server (/default.asp). This is the same as the more traditional CGI SCRIPT_NAME variable.
PATH_TRANSLATED	Returns a system path (i.e. DOS path—not a URL path) pointing to a script page: c:\http\asp\default.asp. This is very powerful for routing scripts and knowing where your application is running from!
QUERY_STRING	Retrieves the full Querystring or URL parameter. Includes everything following the ? in a URL.
HTTP_COOKIE	Contains a full list of cookies that apply. You can also access these with the Cookies collection.

A quick way to see every available server variable is to use the following code, which also demonstrates how to parse the QueryString and Form collections in addition to ServerVariables:

```
<html>
<table Border=1 BGCOLOR="#EEEEEE"
       STYLE="Font:normal normal 9pt 'Verdana'">
<TR BGCOLOR="#CCFFFF"><TH>Form Variable</TH><TH>Value</TH></TR>
<%
For Each lcFormVar In Request.Form
  lcVar =   Request.Form(lcFormVar)
  Response.Write("<TR><TD><b>" & lcFormVar & "</b></TD><TD>" &_
               lcVar & "</TD></TR>")
Next
%>
<TR BGCOLOR="#CCFFFF"><TH COLSPAN=2>Query String</th></TR>
<%
Response.Write("<TR><TD COLSPAN=2><b>" &  "</b>" & _
               Request.ServerVariables("QUERY_STRING") & "</TD></TR>")
For each lcFormVar in Request.QueryString
   lcVar =   Request.QueryString(lcFormVar)
   Response.Write("<TR><TD><b>" & lcFormVar & "</b></TD><TD>" &_
               lcVar & "</TD></TR>")
Next
%>

<TR BGCOLOR="#CCFFFF"><TH>ServerVariable</TH><TH>Value</TH></TR>
<%
For Each lcServerVar In Request.ServerVariables
  lcServer =   Request.ServerVariables(lcServerVar)
  If Len(lcServer) = 0 Then
     lcServer = "n/a"
  End If
     Response.Write("<TR><TD><b>" & lcServerVar & "</b></TD><TD>" &_
               lcServer & "</TD></TR>")
Next
%>
</table>
</html>
```

This code loops through the form and server variables and prints out their values. Keep in mind that some fields won't appear unless they actually apply. For example, HTTP_REFERER, which returns the link that you arrived from, doesn't appear unless you actually arrived from another link—if you simply typed the URL, this value wouldn't exist. However, calling ServerVariables() with these parameters will simply return blank if they're not available. For the same reason, some secure flags don't show up until you run the page under HTTPS, and so on. You can plug this page into any request if you're unsure of what form or server variables are being returned to you—it's a useful debugging tool.

All coded output goes through the Response object

The Response object is the primary output mechanism of your code. Remember that the entire ASP document is treated like one large program. Think of the document much like you would a TEXTMERGE document in Visual FoxPro, where all HTML markup would be delimited with TEXT/ENDTEXT and the rest of the document would contain the program code. Code can be bound around the HTML blocks, and you can even loop through HTML blocks using ASP control structures such as FOR/NEXT DO WHILE and IF/END IF.

When creating dynamic output in script code, you need to use the Response object explicitly as shown in the previous examples. The primary method for sending output to the HTML stream is the Response.Write() method. Any string passed to it is immediately sent to the output stream.

Remember the `<%= %>` expression evaluator construct? Well, in actuality this is simply a shortcut for Response.Write() as well, so the following expressions are equivalent:

```
<%= now %>
<% Response.Write(now) %>
```

The Response object also supports a few other methods (see **Table 3**).

Table 3. Response object methods.

Response Method	What it does
End	Sends all buffered output to the client and stops operation of the ASP script.
Clear	Clears any existing output that has been buffered. It's recommended you use buffered output whenever possible to allow you to manipulate headers while running scripts. (See MSDN for more details.)
Flush	Forces any buffered output to be sent to the client immediately. Don't use if buffering is on.
AddHeader	Adds an HTTP header to output. If buffering is off, AddHeader can only be called prior to any document output being created. Once output is sent, the header cannot be modified. Headers are used for cookies, Cache Control, Redirection and any custom directives for browsers.
Cookies	This collection allows you to add cookies to your request. Pass a name, value and optionally an attribute flag to create a cookie on your request.
Redirect	Allows you to abort the current page and load another HTTP page off the Web. Note that redirects ignore any other HTTP headers, including cookies.

System services through the Server object

The Server object provides system services to an ASP application. The most important and powerful service is the ability to create COM objects. For example:

```
<% Set loVFP = Server.CreateObject("VisualFoxPro.Application") %>

The Visual FoxPro Version on this system is:
<%= loVFP.Eval("Version()") %>
```

Note that in order to create VisualFoxPro.Application you have to adjust IIS in order to allow running EXE servers. See the "Running out-of-process servers with ASP" sidebar for details.

The short script code above causes the Visual FoxPro Application object to load and become available to your ASP application. Using the Eval or DoCmd methods of the application object, you can easily manipulate Visual FoxPro directly from within ASP. On the downside this is rather slow—when you create the VFP object, the entire VFP runtime loads on each page hit as a separate instance of VFP 6.0 starts up. An in-process DLL instead of the out-of-process EXE would be much more efficient here, although it would mean that the runtime would never unload.

More to the point, you can create your own COM objects and call them directly from the ASP page. Thus you have full control over instancing of your server by choosing to build either an out-of-process EXE or in-process DLL. I'll discuss the ability to call VFP COM objects in much more detail later in this chapter.

The Server object provides a handful of useful utility functions such as URLEncode and HTMLEncode, which can take text and make it safe for display as HTML or for embedding into a query string or other mechanism that requires content to be provided in official HTTP safe format.

Using out-of-process servers with ASP

Because VisualFoxPro.Application is an EXE out-of-process server, you need to add some special settings to the IIS metabase. By default, ASP disables loading out-of-process components. You can use the IISAdmin objects to enable the functionality as follows.

Visual FoxPro (6.0 or later only):

```
o = GETOBJECT("IIS://LOCALHOST/W3SVC/1/ROOT")
? o.AspAllowOutOfProcComponents
o.AspAllowOutOfProcComponents = .T.
? o.AspAllowOutOfProcComponents
o.SetInfo() && Save changes
```

Active Server Pages:

```
<%
Set o = GetObject("IIS://LOCALHOST/W3SVC/1/ROOT")
Response.Write(o.AspAllowOutOfProcComponents)
o.AspAllowOutOfProcComponents = True
Response.Write(o.AspAllowOutOfProcComponents)
o.SetInfo
%>
```

Keeping state with Session and Application objects

One of the neatest features of ASP is the inclusion of a built-in Session object. As you know, HTTP is a stateless protocol, which means that each Web request essentially knows nothing about the request that preceded it. Requests fire out of order for different users, and ideally a Web application should reset state at the end of each request to the way it was found on startup. Statelessness is great for scalability, but it's lousy for applications that require you to keep track of what users are doing while navigating through a site.

To get around this, most Web applications require a mechanism to keep state. Most commonly this mechanism is implemented via HTTP cookies that serve as IDs that are looked up on each request. The cookie is then used to reestablish the user's context, which could be as simple as saying, "Yup, this guy was here before," or as complex as figuring out the parameters for the user's last query. See the sidebar "Cookie Monsters" for more details.

The Session object uses cookies to manage a session, but it hides that fact from your ASP application. The Session object basically wraps a persistent container that allows you to keep values and even object references for each user on a site. A common use for Session objects is for caching object references.

Look again at the VFP example above where the VisualFoxPro.Application object was reloaded on each hit. Run the example again and note how long it takes to refresh the page. Now change the code to the following and try again:

```
<%
If IsObject(Session("oVFP")) Then
   Set loVFP = Session("oVFP")
Else
   Set loVFP = Server.CreateObject("VisualFoxPro.Application")
   Set Session("oVFP") = loVFP
End If
%>
```

You'll notice that the first hit takes quite a while but a second hit is very quick—almost instant. This is because you've cached a reference to the VFP object in a session variable and the VFP runtime does not have to reload.

This is very powerful if you think about it! You can create a COM object with a user's scope and keep that object alive, including any settings that are made on the object. For example, you might run a query as part of the object and then come back on the next hit and still have the result set open and selected in the server upon return. This is a typical stateful scenario that's common for many stand-alone applications where a user hangs on to objects for the duration of the application. It's also quite powerful, because this is typically very tough to do with Web applications; ASP provides this mechanism quite easily through the Session object.

Be careful with sessions. The convenience they provide is an invitation to build applications that won't scale well. The above example is actually a good reason why you should be wary. In the example each new session creates a new instance of Visual FoxPro! Run the example once with your browser, and then fire up another instance of the browser (make sure that you have two IExplorer.exe listings in Task Manager with IE or else you'll reuse the same session) and rerun the page. You'll find that you now have two instances of VFP.exe in memory. Now imagine that you have hundreds of users on your site! You'll run into a very serious problem with running out of resources as each user gets her own copy of VFP.exe. The same goes for caching ADO recordsets (which we'll talk about in a minute)—it's possible to hang on to a SQL result between requests with a Session object, but if you have a lot of users the resource requirements might be too heavy. The bottom line is that the Session object can provide great convenience by providing state, but stateful applications inherently don't scale well.

Whether to use sessions for resource-intensive objects and tables is something you need to weigh carefully depending on your type of application and expected load. You should be especially mindful of this if you're using Visual InterDev because its wizards crank out a lot of code with Session variables that don't scale well. Beware, and know what goes into your sessions. Above all, test your code under load to see exactly what the resource requirements are on your server!

Cookie Monsters

What's a cookie? An HTTP cookie is nothing more than a special HTTP header that is passed back and forth between the browser and the Web server. Cookies are typically originated by a Web server and sent to the client via an HTTP header that looks like this:

```
Set-Cookie: wwUserID; expires=Mon, 01-Jan-1999 06:00:00 GMT; path=/
```

This header tells the browser to create storage for a cookie. By default, cookies have a lifetime as long as the browser is running, but you can create permanent cookies that persist beyond the browser's lifetime by setting the *expires* tag to some time in the future (make sure you use a valid date, including the right day of the week—otherwise the cookie will not save!). The browser receives this cookie request and adds it to its list of cookies. If the cookie has an expiration date, it's saved to disk in the Temporary Internet Files directory; otherwise it remains in memory. Note that the Path= of the cookie string describes where the cookie is valid on the target site. The path can be global for the site (/) or apply to a specific virtual directory.

Once the browser has the cookie, it returns it on every request to the server as part of the HTTP request information, and you can query for it with the Request.Cookies collection. The typical scenario is this: Every request checks to see whether the user has a cookie— if not, one is added to the current request, possibly redirecting the user to a start or login page. Once the user has a cookie, he has access and can go where he pleases.

Use cookies sparingly! Don't send a cookie on each request—validate once and assign the cookie and then reread the cookie each time after that. Write once, read many! Second, don't store lots of information in cookies—use a table on the server to store that information instead, and use the cookie to store a lookup ID in the table. People are a lot more willing to accept a cookie if there appears to be no useful data saved in it. Finally, if you plan to use cookies, you might want to warn users because some of them have cookies turned off. At the very least, provide some useful feedback if a cookie is rejected, with an explanation of why the cookie is required.

Like the Session object, the Application object allows you to create persistent data that's accessible to all ASP pages. Think of Application variables as global variables. (Sessions are more like user-specific static variables.) The Application object works just like the Session object for assignment of variables and references, but because an application object is global you need to make sure you protect writing to any Application variable with the Application.Lock function. If you're familiar with multi-threaded programming or record locking in a database application, you know what Lock() does—it locks the application object and doesn't allow another page access to it. Use Lock() sparingly and only for the shortest possible intervals before calling Unlock to free the Application object again. Use Application-scope variables only if absolutely necessary, because locking can have disastrous effects on busy sites where lock collisions might be frequent. Also keep in mind that if you attach objects to the Application object, you're essentially attaching a *single* object reference that is used by all users hitting your ASP pages—only one page at a time can access the object. This might be what you want (unlikely with VFP and VB COM objects, but okay with multi-threaded C++ objects), but in most cases it's unacceptable.

> ❗ **Session and Application objects and multiple servers**
> *Because Session and Application objects are implemented as in-memory objects, they cannot scale to multiple servers. If you plan to use multiple Web servers for load balancing, there's no guarantee that users will hit the same server on each request. Because Session and Application objects can't work across machines, you won't be able to use them for such applications.*

Getting down to business—Simple data access with ASP and ADO

It's time to look at a simple example that demonstrates what I've described so far and also introduces data access. Let's start with a small utility application that counts hits to a particular page on a Web site and logs the information into a table. I'll log each hit as the user accesses the page for the first time only. In order to do something useful with the information, I'll also create a simple query page that lets me see the hits that were incurred on a particular page.

> ❗ **Making temporary security settings**
> *The majority of problems related to Active Server development stem from security issues with Web applications not having access to server resources. To make sure all of the samples work, I recommend that you **temporarily** adjust your security setting for the IUSR_ anonymous user account (if you're running NT with IIS). I'll discuss the exact security issues later, but for now it'll be best if you assign Administrator rights to this account. To do this, go into User Manager, select the IUSR_MACHINENAME account and add it to the Administrator group. Save your changes and exit. You'll want to stop the Web server to make those changes take—do so from the Services Manager in Control Panel and stop the World Wide Web Service and IIS Admin Service. Then restart the services.*

First I need to create a table to contain the logging information. It's easiest to do this from within Visual FoxPro by placing the following code into a program and running it (replace the path with something convenient for you):

```
CREATE TABLE c:\webbook\asp\data\wwPageLog ;
(  PAGE        C (30),;
   TIMESTAMP   T ,;
   BROWSER     M,;
   REFERER     M ,;
   IP          C (15),;
   OTHER       M)
```

Creating an ODBC data source
Once the table is created, you need to create an ODBC System Data Source to point at the directory that contains this file. I'll call this DSN RASLOG; its ODBC configuration screen should look something like **Figure 4.3**.

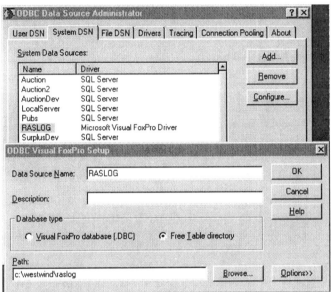

Figure 4.3. *Setting up an ODBC data source is required in order to access data with ADO. Create a System DSN and point it at your Fox data. The database type can be either a .DBC or a directory that becomes the equivalent of a database.*

Working with the demo code
To set up the demos included with the Developer's Download Files at www.hentzenwerke.com, follow these steps:

1. Find the source code directory called WebBook_HTML.
2. Copy it to your hard disk to a directory of your choice.
3. Create a virtual directory from this directory:
    *   Go into the IIS Management Console and select the root Web site.
    *   Right-click and select New/Virtual Directory.
    *   Name it *WebBook* (or the name of your choice).
    *   Point it at the directory where you copied the WebBook_HTML files.
        Make sure you enable the Script rights.
4. To access the samples for this chapter, you can then use http://localhost/webbook/asp/.

As I pointed out earlier, I'm not going to discuss in great detail how to use any tool in particular, but it's appropriate to mention how to set up Visual InterDev to view your ASP documents at this time. VID's site display features are handy for finding files as well as providing a nice highlighting HTML editor. To create a project in VID, follow these steps:

1. Start up VID and select New Project.
2. When prompted for a Web site, type *localhost* to use the local Web server.
3. Next you'll be prompted for a Web application name. This is the name of a virtual directory that VID will use or create if it doesn't exist. This is the "live" Web path where the final pages go.
4. Leave the styles blank for now.
5. Click Finish to create the project.

Once the VID project is created, you can view and edit files. When editing files you'll be prompted whether to get the *Working Copy* of a file—this essentially checks out a file. Other users of the same project will see this file as locked so only one copy is checked out at a time. When you save changes to a working copy of a file, you save the changes directly back to the live Web site.

Creating the ASP document

If you don't use VID, you can create the following files independently in the \webbook\ASP HTML directory. Using VID, select the ASP subdirectory and click Add Server Page from the Add menu.

Let's create an ASP page that does the following:
*   Checks to see whether the user has already visited this page. Logs her only if she hasn't been here before.
*   Connects to the database.
*   Retrieves the various pieces of information to log from the Request object.
*   INSERTs the data into the wwPagelog table.
*   Displays the body of the page.

Here's the code for this page:

```
<%
'*** If visitor doesn't have a cookie, log the hit as a new visitor
If Request.Cookies("wwDefault") = "" Then
    '*** First time hit - create a cookie for the user
    Response.Cookies("wwDefault") = "Yes"

    Set Conn = Server.CreateObject("ADODB.Connection")
    Conn.Open("dsn=RasLog")

    sql = "INSERT INTO wwPageLog (Page, TimeStamp, Browser, Referer, IP)"
    sql = sql + "VALUES ('Default.asp',"

    sql = sql + "datetime(),"
    sql = sql + "'" & Request.ServerVariables("HTTP_USER_AGENT") & "',"
    sql = sql + "'" & Request.ServerVariables("HTTP_REFERER") & "',"
    sql = sql + "'" & Request.ServerVariables("REMOTE_HOST") & "')"
```

```
   ' Response.Write(sql)     ' Debug

   Conn.Execute(sql)
   Conn.Close
   Set Conn = nothing
End If
%>
<html><head>
<title>ODBC Logging</title>
</head><body bgcolor="#FFFFFF">
<h1>This could be your custom logged homepage</h1>
<hr>
This request has been logged into a VFP database using ADO.
To view the list of recent hits to this page click below:
<ul>
<li><a href="../ASP/ShowODBCLog.asp">Show hits on this page...</a>
</ul>
</body></html>
```

This document has two very distinct sections: The Active Server code at the top and the plain HTML text at the bottom. In this case, the two are very distinct because the insertion code happens prior to the page being displayed, but, as you'll see in the next example, you can also mix code and HTML.

The insertion code demonstrates several ASP features that I discussed in the previous sections. It starts out by checking for the existence of a cookie called wwDefault (Default for my default or home page) using the Request.Cookies collection. When a user arrives at this page for the first time, the cookie will not exist so the code enters the IF statement. As it does, it immediately adds a cookie to the request header using the Response.Cookies collection. Once set, the next time the user comes to this page while the same instance of her browser is running, the cookie will still exist and the IF block will *not* be executed. This basic code demonstrates how to execute code only once per user on a given page (you could also use a Session object variable for this—but more on that later).

The rest of the ASP code deals with accessing the database and inserting a record into it. To do so, the ADO object is used. ADO is a COM component that must first be created with:

```
Set Conn = Server.CreateObject("ADODB.Connection")
```

which is a Connection object. Several different objects are available in the ADODB component, such as the Recordset and Parameters objects, which you can also create explicitly. In fact, you can take a number of approaches to open a table, using ADO objects that have overlapping functionality. Here I choose to use a Connection object and simply run an Execute against the connection, since that's the easiest way to go with the least amount of code. I'll look at other ways in later examples.

To actually open a connection, you need to call the Open method and pass along a connection string. For VFP ODBC data sources, this means simply passing the DSN name:

```
Conn.Open("DSN=RASLOG")
```

It's also possible to use a full connection string that doesn't require a DSN, but this is not advisable because it can *possibly* expose the location of the data source if access can be gained to the ASP file's source code. Here's the code:

```
Conn.Open("driver=Microsoft Visual FoxPro Driver;Exclusive=No;" &_
          "SourceType=DBF;SourceDB=C:\westwind\raslog;uid=;pwd=")
```

With the connection open, it's possible to call the Execute() method of the Connection object to run a SQL command. In this case I'll build a SQL string into a memory variable first. I then pass the full string to the Execute() method. The string retrieves the browser, the referring link and the remote user's IP address, and builds the whole thing into one large INSERT statement. If you've worked with SQL Passthrough in Visual FoxPro, you'll be familiar with building SQL statements as strings.

Error handling with ASP and ADO

What about error handling? Well, VBScript doesn't have much support for error handling—it only has an ON ERROR RESUME NEXT statement, which can't be unset once it's set (in other words, you can't just go ON ERROR to reset default error handling as you can in VFP). ADO itself supports an error object, but whenever an error occurs it fires an error event in the client code (ASP in this case). If you don't have ON ERROR RESUME NEXT enabled, you get an ASP error message, which is fine for debugging but not optimal for end users.

Here's what the code looks like adjusted for manual error handling of the Connection object. To make the ON ERROR fire, change the SQL statement to an invalid statement and then rerun the page with the following code:

```
On Error Resume Next
Conn.Errors.Clear

Conn.Execute(sql)

If Conn.Errors.Count > 0 Then
  %>
  <b>A SQL error occurred while executing the Insert:</b><BR>
  <%
  Response.Write(Conn.Errors(0).Description )
  Response.End
End If

Conn.Close
Set Conn = Nothing
```

Note that the error's collection is zero based! Keep in mind that any error in your code after that ON ERROR RESUME NEXT statement will be ignored. Ideally, you should take it out while debugging and then add it in when you're ready to deploy.

Displaying the logging results

Now that I've logged the hits to the default page, I need a mechanism to retrieve the information. **Figure 4.4** shows the results of the log display page.

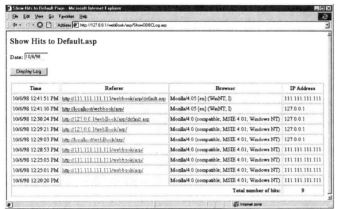

Figure 4.4. *The logging results are displayed in an HTML table. Note that the form serves as an input and output form at the same time.*

This page acts both as a display and query page. You can input a different date to update the display. When the page first loads, the date defaults to today's date. Here's the ASP code that makes this page work:

```
<% '*** This code always loads the table with the log
   Set Conn = Server.CreateObject("ADODB.Connection")
   Conn.Open("dsn=RasLog")

   '*** Retrieve the date from the Input form
   lcDate = Request("LogDate")

   '*** Handle ALL selection
   If Ucase(lcDate) = "ALL" Then
      lcWhere = ""
   Else
      '*** If Empty default to today's date
      If lcDate = "" Then
        '*** On Empty date show all entries
         lcDate = cDate(Date)
      End If

      lcWhere = "WHERE ttod(timestamp) = ctod('" & lcDate & "')"
   End If

   '*** Build the SQL Statement And Execute into a RecordSet
   SQL = "SELECT TimeStamp,Referer,Browser,IP FROM wwPageLog " & _
          lcWhere & " GROUP BY 1 ORDER BY 1 DESCENDING"

   Set rs = Conn.Execute(sql)
%>
<html>
<body bgcolor="#FFFFFF">
<h2>Show Hits to Default.asp</h2>

<form action="ShowODBCLog.asp" method="POST">
```

```
   <p><strong>Date:</strong>
  <input type="text" size="8" name="LogDate" value="<% =lcDate%>">
    <p>
  <input type="submit" name="btnSubmit" value="Display Log">
  </p>
</form>

<table border="1" cellpadding="3" width="100%" bgcolor="#EEEEEE" border="3">
    <tr>
        <td align="center" bgcolor="#FFFDCA"><strong>Time</strong></td>
        <td align="center" bgcolor="#FFFDCA"><strong>Referer</strong></td>
        <td align="center" bgcolor="#FFFDCA"><strong>Browser</strong></td>
        <td align="center" bgcolor="#FFFDCA"><strong>IP Address</strong></td>
    </tr>

<% Do While Not rs.EOF  %>     <tr>
        <% lctext=rs("Referer") %>
        <td><% =rs("Timestamp")%></td>
        <td><a href="<% =lcText%>"><% =lcText%></a></td>
        <td><% =rs("Browser")%></td>
        <td><% =rs("IP")%></td>
    </tr>
<%
rs.MoveNext
Loop

'*** Now Calc the total
sql = "SELECT COUNT(*) as TotalHits FROM wwPageLog "  & lcWhere
Set rs = Conn.Execute(Sql)
%>     <tr>
        <td colspan="3" bgcolor="#FFFDCA" align="RIGHT"><b>Total number of
hits:</b></td>
        <td align="center" bgcolor="#FFFDCA"><b><% =rs("TotalHits")%></b></td>
    </tr>
<%
rs.Close
Conn.Close
%></table></body></html>
```

The code starts by opening a connection to the database the same way it did on the previous page. Next it tries to retrieve the LogDate form variable. I say "it tries," because in most cases this variable won't actually be available because the page was not loaded as a form, but rather directly from a link:

```
lcDate = Request("LogDate")
```

This line retrieves the value of the LogDate input field if and only if the user clicked on the Display button on the form. Otherwise this value is blank and defaults to today's date. If you look into the HTML section of the document you'll find lcDate referenced in a form:

```
<input type="text" size="8" name="LogDate" value="<%= lcDate %>">
```

This forces the updated value to be displayed in the input box. The `IF UCASE(lcDate) =` `"ALL"` block deals with converting the date input, whether it exists or not, into a valid WHERE string—lcWhere—that will be used in the SQL statement to retrieve the records. The code to build the SQL string and actually run it looks like this:

```
'*** Build the SQL Statement And Execute into a RecordSet
SQL = "SELECT TimeStamp,Referer,Browser,IP FROM wwPageLog " & _
          lcWhere & " GROUP BY 1 ORDER BY 1 DESCENDING"

Set rs = Conn.Execute(sql)
```

When Conn.Execute() runs, it returns an ADODB.Recordset object and the code stores this object in a variable called *rs*. The rs object is used to navigate the result set and get at the individual field values. Think of a recordset as a result cursor from a SQL statement. Recordsets can take on various different forms, from true connections to database tables to result cursors to disconnect tables that are not updated on the server until you issue a batch update. In this example, the result is a read-only, forward-only cursor.

Looping through the recordset

I now have a recordset and it's time to dump it out into the display as an HTML table. To do so, use the Recordset object and loop through all the records, printing the field information for each into a table cell:

```
<% Do While Not rs.EOF  %>     <tr>
        <% lctext=rs("Referer") %>
        <td><% =rs("Timestamp")%></td>
        <td><a href="<% =lcText%>"><% =lcText%></a></td>
        <td><% =rs("Browser")%></td>
        <td><% =rs("IP")%></td>
    </tr>
<%
rs.MoveNext
Loop
%>
```

Notice that I decided to make the referring link a clickable HREF link, so that if you're curious where people are coming from you can go right to the page that sent them to your site. Field values are embedded into the output stream by using the `rs("FieldName")` syntax. This is a shortcut for the `rs.fields("FieldName")` collection—ADO supports default methods and properties that make the rs() lookup look like a function, which it actually is not. You're actually calling an object in the hierarchy.

The code finally goes through and runs another query to calculate the total number of hits. Note that I simply reuse the rs object reference and force another query to run off the Connection object with the Execute() method call:

```
Sql = "SELECT COUNT(*) as TotalHits FROM wwPageLog "  & lcWhere
SET rs = Conn.Execute(Sql)
```

The lcWhere clause is reused from the initial date parsing block, so it's guaranteed to run against the same data as the list display.

Other ways to handle ADO
As I pointed out above, there are other ways to do pretty much the same thing in terms of querying data via ADO. The reason is that the various ADO objects are tightly interrelated and allow access from each other. I explained how to create a Recordset object by running a Connection.Execute() method call, but you can also go the other way—creating a Recordset object, passing a connection to it, then running a query on the recordset that uses this connection:

```
Set Conn = Server.CreateObject("ADODB.Connection")
Set rs = Server.CreateObject("ADODB.Recordset")

Conn.Open("DSN=RASLOG")
rs.Open "SELECT * FROM RASLOG",Conn,adKeyset
```

Why would you want to do this? It allows you more flexibility in how the result cursor is created, which is not possible if you use the Connection's Execute method. In the above example, adKeyset specifies that the cursor is actually linked to the Fox database table, so any updates are immediately visible to you and any other users of the database—it's sort of like doing a USE on the table in question and then using SCAN and update commands like REPLACE on it.

There isn't enough space here to go into the details of how ADO works and interacts with the database, much less how to optimize database access. But I encourage you to review the MSDN documentation to at least get a feel for the options that are available, and experiment with them. It's amazing what little changes in some of these parameters can do for performance! I haven't found a really good reference on what works well and in what situations, so most of what you find will be based on trial and error. In due time there will be articles, books and white papers, but for now there's not much to go by other than figuring it out the hard way.

A TasTrade invoice viewer application
The example I've shown so far isn't terribly useful, nor does it make really good use of a database connection. But I hope it's given you a basic idea of how ASP works and how you can use ADO to get at data. In this section I'll discuss a sample application that acts as an invoice viewer for the TasTrade application that ships with Visual FoxPro. I won't show as much ASP code to clutter up the text, but will focus on the special issues that are related to this invoice sample.

The application starts out with an invoice-selection form like the one shown in **Figure 4.5**. The idea is that you can select a few options and pull up a list of matching invoices. What's nice about this form is how it groups the orders by customer and breaks each customer down by orders.

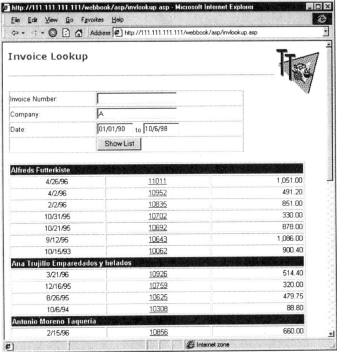

Figure 4.5. *The TasTrade Invoice Lookup application in action. The query form allows retrieval of invoices based on search criteria and displays a one-to-many view of customers and their individual orders.*

Watching out for unnecessary data display

As in the ODBCLog display example, this form serves as both a query and result form. One thing that's crucial is that on startup I don't want to run a query for all orders because this display takes a fair amount of time to build. So rather than assuming that the user wants to see everything, the code checks to see whether all fields are blank and, in that case, displays only the query form:

```
lcCompany = Request("txtCompany")
lcInvNo = Request("txtInvoiceNo")
lcFromdate = Request("txtFromDate")
lcToDate = Request("txtToDate")

llFirstHit = False
If Len(lcToDate) = 0 and LEN(lcFromDate) = 0 Then
    llFirstHit = True
    lcFromDate = "01/01/90"
    lcToDate = FormatDateTime(now,vbShortDate)
End If
```

```
If Not llFirstHit Then
  lcWhere = ""

  If Len(lcCompany) > 0 Then
     lcWhere = " AND Upper(Company) like '" & UCase(lcCompany ) & "%' "
  End If
  If Len(lcInvNo) > 0 Then
     lcWhere = lcWhere & " AND orders.order_id = '" & lcInvNo &    "' "
  End If
  lcSQL = "Select customer.company, customer.cust_id, " &_
           "orders.order_id,orders.order_date, Order_amt " &_
           "FROM orders, customer " & _
           "WHERE customer.cust_id = orders.cust_id " & lcWhere &_
                 "ORDER BY company,order_date DESC"

  Set rs = Conn.Execute(lcSQL)

End If
```

When *llFirstHit* is True (it's tied to whether or not the date is empty), no query is run, and in the actual HTML text following the form there's a small snippet that aborts the output before creating the table output:

```
<% '*** On the first hit don't show list
   If llFirstHit Then
      Response.End
   End If
%>
```

I do want to run a query if the user entered one, so the code inside the IF NOT llFirstHit executes the creation of the WHERE clause and the actual SQL command result into the rs Recordset object. The table is built again by running through the recordset and outputting the RS("FieldName") values into the table. Before creating the table I added a Response.Flush:

```
<table border="1" width="570" class="bodytext">
<% Response.Flush
   lcLastCompany = "  "
   Do While Not rs.EOF
   If rs("cust_id") <> lcLastCompany Then %>
 <tr>
   <td bgcolor="#000000" colspan="3" width="564"><font face="Arial"
   color="#FFFFFF"><strong><%= rs("Company")%></strong></font></td>
 </tr>
<%lcLastCompany = rs("cust_id")
   End If %>
```

This forces all buffered output to be displayed immediately, before building the possibly large table. This indicates to the user that the rest of the page will appear in a moment. Remember that tables don't render until every element has been received, and if you're generating the full list of invoices the table can take a while to render (this will change in IE 5.0 if you use fixed-width columns but it's the first browser to support this feature—don't count on this fast rendering mechanism in other browsers).

The code above also demonstrates how the one-to-many display is accomplished. The query that pulls the customer and order information returns a denormalized result set that contains both customer and order data. As the code loops through the table, it keeps track of the last order number. When the number changes, it adds the extra row into the HTML table:

```
<% If rs("cust_id") <> lcLastCompany Then %>
    … display extra row
<% End If
    lcLastCompany = rs("cust_id")
%>
```

The table also displays the invoice number as a hot link:

```
<a href="invdemo.asp?Orderid=<%=rs("Order_id")%>"><%= rs("order_id")%></a>
```

Which is my segue into the next form.

Complex forms and data access
The Invoice Display form is a bit more complex because it contains data from multiple tables laid out in a display that mimics an invoice. I used FrontPage to create the main page layout and then added code with Visual InterDev's code editor. If you design your pages carefully and create script and markup tags explicitly for every bit of non-HTML code, FrontPage works very well even for complex forms that contain a fair amount of code (I do recommend frequent backups, though). Visual InterDev excels at syntax completion and color highlighting in its code editor. My results appear in **Figures 4.6a** and **4.6b**, which show both the final form in the browser and the design mode in FrontPage.

What's interesting is that Visual InterDev can't handle this form in WYSIWYG mode because of the embedded expressions in input fields. When using FrontPage, it's important to create code snippets and expressions with the proper markup tags. If everything is marked up explicitly, FrontPage behaves itself and keeps all of your code intact. You can also input ASP Expressions directly into the various FrontPage property dialogs. For example, the title of the document includes the ASP expression. Same goes for field values and names.

When it comes to writing additional code, use Visual InterDev. The syntax color highlighting and minimal Intellisense features make writing code a bit easier than in FrontPage's HTML editor or, worse yet, the code snippet editor.

How the form works
This form works by calling it *either* with an invoice number on the query string (following the ? on the URL) or by passing a form variable from an HTML form:

```
lcInvToShow = Request("txtInvToShow")
If lcInvToShow = "" Then
    lcInvToShow = Request.QueryString("Orderid")
End If
```

```
If lcInvToShow = "" Then
  '*** Grab the last invoice entered
  SQL = "SELECT MAX(Order_id) as LastOrder FROM Orders"
  Set rs = Conn.Execute(SQL)
  lcInvToShow = rs("LastOrder")
End If
```

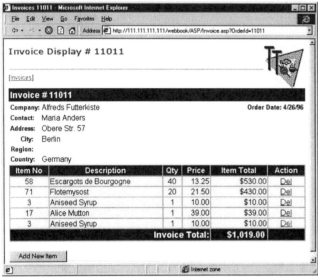

Figure 4.6a. The invoice display form demonstrates some of the design issues when working with complex forms.

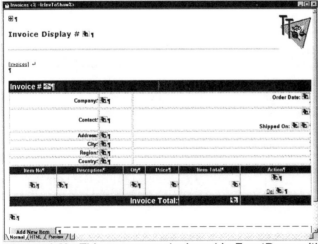

Figure 4.6b. This page was designed in FrontPage with script tags carefully embedded into the HTML layout. The result (Figure 4.6a) is a visually designed form that would have been difficult to lay out by hand.

Note that there's also support for the possibility that no invoice number at all is passed. In this case the code tries to find the last invoice created and retrieves that invoice number instead. After executing this code you always have an invoice number to display!

What follows is a messy SQL statement that retrieves the actual data:

```
SQL = "SELECT * FROM  customer INNER JOIN orders " & _
       "INNER JOIN orditems INNER JOIN products " & _
       "ON  Orditems.product_id = Products.product_id " &_
       "ON  Orders.order_id = Orditems.order_id  " &_
       "ON  Customer.cust_id = Orders.cust_id " & _
       " ORDER BY Orders.order_id "

  SQLWhere =   "WHERE orders.Order_Id = PADL('" & lcInvToShow & "',6)"

  Set rs = Conn.Execute(SQL + SQLWhere)

  If rs.EOF Then
    '*** Grab the last invoice entered
    SQL2 = "SELECT MAX(Order_id) as LastOrder FROM Orders WHERE !DELETED()"
    Set rs = Conn.Execute(SQL2)
    lcInvToShow = rs("LastOrder")

    SQLWhere =   "WHERE orders.Order_Id = PADL('" & lcInvToShow & "',6)"

    Set rs = Conn.Execute(SQL + SQLWhere)
    lcInvToShow = rs("Order_Id")
  End If

  If Datediff("yyyy", rs("Shipped_On"),Date) > 10 Then
      llShipped = False
  Else
      llShipped = True
  End If
```

Note the use of rs.EOF to determine whether any records were returned from the query. Incidentally, this is the only way to find out whether a query worked correctly—rs.RecordCount always returns -1 against the VFP ODBC driver and a useful value only against data sources that support bookmarks (approximate record pointers). The VFP ODBC driver currently does not support many of the advanced OLE DB features.

The end of the statement contains a little snippet that figures out whether the order has shipped; it uses the VBScript DateDiff function. This value is used in several places to decide whether the Shipped On date is to display and whether items can be added and deleted from the order. For example, here's the logic for the Add button:

```
<%If Not llShipped Then%>
<form action="ItemList.asp?Orderid=<%= LTRIM(lcInvToShow)%>" method="POST">
  <p><input type="SUBMIT" name="btnSubmit" value="Add New Item"> </p>
</form>
<%End If%>
```

When you click the Add New Item button, a list pops up. This list simply runs a query against the products table and displays the data in an HTML table—nothing you haven't seen before. The EditItem.asp form then displays an individual item; you can add it to the order by selecting the quantity using the single input form element and clicking the Add button on the form. **Figure 4.7** shows these two forms in operation.

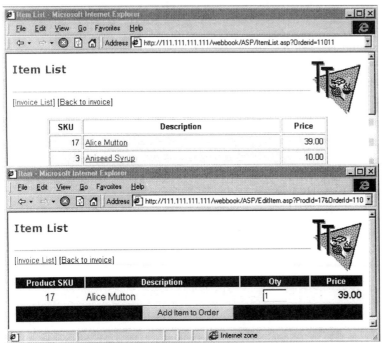

Figure 4.7. *Selecting and adding items to an invoice.*

What's interesting in the form submission for the item is that it uses what I call an *action page*. The form is submitted to ItemAction.asp, which, unlike all other pages I've described so far, does not contain HTML. Rather, it's a handler that deals with operations related to the order items—in this case adding and deleting items from the order. The reason for this is fairly straightforward: When you add or delete an item, you really don't need a custom page of any sort, but rather you want to redisplay the original invoice form with the updated invoice information. This is easy to do with an HTTP Redirect, and looks something like this for the DELETE operation:

```
lcAction = Request.QueryString("Action")
lcOrderId = Request.QueryString("Orderid")
lcProdId = Request.QUeryString("ProdId")
lcLineId = Request.QueryString("Line_no")
```

```
If UCASE(lcAction) = "DELETE" Then
    '*** Lineitems first
    SQL = "DELETE FROM OrdItems " & _
        " where Order_Id = PADL('" & lcOrderId & "',6)  AND ;
        Line_No =  VAL('" & lcLineId & "')"
    Conn.Execute(SQL)

    '*** Redisplay the invoice form
    Response.Redirect("Invoice.asp?Orderid=" & lcOrderId)
End If
```

The key in this code is the Action query string parameter that determines which operation to perform—in this case, DELETE. The code then branches into an IF statement for each action that is to be performed. Here it simply runs a SQL DELETE for the items selected. The key piece that makes this work is the Response.Redirect() method call, which sends back a message to the browser: "Sorry, I have no output for you, but you can go to this page instead and find it there." In reality the server returns an HTTP header that the browser reads and uses to access the new page.

While I'm on this page, I should also talk about the Add operation, which turns out to be a little more complicated because it involves data from a number of tables. Here's the code:

```
If UCASE(lcAction) = "ADD" Then
    lcQty=Request.Form("txtQty")

    '*** Retrieve last ID and total price
    SQL = "SELECT MAX(Line_no) as NewId,SUM(Unit_price *quantity) as
OrderTotal FROM OrdItems WHERE Order_Id=PADL('" & lcOrderId  & "',6)"

    Set rs = Conn.Execute(SQL)

    lnNewId = CInt( RS("NewId") ) + 1
    lcNewId = CStr(lnNewId)
    lnTotal = RS("OrderTotal")

    '*** Retrieve item information
    SQL = "SELECT Product_id,prod_name, unit_price FROM products " & _
        "WHERE product_id = PADL('" & lcProdId & "',6)"
    Set rsProduct = Server.CreateObject("ADODB.RecordSet")
    rsProduct.Open SQL,Conn

    lnPrice = rsProduct("Unit_price")

    '*** Now insert the new lineitem into the database
    SQL = "INSERT INTO OrdItems " & _
        " VALUES(" & lcNewId & ",PADL('" & lcOrderid & _
        "',6),PADL('" & lcProdId & "',6)," & lnPrice &"," & lcQty & ")"

    Conn.Execute(SQL)

    '*** Update the order total -
    '*** if the database had a trigger we wouldn't need this
    lnTotal = lnTotal + (lnPrice * CInt(lcQty))
```

```
   SQL = "UPDATE ORDERS where Order_id = PADL('" & lcOrderId & _
         "',6) SET Order_amt = " & lnTotal

   Response.Write(SQL)
   Conn.Execute(SQL)

   '*** Redisplay the invoice form
   Response.Redirect("Invoice.asp?OrderId=" & lcOrderId)
End If
%>
```

Note that there are four SQL statements executed in this request:

1. Retrieves the highest line-item number and the current total for the order (note that this might be a multi-user issue if multiple people are allowed access to the same record).
2. Retrieves information about the individual item—most importantly the price.
3. Runs the actual INSERT statement into the ORDITEMS table to add the item.
4. Updates the Order total so the total is correct when we redisplay our invoice (this really belongs in an INSERT TRIGGER, but the TasTrade sample doesn't have one).

A few reservations about VFP and ADO

Given the fact that this is a demo and doesn't include error handling, you can probably appreciate Visual FoxPro's ability to do this with real record pointers and SQL statements that are part of the language. Code like the stuff above takes awhile to write and debug with ASP— there's a lot of trial and error involved, even once you're familiar with the syntax. And because error handling is so minimal, it's difficult to write smart interfaces that can handle updates to the database safely from ASP code directly. Can it be done? Yes! But keep in mind that to write solid ASP applications that use data access, you need to be thorough. Prepare to put in your time—it's not as easy as the Visual InterDev wizards would have you believe!

You'll also want to consider the limitations of the VFP ODBC driver. There are currently problems with Memo field updates, and NULL values can cause problems because ADO and VFP don't quite agree what constitutes a NULL. VFP also doesn't support most of the different cursor type modes that are available in ADO, so using updateable recordsets doesn't work. This means that if you use VFP you have to use SQL statements rather than the sometimes easier field update functionality provided by rs::EditMode and rs::Update. These features work with SQL Server, so these issues don't apply.

There are workarounds for each issue, but they aren't very intuitive. You can't execute stored procedures directly, even with a SQL statement (SELECT StoredProc() FROM SomeTable WHERE RECNO() = 1). This means some tasks that could be greatly simplified by creating an update routine as a stored procedure are not available to you as options to abstract code. Triggers and validation code will fire in your database, but you can't access that code directly through ADO. ODBC opens VFP tables and does not release them if you have connection pooling enabled. This means if you need to run maintenance operations like PACK or INDEX—good luck. The only way you can do these maintenance operations is to take the data offline. In most cases this means shutting down the Web server.

The VFP ODBC driver is also single threaded and cannot process multiple queries simultaneously. This means VFP data doesn't scale well. Because VFP data access is fast, this probably won't be noticeable until you run a monster query that takes a few long seconds to run while others are trying to access the same data source. Beware and test your load carefully!

This isn't meant to discourage you from using VFP data. The VFP ODBC driver continues to be the fastest ODBC data source available, and as long as you understand these issues you can probably work around them.

Scripting as an application environment?

The sample application above gives you an idea of what it takes to write an application using only ASP script and ADO to access data. Compared to development within Visual FoxPro—where you can take advantage of the rich development environment, a sophisticated debugger and all of the classes that you've previously created in a basic application framework—scripting sure feels like taking a huge step back. The concept is simple enough, and in terms of getting code online it's the easiest mechanism and makes a lot of sense. However, in terms of code maintenance and the application-development environment, scripting leaves a lot to be desired. Searching through documents containing both HTML and code is tedious at best. VBScript and JScript are limited languages.

On their own, these languages have one-tenth of the general-purpose functionality that VFP supports, which means you have to write a lot more code to do operations that take single commands inside VFP. Finally, also keep in mind that these scripting languages are interpreted. They're not terribly fast, even as far as interpreted languages go. You'll notice this mostly when you have code that needs to iterate through large loops. A good example is the Invoice List discussed earlier with the TasTrade demo—90% of that slow request's time is spent generating the HTML table by looping through the recordset.

I've already discussed error handling as a seriously lacking issue in the scripting engine. Without decent error handling, it's difficult to build solid applications that can gracefully survive the many unexpected problems that can occur with applications that support high-volume access.

So, think of these things as you approach your ASP projects. Much of ASP's simplicity is based on the assumption that you will use scripting to create the application. In the next section, I'll talk about integrating ASP with external COM objects, which addresses some of the issues discussed above. But keep in mind that at that point you're greatly increasing the complexity of the environment in terms of implementation, administration and even deployment.

Taking advantage of COM with Active Server Pages

Direct database access provides the easiest way to get at FoxPro or other ODBC data quickly. But as I pointed out in the last section, there are some rather serious issues with ASP scripting that come down to the limitations of the scripting model and the limited support for error handling. These issues make it relatively hard to build mission-critical, bulletproof code with scripting. Furthermore, the scripting nature that mixes code and HTML can easily lead to heinous spaghetti code that's hard to debug and even harder to fix a few months after the application goes live. Also, doing everything in script code violates a fundamental rule of good application design: Separate the user interface from the data access code. While it's possible to do all these things with scripting code, the environment does not encourage it. Scripting requires you to maintain strict discipline, which may result in your bypassing many of the conveniences that make ASP such an attractive solution in the first place.

There is another way: COM. Microsoft has long realized that no development tool is an island, and thus should be extensible. Active Server Pages is no different. With ASP you have the ability to create any Automation-capable (IDispatch-compatible) COM object using the Server.CreateObject() method. Once that object has been created, you can access its methods and properties the same way you can in Visual FoxPro, Visual Basic or any other Automation-capable client.

You've already seen the COM interface in action: Every time I created a connection for ADO I explicitly created a COM object and internally accessed its methods and properties, such as Execute and the various collections. Even the Request, Response, Session and Application objects are COM objects, although ASP creates them internally and passes them forward to your ASP page as part of a ScriptingContext object. I'll talk about this a little later.

Here's a look at how this works. In the beginning of this chapter I showed how to use VisualFoxPro.Application and the Eval and DoCmd methods to make VFP operate as if you were sitting at the command window. You can do a lot with that alone, but it's really not that flexible because you're dealing with the entire development environment and the limited interface of these two methods. However, you can create your own full-fledged COM server objects with Visual FoxPro code. The object can access any FoxPro code, including database access, using the fast, native VFP data engine.

I'll show you several different mechanisms to use VFP COM objects in ASP:

- As a typical business object using properties and methods.
- As an HTML-generation engine through method calls.
- Using objects to communicate and interact directly with Active Server Objects.

Calling all VFP servers
Let's start with a very simple COM example that you might also find useful. I'm sure you've seen the counters in use by many Web sites. I'll implement one with Visual FoxPro by creating a COM object that counts up hits in a database file. In this example, ASP is used to handle all the HTML and Web-related tasks while VFP provides the business logic (however simple it might be in this example).

Here's the skeleton server code and the implementation of the IncCounter method:

```
******************************************************************
DEFINE CLASS ASPTools AS Custom OLEPUBLIC
******************************************************************

cAppStartPath = ""
lError = .F.
cErrorMsg = ""
***********************************************************************
* WebTools :: Init
*****************************
***   Function: Set the server's environment. VERY IMPORTANT!
***********************************************************************
```

```
FUNCTION INIT

SET RESOURCE OFF
SET EXCLUSIVE OFF
SET CPDIALOG OFF
SET DELETED ON
SET EXACT OFF
SET SAFETY OFF
SET REPROCESS TO 2 SECONDS

*** Utility routines like GetAppStartPath etc.
SET PROCEDURE TO wwUtils ADDITIVE

THIS.cAppStartPath = GetAppStartPath()

*** Important: We need to get at our data
SET PATH TO (THIS.cAppStartpath)
DO PATH WITH "DATA"

ENDFUNC

****************************************************************************
* WebTools :: IncCounter
******************************
***   Function: Increments a counter in the registry.
***     Assume: Key:
***             HKEY_LOCAL_MACHINE\
***             SOFTWARE\West Wind Technologies\Web Connection\Counters
***       Pass: lcCounter  -  Name of counter to increase
***             lnValue    -  (optional) Set the value of the counter
***                          -1 delete the counter.
***     Return: Increased  Counter value  -  -1 on failure
****************************************************************************
FUNCTION IncCounter
LPARAMETER lcCounter, lnSetValue
LOCAL lnValue

lnSetValue=IIF(EMPTY(lnSetValue),0,lnSetValue)

IF !USED("WebCounters")
   IF !FILE(THIS.cAppStartPath + "WebCounters.dbf")
        SELE 0
        CREATE table (THIS.cAppStartPath + "WEBCOUNTERS") ;
      (   NAME        C (20),;
          VALUE       I )
        USE
   ENDIF
   USE (THIS.cAppStartPath + "WEBCOUNTERS") IN 0 ALIAS WebCounters
ENDIF

SELECT WebCounters

LOCATE FOR UPPER(name) = UPPER(lcCounter)
IF !FOUND()
   INSERT INTO WEBCounters  VALUES (lcCounter,1)
   lnValue = 1
```

```
ELSE
    IF RLOCK()
        IF lnSetValue > 0
            REPLACE value with lnSetValue
        ELSE
            IF lnSetValue < 0
                REPLACE value with 0
                DELETE
            ELSE
                REPLACE value with value + 1
            ENDIF
        ENDIF
        lnValue = value
        UNLOCK
    ENDIF
ENDIF


RETURN lnValue
ENDFUNC


****************************************************************************
* aspTools :: Get/Set Default
****************************
FUNCTION GetDefault
RETURN SYS(5) + CURDIR()

FUNCTION SetDefault
LPARAMETER lcPath
CD (lcPath)
RETURN


****************************************************************************
* aspTools :: Error
*******************************
***   Function: Error Method. Capture errors here in a string that
***             you can read from the ASP page to check for errors.
****************************************************************************
FUNCTION ERROR
LPARAMETER nError, cMethod, nLine

THIS.cErrorMsg=THIS.cErrorMsg + "<BR>Error No: " + STR(nError) + "<BR>  Method:
" + cMethod + "<BR>  LineNo: " +STR(nLine) + "<BR>  Message: "+ message() +
Message(1) + "<HR>"
ENDFUNC
```

You should become familiar with a few important issues right from the start. First, the Init event of the server is used for setting the environment. It's crucial at this point that you set all settings that you expect your server to have. Most importantly, you want to turn off EXCLUSIVE access on startup or you'll run into problems when multiple instances of your server try to access data. This is probably the most common error that hangs servers! It's a good idea to turn off the resource file for the same reason. Any environment settings you expect to be in place should also be set at this time. SET DELETED and SET EXACT are a couple that I always set.

Your server should also contain an error handler. This is vital, because any error that occurs will hang your server to the point that you'll have to kill the process (if it's an EXE) or the client process (if it's a DLL server). Trapping the error will prevent this tragic end of your server's life in most circumstances.

Unloading your COM objects

IIS loads in-process COM objects into its address space and never releases them! This means that once IIS has them loaded, you can't rebuild your server! There are a couple of ways you can accomplish this:

- *Stop the IIS service and restart it. You can do this manually through the NT Service Manager. (You can't stop the IIS service through the Management Console. Stopping does not actually unload the service.) Or you can do it with a batch file using the KILL utility from the NT Resource Kit as shown in Figure 4.8.*

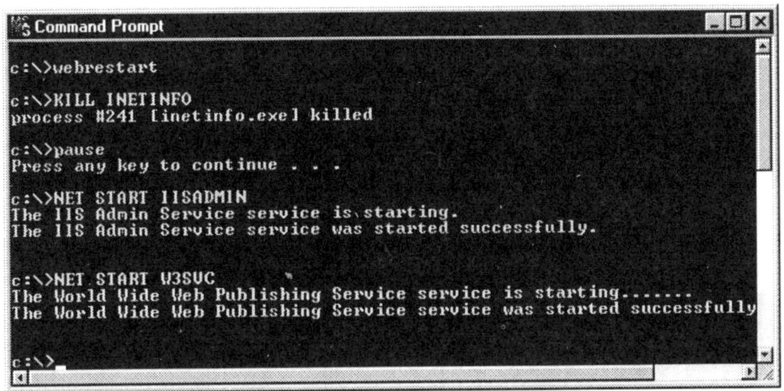

Figure 4.8. Releasing COM objects by shutting down IIS completely. Use the NT Resource Kit's KILL utility for a quick shutdown.

You can start any other services like SMTP, FTP and Gopher here if they were running, but for quick startup use the above only.

- *Use "separate application" virtual directories. When you create a virtual directory, you have the option to create it as a "separate application" in IIS 4.0. See Figure 4.9. This option sets up the entire virtual directory in its own Microsoft Transaction Server context object, which, among other things, has the ability to be unloaded separately from the Web server.*

COM objects loaded in one of these "applications" do not load into IIS, but into this Transaction Server module. With it you also get a separate security environment, and a crash in this application will not affect the Web server as a whole. The most important feature in this context is the Unload button, which becomes active once you've accessed an ASP page in the application.

Pressing this button unloads the entire MTX session along with any loaded COM objects inside it. I've had some problems with running applications separately, and there is some performance overhead involved in running applications this way, so decide carefully if you want to implement this. For debugging, however, it's a good solution because you can easily unload your servers—although it still takes three or four clicks to do so.

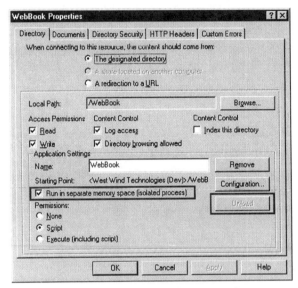

Figure 4.9. *Applications can be set up in a separate memory space, which allows them to be unloaded independently of the Web server as a whole. This can be configured in the IIS Management Console for each virtual directory.*

Okay, so much for infrastructure. The actual application code for our hit counter is pretty simple. The counter is stored in a table, which is created if it doesn't exist. The app looks for the counter name in the table and, if found, it's increased by one and returned. If the counter doesn't exist, a new entry is added. The method supports deleting counters by passing a negative value and setting counters to an arbitrary value by passing an optional, second integer-value parameter.

You can build a COM object from the server by following these steps:

1. Create a project and name it *ASPDemos*.
2. Add the AspTools.prg created above to the project.
3. Build the project into a DLL.
4. Go back and bring up the Project Info dialog and make sure your ASPTools server is marked for multi-use and rebuild.

Once you've built the DLL, you can test basic operation of the COM object from within VFP:

```
o=create("aspdemos.asptools")
? o.IncCounter("Test1")       && 1
? o.IncCounter("Test1")       && 2
? o.IncCounter("Test1",20)    && Set to 20 - 20
? o.IncCounter("Test1")       && 21
? o.IncCounter("Test1",-1)    && Delete counter - 0
```

Note that this server was built as an in-process DLL. If you look at Task Manager, you'll see that there's no separate aspDemos application running—this is because aspDemos.dll loaded into the calling process, which in this case is Visual FoxPro. You should see the memory usage of your VFP6.exe jump by about 3-4 meg when you start up this server. Because the DLL runs in process and happens to also be a VFP object, operation is very snappy.

If this works, move the server onto an ASP page and use the following code:

```
<html>
<head>
<title>VFP COM Servers in Active Server</title>
</head>
<body bgcolor="#FFFFFF">
<h2>Visual FoxPro COM Counter</h2>
<hr>
<p>This page has been hit:<strong>
<%
    SET oServer = Server.CreateObject("aspDemos.AspTools")
    Response.Write(oServer.IncCounter("ASPDemoCounter"))
%> </strong>times.</p>
<hr>
    <b>Application DLL Path:</b> <%= oServer.cAppStartpath %><br>
    <b>Application's current Path:</b> <%= oServer.getdefault()  %>
</body>
</html>
```

Save the text document as COMCounter.asp and run it through the browser. You should see something like **Figure 4.10**.

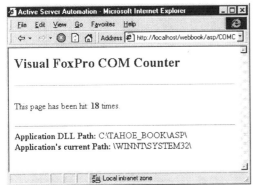

Figure 4.10. *The Hit Counter example uses a VFP table to increment a counter value. Note the COM DLL's actual location and the startup path in the SYSTEM directory.*

As you click the page, the counter is incremented on each hit as the IncCounter method is called on each request. Notice that the first hit takes a few seconds as the VFP runtime loads into IIS's process. Subsequent hits appear to be almost instant because VFP is already loaded in memory.

The key functionality of ASP is its ability to create COM objects using the Server object's CreateObject method:

```
SET oServer = Server.CreateObject("aspDemos.AspTools")
```

Once created, the server can be accessed like any other variable in the ASP script code and expressions:

```
Response.Write(oServer.IncCounter("ASPDemoCounter"))
```

Or it can be embedded inside HTML:

```
Counter value is: <%= oServer.IncCounter("ASPDemoCounter") %>
```

Beware of errant paths!

I'll demonstrate how paths work at this point because this happens to be the most common problem with first ventures into COM servers loaded into IIS. If you look back at the server code, you'll see in the Init event of the object:

```
THIS.cAppStartPath = GetAppStartPath()

*** Important: We need to get at our data
SET PATH TO (THIS.cAppStartpath)
DO PATH WITH THIS.cAppStartPath + "DATA"
```

This code is vital in making sure that the server can find the data it needs. The reason for this can be seen in the Web page and the result from:

```
<b>Application's current Path:</b> <%= oServer.getdefault()   %>
```

which is your SYSTEM directory, rather than the directory where the DLL server lives. There are a couple of problems with this: First, the SYSTEM path is a bad place to run any application that generates as many temporary files as VFP does; because this directory contains thousands of other files, access to it is deadly slow. Second, you don't have access to your data from there. You have a few choices in the Init event code. The GetAppStartPath() utility function (in wwUtils.prg) figures out the location of the server, regardless of how the server was started, and stores it in a property. Now, whenever you try to access any files, that path is used to prefix the filename. Just don't forget that the default path remains the SYSTEM directory. If you create temporary files and cursors, be sure to create them in a different location, such as the TEMP directory, by explicitly providing a path.

> ❗ ***In-process COM servers and the default path***
> *Another option is to do CD (THIS.cAppStartPath) or SET DEFAULT TO (THIS.cAppStartPath), but be careful with this because it changes the path of the client process (IIS in this case) as well! There's only one "default path" per process, and if several COM objects all try to monopolize the default path and make assumptions based on it, you're in trouble. Therefore it's not recommended to use SET DEFAULT or CD from your COM object unless you know exactly what other components in the application are doing. This is an issue only with DLL-based COM objects—EXE servers run in their own process and get their own default path.*

Understanding server security

Another frequently problematic issue concerns the security environment under which your server runs. When you test your server, there's often no problem because you call it from your VFP application while you're logged onto the machine—using an administrator account or, at the very least, a user account that has access to the files that the server is likely to need.

When you run your server inside IIS, however, it's not your logged-on account that determines the security of your server. In most cases this user will be the machine's IUSR_MachineName account—the anonymous Web user (where *MachineName* is the name of your Windows NT/95 workstation).

To demonstrate, add the following method to your server:

```
********************************************************************
* ASPTools :: GetUsername
********************************
*** Function: returns the currently active username
********************************************************************
Function GetUserName

DECLARE Integer GetUserName ;
   IN WIN32API AS GUserName ;
   STRING @nBuffer, ;
   INTEGER @nBufferSize

lcUserName = SPACE(255)
lnLength = LEN(lcUserName)

lnError = GUserName(@lcUserName,@lnLength)

RETURN SUBSTR(lcUserName, 1, lnLength - 1)
```

Then go back to the original ASP page and add this to the bottom of the COMCounter.asp file created above:

```
<b>Current User name: </b> <%= oServer.GetUserName() %>
```

You'll find that the username displays "IUSR_MachineName" (or possibly something like "WAM_USR_APP1" if you created a "separate application"—more on that later).

Now try the following (this will work only if you're running NT with NTFS—make sure you note the permissions on the file before changing them): Open Windows Explorer, select the COMCounter.asp file and change the permissions on it, so that only your user account has access to it. In my case I'll remove IUSR_, Everyone and also Administrator (because my development IUSR_ account has admin rights). So now only my current user account has access to this file. Rerun the request.

You'll be presented with a password dialog box asking for username and password. Type in your account info and now look at the username returned by the ASP page: It's the username you logged in as in the password dialog—in my case *rstrahl*. Once you've tested this, make sure you reset the permission for IUSR_ and Everyone (if it was there before).

This demonstrates how IIS passes down security to your COM object. The good news is that the security of the ASP page determines how your server is accessed. The bad news is that the security of the ASP page determines how your server is accessed! Here's why it's a problem: Normally the IUSR_ account is meant to be a low-impact, user account that has practically no rights other than to read and execute Web pages and scripts on your site.

When your COM object gets called from the Web, it usually will load under the IUSR_MachineName account, which by default will not have rights to read and write data in your application path!

Read the previous sentence again, because it's very important! So how to get around this nasty problem? There are several ways:

- **Give directory access to the IUSR_ account.**
  Assign full access rights to the IUSR_ account for every directory in which you'd expect to write data. This is tedious and prone to many errors because the directory permissions must be configured on every machine that you move files to. You also need to remember that this may include the system TEMP path and the SYSTEM path in order to make Windows API calls! It also opens up your system to serious security issues. This option is not recommended.

- **Give the IUSR_ account additional rights.**
  You can add the IUSR_ account to the Administrator group, and all your COM objects will magically have access to the system! Sure, but so will anybody else who accesses your system over the Web. If they can find a way into a directory (via Web Mapping, or whatever) the system is open to them. This may be a bad idea for a production system, but it's probably the best way to work on your development system—just be sure to test with the Admin rights off before you take your application online!

- **Use Microsoft Transaction Server for your COM object.**
  MTS allows you to configure a security role for your COM component, and by running through MTS you're allowing MTS to manage the security context for you. By doing so, you're changing the security only for the component—not the entire Web site. This is a decent way to implement security, but it complicates both installation and development of

applications. Use this only as a deployment solution. See Chapter 9 for more information about using MTS.

- **Impersonate a user account from within your COM object.**
  NT supports a concept called *user impersonation,* which allows you to temporarily change the user context to another user and then reset it to the original. In fact, this is how IIS itself handles user contexts such as IUSR_ that it passes to you. Setting user accounts is complex and requires usernames and passwords, which is unsuitable for generic applications. However, knowing how IIS creates user accounts can help here: IIS is a service so it runs under the SYSTEM account, but it impersonates the Web user to become whatever user is logged in. An API function called *RevertToSelf()*strips off all impersonations. When you do this to a Web request in your COM object, the server reverts to the SYSTEM account, which typically does have rights in most places on your system unless it was explicitly disabled.

The most consistent mechanism is the last item, so here's how to implement it. Add the following to the top of the GetUserName method presented above:

```
Function GetUserName
LPARAMETER llForceToSystem

IF llForceToSystem AND "NT" $ OS()
  DECLARE INTEGER RevertToSelf ;
      IN WIN32API
  RevertToSelf()
ENDIF
```

and add the following to the COMCounter.asp page:

```
<b>Current User name: </b> <%= oServer.GetUserName() %>
<b>Current User name: </b> <%= oServer.GetUserName(True) %><br>
<b>Current User name: </b> <%= oServer.GetUserName() %>
```

When you run this, you get:

```
Current User name: IUSR_RAS_NOTE
Current User name: SYSTEM
Current User name: SYSTEM
```

This demonstrates that an anonymous user comes in as IUSR_RAS_NOTE, and then the IIS Impersonation is removed with RevertToSelf() and switches to SYSTEM. (Note: If you're logged into the Web server somehow, like through VID debug mode, your user account might show up instead of SYSTEM.) The last call is in there to demonstrate that once you've changed the user context it doesn't change back for each method call but is scoped to the current page. There is no easy way to reset it back to IUSR_ unless you know the password. Generally this should not be a problem.

What does this mean? Since IUSR_ is not supposed to have any rights, you can run into problems with accessing data in paths where IUSR_ doesn't have rights. When running your COM components, you can use RevertToSelf() to essentially grant the user temporary rights while you're executing the current ASP page. So once you've reverted to the SYSTEM or specific user account, the user has rights to access the system as needed, be it for data or the registry or a network resource. Once the page completes, the lax security is released and reverts back to IUSR_ on the next access to the Web server.

Keep in mind that the SYSTEM account is a local account! It most likely will not have access to remote machine drives across the network. If that's required, you might have to set up a specific account to impersonate and use it for remote access, or else use the Transaction Server mechanism mentioned in the bullet list above.

I've detoured a little in this section to demonstrate how you can do useful things with your COM servers to provide debugging information. Although this is not what you'll focus on most when you build your application, this mindset is advantageous when you do run into problems. Utility methods that return a set of debug or informational values, or set properties like the *cErrorMsg* property of the server, are good features that you should consider building into all of your servers at the base class level for your ASP components.

Using VFP to generate HTML

The code above also demonstrates the most obvious use of ASP COM objects: accessing methods and properties directly as business objects. You get individual pieces of information via Property or Method access, and then return them back to the server page. The ASP page then takes the result and uses it as part of the VBScript code and displays output based on it. This is similar to using an object inside a VFP application.

Another approach is to use VFP to do most of this work, and then simply return the output back to the ASP page to display. Physically this approach is no different from using method calls and properties directly, but conceptually it's changing the role of the VFP server into an HTML-generation tool in addition to processing the business logic.

I'll add a few more methods to the ASPTOOLS server now. The following code queries the same data from the TasTrade customer and invoice tables as in the ADO sample above, pulling a customer list and displaying it as an HTML table:

```
***************************************************************************
* AspTools :: CustList
*******************************
***   Function: Retrieves a customer and returns an object ref to it
***************************************************************************
FUNCTION Custlist

*** VFP Sample Data Path
lcDataPath = home(2)+"data\"

lcWhere = ""
IF !EMPTY(THIS.cCompany)
   lcWhere = " AND Company = THIS.cCompany "
ENDIF
```

```
IF LEN(THIS.cInvNo) > 0
  lcWhere = lcWhere + " AND orders.order_id = PADL('"  +THIS.cInvNo +    "',6) "
ENDIF

SELECT customer.company, customer.cust_id, orders.order_id,orders.order_date,
Order_amt ;
   FROM (lcDataPath + "Orders"), (lcDataPath + "Customer") ;
   WHERE customer.cust_id = orders.cust_id &lcWhere ;
   ORDER BY company,order_date DESC ;
   INTO CURSOR TQuery

lcLastCustId = " "
lcOutput = ""
SCAN
lcOutput = lcOutput + ;
[<table border="0" width="570" class="bodytext">]
  IF lcLastCustId <> Tquery.Cust_id
  lcOutput = lcOutput + ;
  [<tr><td bgcolor="#000000" colspan="3" width="564"><font face="Arial"
color="#FFFFFF"><strong>] + Trim(Tquery.Company)
+[</strong></font></td></tr>]+CHR(13)+CHR(10)
  ENDIF
  lcLastCustId = Tquery.Cust_Id

  lcOutput = lcOutput + [<tr>]+;
  [<td align="center" width="179">] + Transform(TQuery.Order_date) + [</td>] +
;
  [<td align="center" width="198"><a
href="Invoice.asp?Orderid=]+TQuery.Order_id+[">]+Tquery.Order_id+[</a> </td>]+;
  [<td align="Right" width="175">]+ Transform(order_amt) + [</td>]+;
  [</tr></table>] + CHR(13)+CHR(10)
ENDSCAN

USE IN TQuery

RETURN lcOutput
```

This code looks at several input properties to determine the values of the submitted values from the ASP page, which looks like this (truncated for size):

```
<%
  Set oServer = Server.CreateObject("aspdemos.asptools")

  lcCompany = Request("txtCompany")
  lcInvNo = Request("txtInvoiceNo")
  lcFromdate= Request("txtFromDate")
  lcToDate = Request("txtToDate")

  llFirstHit = False
  IF LEN(lcToDate)=0 and LEN(lcFromDate)=0 then
     llFirstHit = True
     lcFromDate = "01/01/90"
     lcToDate = FormatDateTime(now,vbShortDate)
  END If
%>
```

```
<form action="COMinvlookup.asp" method="POST">
  <table border="1" cellPadding="1" cellSpacing="1" width="75%"
class="bodytext">
    <tr>
      <td>Invoice Number: </td>
      <td><input id="txtInvoiceNo" name="txtInvoiceNo" size="20" value="<%=
lcInvNo %>"></td>
    </tr>
    <tr>
      <td>Company: </td>
      <td><input id="txtCompany" name="txtCompany" size="20" value="<%=
lcCompany %>"></td>
    </tr>
    <tr>
      <td>Date:</td>
      <td><input id="txtFromDate" name="txtFromDate" size="8" value="<%=
lcFromDate %>"> to <input id="txtCompany" name="txtToDate" size="8" value="<%=
lcToDate %>"></td>
    </tr>
    <tr>
      <td> </td>
      <td><input type="submit" value="Show List" name="btnSubmit"></td>
    </tr>
  </table>
</form>

<% oServer.cCompany = lcCompany
   oServer.cInvNo = lcInvNo
   oServer.CFROMDATE = lcFromDate
   oServer.CTODATE = lcToDate
%>

<%= oServer.CustList() %>
```

As with the ADO page, the form acts as both an input and output form. The difference here is that Visual FoxPro is used to do all data access, as well as providing the majority of the HTML generation for the table list below. The key code is in the last five lines of the ASP page, which populates the query properties and then calls the Custlist method to render the HTML, which is returned as a string.

If you look back at the COM server-to-HTML VFP code, you might be telling yourself, "This is some ugly code," since it's generating HTML manually via code. It might not be very easy to type this stuff, but it is very fast and efficient code. In addition, once you start using VFP for HTML generation you'll quickly take to creating some base classes that can create HTML automatically for many tasks. I don't want to get into this too much here—there's a lot of detail on HTML-generating routines in Chapter 5, *FoxISAPI*. All features of the FoxISAPI Response object can also be used with ASP! So, if the concept of mixing ASP and Visual FoxPro for HTML generation appeals to you, be sure to take a look at Chapter 5.

Getting around slow HTML tables

Although this code matches the ASP-based INVLOOKUP almost exactly, there are a couple of interesting twists. For one thing, the order list can get very long—the VFP demo data contains more than 1000 records. One problem that you run into is how to display all that data at once. Surprisingly, getting the data and generating HTML is relatively fast—what's really slow is the table rendering inside the browser. HTML tables in IE don't display until all data for that table has been retrieved, including the final </table> tag. This means the entire set of data needs to download and then IE must recalculate the table widths and render it. When you run the ASP table, you'll find that the table is not available for 10 to 20 seconds (on my P200 notebook).

To speed things up, there's a little trick you can use: Rather than rendering the entire output as one huge table, the Fox code creates each row as its own table. The tables stack on top of each other, and if you remove the borders from the tables you can't tell the difference. Now the table starts rendering immediately as soon as any data is returned, even while it's downloading the remainder of the data. The apparent performance of the INVLookup.asp page and the COMINVLookup.asp are like night and day. Note that you can do the same thing to the ASP-only code as well. But even then the VPF code performs notably better than the scripted ASP page.

Besides performance, you get the advantage of the flexibility of VFP code. If you need to perform complex conditional logic or run a lot of separate queries and subqueries, creating HTML in Visual FoxPro may be a smart solution. On the downside, VFP HTML generation means that you have to recompile your server in order to change the visual aspects of the generated code.

Using ASP objects with your VFP COM server

When building Web applications, it's vitally important to have access to the input that the Web server makes available. As you've seen in this chapter, you can do this with ASP by using the Request and Response objects for input and output. Because these are COM objects they can also be passed into your Visual FoxPro Automation servers as parameters. We've already seen how to pass plain parameters to your VFP COM objects, but COM also makes it possible to pass another COM object as a parameter. This makes it much more convenient to pass information to Visual FoxPro. Rather than passing 50 parameters of an insurance submission form, you can pass a single object containing the request information. For example, to pass the Request object to your VFP server you can simply do this:

```
<% Set oServer = Server.CreateObject("ASPDemos.ASPTools")
   oServer.ProcessRequest(Request)
%>
```

Sounds simple enough—I pass the single, compound Request object to Visual FoxPro and then use VFP to pull the request information from the object itself. There's a rub, however: VBScript's concept of default methods and objects is unsupported by Visual FoxPro, so the following code *does not work* in Visual FoxPro as it does in VBScript:

```
* VFPClass::ProcessRequest
FUNCTION ProcessRequest
LPARAMETER loRequest, loResponse

lcLast = loRequest("Last")

ENDFUNC
```

This code *does not work* as is! It results in an error because VFP does not recognize loRequest() as an object, but rather thinks it's a function. The key to making this work is to understand how the object model works without the VBScript defaults. If you take out all the default property and method calls, you come up with the following:

```
loRequest.Form("Last").Item()
```

This looks kind of funky, but it's the right way to access the Form object and one of its collection values. The Form collection is the default property for the Request object, and the Item() method is the default method for the Form collection, which makes Request("FormVar") work in VBScript. In Visual FoxPro you always need to use the longhand to make this work. Knowing this, you can now access all of the other Request object collections.

A call to the object from the ASP page looks like this:

```
<%= oServer.ProcessRequest(Request,Response,Session) %>
```

You can handle it like this:

```
* VFPClass::ProcessRequest
FUNCTION ProcessRequest
LPARAMETER loRequest, loResponse, loSession

lcLast = loRequest.Form("Last").Item()
lcBrowser = loRequest.ServerVariables("HTTP_USER_AGENT").Item()
lcParameter = loRequest.QueryString("UserId").Item()

lcSessionValue = loSession.Value("TestVar")

loResponse.Write("Your last name is: " + lcLast + "<BR>"+;
                "The browser you use is: " + lcBrowser
Return .T.
```

Slick! As you can see, the various Request collections like ServerVariables, Form and QueryString all use the same syntax for accessing the item values with the Item() method. I also decided to pass the Response object to the VFP object to write output directly to the ASP output stream, rather than passing the result back to the ASP page as a string. Using the Response object directly can be more efficient when creating large amounts of text in some situations, as well as allowing your code to send intermediate output to the HTML stream, rather than buffering output until generation is complete. By doing so you can essentially create an entire HTML page with this complete ASP page:

```
<% Set oServer = Server.CreateObject("ASPDemos.ASPTools")
   Response.Write(oServer.ProcessRequest(Request,Response,Session) )
%>
```

I also pass a Session object—you can use its Value() method to retrieve any session values that you stored in an object. The same goes for the ASP Application object. Notice the inconsistency here with a value method rather than an item.

The Response object is a little easier to deal with. All you have to do is call the Write method to send output directly into the ASP output stream. Note that it's much more efficient to write to the Response object once with a single large string rather than sending a lot of small strings in a loop, since each call to the Response object is a COM method call.

The IScriptingContext interface

You've now seen how to access the Request and Response objects by passing parameters to a COM object method. There is another way to make these two objects, as well as ASP's Session, Application and Server objects, available to your servers automatically.

Automation servers called from an ASP page can choose to implement the IScriptingContext interface that consists of two methods: OnStartPage() and OnEndPage(). The OnStartPage() method receives a single object parameter: oScriptingContext. This object is nothing more than a container that can provide object references to all of the built-in ASP objects. This is quite useful to generically capture the scripting context and store it to a property of your Automation server so it's automatically available for each request:

```
DEFINE CLASS MyAutoServer AS CUSTOM OLEPUBLIC

oScriptingContext = .NULL.

FUNCTION OnStartPage
LPARAMETER loScriptingContext
THIS.oScriptingContext = loScriptingContext
ENDFUNC

Function EchoBrowser
loRequest = THIS.oScriptingContext.Request
loResponse = THIS.oScriptingContext.Response
lcBrowser = LoRequest.ServerVariables("HTTP_USER_AGENT").item()
loResponse.Write(lcBrowser)
RETURN

ENDDEFINE
```

This interface's main purpose is to give you hooks at the beginning and end of a page to perform cleanups and to make it easier to get access to the various objects that ASP exposes. Keep in mind, though, that you cannot use any of the client object's methods in the OnStartPage() and OnEndPage() "events" because they're not properly initialized in these methods. All access to these objects must occur only in your actual request methods, such as EchoBrowser() in the class above.

Objects from Visual FoxPro

It's easy to pass objects to your Visual FoxPro server, but it also works the other way around: You can create objects in Visual FoxPro and pass them back to an ASP page.

Here's a simple example of a VFP method that retrieves a record from a table, uses SCATTER NAME MEMO to create an object from the record, and passes it back to ASP:

```
**********************************************************
* ASPTools :: GetCustObject
********************************
***   Function: Retrieves customer and returns an object
***       Pass: lcCustId  -  Cust ID No (no left padding)
***     Return: loCustomer -  Customer Object
**********************************************************
FUNCTION GetCustObject
LPARAMETERS lcCustId

IF !USED("TT_Cust")
   USE (THIS.cAppStartPath + "data\TT_Cust") IN 0
ENDIF

SELECT TT_Cust

LOCATE FOR CustNo = PADL(lcCustId,8)
IF FOUND()
   SCATTER NAME loCustomer MEMO
   RETURN loCustomer
ENDIF

SCATTER NAME loCustomer MEMO BLANK
RETURN loCustomer
* WebTools :: GetCustObject
```

Isn't that cool? Any object you create from within Visual FoxPro is automatically turned into a COM-compatible object that's marshaled back to the calling COM client—ASP in this case. Inside your ASP page you can now simply use that object:

```
<%
lcCustNo = Request.QueryString("CustNo")

'*** Instantiate VFP Object
SET oServer = Server.CREATEOBJECT("aspdemos.asptools")

'*** Retrieve Customer Object
SET loCustomer = oServer.GetCustObject( (lcCustNo) )
%>
<PRE>
Company: <%= loCustomer.Company %>
Name  : <%= loCustomer.CareOf %>
Phone : <%= loCustomer.Phone %>
</PRE>
```

Objects can be nested, so you can create a VFP object that contains other member objects, and you can reference those objects and its methods from ASP as well. Powerful, don't you think?

Example—an object-based customer browser

Let's look at a simple example that allows browsing, editing and adding to a customer list—all using a single ASP page and three separate methods of a VFP Automation Server. **Figure 4.11** shows the simple form.

Everything happens on a single ASP page, which can run in three modes: Default View, Customer View or Save Mode. Customer View occurs when you click on a company hot link, which retrieves the customer information and fills the individual fields above the list with the customer values. Saving occurs when you click the Save button, which causes the ASP page to run with a Querystring of ASPObjects.asp?Action=Save. The Save flag is used by the page to decide whether to update or add a new object.

The ASP page acts as the "navigator" that simply controls the VFP back-end object. Here's the ASP/HTML code:

```
<html><head>
<title>Active Server Objects to VFP</title>
</head><body>
<%
Set oServer = Server.CREATEOBJECT("aspdemos.asptools")

lcAction = Request.QueryString("Action")
lcCustno = Request.QueryString("Custno")

If lcAction = "Save" Then
    Set loCustomer = oServer.SaveCustomer(Request, Response, Session)
    lcCustno = loCustomer.Custno
Else
    Set loCustomer = oServer.GetCustObject( (lcCustNo) )
End If
%>

<form method="POST" action="aspObjects.asp?Action=Save">
  <input type="hidden" name="CustNo" value="<%= lcCustNo%>"><table border="0"
width="72%">
    <tr>
      <td width="16%" align="right"><strong>Company:</strong></td>
      <td width="84%"><input type="text" name="txtCompany" size="45"
value="<%=loCustomer.Company%>"></td>
    </tr>
...remaining fields omitted for space
</table>
</form>
<%
Response.Write( oServer.HTMLCustList() )
%>
</body></html>
```

Notice the retrieval of the "Action" form variable, which is responsible for routing calls to the appropriate server method. There's also a hidden CustNo form variable that lets the server know which customer to save when the user clicks the Save button. Although the form variable is hidden, it does appear in the Request object.

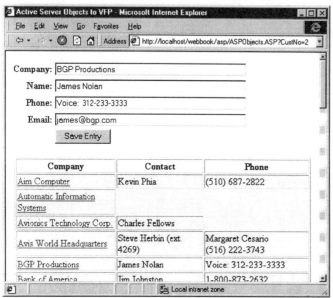

Figure 4.11. *This example uses Visual FoxPro and ASP objects that are passed back and forth between the ASP page and the VFP COM component. ASP passes its objects like requests to the VFP component, which returns full business objects that are used in the ASP code to display the page.*

Here are the three Visual FoxPro methods in the VFP COM object:

```
*******************************************************************
* AspTools :: GetCustObject
**********************************
***   Function: Retrieves a customer and returns an object ref to it
***        Pass: lcCustId   -   Customer ID (may not be Left padded)
***      Return: loCustomer  -   Customer Object
*******************************************************************
FUNCTION GetCustObject
LPARAMETERS lcCustId

IF !USED("TT_Cust")
   USE (THIS.cAppStartPath +"data\TT_Cust") IN 0
ENDIF

SELECT TT_Cust

LOCATE FOR CustNo = PADL(lcCustId,8)
```

```
IF FOUND()
   SCATTER NAME loCustomer MEMO
   RETURN loCustomer
ENDIF

SCATTER NAME loCustomer MEMO BLANK
RETURN loCustomer
ENDFUNC
* ASPTools :: GetCustObject


****************************************************************************
* ASPTools :: SaveCustomer
********************************
***   Function: Saves a customer based on a CustId and returns an object
***             ref to the customer.
***       Pass: ASP Request Object
***     Return: loCustomer object
****************************************************************************
FUNCTION SaveCustomer
LPARAMETERS loRequest, loResponse, loSession

lcCustno = loRequest.Form("CustNo").item()
lcCompany = loRequest.Form("txtCompany").item()
lcName = loRequest.Form("txtCareOf").item()
lcPhone = loRequest.Form("txtPhone").item()
lcEmail = loRequest.Form("txtEmail").item()

IF !EMPTY(lcCustNo)
   UPDATE (THIS.cAppStartPath + "data\tt_cust") ;
     SET Company = lcCompany,CareOf = lcName, Phone = lcPhone, Email = lcEmail;
     WHERE CustNo = PADL(lcCustno,8)
ELSE
   INSERT INTO (THIS.cAppStartPath  + "data\tt_cust") ;
      (Company, CareOf, Phone, Email,CustNo) VALUES ;
      (lcCompany, lcName, lcPhone, lcEmail, SYS(3))
ENDIF

SELECT TT_Cust
LOCATE FOR Custno =  PADL(lcCustno,8)
lcOutput = "<b>" + TRIM(Company) + " has been saved...</b><br>"
loResponse.Write(lcOutput)

SCATTER NAME loCustomer MEMO

RETURN loCustomer
ENDFUNC
* WebTools :: SaveCustList


****************************************************************************
* ASPTools :: HTMLCustList
********************************
***   Function: Test Method that retrieves a customer list based on
***             a name passed.
***       Pass: lcCompany  -  Name of the company to look up
***     Return: HTML of the list
****************************************************************************
```

```
FUNCTION HTMLCustList
LPARAMETERS lcName

lcName = IIF(type("lcName") = "C", UPPER(lcName), "")

*** Run Query - Note I'm creating the Hotlink right in the query
***              to be able to use the ShowCursor method to display the
***              cursor with a single command!
SELECT [<A
HREF="ASPObjects.ASP?CustNo=]+URLEncode(tt_cust.custno)+[">]+tt_cust.company+[<
/a>] as Company,;
      careof as Contact, Phone ;
 FROM (THIS.cAppStartPath + "data\TT_CUST") ;
 WHERE UPPER(tt_cust.company)=TRIM(lcName) ;
 INTO CURSOR TQUERY ;
 ORDER BY company

*** Stolen from wwFoxisapi
RETURN THIS.ShowCursor()
ENDFUNC
* HTMLCustList
```

Notice how little code is involved in making this work, and how the HTML display logic and the business logic has been, for the most part, separated: The ASP page has the HTML display logic and the VFP COM object has the business rules.

Compare this version of HTMLCustList with the version used in the previous section where the HTML was built by hand. Here I use a generic method called ShowCursor, which can render any cursor as an HTML table with this single line of code. Methods like this can make very short work of creating results. Take a look at the 30 or so lines of code that make this work in the source code, or see Chapter 5 for more details about this method.

The key concept to walk away with from this exercise is that it's easy to have Visual FoxPro and Active Server Pages communicate with each other using business objects that you can create or may have already created with Visual FoxPro.

Sharing data with ASP—passing ADO objects

In addition to the powerful functionality of passing generic objects back and forth, you can also pass data directly by using ActiveX Data Objects! To demonstrate, I'll show an example that accesses a SQL Server database and passes the data to your VFP server. You can, of course, do this directly from ASP using ADO and then looping through the recordset or using action operation to update the data directly from ASP code.

Let's do something a little different—open the SQL Server Pubs Author table as a cursor instead, pass it to the VFP Active Server Component and add a record to it within the VFP code. To do this, set up a System DSN to the SQL Server Pubs database and name it Pubs. You might also have to set up some additional default values for the Authors table in order to allow inserts with only a few fields filled in, as I did in **Figure 4.12**.

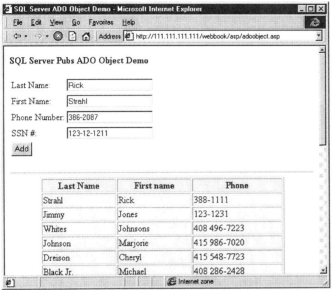

Figure 4.12. *Using Visual FoxPro to process an ADO recordset created by an ASP page allows you to put the business logic where it belongs—in the VFP COM object.*

Here's the ASP code to open the Authors table as a cursor (note that some of the constants defined in the ADO documentation don't work, so the literal values must be used):

```
<form method="POST" id=form1 name=form1>
<Table>
<TR><TD>Last Name:</td><td> <INPUT type="text" name="txtLName"></td></tr>
<TR><TD>First Name:</td><td> <INPUT type="text" name="txtFName"></td></tr>
<TR><TD>Phone Number:</td><td> <INPUT type="text" name="txtPhone"></td></tr>
<TR><TD>SSN #:</td><td> <INPUT TYPE="Text" name="txtSSN"></td></tr>
<TR><TD><INPUT type="submit" value="Add" name=btnSubmit></td><td> </td></tr>
</table>
</form>
<hr>
<%
   Set oServer = Server.CREATEOBJECT("aspdemos.asptools")

   Set Conn = Server.CreateObject("ADODB.Connection")
   Conn.Open("dsn=pubs;uid=sa;pwd=")

   Set rs = Server.CreateObject("ADODB.Recordset")

   rs.CursorType = adOpenKeyset
   rs.LockType = 2 ' adLockOptimistic
   rs.Open  "authors", conn  , , , 2    'adCmdTable

   If Len(Request("txtLName")) > 0 Then
     oserver.AddAdoRecord rs,Request
     rs.Update
   End If
```

```
      rs.Movefirst
%>


Here's a list of records:<p>

'*** Display the record set from inside of VFP
<%= oServer.ShowAdoRS( rs ) %>
```

Inside Visual FoxPro, you can now do several things. First take a look at the code that displays the recordset at the end:

```
FUNCTION ShowAdoRs
LPARAMETER rs

   lcOutput = "<table border=1 bgcolor=#eeeeee width=80% >"

   do while !rs.eof
     lcOutput = lcOutput + "<TR><TD>" + ;
                  rs.fields("au_lname").value + "</td><td>" + ;
                  rs.fields("au_fname").value + "</td><td>" + ;
                  rs.Fields("phone").value + "</td></tr><BR>"
     rs.movenext()
   ENDDO

   lcOutput = lcOutput + "</table>"

RETURN lcOutput
ENDFUNC
```

This is probably not a good use of a VFP object, since you could run it more efficiently inside the ASP code as described in the last example. However, it demonstrates how you can access ADO object properties inside your VFP component. Like the Request object, the Recordset object has many default properties; in order to get at the collection values, use the Value property to retrieve the actual field name, like this:

```
rs.fields("UserId").value
```

To update the cursor created in the ASP page, use the AddAdoRecord method:

```
PROCEDURE AddAdoRecord
LPARAMETER rs, Request
   rs.AddNew
   rs.Fields("au_lname").value =  Request.Form("txtLName").item()
   rs.Fields("au_Fname").value =  Request.Form("txtFName").item()
   rs.Fields("phone").value =  Request.Form("txtPhone").item()
   rs.Fields("au_id").value = Request.Form("txtSSN").item()
   rs.Fields("zip").value = "97031" 'Lazy but required for constraints
   rs.Fields("state").value = "OR"
   rs.Update
RETURN
```

This simple method adds a new record and populates the fields. Note the use of the Request object to retrieve the previous link that led to the current link. (If you try this on your own, this value will be blank unless you arrived at the test page from a link.) This is probably not a good use of passing a recordset because nothing useful really happens in this request—you could just as easily do this without the COM method call from the ASP page. But you could, of course, run extensive Visual FoxPro code prior to actually inserting the record into the ADO result set, which is where the power comes in. You could run your own query against local VFP data and then update the ADO cursor for return to the ASP page, which might do something further with the data. Or you could run a query in the ASP page to prepare the data and then pass it to Visual FoxPro to properly format certain columns of the result. It's easy to do by accessing the ADO object directly.

An objective warning

Using objects is a great way to pass data between VFP and ASP, but keep in mind that passing this data and accessing the individual object properties takes place over COM, which provides the communication infrastructure between ASP and VFP. For this reason, reading properties and calling methods in your COM object is slow and imposes serious scalability issues. Repeatedly creating objects in a loop and retrieving properties from that object in each iteration—only to send them to output with the Response object—might not be the most efficient approach. For example, your ASP page may do this:

```
<%
oServer.RunQuery()  ' creates a VFP cursor
do while oServer.GetNext()  ' retrieve the next rec and store to object
  Last name: <%= oServer.oRecord.LastName %>
  Company: <%= oServer.oRecord.FirstName %>
<% loop %>
```

This code will run perfectly well, but because each GetNext() call and each property access occurs over COM, there's significant overhead (as well as potential blocking issues I'll discuss later). When using objects and COM, you should try to minimize the number of round trips made between the ASP page and your server. In this scenario it might just be easier to have VFP run the query, execute the loop and generate the HTML internally, and then pass back a string that gets embedded:

```
<%= oServer.ShowCustList() %>
```

In iterative situations, using the Response object directly in your VFP methods or passing back a complete string with the result output from VFP can be vastly more efficient than constantly creating and deleting objects over COM. Weigh convenience versus performance, and test different scenarios if you feel your request is slow. Refer to the Object Customer browser example above, where the output routine directly wrote to the Response object.

Keep in mind that there are a number of options available to accomplish the same job, and performance between approaches can vary considerably. With COM in particular, the performance rules aren't always cut and dried—what works well in one request may perform horribly in another.

Understanding ASP/COM scalability

As you've just seen, it's easy to extend ASP with your own Visual FoxPro COM objects. When you're testing you'll see that your server code performance is very fast—operations run at native Visual FoxPro speed, so data access in particular is fast; it's noticeably faster, in fact, than using ADO with the Visual FoxPro ODBC Driver for similar requests.

What's not so obvious is that Visual FoxPro 6.0, in its initial release, has serious scalability problems to consider. In order understand this, you must understand how IIS creates new instances of COM objects when called from ASP pages. Many of these issues will be addressed in an upcoming interim release of Visual FoxPro—I'll discuss some of the new features of this version later.

What is Apartment Model Threading and why should you care?

Apartment model threading works by allowing multiple, simultaneous instances of your component to be created on separate threads. The operation is transparent and the logistics for the threading model are built into the Windows COM subsystem, with Visual FoxPro 6.0 complying to the apartment-thread model. Although COM makes it possible through this mechanism to run your COM servers as multi-threaded objects that can operate simultaneously, your program has little control over the multi-threading environment. In other words, the system controls the threading model and your application behaves just as a stand-alone application running in a multi-user environment.

To take advantage of apartment model threading, simply create an in-process component (build a COM DLL in the Project Manager, making sure each OLEPUBLIC class is marked for multi-use operation!) and then instantiate your component via CreateObject() or an equivalent function call from any COM-compliant client. If the client is multi-threaded it can take advantage of the scheduling magic that COM performs to allow your server to be called on multiple, simultaneously operating threads. In the case of Active Server Pages, the client is IIS using an ASP page that has created an object reference of your component via the Server.CreateObject() method.

Note that, starting with VFP 6.0, you can create application-level objects that are instantiated in Global.asa using the <OBJECT> tag. This is a new feature that is made possible by the new threading model of in-process servers. Here's an example from my Global.asa:

```
<OBJECT RUNAT=SERVER SCOPE=APPLICATION
  ID=oWebTools
  ProgId="aspdemos.asptools" >
</OBJECT>
```

Once instantiated here, the object can be called on any page that is in the same virtual path hierarchy as the Global.asa file. Understand that this object is global, not only to the current page and user, but to all users on the site! This means a *single* instance is held and serialized by ASP, regardless of whether the component is multi-instance-capable or not. For this reason, application-level objects don't scale well unless they are implemented as true multi-threaded and reentrant object classes. This can't be done with high-level tools like Visual FoxPro or Visual Basic, but requires C++, Delphi, Java or any other language that supports multi-threaded code from within the language itself.

Regardless of how you create your object, Active Server invokes your object on a specific thread and guarantees that it's always called on the same thread for the duration of its lifetime (typically an ASP page); or in Microsoft-speak, "the same apartment." Actually, this is not a function of the Active Server client, but of the COM subsystem in Windows that handles the logistics of marshaling requests on your component to the appropriate thread if necessary. If the thread calling your component is already the correct thread, no marshaling takes place. If you create and destroy your object on each page, then marshaling is not an issue, but if you use objects with Session and Application scope, these objects potentially require marshaling. Keep in mind that if you use an application-scope object, a single instance of that object is shared by all simultaneous pages. There's no marshaling in that scenario, but also no multi-threading of any sort. For this reason you should think carefully about whether you really need to implement Application objects.

It's important to understand that apartment model threading is only available to DLL/in-process COM objects; EXE/out-of-process servers will suffer the same blocking issues as before with serious performance limitations on the server's COM subsystem. Note also that in-process DLL servers in Visual FoxPro 6.0 can no longer have any user interface—this means no forms, no message boxes, and no error dialogs. Even WAIT WINDOW and INKEY() are disallowed! All access to the UI will generate a VFP exception in your COM server. (You can still "run" forms in VFP without generating an error, but the UI is invisible. It's equivalent of DO FORM NOSHOW.)

Okay, that all sounds good, but there's a problem in the initial release of Visual FoxPro 6.0. Unlike VFP 5.0, version 6.0 *does* support apartment model threading, but it *blocks access to the same server while another call to that same server is executing*. The server is blocked at the component level, which means that the component starts up on a new thread, but has to wait for a blocking lock to clear before it can enter the processing code. This means that if two requests are hitting a page that uses the same COM server (not object, but server—each server can contain multiple objects) the requests will queue. If you have a 10-second request and a 1-second request following it, the 1-second request may have to wait up to 11 seconds to get its result returned. That's very limiting for an Active Server Page on a busy Web server with perhaps hundreds of simultaneous users!

This behavior is addressed in a forthcoming Service Pack for Visual FoxPro. It provides a new multi-threaded runtime that handles thread isolation and does not block simultaneous method calls. I'm currently using an early beta version of this release, and it's possible to get unlimited instances of your server to fire up simultaneously. **Figure 4.13** shows six instances of a component processing simulated slow requests simultaneously. The thread IDs and completion times clearly show that requests run simultaneously.

Here's what the code looks like. Add another method to the ASPTools object called SlowHit, which allows you to force a request to take a certain amount of time:

```
***********************************************************************
* ASPTools :: SlowHit
*********************************
*** Function: Allows you to simulate a long request. Pass number of
***           seconds. Used to demonstrate blocking issues with
***           VFP COM objects.
***********************************************************************
```

```
FUNCTION SlowHit
LPARAMETER lnSecs
LOCAL x
lnSecs = IIF(EMPTY(lnSecs), 0, lnSecs)

DECLARE Sleep IN WIN32API INTEGER
FOR x = 1 to lnSecs
  FOR x = 1 to lnSecs
     Sleep(1000)
  ENDFOR
ENDFOR

DECLARE INTEGER GetCurrentThreadId IN WIN32API

RETURN GetCurrentThreadId() && "waited for " + TRANSFORM(lnSecs) + "..."
```

Note that you can't use WAIT WINDOW, INKEY or DOEVENTS because these are UI operations that are not allowed in a DLL server. I use the Sleep API to wait without hogging all of the system's CPU in a tight loop.

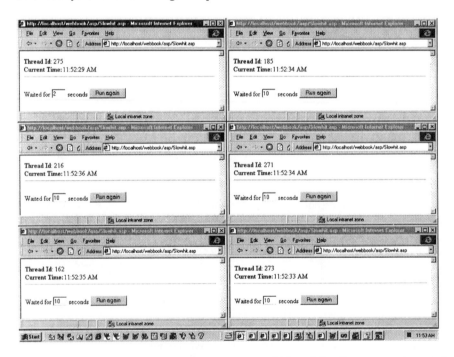

Figure 4.13. *A forthcoming interim release of Visual FoxPro supports running multiple simultaneous instances of objects. This example shows that each page ran the component on its own thread, with multiple components executing requests of various lengths at the same time. This would not work with the original release version of VFP 6.0—you'd see separate threads but queued operation.*

To exercise this method, create an ASP page called Slowhit.asp:

```
<%
   lnSecs = Request("txtSeconds")
   IF LEN(lnSecs) < 1 then
      lnSecs = "3"
   End If

   lnSecs = CLng(lnSecs)
   Set oServer = Server.CreateObject("AspDemos.AspTools")

      Response.Write( "<b>Thread Id</b>: " & oServer.SlowHit((lnSecs)) &
"<br>")
   Response.Write( "<b>Current Time:</b>" & FormatDateTime(now,vbLongTime))
%>
<hr>
<form method="POST" action="Slowhit.asp">
Waited for <INPUT type="text"  name=txtSeconds size="3" value="<%= lnSecs %>">
seconds
<INPUT type="submit" value="Run again"name=button1>
</form>
```

> ❗ ***Beware of browser session with IIS 4.0***
> *Make sure you open multiple, **separate** browser windows to test any multi-threading samples. If you're using IE, make sure you set the option to have each new instance start up as a separate process (Advanced Options).Once set, click on the Start Menu or Desktop icon to start the new instance—do not use Ctrl-N or New Window from within an existing browser window! Ideally you should use different browsers altogether to simulate multiple clients. Why? ASP tracks sessions by browser and appears to have logic that picks up on this session. When you run multiple requests from the same browser, each server request gets queued to the same thread. If you fire up separate instances, you might still get the same thread occasionally, but if a thread is busy it will start up another for the other session.*

To run this sample, load two instances of the SlowHit.asp page into separate browser windows. Change the timeout values so that one runs for two seconds and one for 10 seconds. With the original version of VFP 6.0 you'll see that both instances run on different threads, but you'll also find that the two-second request is blocked by the 10-second one. Full blocking makes this a serialized request operation. With the updated version of VFP, you'll see the two-second request complete before the 15-second one, and you'll see each request on a separate thread.

As you might expect, VFP 6.0 can present a serious scalability issue, which applies not only to Active Server Pages but also to any multi-threaded environment that loads more than one instance of your server. Another very obvious application with which VFP has the same issues is Microsoft Transaction Server. As with ASP, the updated, multi-threaded runtime allows multiple objects to run simultaneously inside MTS.

With the updated version of VFP 6.0 you can build a new type of DLL called a *multi-threaded DLL* that employs a new, multi-threaded runtime file that avoids the blocking issues. To build your servers with the multi-threaded runtime, use:

```
BUILD MTDLL aspDemos FROM aspDemos
```

BUILD MTDLL and a new option in the Project Build dialog allow servers to be built this way. The new version of the runtime strips some functionality from the VFP runtime (menu support, reports, old @say..get, and so on) so it is more lightweight, but you might want to check your code to make sure you don't run into some of the missing features. Additionally, Microsoft suggests that the multi-threaded runtime might be slightly slower than the regular runtime because it has to access data using thread-specific local storage, which tends to be slower than direct memory access. Overall this should be a fair tradeoff, though, and the performance difference is expected to be minor.

Chapter 9 provides a more detailed discussion about the COM model that VFP provides and how it relates to multi-threaded server access in ASP and MTS.

Summing up

Active Server Pages provide a rich solution for building server-side Web solutions. Microsoft has put its weight behind this scripting technology and has done a good job of providing an easy tool for the job. In addition, through the extensibility of COM, Active Server Pages can grow as the needs of your applications grow.

Data access is integrated into ASP indirectly through COM-based ADO support, which is accessible through your page's ASP code, or from within COM components you build on your own. ADO data access is decidedly more complex than using the FoxPro Data Manipulation Language (DML), but if you're quick with SQL and have patience through the testing process, ADO provides most of the functionality you'd expect for data access—it's just a lot more work.

The ability to pass objects between the ASP page and COM components makes it possible to build sophisticated servers that can share data and the base tools from an ASP page. It also gives you the ability to use Visual FoxPro's DML directly for data access, for increased performance of native VFP data access, and the flexibility of the language to perform fast, complex data formatting. FoxPro's strengths with data access speed, the data-centric language and string performance really shine here to give you the best of both worlds.

While at first glance it seems easy to get started with the scripting metaphor, keep in mind that complexity and administration go way up once you step beyond the basics. At that point you need to look into extensibility via COM.

ASP pros:
- Very easy to get started with.
- It's the official Microsoft technology for server-side Web development.
- It's free and part of any Microsoft Web server (no extra installation).
- Script-based metaphor makes for quick developer startup.
- Low-impact deployment of new code and code changes in scripts—as easy as updating a file on the Web server.

- COM capabilities allow extensibility.
- Budding third-party market for COM ASP components.

ASP cons:
- Code maintenance for anything but simple applications is difficult.
- Development environment is not nearly as rich and well implemented as standard desktop development tools such as VFP and VB, even with tools like Visual InterDev, HomeSite 4, and so on.
- Requires COM for most substantial applications.
- Complexity of development, deployment and administration goes way up once custom COM components are required. An understanding of how IIS security and administration works is a must!
- Initial development startup requires solid understanding of HTML. There's not much help in HTML generation functionality.
- Not well supported by Microsoft. Several serious bugs in the past have never been addressed or acknowledged publicly. If you have system-level problems, tracking down the source is nearly impossible because of the interdependencies.

ASP resources
http://www.ActiveServerPages.com/
http://www.15seconds.com/
http://www.ServerObjects.com/

Chapter 5
FoxISAPI

The last chapter introduced you to Active Server Pages, which is Microsoft's flagship strategy for building Web applications in a scripting and component environment. FoxISAPI represents a slightly different approach that follows the more traditional CGI/ISAPI model of a direct interface between the Web server and the back-end application. With FoxISAPI you use Visual FoxPro COM objects in direct response to links and forms in an HTML page. Because FoxISAPI provides a direct path to your FoxPro code, it allows you more flexibility and control over what you can do with your servers and the FoxPro code within them. FoxISAPI is also the fastest and most scalable mechanism available from Microsoft to run Fox code off your Web server at this time.

What is FoxISAPI?

Microsoft provides FoxISAPI as a "sample" application. This means it does not officially support this product and you won't be able to call tech support to get help. Don't let that scare you off, though—FoxISAPI provides a lot of power that makes it worth looking past this disclaimer. Microsoft provides FoxISAPI with full source code, including the C++ source files to the ISAPI DLL. This should also give you an idea of the complexity level involved with this tool. Whereas it's easy to get started with Active Server Pages and more difficult to build high-end applications, FoxISAPI starts with more complex configuration and setup but has a simple implementation that can easily scale up. In other words, FoxISAPI has a steeper learning curve, but it's easier and more consistent to work with once you get past the initial installation and configuration.

The initial learning curve is worth it: FoxISAPI provides what Active Server Pages cannot provide very well, namely the ability to build truly scalable Web applications using native data access that can bypass ODBC altogether if desired. As you learned in the final section of the last chapter, Active Server Pages has problems with Visual FoxPro COM objects running simultaneously. FoxISAPI works around this nasty problem by providing its own implementation of a pool manager for managing multiple COM objects. In addition, FoxISAPI focuses much more heavily on the FoxPro end of the development cycle, making it a more comfortable solution for those familiar with the Fox language and those not willing to work with a limited scripting language. You also get the flexibility to implement your own high-level Web application framework. In this chapter I'll show the basics of a framework along with some useful tools that rival the functionality of Active Server Pages—all driven through the FoxPro engine.

On the highest level, FoxISAPI:

- **Is a server-side Web development tool.**
  FoxISAPI runs on the back end as an IIS ISAPI extension. Clients do not need Visual FoxPro to run your application over the Web. The application is maintained in one place and you can build true thin client applications with it.

- **Offers a high-performance, direct interface to Visual FoxPro code and data.**
  For calling Visual FoxPro back ends from a Web page, FoxISAPI is very efficient. In fact, it's the most efficient tool available from Microsoft for access to Visual FoxPro data. You don't need ODBC or OLE DB to access your Fox data.

- **Is an Internet Server API (ISAPI).**
  FoxISAPI is built as an ISAPI extension that communicates with a Visual FoxPro COM object. ISAPI's multi-threaded, system-level implementation allows for maximum performance and flexibility in the connector application that calls your Visual FoxPro COM object.

- **Uses COM for messaging.**
  ISAPI provides the low-level interface to the Web server and uses COM to talk to your Visual FoxPro application. Your application is built as a COM object that acts as a server to the FoxISAPI connector, which becomes the client to your app.

- **Includes a built-in COM pool manager.**
  FoxISAPI can circumvent the concurrency issues with Active Server Pages discussed in the last chapter. A built-in COM object manager makes it possible to load multiple instances of your server and have FoxISAPI call servers from this pool, allowing multiple requests to run concurrently, giving a simulation of multi-threading to VFP servers. Note: The pool manager works best with out-of-process, single-use EXE servers, although you can use in-process objects as well.

- **Creates HTML output from your Visual FoxPro code.**
  Once your server is called by the ISAPI DLL, it's responsible for retrieving input from the server in the form of several parameters and then generating HTTP-compliant output, which in most cases is HTML.

All of these features add up to a quick and efficient engine that is very direct and wastes no time with high-level components. A request is directly routed to your FoxPro code, which can get to work processing business logic and creating HTML output to send back to the Web server.

At first thought, the idea of having to create HTML in code might sound like a huge step back from a scripting engine. However, using code directly provides tremendous speed advantages and also gives you full flexibility in how you want to generate the HTML. In fact, it's reasonably easy to build a scripting engine with FoxPro code that simulates 95 percent of what Active Server Pages does with a couple hundred lines of generic, reusable code. I'll show you how later on in this chapter.

How it works

FoxISAPI consists of two basic components which are required to make it tick: the Foxisapi.dll and your implementation code created as a Visual FoxPro COM object. See **Figure 5.1**.

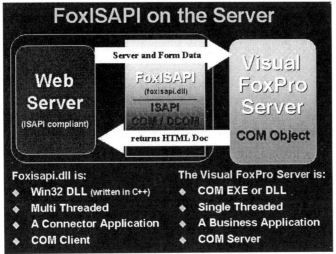

Figure 5.1. *The inner workings of FoxISAPI. The ISAPI extension communicates with a Visual FoxPro COM object.*

When the browser makes a request on the Web server, it asks to load Foxisapi.dll via a URL link such as this:

```
http://someserver.com/scripts/foxisapi.dll/YourServer.YourClass.YourMethod
```

This link causes the Web server to load FoxISAPI into its memory space. Because Foxisapi.dll is a Win32 DLL, it loads once and stays loaded in the calling process of the Web server; it never unloads. The DLL is also multi-threaded, which means it can take multiple, simultaneous requests from the multi-threaded Web server. If 10 people request the same URL that takes 10 seconds to process, you can have 10 threads asking to access your COM object. Unfortunately, Visual FoxPro is single-threaded and cannot walk and chew gum at the same time, so in its default implementation Foxisapi.dll will have to queue these incoming requests. However, FoxISAPI includes a pool manager to manage multiple simultaneous instances of the COM objects, which makes it possible to run requests concurrently. (More on that later.)

Once loaded, Foxisapi.dll tries to create an instance of the COM object specified on the URL—Yourserver.YourClass—by issuing the equivalent of:

```
o=CREATEOBJECT("YourServer.YourClass")
o.YourMethod("FormVar1=Test+Value","c:\http\foxisapi\XXX.ini",0)
```

The COM server must exist and be registered in the Windows Registry in order for FoxISAPI to create the object from the ProgID passed on the URL command line. FoxISAPI works with either out-of-process (EXE) or in-process (DLL) components, but it's better to use EXE servers, both for stability and scalability. To register your EXE COM object you can run it from the Command Prompt:

```
YourServer /regserver
```

Make sure the type library file (.tlb) is in the same directory as the server when registering it. Always copy the type library along with the server.

If you look back on the URL you'll see that all three pieces of the server—the server, class and method—are described in the *YourServer.YourClass.YourMethod* URL. The server link follows Foxisapi.dll with a slash (this is known as the *Logical Path*) in order to allow the two above commands to be described as a single string. Very direct, but it also makes for a rather lengthy and unsightly URL.

At this point Foxisapi.dll has created an instance of the COM object and has called your method in this server. FoxISAPI is smart enough to load an instance and then keep the reference to the server alive until you explicitly unload it. This means that the first hit on the server will be slow as the entire VFP runtime loads into memory, but subsequent hits are very fast because they access a server that is already loaded in memory.

> ❗ *Due to a quirk in the DCOM subsystem of Windows NT, servers can be unloaded by the system after approximately eight minutes of idle time when loaded from IIS. The servers disappear even though FoxISAPI continues to hold a reference to the server. Internally, Foxisapi.dll checks for this particular condition and reloads the server on the next hit.*
>
> *So, if you see your COM objects disappearing off the task list when things get slow on your server, consider that normal behavior. In a way this is a useful "feature"— this makes it possible to load a large pool of servers, which will be active only if the server is busy enough to keep them all exercised. When activity slows, the less busy servers automatically are unloaded, freeing up system resources.*

Build your application code with Visual FoxPro

What happens next? FoxISAPI has called a method in your server with a set of parameters, and you have received a blank check from the Web server to go wild and run Visual FoxPro through its magic paces. You can run any queries, inserts and updates, access ODBC data sources to SQL servers, or call business logic in business objects or stand-alone functions. You can even write straight procedural spaghetti code if you wish—all of Visual FoxPro is available to you.

Well, not all of it actually. You can't run interactive code that requires user intervention. You can't run a form or pop up a dialog box to have a user start entering data. By the time the request reaches your FoxPro code, you're essentially looking at building a one-way transaction-based request handler. The Web server is waiting for a single response from your code in the form of a complete HTML document. There's no interactivity happening at this point. Your entire user interface needs to be generated as HTML that is sent back as the character return value from your COM object method.

Any attempt to call an interactive form or dialog will cause the server to hang. It's very important to understand this! Any prompt in your code, whether voluntary (forms, MessageBox, etc.) or involuntary (a File Open dialog, a program error) will cause your server to hang and no longer be available to serve requests! Error handling is an obvious requirement, and we'll discuss this a little later on when talking about the framework classes.

Once your code is complete, it needs to return a string to Foxisapi.dll as the return value. This string must contain *HTTP*-compliant output. In most cases this output will be an HTML document. But because FoxISAPI doesn't *require* an HTML result, you can send any valid HTTP response, including direct HTTP requests asking for user authentication, redirection to other pages, and so on. You can also send other content types such as graphics, binary documents such as Microsoft Word or Adobe Acrobat PDF documents, as long as you provide the proper Content Type header for the text. It's even possible to send data directly over the wire to the client. How about sending a DBF file back to the client? Thismight be very useful if the client is not a Web browser but another FoxPro application. FoxISAPI can do all of these things because it expects an HTTP response rather than HTML.

Building the COM server

What does a FoxISAPI-compliant COM server look like in terms of FoxPro code? You might be surprised that a "Hello World" application with FoxISAPI takes fewer than 10 lines of code! The most basic FoxISAPI-compatible COM server that you can build looks like this:

```
*** System Defines
#DEFINE CR CHR(13)+CHR(10)

DEFINE CLASS TFirstServer AS Custom OLEPUBLIC

FUNCTION Helloworld
LPARAMETER lcFormVars, lcIniFile, lnReload

lnReload = 0  && Keep server loaded

lcHeader = "HTTP/1.0 200 OK"+CHR(13) + CHR(10) +;
           "Content-type: text/html" + CHR(13) + CHR(10) + CHR(13) + CHR(10)

lcOutput = "<HTML><BODY>" + ;
           "<h1>Hello World From Visual FoxPro!</H1><HR>" + CHR(13)+CHR(10) +;
           "<b>Version: </b>" + Version() + "<BR>"+;
           "<b>Time:    </b>" + Time() +;
           "</BODY></HTML>"

RETURN lcHeader + lcOutput

ENDDEFINE
```

First, the class created must be defined as OLEPUBLIC in order to be accessible as a COM object once compiled. If you use a visual class, set the OlePublic flag in the Class Options dialog. Note that you can use a single server that contains multiple publicly accessible classes by using several OLEPUBLIC classes in the same project.

The method takes three input parameters, which we're not yet using. All methods called directly from FoxISAPI must accept those three parameters or a COM error will occur and display in the browser through Foxisapi.dll's limited error reporting screen. The routine then builds a simple HTML string containing the VFP version number and current time to demonstrate something dynamic that changes with each request. The string is returned to FoxISAPI by way of the RETURN value. The method builds both the HTML for display in the page as well as the HTTP header, which is required to let the browser know it's dealing with an HTML document.

> **!** *While you're looking at this rocket science example: You should make a point of always including a very basic request in your server, so that you can easily test its operation through the Web page without fear of potentially causing an error based on permissions or faulty program logic. I'll discuss more on error handling later, but I suggest you include a very simple method, which simply takes three parameters and returns a string:*

```
Procedure ServerTest
LPARAMETER lcFormVars, lcIniFile, lnRelease
RETURN "<HTML>FoxISAPI Test Request</HTML>"
```

After you've built the FoxISAPI request handler class, test your server inside Visual FoxPro as a native class:

```
o=CREATEOBJECT("TfirstServer")
? o.HelloWorld()
```

This will print out the HTML response as text on the VFP desktop. If you need to work with form variables, you can simulate URL encoding manually. For example:

```
o=CREATE("TfirstServer")
? o.HelloWorld("Name=Rick+Strahl&Company=West+Wind+Technologies")
```

and so on. It gets tedious quickly with more than a few parameters, but it's a good idea to test forms inside VFP first before building them into COM objects, which can't be interactively debugged because they are compiled EXE files.

Next, build your server into an out-of-process EXE COM object. Add the PRG file into a project and call it FirstServer. To build you can use:

```
BUILD EXE FirstServer FROM FirstServer RECOMPILE
```

or you can use the Project Manager interactively. You should then see the server listed in the Project Manager on the Servers tab as shown in **Figure 5.2**. You should build your server as a single-use EXE for best results. Once set, you don't have to worry about this setting again.

Then check for operation of your server as you did with the native class, but use the COM ProgID for the server's creation instead:

```
o=CREATEOBJECT("FirstServer.TfirstServer")
? o.ServerTest()
```

You should see the result from the method just as you did before, except you've now used 4M of memory for another instance of the VFP runtime. You're now running a COM object that you can see in Task Manager, showing as FirstServer.EXE.

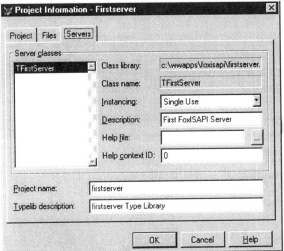

Figure 5.2. *Your compiled COM object should show up in the Project Information dialog's Server tab as a Single Use server.*

Now it's time to move it onto the Web. I'm going to skip the configuration step for now and jump directly to using the server from a Web page. With the COM EXE built, you can call this server through FoxISAPI by typing the following URL into the browser's location window, as shown in **Figure 5.3**:

```
/localhost/foxisapi/foxisapi.dll/TFoxServer.TFoxIsapi.HelloWorld
```

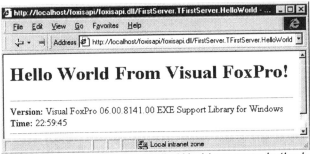

Figure 5.3. *Running the Hello World program in the browser.*

Whoopee—isn't it exciting what can be accomplished with a 4M EXE file? The above server is pretty simple and doesn't do anything terribly useful, but it does demonstrate the key pieces that each FoxISAPI method called from a Web link must support.

Server configuration

And now back to our regularly scheduled program. I skipped the server configuration to show you the result and how to call it first. If you try loading the server before performing the following configuration steps, your request will likely fail with a COM error ("Catastrophic Failure in IIS 4" or "Access Denied in IIS 3"). The Web server imposes several security requirements that must be addressed before a COM object can be called from within the Web service's security environment.

This is necessary to prevent unauthorized access to servers. For example, FoxISAPI essentially makes it possible to run any COM component on your computer. Without the default security on the server, it would be possible for a client to invoke word.application (Microsoft's Word Automation Server), for example. So by default, security is set restrictively to disallow any access to objects for the Internet user account, which is IUSR_Machinename, where *Machinename* is the NetBios name of your Web server.

Copy Foxisapi.dll into a Web script directory
In order to call Foxisapi.dll from a Web page, it needs to be accessible to the Web server in a directory with Execute rights. The Microsoft examples put it into the server's script directory, but I prefer putting it into its own FoxISAPI virtual directory and setting Execute rights as shown in **Figure 5.4**.

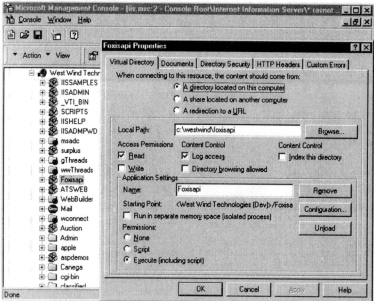

Figure 5.4. Place FoxISAPI in a virtual directory with Execute rights.

You'll also want to copy Foxisapi.ini into the same directory. It contains various configuration information about how FoxISAPI runs. In order for Foxisapi.dll to create the INI files in this directory, you should also give Change rights to the IUSR_ account using Windows Explorer, as shown in **Figure 5.5**.

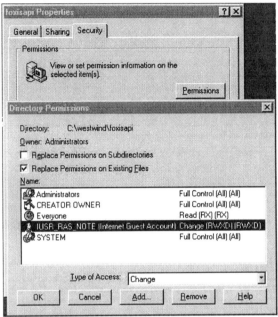

Figure 5.5. *The FoxISAPI script directory needs Change rights in order to write temporary files.*

Run DCOMCNFG to configure your server

And now for the really fun part—NOT! In order to properly run your COM object inside IIS, you need to configure it for the proper *impersonation* of an NT User account. Impersonation lets the server run in the context of the specified user. When the server starts up, it gets all rights of the impersonation account assigned to it. Without this impersonation your server will run under the IIS default user account called IUSR_MachineName. Mine is IUSR_RAS_NOTE, as you can see in Figure 5.5.

The problem is that the IUSR_ account has next to no rights on your computer by default, and without impersonation you'll run into problems accessing resources on your machine. This affects data stored in directories that don't allow IUSR_ access, ODBC data sources, the registry, and so on. IUSR_ is very limited and by default has only Read and Execute rights in the Web directories. Impersonation makes it possible to temporarily assign the IUSR_ account rights to run a COM object without opening up the entire system to this guest account.

To get around this problem, you can use impersonation on all EXE-based COM objects with a utility called DCOMCNFG. You should make two settings—global settings and settings for your individual server.

Global default settings allow you to configure all servers for default launch and access rights. These rights determine whether a given NT account will have the rights to launch and access your server. I'm not sure why you'd want to separate these options—launching and not accessing would be kind of silly—but you have to set both rights. **Figure 5.6** shows the dialog.

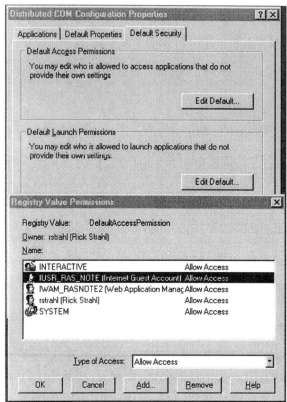

Figure 5.6. *The Default Security settings of DCOMCNFG let you set launch and access rights for all servers on your system. These can be overridden at the individual server level.*

Set up the IUSR_ account in this fashion for both the Default Access and Default Launch permissions. You can also configure this option directly on your specific server, but I prefer to do it here on my Dev box, so I don't have to worry about it for each server I build. On an online machine, you probably want to set these for each server individually for more controlled security.

The next step is to configure the individual server. Click the Applications tab, then find the name of your server (TFirstServer) or the descriptive name you gave the server in the Project Manager (First Server Example). Note that you are looking for the "Class" name or the Description if you changed it in the Project Manager's Servers tab. If your server contains multiple OLEPUBLIC classes, only the first one will show up in DCOMCNFG, but the rights you set apply to all classes in the server. In the earlier example, I typed **First FoxISAPI Server**, which is the entry you see in **Figure 5.7**.

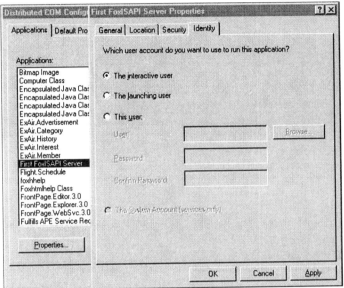

Figure 5.7. *Configuring the individual server inside DCOMCNFG. Use "The interactive user" whenever possible.*

By setting the impersonation level to "The interactive user" you are telling COM to use whoever is logged on currently, or the SYSTEM account if nobody is logged on as the controlling account for your COM object. So if you're logged on as an Administrator, the server will use that account while running.

> *Be careful with SYSTEM account logons. The SYSTEM account rights may or may not allow access to your data and application directories—make sure you check permissions on these directories explicitly if you plan to run your FoxISAPI application prior to logon. Operation without a logon is very tricky and varies with IIS and NT Service Pack versions—in general FoxISAPI is not well suited for running without a logon, but it can be done with some security tweaking of the IUSR_ and SYSTEM accounts.*

Updated in VFP 6.0
Visual FoxPro 6.0 no longer blows away the DCOMCNFG registry settings, as VFP 5.0 did every time you rebuilt your project. Unless you rename your servers or you explicitly tell them to generate new ClassIDs when building, the settings you make in DCOMCNFG on a particular server remain intact each time you rebuild. Keep in mind you still have to make the setting at least once before running the server.

You can also set the account to a specific NT user account by supplying a username and password. This will work fine and is useful especially if you plan to run your server with no users logged onto the system.

I recommend using "The interactive user" at least when running on your development machine. This setting allows user interfaces to be visible—you can build a FoxISAPI server as a form class and keep the form visible as a status window, for example. The interactive user also provides the same user context that you're currently running in while debugging, and you can expect consistent behavior between your testing of the COM object and IIS calling it.

A final word on permissions: I highly recommend running NTFS partitions on your servers because it is the only way to properly configure the security settings for individual directories. When running FAT partitions you have to mess around with file shares, which is a lot more difficult to control. You also lose the ability to control access to individual files with FAT. If you happen to be running on Windows 95/98, none of the security issues described here apply because the Web server account has open access to the system.

Unloading and managing servers

Because IIS loads your COM object, the object stays loaded in memory by default. This means when you build your server, you first have to unload your servers or you get a "File Access Denied" error. Foxisapi.dll includes a built-in request that releases all COM references using a RESET command string:

```
/foxisapi/foxisapi.dll/RESET
```

Actually, RESET is the default value, but you can set the value in Foxisapi.ini in the same directory as Foxisapi.dll.

RESET will unload your servers, but it makes no guarantee that they stay unloaded. Take the scenario of a busy Web server: You unload the server, but servers immediately reinstantiate because new requests coming in force a new instance to be loaded immediately. On busy sites the only reliable way to unload and update servers is to stop the Web server. (For what it's worth, the same rules apply to Active Server Pages and COM objects loaded from there.)

(i) *When building an application with FoxISAPI, you'll have to build and rebuild your server quite frequently. Because rebuilding your servers requires unloading them first, it can be cumbersome to have to select the Web page and click the FoxISAPI Reset link to unload your servers.*

The framework included with the Developer's Download Files at www.hentzenwerke.com includes a utility class called wwIPStuff, which allows you to programmatically access HTTP links. With it you can write a program to unload the FoxISAPI server and then rebuild your EXE file:

```
SET CLASSLIB TO wwIPSTUFF ADDITIVE

*** Force the server to unload so we don't have to
*** do it manually.
o=CREATE("wwIPSTUFF")
o.HTTPGet("http://localhost/foxisapi/foxisapi.dll/Reset")
```

```
*** Release it so we can include it in the project
o=.f.
RELEASE CLASSLIB wwIPStuff

*** Server Cleanup takes a sec after request returns
wait window "Hang on waiting to unload server..." TIMEOUT 2
BUILD EXE FIDEMO FROM FIDEMO RECOMPILE

IF FILE("FiDemo.err")
   MODI COMM FIDEMO.ERR NOWAIT
ENDIF
WAIT CLEAR
RETURN
```

*You can modify this program with your server name or pass a parameter. I don't like the extra typing required to pass a parameter—I would rather name the program something short like Bld.prg so I can just type **DO BLD**.*

COM server instancing

The configuration options discussed in the previous section apply only to EXE, out-of-process components. FoxISAPI works best with out-of-process components, but it's possible to use in-process components if you plan to use only a single instance of your server. In-process objects cannot be pooled by the pool manager. They will run in the pool manager, but each server request blocks until the previous one returns. In other words, it's no better than running a single server in the first place. (This will be fixed by the multi-threaded runtime update in a forthcoming Service Pack—but even with this update, out-of-process servers tend to be a better choice.)

Let's compare the different COM instancing modes available to FoxISAPI applications.

In-process COM objects

These objects have the following characteristics:

- **Very fast call interface**
  Affects only the DLL->COM object parameter and return value passing, not operation of your VFP server code. This can provide slightly better performance on short requests.

- **Crash it—crash the Web server**
  If you crash your COM DLL, there's a good chance you'll take the Web server or the current IIS 4.0 application down with it. At the very least, a stuck session will hang your application with no way to unload it.

- **Can't be unloaded completely**
  Once a COM DLL has been loaded into IIS it cannot be unloaded. This is a problem for development because you're likely to update your servers frequently while debugging. Even live sites suffer because there's no chance to do online updates on busy sites without shutting down the Web server.

- **Security issues—no configuration available**
  COM DLL objects run in the calling process and inherit that process' security attributes. Under IIS that means your server gets called using the IUSR_machinename account, which has limited rights. If you need access to a resource that IUSR_ doesn't have rights to, your only avenue is to change permissions on the IUSR account, which can affect other security settings. Unlike out-of-process servers, in-process servers cannot be configured externally to impersonate another account—this can be done only by using complex Win32 API calls.

  If you change security rights on the IUSR account, review the options and settings carefully!

- **VFP 6 does allow multiple COM DLL instances**
  Visual FoxPro 5.0 was unable to handle more than one instance of a COM DLL in the same process. Visual FoxPro 6.0 does allow multiple instances, so in theory you can get multiple instances to run in the pool manager. However, due to limitations in the Visual FoxPro runtime, these instances cannot process requests at the same time, rendering this new feature practically useless. The forthcoming service pack will allow multiple simultaneous in-process instances in the pool manager, but it remains to be seen how stable this environment will be—in the past, multiple in-process servers in FoxISAPI caused mysterious lock ups.

Out-of-process COM objects

These objects have the following characteristics:

- **Slightly slower call interface**
  The call interface for out-of-process components always requires cross-process marshalling, which is slower than in-process calls or even in-process marshalling. However, before considering claims that in-process calls are hundreds of times faster, keep in mind that FoxISAPI makes a single method call per request. Although cross-process marshalling can be much slower, we're talking less than a millisecond of overhead for both the call and retrieving the result value—hardly something to worry about when building a request that accesses a database and is likely to take at least a few hundredths of a second.

- **Crashes don't affect the Web server**
  Out-of-process components run in a separate process and thus are not as vulnerable to the host environment. Stability tends to be much better running in a separate EXE because the Web server environment does not directly impact your server. IIS has its own instabilities, and I find it best to isolate my code from it whenever possible. When a server does crash it doesn't affect the Web server much, other than the request itself failing. With some logic built into the COM manager, it can also potentially handle reloading the server. (FoxISAPI doesn't do this natively, but it can be implemented rather easily.) The server might be able to detect the error, unload or kill the original server, and load a new copy.

- **Servers can be unloaded easily**
  Servers are easily unloaded with FoxISAPI's Reset option. Unlike in-process components, releasing the server object removes it from memory because it's not running inside the Web server's address space.

- **Allow multiple simultaneous servers**
  FoxISAPI's built-in pool manager can effectively manage several instances of out-of-process components. This makes it the most scalable solution that Microsoft ships for building FoxPro code running on the Web.

- **Support for running objects remotely over DCOM**
  Distributed COM makes it possible to run any EXE-based COM object on another computer. No changes are required in the code of the server (other than potential pathing issues with a remote machine). This feature is not available to DLL-based COM objects unless they run in Microsoft Transaction Server at considerable overhead. This makes it possible to scale an application to other machines easily when load gets heavy.

Personally, I don't see any good reason to use in-process components with FoxISAPI. There's no pressing advantage except a very slight performance gain, but a huge downside in terms of management and stability. Finally, the lack of scalability for in-process objects makes DLL components a bad choice for anything but low- to medium-volume applications that deal only with sub-second requests.

Building FoxISAPI requests

You now know the mechanics of how FoxISAPI works and how you can create your own server. Now let's take it step by step and create a few requests while looking a little closer at the inputs and outputs that FoxISAPI requires.

When FoxISAPI calls your COM server, it passes along three parameters to each request method called. While you might not need to do anything with these parameters, your method *must* support them to prevent a COM error when the method is called.

lcFormVar

The first parameter is the most important because it contains form variables retrieved from an HTML form via an HTTP GET or POST. When a user enters information into a Web page, lcFormVar will contain the values the user entered in an encoded format called URLEncoded. The URLEncoding mechanism creates a "safe" string that translates any non-keyboard and control characters into characters that can be interpreted by any platform or development tool that supports 7-bit characters (typical Windows ANSI character sets are 8-bit). For example, consider the login HTML form with fields named txtUserId and txtPassWord in **Figure 5.8**.

The HTML for the form (minus the formatting) looks like this:

```
<form method="POST"
 action="foxisapi.dll/FServer.TFServer.ServerTest">
   User ID: <input type="text" name="txtUserId"
            size="20" value="Rick Strahl">
```

```
Password: <input type="text" name="txtPassword"
          size="23" value="BIGKAHUNA 123 !@#$">

<input type="submit" value="Login"
      name="btnSubmit"> </font></small></td>
</form>
```

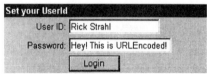

Figure 5.8. HTML form that prompts for user ID and password. The fields are URLEncoded and sent to your FoxISAPI server in the lcFormVar parameter.

The resulting URLEncoded string looks like this:

```
txtUserId=Rick+Strahl&txtPassword=Hey%21+This+is+URLEncoded%21&btnSubmit=Login
```

The parameter string contains a key/value pair for each of the form variables. Here are the rules for URLEncoding/Decoding:

- Key value pairs are separated by **&**.
- Spaces are converted to + signs.
- All "extended" characters are converted to hexadecimal escape codes. The escape code uses a percent sign (%) plus a hex number to store the ASCII code of the characters. For example, a carriage return (ASC(13)) is encoded as **%0D**. This encoding makes it possible to safely send binary data between platforms—even those running 7-bit character sets.
- Both keys and values are URLEncoded.

The FoxISAPI framework discussed later in this chapter takes care of decoding form variables and the querystring using the Form() and QueryString() methods.

lcIniFile

This parameter contains the path to an INI file that contains all the server, browser and system variables. The INI file is created by Foxisapi.dll before control passes to your OLE server and is deleted after your method call returns. You can retrieve these with calls to the GetProfileString API call (or use the wwFoxISAPI::ServerVariables(cVarname,cSection) from the listings below). You can see what's available by looking at the following INI file by the password dialog request:

```
[FOXISAPI]
Request Method=POST
Query String=Method=ServerTest
Logical Path=/FirstServer.TFirstServer.Process
Physical Path=c:\westwind\FirstServer.TFirstServer.Process
FoxISAPI Version=FoxISAPI v1.2
Request Protocol=HTTP/1.1
```

```
Referer=/foxisapi/foxisapi.dll
Authenticated Username=rstrahl
Server Software=Microsoft-IIS/4.0
Server Name=localhost
Server Port=80
Remote Host=127.0.0.1
Remote Address=127.0.0.1
[ALL_HTTP]
HTTP_ACCEPT=application/msword, application/vnd.ms-powerpoint, image/gif,
image/x-xbitmap, image/jpeg, image/pjpeg, */*
HTTP_ACCEPT_LANGUAGE=en-us
HTTP_CONNECTION=Keep-Alive
HTTP_HOST=localhost
HTTP_REFERER=http://localhost/foxisapi/
HTTP_USER_AGENT=Mozilla/4.0 (compatible; MSIE 4.01; Windows NT)
HTTP_COOKIE=SOURCESITE=default0598|1669.92|6; WWTHREADID=VA1D7SY5;
TRACKSOURCE=DF1
HTTP_CONTENT_LENGTH=78
HTTP_CONTENT_TYPE=application/x-www-form-urlencoded
HTTP_ACCEPT_ENCODING=gzip, deflate
[Accept]
*/*=Yes
[SYSTEM]
GMT Offset=-28800
```

Typically you'll use only a few keys from the INI file. The *Query String* is frequently read to figure out what "parameters" were passed to a form or link. These things are very similar to parameters to a function. For example, the query string may include a UserId that identifies the user for tracking. Or in a table-browsing routine a RecordId may be used to tell the request which record to navigate to or start from.

The *User Agent* can help you to determine whether the user's setup allows you to show browser-specific features. The Referer tells where the user was coming from—*HTTP_REFERER* contains the link the user clicked to arrive at the current location. HTTP *Cookies* can be retrieved using a browser-stored ID that you can use to track a user over several requests through a site. The *Physical Path* usually contains the name of the running script file (Foxisapi.dll) or the name of the document if it's a document script map—this is a very important feature for creating a scripting engine, which I'll discuss later in this chapter.

InReleaseFlag
This parameter concerns itself with the persistence of the COM object. By default, FoxISAPI contains logic to create COM instances and unload those instances from memory. By keeping instances loaded, successive accesses to the same server are quite fast because the server is already loaded in memory. In essence, each COM object called maintains only one persistent instance in memory at any time. The lnReleaseParameter can have two values:

- **0** — Keep Server Reference
- **1** — Release Server Reference *(default)*

lnReleaseFlag allows you to unload the current instance from within a request by changing the lnReleaseFlag parameter to 1, which is the default. A bad default, really: We want our server to stay loaded, so you should always change this passed parameter to 0.

> *The wwFoxISAPI class discussed a little later includes a flag called ISaveRequestInfo. When set to .T. this flag causes the framework to write a temporary file of all request form variables and the contents of the INI file to your TEMP directory and a file called TEMP.ini. It also captures the output generated by your code into TEMP.htm.*
>
> *You can use this file to debug your input and even to retrieve the string and INI file to build "fake" requests that you can run against your object from within Visual FoxPro's IDE.*

Returning HTTP output

FoxISAPI has now passed off control to you! You've accepted the parameters and you're ready to roll. Once your code gets control you can use VFP as you see fit to run queries or any other kind of transaction or logic operation using FoxPro code. The end result of each exit point of your method must be an HTTP-compliant string.

In most cases the output will be an HTML string that you generate within your code. You can certainly hand-code all HTML by building strings using `lcOutput = lcOutput + "More Text"`. But it doesn't necessarily mean you have to hand-code it all. You can, for example, load a file from disk into a string and translate values inside the string to insert fields and other dynamic content. Or use generic routines that can create HTML from tables, and so on.

Regardless of how you create your output, it should always include an HTTP header plus the actual display content. For an HTML document it looks like this:

```
HTTP/1.0 200 OK
Content-type: text/html

<HTML>
<H1>Hello World</H2>
</HTML>
```

The HTTP header and Content-type are important because not all browsers will support headerless results. Leaving off the header can result in an "Invalid Response" error on some browsers. (IE 4 doesn't complain, but most versions of Netscape, IE 3 and most others will!)

An HTTP header consists of three things:

- **An HTTP status string**
  These are status codes that the server uses to determine what to do. Codes in the 200's indicate success; in the 500's they indicate errors; and in the 400's they indicate access errors and authentication requests. In most cases a 200 result is used; sometimes you might dip into the 400 numbers for authentication or denying access. 500 errors are usually generated by the Web server itself when an error occurs.

- **A set of client directives**
  These are sent and interpreted by the browser. Content-type is the only one required by a browser—most others are optional. You can set things like cache status, page expiration, whether the page can be loaded from another URL, and so on. You can also attach HTTP cookies with these directives using the Set-Cookie: key (you can see a retrieved Cookie in the INI file listing above).

- **A blank line**
  This is very important. The Web server and browser need the blank line to determine the end of the header.

Each line of the header must be separated by a CHR(13)+CHR(10) and the final header line must be followed by a blank line containing only the CHR(13)+CHR(10).

Content types
While you will almost always return an HTML document, it's possible to generate other content as well. For example, the following returns an Adobe Acrobat (PDF) document:

```
HTTP/1.0 200 OK
Content-type: application/pdf

%PDF-1.2
... the above is the start of the binary PDF file
<remainder of binary PDF document here>
```

You can also send images, Word documents and even raw data in this fashion. Note that the Content-type is used by the browser to determine what to do with the content. If a viewer or plug-in/control is available for a certain content type, it will start automatically. This is essentially how viewers and ActiveDocuments work.

HTTP directives
In addition to different content types, you can call on HTTP directives. For example, if you wanted authentication to occur you might return:

```
HTTP/1.0 401 Not Authorized
WWW-Authenticate: basic realm=localhost

<HTML>
Get out and stay out!!!
</HTML>
```

An authentication box that was initiated from a Web request (see **Figure 5.9**) forces authentication against the NT user/security manager if Basic Authentication is enabled in the Web server.

Figure 5.9. *An HTTP header directive allows you to bring up an authentication dialog.*

Here's a FoxISAPI method that handles authentication of a user (using some logic from the wwFoxISAPI class):

```
*****************************************************************
TFirstServer :: Authenticate
*******************************
LPARAMETER lcFormVars, lcIniFile, lnReleaseFlag

*** I'll get to this shortly... Parses the inputs into objects
THIS.StartRequest(lcFormVars,lcIniFile,@lnReleaseFlag)

*** Retrieve the user name from the Ini File
lcUserName=Request.ServerVariables("Authenticated Username")

*** Check if we have a validated user
IF EMPTY(lcUserName)
    *** Nope - Send Password Dialog
    Response.Write("HTTP/1.0 401 Not Authorized"+CR+;
                "WWW-Authenticate: basic realm=localhost"+CR+CR+;
                "<HTML>"+CR+;
                "Get out and stay out!!!"+CR+;
                "</HTML>"+CR+;
    RETURN THIS.cOutput
ENDIF

*** Go on processing - user has been authenticated
THIS.StandardPage("You're Authenticated",;
                "Welcome <b>"+lcUsername+"</b>. "+;
                "You may proceed to wreak havoc!")

RETURN THIS.cOutput
ENDFUNC
```

This causes the browser to open an authentication box unless the user accessing the link was previously authenticated. If the user was not authenticated, the password box pops up. If the user types an invalid password, an error message is returned ("Get out and stay out" in this case)—otherwise, the same link is re-executed and the now-validated user can get past the password check to see the HTML page confirming the access. You can then check the password as passed back in the *Authenticated Username* Request variable to determine whether to allow the user in. (NT will first authenticate the user and fail if the user is not valid, as per the User Manager.) If the authentication login succeeds, the browser reruns the request—now the user will be shown as authenticated, pass the IF EMPTY() check, and go on to request processing.

But I'm jumping the gun again. Let's first look at some requests that use the basic FoxISAPI mechanism to access some data.

A word about the samples

As you read the text here, you can bring up the demo page in the directory where you installed the samples. Find the FoxISAPI demo directory and do the following:

1. Start the IIS Service Manager and go to the default Web site.
2. Add a new virtual directory. Call it *FoxISAPI* and point at <SampleInstallPath>\FoxISAPI\HTML.
3. To access the demo page, connect to http://localhost/foxisapi/default.asp.

This installs the FoxISAPI virtual directory and lets you access the demos. Before you run any of the demos you have to compile the demo servers. To start up VFP in the demo path, follow these steps:

1. Start up Visual FoxPro.
2. Change path to <SampleInstallPath>\FoxISAPI.
3. SET PATH TO .\DATA;.\CLASSES;.\Forms;.\wconnect\;.\wwDemo;.\http
    (You can skip this step if you create a shortcut on the desktop and start up directly in the Foxisapi directory—the Config.fpw file there will set the path at startup. I recommend this approach!)

Once you're there you can now compile the demos. I suggest you follow along with the text here, but you can compile the servers to check out the samples first. To compile:

1. BUILD EXE FirstServer FROM FirstServer
2. BUILD EXE FiDemo FROM FiDemo

Finally, don't forget to use DCOMCNFG on these servers:

1. Set up or make sure Default security is set.
    a. Open the Default Security tab.
    b. Add IUSR_MachineName to the Allow Access permissions.
    c. Add IUSR_MachineName to the Default Launch permissions.

2. Configure each of the individual servers (note that the server IDs might vary on your machine).
3. Click the Applications tab.
4. Double-click *First FoxISAPI Server* in the list.
5. Click the Identity tab and select *Interactive User*.
6. Double-click the *Tregister* (or *FIDemo* or *HTTPDemo*) entry and repeat step 5.

Default.htm is the demo page that contains links to all samples discussed in this chapter. It also contains links to the FoxISAPI maintenance requests, such as unloading servers and showing server status.

Most samples also contain a link to show the source code of the class method responsible for handling the request. They do this by using a FoxISAPI request in the wwFoxISAPI class that looks at the source file located in a specified code directory, searches for the method and extracts the code from it. It's a useful feature that can be implemented with only a few lines of code:

```
FUNCTION ShowCode
******************************************************************************
* wcFoxISAPI :: ShowCode
*********************************
*** Function: Routine displays code for a given routine
***      Assume: Url: ?Method=ShowCode&ShowMethod=FirstQuery&PRG=Test.prg&
******************************************************************************

lcMethod=Request.QueryString("ShowMethod")
lcFile = Request.QueryString("PRG")

IF EMPTY(lcFile)
   lcFile = FORCEEXT(PROGRAM(),"PRG")
ENDIF
lcProgram = FileToString(lcFile)

lcCode=Extract(lcProgram,"FUNCTION "+lcMethod,"FUNCTION ")

Response.ContentTypeHeader("text/plain")
Response.Write(lcCode)

ENDFUNC
* wcFoxISAPI :: ShowCode
```

This just shows the power of what you can do with a request handler and a little ingenuity.

Show me the data!
Up to now I haven't shown how to do anything with data. Well, here you go with a simple example that queries a customer database, demonstrating all you've learned about parameters and return values:

```
******************************************************************
* TFirstServer :: FirstQuery
*********************************
FUNCTION FirstQuery
LPARAMETER lcFormVars, lcIniFile, lnReleaseFlag

*** Don't release the server
lnReleaseFlag=0

lcOutput="HTTP/1.0 200 OK"+CR+;
         "Content-type: text/html"+CR+CR

SELECT  Company, Careof, Address, custno, phone ;
   FROM (".\data\TT_CUST") ;
   ORDER BY COMPANY ;
   INTO Cursor TQuery

lcOutput = lcOutput + ;
  [<HTML><BODY BGCOLOR="#FFFFFF">] + ;
  [<H1>Hello World with Data </H1><HR>] + ;
  [Matching found: ]+STR(_Tally)+[<p>] + ;
  SHOWCODEFOOTER

lcOutput = lcOutput + ;
  [<TABLE CELLPADDING=4 BORDER=1 WIDTH=100%>]+CR+;
  [<TR><TH>Name</TH><TH>Company</TH><TH>Address</TH></TR>]+CR

SCAN
   *** Build the table row
   lcOutput = lcOutput + [<TR><TD>]+;
          TRIM(IIF(EMPTY(TQuery.Careof),"<BR>",Tquery.CareOf))+[</TD><TD>]+;

TRIM(IIF(EMPTY(Tquery.Company),"<BR>",TQuery.Company))+[</a></TD><TD>]+;

TRIM(IIF(EMPTY(Tquery.Phone),"<BR>",STRTRAN(TQuery.Phone,CHR(13),"<BR>")))+;
          [</TD></TR>]+CR
ENDSCAN

lcOutput = lcOutput   + [</TABLE><HR>] + ;
                        [</BODY></HTML>]

USE IN Tquery
USE IN TT_Cust

RETURN lcOutput
```

This code generates an HTML table as seen in **Figure 5.10**. The code is straightforward: The request hits the page and the code runs a query. It then loops through and builds an HTML-formatted table using an lcOutput string variable, which is eventually sent back as the return value.

Easy enough, but the problem with the above request is that it doesn't interact with the Web page at all. We're simply running a query, but we're not parameterizing that query in any way. I haven't shown the tools to decode the form variables and perform some basic HTML generation automatically. Time to start building some basic framework functionality.

Figure 5.10. *The results of querying a customer database.*

Decoding form variables

Let's start by looking at the code that's responsible for decoding form variables. This is useful functionality beyond FoxISAPI. Any CGI/ISAPI application has a need to decode URLEncoded context, and the following functions provide the functionality to pull out a value based on a key passed to the GetUrlEncodedKey() function. URLDecode handles the actual decoding, and Extract is a helper function that extracts text between a set of delimiting strings:

```
************************************************************************
FUNCTION GetURLEncodedKey
*********************************
***    Function: Retrieves a 'parameter' from the query string that
***              is encoded with standard CGI/ISAPI URL encoding.
***              Typical URL encoding looks like this:
***      "User=Rick+Strahl&ID=0011&Address=400+Morton%0A%0DHood+River"
***        Pass: lcUrlString   -   Full string of key/val pairs
***              lcKey         -   Form Variable to retrieve
***      Return: Value or ""
************************************************************************
LPARAMETERS lcURLString, lcKey
LOCAL lnLoc,c2, cStr

lcURLString=IIF(EMPTY(lcURLString),"","&"+lcURLString)
lcKey=IIF(EMPTY(lcKey)," ",lcKey)
lcKey=STRTRAN(lcKey," ","+")

*** First try locating the key with & in front
lnloc=ATC("&"+lcKey+"=",lcURLString)
```

```
lcRetval=Extract(lcUrlString,"&"+lcKey+"=","&",,.T.)

RETURN URLDecode(lcRetval)
ENDFUNC


****************************************************************************
FUNCTION URLDecode
******************
***   Function: URLDecodes a text string to normal text.
***     Assume: Uses wwIPStuff.dll
***       Pass: lcText    -   Text string to decode
***     Return: Decoded string or ""
****************************************************************************
LPARAMETERS lcText
LOCAL lnSize

*** Use wwIPStuff for large buffers
IF LEN(lcText) > 1024
   DECLARE INTEGER URLDecode ;
      IN WWIPSTUFF AS API_URLDecode ;
      STRING @cText

   lnSize=API_URLDecode(@lcText)

   IF lnSize > 0
      lcText = SUBSTR(lcText,1,lnSize)
   ELSE
      lcText = ""
   ENDIF


   RETURN lcText
ENDIF

*** First convert + to spaces
lcText=STRTRAN(lcText,"+"," ")

*** Handle Hex Encoded Control chars

lcRetval = ""
DO WHILE .T.
   *** Format: %0A  ( CHR(10) )
   lnLoc = AT('%',lcText)

   *** No Hex chars
   IF lnLoc > LEN(lcText) - 2 OR lnLoc < 1
      lcRetval = lcRetval + lcText
      EXIT
   ENDIF

   *** Now read the next 2 characters
   *** Check for digits - at this point we must have hex pair!
   lcHex=SUBSTR(lcText,lnLoc+1,2)

   *** Now concat the string plus the evaled hex code
   lcRetval = lcRetval + LEFT(lcText,lnLoc-1) + ;
      CHR( EVAL("0x"+lcHex) )
```

```
      *** Trim out the input string
      IF LEN(lcText) > lnLoc + 2
         lcText = SUBSTR(lcText,lnLoc+3)
      ELSE
         EXIT
      ENDIF
ENDDO


RETURN lcRetval
ENDFUNC
* EOF URLDecode


**************************************************************************
FUNCTION Extract
******************
***   Function: Extracts a text value between two delimiters
***      Assume: Delimiters are not checked for case!
***             The first instance only is retrieved. Idea is
***             to translate the delims as you go...
***        Pass: lcString    -  Entire string
***              lcDelim1   -  The starting delimiter
***              lcDelim2        -  Ending delimiter
***              lcDelim3        -  Alternate ending delimiter
***              llEndOk   -  End of line is OK
***      Return: Text between delimiters or ""
**************************************************************************
PARAMETERS lcString,lcDelim1,lcDelim2,lcDelim3, llEndOk
PRIVATE x,lnLocation,lcRetVal,lcChar,lnNewString,lnEnd

lcDelim1=IIF(EMPTY(lcDelim1),",",lcDelim1)
lcDelim2=IIF(EMPTY(lcDelim2),"z!x",lcDelim2)
lcDelim3=IIF(EMPTY(lcDelim3),"z!x",lcDelim3)

lnLocation=ATC(lcDelim1,lcString)
IF lnLocation=0
   RETURN ""
ENDIF

lnLocation=lnlocation+len(lcDelim1)

*** Crate a new string of remaining text
lcNewString=SUBSTR(lcString,lnLocation)

lnEnd=ATC(lcDelim2,lcNewString)-1
IF lnEnd>0
   RETURN SUBSTR(lcNewString,1,lnEnd)
ENDIF
IF lnEnd = 0
   *** Empty Delimited string
   RETURN ""
ENDIF

lnEnd=ATC(lcDelim3,lcNewString)-1
IF lnEnd>0
   RETURN SUBSTR(lcNewString,1,lnEnd)
ENDIF
```

```
IF llEndOk
  *** Return to the end of the line
  RETURN SUBSTR(lcNewString,1)
ENDIF

RETURN ""
*EOP RetValue
```

Note that the URLDecode code calls on a routine in a DLL to handle decoding if the buffer gets large. The reason for this is that the process of decoding is very slow in Visual FoxPro because the string has to be constantly rewritten. The C code in the DLL is much more efficient because it can simply walk and write the string directly, without constantly reassigning the string to a variable.

 wwIPStuff.dll and the API_URLDecode method are included with the Developer's Download Files at www.hentzenwerke.com (wwIPStuff contains other useful stuff, which I talk about in Chapters 6 and 7.)

The above code lets you retrieve a form variable name. So I'll change the query I created previously and use an HTML form to query for a company name selection:

```
<form method="POST"
action="/foxisapi/foxisapi.dll/FirstServer.TFirstServer.FirstQuery2">
  Company Query by name:<br>
  <input type="text" name="Company" size="20">
  <input type="submit" value="Run Query" name="btnSubmit">
</form>
```

I can now use GetUrlEncodedKey to retrieve the company name and build a filtered SELECT statement query with the company name retrieved:

```
FUNCTION FirstQuery2
*********************************************************************
* FirstServer :: FirstQuery2
********************************
***   Function: Like FirstQuery, except this query allows the query
***             to accept an HTML field value for filtering the result.
*********************************************************************
LPARAMETER lcFormVars, lcIniFile, lnReleaseFlag

lcCompany = GetUrlEncodedKey(lcFormVars,"COMPANY")

*** Don't release the server
lnReleaseFlag=0

lcOutput="HTTP/1.0 200 OK"+CR+;
         "Content-type: text/html"+CR+CR

SELECT  Company, Careof, Address, custno, phone ;
   FROM .\data\TT_CUST ;
   WHERE Company = lcCompany ;
   ORDER BY COMPANY ;
   INTO Cursor TQuery
```

```
lcOutput = lcOutput + ;
  [<HTML><BODY BGCOLOR="#FFFFFF">] + ;
  [<H1>Hello World with Data</H1><HR>] + ;
  [Matching found: ]+STR(_Tally)+[<p>]

<... The rest of the code is identical to FirstQuery1>

RETURN lcOutput
```

By the way, notice that this request will also work if called from a static hyperlink such as `http://localhost/foxisapi/foxisapi.dll/FirstServer.TfirstServer.FirstQuery2`. The result from GetUrlEncodedKey() will be an empty string, which will result in the SELECT statement retrieving all records from the table.

Even better, because of the way FoxISAPI works, if there is no form involved it uses the query string as form variable parameters. Query strings, like form variables, should always be URLEncoded so the same logic works. So you can run the query above also as:

`/foxisapi/foxisapi.dll/FirstServer.TfirstServer.Firstquery2?Company=B`

Keep in mind this will work only if you don't have a form that you are submitting. To retrieve the query string properly, you can retrieve it from the ServerVariables INI file.

Retrieving ServerVariables from the INI file

In addition to the form variables, it's important to be able to retrieve the variables from the INI file, which I call ServerVariables (in Active Server Pages lingo). The following function retrieves values from the INI file:

```
*********************************************************************
FUNCTION GetServerVariable
*********************************
*** Function: Generic Request access routine that allows retrieving a
***           value from the INI ContentFile.
***      Pass: lcVariable  -  Variable to return value for
***            lcSection   -  Section in the INI file
***    Return: "" if not found or string otherwise
*********************************************************************
LPARAMETERS lcVariable, lcSection
LOCAL lcResult,lnResult

IF EMPTY(lcSection)
   lcSection="FOXISAPI"
ENDIF

*** Initialize buffer for result
lcResult=SPACE(512)

DECLARE INTEGER GetPrivateProfileString ;
   IN WIN32API ;
   STRING cSection,;
   STRING cEntry,;
   STRING cDefault,;
```

```
    STRING @cRetVal,;
    INTEGER nSize,;
    STRING cFileName

lnResult=GetPrivateProfileString(lcSection,lcVariable,"*NONE*",;
                        @lcResult,LEN(lcResult),THIS.cContentFile)

*** Trim off the NULL
lcResult = SUBSTR(lcResult,1,lnResult)

IF lcResult="*NONE*"
  lcResult=""
ENDIF

RETURN lcResult
ENDFUNC
* GetServerVariable
```

Now I'll look at the query request again and rewrite it, this time using the URL's QueryString (the text following a question mark in the URL) to get the company to look up.

I'll modify the query in FirstQuery2 to include a URL reference in the SELECT statement, such as this:

```
SELECT  [<A
HREF="//foxisapi/foxisapi.dll/FirstServer.TfirstServer.ShowCompany?ID=]+;
        LTRIM(CustNo)+[">]+Company+[</a>] AS Company, ;
    Careof, Address, custno, phone ;
    FROM .\data\TT_CUST ;
    WHERE Company = lcCompany ;
    ORDER BY COMPANY ;
    INTO Cursor TQuery
```

The parameter ID will tell me the record ID I want to look up in a request called ShowCompany. The result can be seen in **Figure 5.11**.

> ❗ *Notice the /foxisapi prefix used in the embedded HREF link. Unfortunately, due to the fact that FoxISAPI uses the extra path to denote the Server, Class and Method, you can't simply reference the FoxISAPI DLL, even when you're calling Foxisapi.dll in the same directory as the current request. If you do, the URL will be interpreted incorrectly. To get around this, for now you must always use a full path.*
>
> *A good way to do this is to use /, which is the server root, rather than hard-coding the server name explicitly. I'll show some ways around this by using the FoxISAPI DLL provided with the Developer's Download Files.*

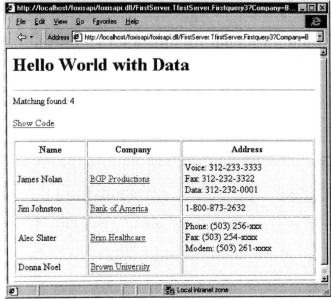

Figure 5.11. *The data query now contains a link embedded via a SQL statement that lets us drill down to the customer detail.*

When you click the link, the following request displays the contents of the company selected in a semi-generic fashion:

```
FUNCTION ShowCompany
***********************************************************************
* TFirstServer :: ShowCompany
*******************************
***   Function: Displays Company information using some generic code
***             to parse field names and values
***********************************************************************
LPARAMETER lcFormVars, lcIniFile, lnReleaseFlag

lcQueryString = GetServerVariable("Query String")
lcCustno = PADL(GetUrlEncodedKey(lcQueryString,"ID"),8)

*** Don't release the server
lnReleaseFlag=0

lcOutput="HTTP/1.0 200 OK"+CR+;
        "Content-type: text/html"+CR+CR

IF !USED("TT_Cust")
   USE (".\data\TT_Cust") IN 0
ENDIF

SELE TT_Cust
LOCATE FOR Custno = lcCustNo
IF !FOUND()
```

```
            lcOutput = lcOutput + "<HTML><b>Invalid Customer</b></HTML>"
            RETURN lcOutput
ENDIF

lcOutput = lcOutput + ;
[<TABLE BGCOLOR="#EEEEEE" Width=400 Border=1>]+CR+;
[<TR><TD COLSPAN=2 ALIGN="CENTER"><b>Customer Information</b></TD></TR>]+CR

lnFields = AFIELDS(laFields)

*** Just loop through fields and display
FOR x=1 to lnFields
            lcfieldname=lafields[x,1]
            lcfieldtype=lafields[x,2]
            lvValue=EVAL(lcfieldname)

            lcOutput = lcOutput + "<TR><TD BGCOLOR=#FFFFCC><b>" + lcFieldName +
":<b></TD>"+;
                                  "<TD>" + TRANSFORM(lvValue) + "</TD></TR>" + CR
ENDFOR && x=1 to lnFieldCount

RETURN lcOutput + "</TABLE>"
ENDFUNC
* TFirstServer :: ShowCompany
```

The request first retrieves the query string of the request from the INI file. It then retrieves the ID value from the URLEncoded query string result and uses it to locate the specified record in the company table. By using AFIELDS and Visual FoxPro's new TRANSFORM() functionality, which converts any value passed to it to a string, you can display any record with just a few lines of code.

You should be starting to feel the power available to you by now. Creating generic routines, like the one above for displaying the actual company information, makes it possible to create functional, reusable code that allows rapid feature implementation.

You've now seen how to build basic requests with FoxISAPI: how to get at Form variables to retrieve user input. I've also shown how to get server variables from the INI file and how to build output. So far I've done things the hard way by hand-coding HTML and parsing the input on every request. There's a better way!

The next step—a basic framework

The first thing you notice when you look at the code for the last request is that a lot of stuff is going on that has very little to do with the business logic of what you're trying to accomplish. You'll find that lots of things are repetitive and need to occur on every request: adding an HTTP header to a request, parsing form variables (which I haven't done yet), sending error messages that are standard pages, parsing form and server variables, and so on. It's not particularly hard to do, but it's tedious. And it's easy to forget some piece of code that's required.

To make life easier, you need a framework that handles the required tasks automatically and reduces repetitive steps to simple method calls. The framework I'm about to describe is loosely based on West Wind Web Connection from West Wind Technologies, and provides a small subset of that Web application framework.

I'll introduce the operation of the framework by providing a reference of functionality and by showing some implementations using it. Other than a few important aspects, I won't describe the implementation in detail here—you can look at the code in wwFoxISAPI in the Developer's Download Files for more information.

Why do you need a framework?

- **Requests are repetitive.**
  The same things need to be done over and over again. Save some time and call a method in your server instead. Just about every request will need to read some input from the Web server, and every request needs to output some text. The framework simplifies this process and provides a logical interface using objects.

- **Common operations should be abstracted.**
  In particular, HTML generation and form variable parsing should be abstracted in an extensible way so that the process of creating your application is simplified. In the framework built here, I'll use support objects and methods very similar to the Active Server Page Objects. *oResponse* is used for output; *oRequest* for input.

- **Generic HTML generation.**
  I'm not going into too much detail here, but it's fairly easy to build routines that render data as HTML. It's handy to have a table generator, for example, that will take any cursor and generate HTML from it.

- **Scripting is essential for HTML applications.**
  Scripting is the key to make it easy to create HTML output without having to recompile your code every time you make a tiny change to the interface. In my opinion, the combination of a code request and a script template page to display is the best possible way to generate an application. I'll look at how to create a scripting engine with this class.

The wwFoxISAPI framework

This framework consists of three main classes (all contained in wwFoxISAPI.prg):

- **wwFoxISAPI**
  The server object from which you subclass your FoxISAPI apps. This is your entry-point class that gets called by the Web link.
- **wwRequest**
  Member object of wwFoxISAPI that handles retrieval of form and server variables to allow you to use information provided by the user and Web server in your requests. Object is: wwFoxISAPI::oRequest.
- **wwResponse**
  Member object of wwFoxISAPI that handles output of all HTML/HTTP. Object is: wwFoxISAPI::oResponse.

wwFoxISAPI

This class represents the basic server object, which is also a container for the wwRequest and wwResponse objects. It has the following properties and methods.

Property	What it does
oRequest	Instance of a wwRequest object used for retrieving HTML form and server variables.
oResponse	Instance of a wwResponse object used for all output to be sent back to the Web server.
lError	Flag that determines whether an error occurred.
cErrorMsg	If lError is .T. this contains an error message.

Method	What it does
Process()	Provides an entry point for *every* request of the server. Optionally called, but recommended to centralize access! Set Method = on the URL. Pass: <cFormVars>, <cIniFile>, <nRelease> Return: returns completed HTML output
StartRequest()	Configures the oRequest and oResponse members from the current request input data. Method is automatically called by Process, or you should manually call it with a FoxISAPI request's input parameters. Pass: <cFormVars>, <cIniFile>, <nRelease> Return: nothing
StandardPage()	Simple HTML page-generation method. Creates a fully functional page from a header and body parameter. Pass: <cHeaderText>, <cBodyText> Return: nothing
ErrorMsg()	Same as StandardPage, but implemented to show error messages differently than standard pages. Pass: <cHeaderText>, <cBodyText> Return: nothing
Error()	Internal, protected error handler method. Important. Calls ErrorMsg() to generate an error response and turns off further output.

wwRequest

This class handles access to the input made available by the Web server, including access to HTML form variables, the Query String and server variables. This object is configured on each call by calling wwFoxISAPI::StartRequest, which sets the cContentFile and cFormVars properties.

Property	What it does
cFormVars	Used to hold the HTML form variables for parsing.
cContentFile	The name of the INI file that holds all server variables.
cQueryString	The full Query String as passed on the URL. This is everything following the ? in the URL.

Method	What it does
LoadRequest()	Initializes the request. This method is called from wwFoxISAPI::StartRequest. Pass: <cFormVars>,<cIniFile> Return: nothing
Form()	Returns an individual HTML form variable entered by the user. Pass: <cFormVarName> Return: content of form variable or "" if it doesn't exist or is empty
QueryString()	Returns named parameters of the Query String. Pass: <cQueryStringKey> or <nPositionalParameter> Return: content for Query String key or ""
ServerVariables()	Returns any of the server variables available In the INI file. See the INI file listing above for details on what keys are available. Pass: <cServerVarKey>,[<cSection>("FoxIsapi")]
GetFormMultiple()	Returns a multivalue HTML form variable into an array. Pass: <@aFormVars>,<cFormVarName> Return: number of formvars retrieved or 0
SetKey()	Forces a form variable to be set to a new value. Used for overriding values on auto updates. Pass: <cFormVar>, <cValue> Return: nothing
aCGIParms()	Creates an array of positional parameters separated by ~'s. For compatibility with Web Connection and the optional positional parameter scheme. Parses into Protected aCGIParms property.
GetCGIParameter()	Returns a positional parameter. You can also use QueryString(nValue) for this, but only after you've called aCGIParms!
GetAuthenticatedUser()	Returns the REMOTE_USER environment variable. User that's logged on to NT on the server.
GetPhysicalPath()	Returns the name of the script. Note: This doesn't work correctly for Foxisapi.dll but it works with script maps. Use this to retrieve the path to a script for template expansion.
GetLogicalPath()	Returns the virtual path to a script-mapped document. Again, doesn't work with Foxisapi.dll but works with script-mapped docs mapped to it.
GetPreviousUrl()	Returns the URL that called this document. If the user typed the URL manually, this value will be blank.
GetBrowser()	Returns the browser's full name.
IsLinkSecure()	Returns .T. if the link is secure. Pass a server as a string if the port is different from 443 (standard SSL port).
GetCookie()	Retrieves an HTTP cookie.
GetRemoteAddress()	Retrieves the client's IP address.
GetServerName()	Name of the server's domain or IP as specified on the client's URL.

wwResponse

This class is responsible for creating output for the Web application. All output should flow through the Write or Send methods of this class in order to properly handle output to different output sources, as well as to handle error responses that allow output to be turned off after an error has occurred and an error message generated.

Property	What it does
cOutput	Property that holds the cumulative HTTP (mostly HTML) output.
lNoOutput	When .T., any request for output doesn't write to the output source. Typically used after an error occurs to prevent further output.

Method	What it does
Write Send()	Low-level output methods that can be called directly and used internally by all framework functions to send output to the output source. If lNoOutput is .T., output is not sent to the output source, but rather returned as a string. All internal methods call Send or Write and return the result to the user—most methods also support the lNoOutput parameter with the same result. Pass: <cText>, <lNoOutput> Return: nothing or the text if lNoOutput is .T.
Rewind()	Clears all output and resets the lOutput flag.
SendLn()	Just like Send or Write, but appends a carriage return for easier source formatting.
GetOutput()	Returns the cumulative output. Doesn't clear the cOutput property.
ContentTypeHeader()	Creates a full Content Type Header Pass: <cContentType (text/html)>, <lNoOutput> Return: "" or header if lNoOutput is .T.
HTMLHeader()	Creates a header for a document. Header includes ContentType Header, title, large text header and background formatting. Pass: <cHeaderText>, <cTitle>, <cBackground>,<cContentType>,<lNoOutput> Return: "" or header if lNotoutput is .T.
HTMLFooter()	Inserts end BODY and HTML tags into the document. Also, allows you to attach extra HTML before the end tags. Pass: <cFooterText>, <lNoOutput> Return: "" or header if lNotoutput is .T.
Authenticate()	Create a request for authentication that pops up a login dialog on the client. Pass: <cDisplayServerName>, <cErrorHTML>, <lNoOutput> Return: "" or header if lNoOutput is .T.
ExpandScript()	Takes an input file and expands the text using program-based evaluation. The page is converted into a TEXTMERGE program that's run by VFP (in compiled mode) or by CodeBlock (interpreted mode). Pass: <cPage>, <nMode>, <lNoOutput> Return: "" or header if lNoOutput is .T. nMode switches: 0 – Auto (compiled in VFP Dev, interpreted in runtime) 1 – Interpreted 2 – Force VFP compiled (must be precompiled in runtime)
ExpandTemplate()	Takes an input file name and expands the text using expression-based evaluation and Codeblocks. Unlike scripting, this mechanism does not support control structures in the HTML page except in distinct Codeblocks. Pass: <cPage>, <lNoOutput> Return: "" or header if lNoOutput is .T.

Looks like a lot of stuff, huh? But it sure makes life easier. Here's a quick look at the previous examples running with the framework:

```
DEFINE CLASS TFirstserver AS wwFoxISAPI OLEPUBLIC

FUNCTION Helloworld2
LPARAMETER lcFormVars, lcIniFile, lnRelease

THIS.StartRequest(lcFormVars,lcIniFile,@lnRelease)

THIS.StandardPage("Hello World From Visual FoxPro",;
                  "This page was generated by VFP at" +time())

RETURN THIS.oResponse.GetOutput()


ENDDEFINE
```

This reduces the Hello World program to three lines of code and does not require you to remember arcane syntax for the HTTP header. Note the RETURN value: It returns the HTML output of the oResponse object back to the client. StandardPage is a simple method that creates a fully self-contained page with an HTTP header, a title, some header text and a body to make it easy to print status messages in a standard format to the browser. This is very useful for error messages—think of it as a Web-based MessageBox or WAIT WINDOW command. The StandardPage method writes output to the oResponse object, so even though it didn't access the response object directly it was used for output, and hence it has to return its content back to the client. You'll want to call THIS.oResponse.GetOutput() on every exit point of your request.

The wwFoxISAPI class has a method called StartRequest, which handles proper setup of all support objects for the class. By passing in the form variables and the name of the INI file, the oRequest object is initialized so it knows from where to retrieve form variables and server variables.

```
PROTECTED FUNCTION StartRequest
LPARAMETERS lcFormVars, lcIniFile, lnUnload

lcFormVars=IIF(!EMPTY(lcFormVars),lcFormVars,"")
lcIniFile=IIF(!EMPTY(lcIniFile),lcIniFile,"")
lnUnload=IIF(EMPTY(lnUnload),0,lnUnload)

*** Set up the Request and Response objects
THIS.oRequest.LoadRequest(lcFormVars,lcIniFile)
THIS.oResponse.Rewind()

THIS.lError = .f.
THIS.cErrorMsg = ""

ENDFUNC
* wwFoxISAPI::StartRequest


* wwRequest::LoadRequest
PROTECTED FUNCTION LoadRequest
```

```
LPARAMETERS lcFormVars, lcIniFile

lcFormVars=IIF(EMPTY(lcFormVars),"",lcFormVars)
lcIniFile=IIF(EMPTY(lcIniFile),"",lcIniFile)

THIS.cContentFile = lcIniFile
THIS.cFormVars = "&" + lcFormVars + "&"

*** Retrieve the query string for parsing
THIS.cQueryString = THIS.ServerVariables("Query String")

ENDFUNC
* wwRequest::LoadRequest
```

When you return from wwFoxISAPI::StartRequest, you have oRequest and oResponse
members that are ready for use, and you don't have to worry about the implementation details.

Now for another look at the data request. The URL to access the list page might look like
this:

```
/foxisapi.dll/FirstServer.TfirstServer.SimpleQuery4?Company=B

FUNCTION SimpleQuery4
LPARAMETER lcFormVars, lcIniFile, lnReload
LOCAL lcCustno
PRIVATE Response, Request

*** Easier reference
Response = THIS.oResponse
Request = THIS.oRequest

*** Objects get initialized in here
THIS.StartRequest(lcFormVars, lcIniFile, @lnReload)

*** Check the QueryString first, then the Form vars
lcCustno = Request.QueryString("Company")
IF EMPTY(lcCustNo)
   lcCustNo = Request.Form("Company")
ENDIF

*** If no custno was passed let's show all custs
IF !EMPTY(lcCustNo)
   lcCustno = PADL(lcCustNo,8)
ENDIF

*** NOTE THE USE OF THE HREF
SELECT ;
  [<A
HREF="/foxisapi/foxisapi.dll/FirstServer.TFirstServer.LookupCustomer?Custno=] ;
  +ALLTRIM(Custno)+[">]+Company+[</a>] as COMPANY,;
  CareOf, phone, custno, company as sort ;
 FROM .\Data\TT_Cust ;
 WHERE CustNo = lcCustNo ;
 ORDER BY Sort ;
 INTO Cursor TQuery
```

```
IF _TALLY = 0
   THIS.ErrorMsg("No customers match the customer number.",;
                "Please retry your request or omit the "+;
                "customer number for a list of all customers.<p>"+;
                [<A HREF="]+THIS.oRequest.GetPreviousUrl()+;
                [">Return to the previous page</a>])
   RETURN Response.GetOutput()
ENDIF


*** Creates Content Type Header and HTML header
Response.HTMLHeader("Simple Customer List")

Response.Write([<TABLE Border=1 CellPadding=3 width="98%">] + ;
 [<TR BGCOLOR="#CCCC88" ><TH>Company</TH>]+;
 [<TH>Name</TH><TH>Phone</TH></TR>])

SCAN
  Response.Write("<TR><TD>" + Company + "</TD><TD>" + Careof + ;
                "</TD><TD>"+ STRTRAN(Phone,CHR(13),"<BR>") +;
                "</TD></TR>")

ENDSCAN

Response.Write("</TABLE>")

RETURN Response.Getoutput()
ENDFUNC
```

Again, note the call to StartRequest to configure the oRequest and oResponse member objects, which are then assigned to PRIVATE Response and Request variables for easier reference and naming compatibility with Active Server Pages. I use the Request.QueryString() method to retrieve the company name. If not found, I also try the form variables for the company value. The resulting company name is then used in the query to retrieve the appropriate customer. If no customer was supplied, I'll display the full list instead.

As before, Response.GetOutput() is used to return the HTML back to the client. Notice that there's an error check if no records are returned from the query. It creates an error message and then also returns the Response output.

This is much better than the previous hard-coded approach. You can quickly generate output with StandardPage and have objects ready to use for retrieving input and sending output that abstract the underlying logic. However, we can take this a little further.

Centralizing the FoxISAPI entry point

Even as I've simplified these tasks through the framework, there's still a lot of duplication in these requests. You still have to remember to call StartRequest() with the parameters passed to your method on each hit, and make sure that you return Response.Getoutput() on all exit points. And there's the issue of cleanly handling an exit from an error.

The solution is to build your server with a centralized method, which I call Process(). Rather than calling each server method directly from the Web page, you'd always call the Process method and tell it which method you'd like to run via a QueryString parameter. You'd end up with a URL like this:

```
/foxisapi.dll/FirstServer.TfirstServer.Process?Method=FirstQuery
/foxisapi.dll/FirstServer.TfirstServer.Process?Method=LookupCust&CustNo=43
```

When calling the method in this fashion, your requests can be centralized and repetitive tasks handled by pre- and post-processing the call to your method. The Process() method can be generic or you can override this functionality with your own, but it must at the very least handle parsing the Method query string parameter and calling the appropriate method. Here's the stripped-down version of the wwFoxISAPI::Process method:

```
************************************************************************
* wwFoxISAPI :: Process
********************************
***   Function: Generic Entry Point Method used for all requests.
***             This method requires that a ?Method=SomeMethod query
***             string is provided on the command line.
***             This method makes it possible to automatically load
***             the Request and Response objects.
***      Assume: Always called from the Web server directly!
***        Pass: lcFormVars
***              lcIniFile
***              lnRelease
***      Return: HTML OUtput
************************************************************************
FUNCTION Process
LPARAMETERS lcFormVars, lcIniFile, lnRelease
LOCAL lcMethod
PRIVATE Response, Request

*** Create PRIVATE object references
Response=THIS.oResponse
Request=THIS.oRequest

lnRelease = 0
THIS.StartRequest(lcFormVars, lcIniFile, lnRelease)
lcMethod = Request.QueryString("Method")
lcPhysicalPath = Request.GetPhysicalPath()

DO CASE
   *** Protect against illegal method calls
   CASE INLIST(lcMethod,"PROCESS","LOAD","INIT","DESTROY")
      THIS.StandardPage("Error","Invalid Method: " +lcParameter)

   *** Handle Template and Script Pages
   CASE ATC(".wcs",lcPhysicalPath) > 0
      THIS.ExpandScript(lcPhysicalPath)
   CASE ATC(".wc",lcPhysicalPath) > 0
      THIS.ExpandTemplate(lcPhysicalPath)

   *** Generic! Method names must be Method= on QueryString
   *** If you use different method names or parameters a custom CASE
   *** should be added *ABOVE* this line!
   ***
   *** Call methods that were specified on the command line's 1st parm
   ***   ie:   wwcgi.exe?Project~Method~MoreParameters
```

```
CASE !EMPTY(lcMethod) AND PEMSTATUS(THIS,lcMethod,5)
   =EVALUATE("THIS."+lcMethod+"()")

OTHERWISE
   THIS.StandardPage("Error","Invalid Method called: " + lcMethod)
ENDCASE

RETURN THIS.oResponse.GetOutput()
ENDFUNC
* wwFoxISAPI :: Process
```

This simple method frees you from a lot of work on each request! It automatically handles the three required FoxISAPI input parameters and sets up Response and Request objects from them. Your method is now called indirectly from `EVALUATE("THIS."+lcMethod)` in the CASE statement. The code first checks to see whether the method exists before executing the `EVALUATE()`; if it doesn't, it displays an error message.

What's nice about this approach is that you've totally centralized your entry point. Request and Response will be available to you without any further code, and you have the ability to override Process to hook any code that needs to occur on *every* hit. For example, a commerce site may need to make sure the user has an HTTP cookie in order to proceed. If not, he might need to be sent to a special login page. Or you might want to check for user authentication on each request. If you didn't use the Process method, you'd have to call a method for these things in *every* handler method you create! With the Process method, this action is centralized and your individual request methods don't need to worry about it.

You can also use Process() to hook up request logging or generate some debug output that captures each request input and output. Here's some useful code that is actually part of the default Process method. It sits at the very end of the Process method and saves all request information and HTML output to a file so you can review it in your TEMP directory after each request:

```
IF THIS.lSaveRequestInfo
   File2Var(SYS(2023) + "\temp.htm",THIS.oResponse.GetOutput())
   lcRequest = "*** Form Data *** " + CR+ lcFormVars + CR + CR + ;
               "*** Server Variables ***" + CR +;
               File2Var(lcIniFile)
   File2Var(SYS(2023) + "\temp.ini",lcRequest)
ENDIF
```

An additional benefit is that you can now make all of your request methods PROTECTED, so the Automation interface that your server exposes is leaner, which results in a smaller footprint and faster load time. This might not matter on small servers you create, but it becomes significant for those that have more than about 50 methods. When you use the Process method approach, you theoretically need to expose only a single method: Process. It also makes your server safer. No longer can you access methods directly, but you are forced through the Process method, which means you can't spoof parameters to your request.

Also, as you can see above, no matter what, THIS.oResponse.GetOutput() will always get called, so you no longer have to worry about remembering to call it on all exit points of your code—the Process method does it for you. You simply write to the Response object and exit, and the Process method sends the result back to the Web server.

All of this results in cleaner code that you write for each request and much easier maintenance of generic code that happens on each hit.

Our Hello World server now becomes a single line of code:

```
DEFINE CLASS MyServer AS wwFoxISAPI

PROTECTED FUNCTION HelloWorld
THIS.StandardPage("Hello World From Visual FoxPro",;
                  "This page was generated by VFP at" +time())
ENDFUNC

ENDDEFINE
```

which you would call like this:

```
/foxisapi/foxisapi.dll/FirstServer.Tfirstserver.Process?Method=HelloWorld
```

Now I'll show you the individual customer display from the customer list example, this time using the Process method syntax:

```
*******************************************************************************
* TFirstServer :: ShowCompany2
*********************************
*** Function: Displays Company information using some generic code
***           to parse field names and values
*******************************************************************************

lcCustno = PADL(Request.Form("ID"),8)

IF !USED("TT_Cust")
   USE (".\data\TT_Cust") IN 0
ENDIF

SELE TT_Cust
LOCATE FOR Custno = lcCustNo
IF !FOUND()
    THIS.StandardPage("Invalid Customer ID",lcCustno)
    RETURN
ENDIF

Response.Write(;
[<TABLE BGCOLOR="#EEEEEE" Width=400 Border=1>]+CR+;
[<TR><TD COLSPAN=2 ALIGN="CENTER"><b>Customer Information</b></TD></TR>]+CR)

lnFields = AFIELDS(laFields)

*** Just loop through fields and display
FOR x=1 to lnFields
        lcfieldname=lafields[x,1]
        lcfieldtype=lafields[x,2]
        lvValue=EVAL(lcfieldname)
```

```
            Response.Write("<TR><TD BGCOLOR=#FFFFCC><b>" + ;
                           Proper(lcFieldName) + ":<b></TD>"+;
                           "<TD>" + TRANSFORM(lvValue) +;
                           "</TD></TR>" + CR)
ENDFOR && x=1 to lnFieldCount

ENDFUNC
* TFirstServer :: ShowCompany2
```

Here's the URL you'd use to access this request:

```
/foxisapi/foxisapi.dll/FirstServer.TFirstServer.Process?Method=ShowCompany2&ID=1
```

Error handling

I haven't talked much about error handling, but it's one crucial aspect of Web applications that can't be overlooked. The wwFoxISAPI class implements a default handler—if you wrote some custom code already, you likely saw it in action when a FoxPro error was displayed on the response page. If errors are not handled by the server's Error method, an error occurs and the server pops up a dialog box, which hangs your server permanently. Obviously, you want to avoid this at all costs.

The first step to protect yourself is to create an error method on your server. If you're using the default FoxISAPI calling convention, the error handler can simply ignore the error or build an error string that you can display before the request returns.

Again, the Process method approach in the wwFoxISAPI class really shines by letting you centralize error handling and by providing a stable point of return for the error code. wwFoxISAPI implements an error method that takes advantage of the framework features for the error display as well as exiting in a predictable manner:

```
*************************************************************************
* wwFoxISAPI :: Error
******************************
*** Function: Limited Error handler. Not much we can do here other
***           than exit. Displays error page.
*************************************************************************
FUNCTION Error
LPARAMETERS nError, cMethod, nLine
LOCAL lcOutput

THIS.lError = .T.

THIS.StandardPage("Hold on... we've got a problem!",;
                  "The current request has caused an error.<p>"+CR+;
                  "Error Number: "+STR(nError)+"<BR>"+CR+;
                  "Error: "+Message()+"<BR>"+CR+;
                  "Code: "+Message(1)+"<BR>"+CR+;
                  "Running Method: "+cMethod+"<BR>"+CR+;
                  "Current Code Line: "+STR(nLine) )

THIS.oResponse.SendLn("<HR>")
```

```
*** Stop further output
THIS.oResponse.lNoOutput=.T.

RETURN TO Process
ENDFUNC
* Error
```

Because the wwFoxISAPI class (or your subclass of it) is at the top of the call stack, its error method will capture *any* error that occurs and is not handled by a local class error. This is useful because we can capture the error using the Response object and report it in the form of an error message that contains error information. You could also log this error into a table, but that's beyond the scope of this discussion.

Test this with the following code from the first server sample:

```
FUNCTION FakeError

oDear = CREATEOBJECT("ObjectThatDoesntexist")
oDear.GetFields()

ENDFUNC
```

You get the HTML result page shown in **Figure 5.12**.

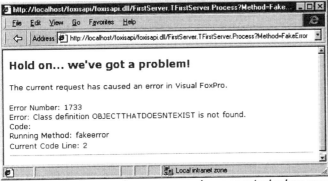

Figure 5.12. *A generic error page is generated when your FoxISAPI code causes an error. The error routine will handle almost any error not handled by your own error handlers in business logic or Web code. The handler can be customized by overriding it in your own implementation class.*

The most important thing about the handler is to avoid popping up an error dialog—the error is ignored and an error message is generated using the oResponse object. The code turns off further HTML output by setting oResponse.lNoOutput to .F.—this means that if the code returns to a calling method, all HTML output will not actually be sent to the output source. When lNoOutput is .T., all output is ignored.

Finally, the code exits by issuing RETURN TO PROCESS. Suppose there's an unhandled error in your request handler method or in one of the functions it calls. The Error method gets control, generates the error message to the Response object, and then issues RETURN TO

PROCESS. It then returns to the line following the EVALUATE() in the Process method, which among other things issues the all-important RETURN THIS.oResponse.GetOutput(), which returns the error message generated in the Error method. You've essentially handled this exception without harming the server and provided a useful error message to the user of your application.

🕸 Get the updated FoxISAPI DLL

The Developer's Download Files for this book (www.hentzenwerke.com) contain an updated Foxisapi.dll, which addresses several problems with the DLL shipped by Microsoft. The DLL also adds a few enhancements that are very useful:

- Allows use of a "default" server method, so that you don't have to specify the server.class.method syntax on the URL. This makes it possible to create script maps and also simplifies the use of the URL.

- Fixes a problem with binary content returned to the Web server. Foxisapi.dll uses string functions that truncate at the first NULL encountered, which causes problems for returning binary data—the updated DLL fixes this problem by using binary functions for output generation to the Web server.

Note that I myself made these fixes—they are not official Microsoft updates. This means if and when Microsoft releases a new version of the DLL, you may be out of sync. The current update is in sync with the shipped version that Microsoft released with Visual FoxPro 6.0. I've submitted my changes to Microsoft and they will likely be incorporated in the next release of FoxISAPI.

Eliminating those long URLs

The Process method approach has all sorts of advantages, and I suggest that this is the only way to reliably build FoxISAPI applications. However, the URLs generated by FoxISAPI in general, and by the Process method approach in particular, are huge. Take the following URL:

```
/foxisapi/foxisapi.dll/FirstServer.TFirstServer.Process?Method=ShowCompany2&ID=1
```

Not only do you have to reference class.server.method, but you also have to add a query string (?Method=) with the method name at the end. Personally I think it's worth the extra typing, but the long URL is a problem for some applications and companies.

To get around this problem (and also to add the ability to create script maps to Foxisapi.dll) I customized Foxisapi.dll with a special option that allows specification of a default server. In Foxisapi.ini I can add:

```
[foxisapi]
DefaultServer=Firstserver.TfirstServer.Process
```

which allows me to run the Company lookup URL as:

```
/foxisapi/foxisapi.dll?Method=ShowCompany2&ID=1
```

If no "extra path" containing the server.class.method is specified, the one in the INI file is used instead. This reduces the URL to a more manageable size and lets it work like any other ISAPI/scripting application. You can find the updated Foxisapi.dll in the Developer's Download Files at www.hentzenwerke.com.

Scripting and Templates

In order to build HTML applications efficiently, it's important to have a mechanism to build the display without having to write a lot of code that must be recompiled every time a minor change is made to the HTML user interface. The combination of code and scripting is an extremely powerful one that can provide the maximum flexibility for your applications: You can run code in a request method as shown above, and then use a template or a script page to actually display the output.

Implementing a scripting engine with Active Server syntax

Now let's walk through the creation of a scripting engine that will allow you to use syntax similar to Active Server Pages but use FoxPro code instead of VBScript. I'll introduce two concepts here: templates and scripts.

- **Templates**

  A template is an *evaluated* document. It primarily uses single expressions or field names to display on a page, but little or no code that can reside in code blocks. A template works through a Visual FoxPro program, parsing the expressions and embedding the result values into the page instead of the expressions or code blocks.

- **Scripts**

  Scripts are a little different—they're turned into a real program that's run by Visual FoxPro either in interpreted mode (using CodeBlock by Randy Pearson) or runtime mode by running a precompiled file from disk. Because these scripts are programs, you can use control structures and HTML in the same document, with HTML in between the control structures. Scripts have a number of issues with compilation that may be difficult to administer, but compiled scripts run at VFP native speed for maximum performance!

Templates with MergeText

Implementing a scripting engine in VFP is simple. You can create both mechanisms with relatively little code. I'll start with templates, using a function called MergeText() (found in wwUtils.prg), which walks through the page loaded from a string and expands the expressions. You call it like this:

```
lcTextToMerge = File2Var ("SomeScriptFile.wc")
lcExpandedText = MergeText(lcTextToMerge)
```

Typically you'll find a file from disk and use File2Var (which is multiuser safe compared to VFP 6.0's FileToStr()) to convert the file to a string that you can feed to MergeText to expand. Inside a template you can use the following syntax:

```
<HTML>
Expression: <%= AnyFoxExpression %>  UDF: <%= UDFFunction() %>
<%  BlockOfCode %>
</HTML>
```

Expressions are evaluated and embedded directly, and can be of any type except Object. Code blocks use Randy Pearson's CodeBlock class to interpret commands sequentially. Several rules apply for CodeBlock:

- LOCAL variables are not allowed.
- Any variables in a control structure must be pre-initialized as PRIVATE and set to a value.
- A codeblock can be only a single function—classes can be created and called but cannot be defined inside a CodeBlock.

Expressions are evaluated using the FoxPro Evaluate() function. This is rather fast because each expression in a page is evaluated only once. CodeBlock is interpreted using a FoxPro parser that uses macro expansion for each line of code. It's therefore rather slow for iterative looped commands, but can provide decent performance for short blocks of commands with non-looped commands. If you find yourself creating more than a few lines of code within a code block, write a UDF as part of your application instead, and use an expression to call it:

```
<%= CreateListTable() %>
```

Note that you can do things like this with CodeBlock:

```
<% PUBLIC o
   o=CREATE("SomeClass")
%>
<HTML>
<h1>Hello World from </h1><%= Version() %>
The time is: <%= TIME() %>

<%= o.ShowHTMLTable() %>

</HTML>
<% RELEASE o%>
```

Because *o* is declared as PUBLIC in the template, it's still visible at the end of the page. This would not work if *o* were declared PRIVATE because each code block is its own self-contained function—the PRIVATE variable would go out of scope when the individual code block completes.

Here's an example of a request you might want to run using a template. You may have a snippet of code like this:

```
#define HTMLPAGEPATH "c:\westwind\foxisapi\"
PROCEDURE ShowCustomer

lcCustno = Request.QueryString("CustNo")
USE TT_CUST
LOCATE FOR CUSTNO = lcCustNo
IF !FOUND()
   THIS.ErrorMsg("Customer Not Found")
   RETURN
ENDIF

*** Must add an HTTP Header
Response.ContentTypeHeader()

*** Load and evaluate the template page
Response.ExpandTemplate(HTMLPAGEPATH + Customer.wc")

ENDPROC
```

The Response object's ExpandTemplate class simply calls MergeText behind the scenes and loads the HTML template in Customer.wc (Web Connection Template), which looks like this after setting it up in FrontPage (see **Figure 5.13**):

```
<html>
<body>

<table width="400">
  <tr>
    <td bgColor="#ffffcc" vAlign="top" width="212"><strong><font
face="Arial">Company</font></strong></td>
    <td width="180"><strong><font face="Arial"><%= Tquery.Company %>
</font></strong></td>
  </tr>
  <tr>
    <td bgColor="#ffffcc" vAlign="top" width="212"><strong><font
face="Arial">Name</font></strong></td>
    <td width="180"><strong><font face="Arial"><%= CareOf %>
</font></strong></td>
  </tr>
  <tr>
    <td bgColor="#ffffcc" vAlign="top" width="212"><strong><font
face="Arial">Phone</font></strong></td>
    <td width="180"><strong><font face="Arial"><%=
STRTRAN(Phone,CHR(13),"<BR>") %> </font></strong></td>
  </tr>
<% IF TQuery.Billrate > 0 %>
  <tr>
    <td bgColor="orangered" width="212"><strong><font face="Arial">Billable
Customer at $<%= BillRate %></font></strong></td>
  </tr>
<% ENDIF %>
</table>
</body>
</html>
```

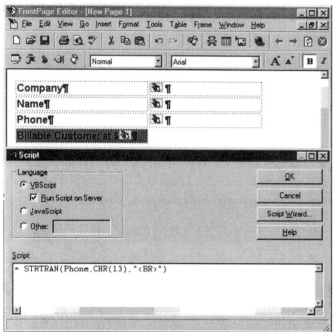

Figure 5.13*. A template page as seen inside Microsoft FrontPage.
The template tags using Active Server-type tags with FoxPro expressions
and code show up as script tags that you can edit.*

In FrontPage all expressions show up as script tags. If you embed input fields, those fields will display the `<%= Expression %>` as the display value of the field. If you have a code block, it'll also be editable inside the editor here using Visual FoxPro code (even though the check box says VBScript). Because MergeText and ExpandTemplate use ASP syntax, FrontPage and most other HTML editors will treat these FoxPro script tags as if they were native Active Server tags. For example, in Visual InterDev the tags are highlighted as code, just as with VBScript, and most keywords even show up in the proper syntax color highlights.

You can call MergeText in your own methods or you can use the wwFoxISAPI::ExpandTemplate() or the wwResponse::ExpandTemplate() methods. The wwFoxISAPI version creates a freestanding request including content type header, and the Response method sends the template right to the Response output source. The Response version only expands the template without any adornments.

Scripting—more power and more work
Templates are very nice, but using CodeBlock is too slow for truly freestanding scripts. While I believe the best way to build Web apps is with a combination of code and scripts/templates, scripting makes it possible to do it all in a single scripted page without any code that needs to be compiled into the application.

Like templates, scripts use Active Server syntax. All features of a template also work with scripts, so you can embed expressions as well as CodeBlocks. However, scripts provide some additional functionality: They allow creation of structured statements that can mix FoxPro code and HTML. For example, the following SCAN loop and IF statement will work only in a script page:

```
<HTML>
<% SELECT * FROM TT_CUST INTO Tquery
   SCAN %>
Name: <%= Company %>
<% IF Billrate > 0 %>
   Rate: <b><%= Billrate %></b>
<% ENDIF %>
<HR>
<% ENDSCAN %>
</HTML>
```

The reason this works is that scripts are actually converted into full programs that are run by Visual FoxPro. The script above is converted into a text-merge document that looks something like this:

```
TEXT
<HTML>
ENDTEXT
   SCAN
TEXT
Name: << Company >>
ENDTEXT
IF BillRate > 0
TEXT
      Rate: <b><< Billrate >></b>
ENDTEXT
ENDIF
ENDSCAN
TEXT
</HTML>
ENDTEXT
```

The wwVFPScript class takes the original script file and converts it into this type of TEXTMERGE code, and then actually runs the code to create a temporary output file that contains the generated HTML.

You can look at wwVFPScript for more details on how this is accomplished. Scripts can run in two different modes: compiled and interpreted. Interpreted pages are truly dynamic and can be changed online, while compiled pages require Visual FoxPro to compile the pages before any changes are visible on the Web site.

The ConvertPage method can convert the HTML scripting into a MergeText-compatible VFP program. The code is then passed to the RenderPageFromVar() method, which actually runs CodeBlock to evaluate the page. CodeBlock interprets the code one line at a time and is rather slow if you're doing anything inside of a loop.

You can also run a page in compiled mode. However, because COM objects are compiled EXE files and can't compile code on their own, this option requires you to compile the pages. The pages you run are separate from the projects and are always unloaded on each request.

While they need to be compiled, they don't require recompilation of the project as a whole. Rather, you can run a separate routine to recompile the pages outside the application while the online application continues to run. To do this, use the wwVFPScript class with the following methods:

```
o=CREATE("wwVFPScript","c:\westwind\foxisapi\somepage.wcs")
o.ConvertPage()
o.CompilePage()
```

This takes the input file and converts it into a Program file, which is compiled into an FXP that can be run by the server application. In the Developer's Download Files at www.hentzenwerke.com, the program called WCSCompile.prg accomplishes this task with a simple parameter interface:

```
SET PROCEDURE TO wwUtils Additive
DO WCSCOMPILE WITH "c:\westwind\foxisapi\*.wcs"
```

The idea is that you can run scripts in interactive mode while debugging, and then compile them to run them at full speed. Once they're compiled, making changes requires recompilation.

Hooking it in...

Templates and scripts called from code are very powerful. ExpandTemplate and ExpandScript make this easy by providing a document file to read from. They give you the opportunity to call a template *after* you've done your processing logic, and even run minimal code and expression logic inside the HTML page.

Now I want to take this a step further so that no code is required and you can fire off a scripted page automatically.

> The following discussion relies on the updated Foxisapi.dll from the Developer's Download Files at www.hentzenwerke.com. Script mapping requires that you do not use the server.class.method syntax. The new DLL can avoid this by using the DefaultServer= key in FoxISAPI.ini to route requests to your code with the proper path names for scrips intact.

Microsoft Internet Information Server provides a mechanism called Script Mapping, which makes it possible to map a file extension to an executable—in this case, Foxisapi.dll. What I want to do is map .WC and .WCS to Foxisapi.dll. To make this work you need to use the Foxisapi.dll included with the Developer's Download Files at www.hentzenwerke.com, rather than the one that ships with VFP, because the syntax using the server.class.method on the extra path is not allowed for script maps.

Follow these steps:

1. Make sure you're using the DLL provided with the Developer's Download Files at www.hentzenwerke.com, not the stock Foxisapi.dll that shipped with VFP. Script mapping will not work with the stock DLL!

2. Modify the FoxISAPI.ini file and add
    DefaultServer=FirstServer.TfirstServer.Process or whatever your server name is. It
    doesn't really matter which server because the functionality is handled by the
    wwFoxISAPI framework, which contains the logic to route .WC and .WCS pages.
3. Create a script map for .WC and .WCS on the Web server. To do so, open up the
    Microsoft Management Console for IIS configuration.
4. Select either your default Web site (if you want the script map to be accessible from all
    directories) or the virtual directory to which you want to assign the map.
5. Right-click and select Properties HomeDirectory (or Virtual Directory)|Configure.
6. Set up two script maps for .WC and .WCS and point them both to your copy of
    Foxisapi.dll. **Figure 5.14** shows what you'll see in the IIS Management Console.

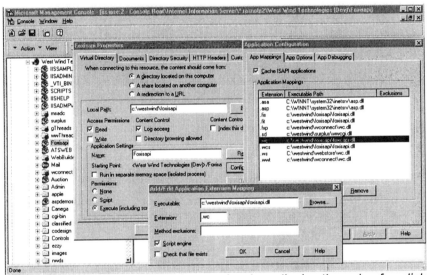

*Figure 5.14. Configuring a script map involves digging through a few dialogs
of the IIS Management Console. You can configure the script map to be
server-wide or specific to a virtual directory.*

If you're using Personal Web Server 4.0 for Windows 95 or NT Workstation, you won't
find an option to configure script maps visually. For PWS on NT you need to make sure you
install the IIS Management Console explicitly from the NT Setup CD. With PWS Windows 95
you can add a registry key:

```
HKEY_LOCAL_MACHINE\SYSTEM\CurrentControlSet\Services\W3SVC\Parameters\Script Map
```

Make sure to reboot Windows 95 after making this change. For NT Workstation you need to
programmatically configure the script maps. You can go to www.west-wind.com/webtools.htm
to find a utility that allows you to programmatically set up script maps, virtual directories and a
few other operations.

Once you have a script map for your DLL, you can run your script pages without having to hook any code in the COM servers you build. For example, to run the previous customer lookup page you can now simply do this:

```
http://localhost/foxisapi/Customerlookup.wc
```

This call will fire up your Automation server through the script mapping and interpret that page by virtue of the logic built into the Process method of the wwFoxISAPI class. This works by capturing the physical path of the request:

```
lcPhysicalPath = Request.GetPhysicalPath()
```

The physical path returns the full path of the location of the script file that was executed by the Web server. In other words, you get a full path to the template, in this case c:\westwind\foxisapi\Customerlookup.wc. Once I know where the template lives, I can read it in with the ExpandTemplate method, which parses the template and sends it back to the Web server.

The hook for capturing the physical path is in the Process method, which checks for the .wc and .wcs extensions that indicate a generic script:

```
lcPhysicalPath = Request.GetPhysicalPath()

DO CASE
   …
   *** Handle Template and Script Pages
   CASE ATC(".wcs",lcPhysicalPath) > 0
      THIS.ExpandScript(lcPhysicalPath)
   CASE ATC(".wc",lcPhysicalPath) > 0
      THIS.ExpandTemplate(lcPhysicalPath)

   CASE !EMPTY(lcMethod) AND PEMSTATUS(THIS,lcMethod,5)
      =EVALUATE("THIS."+lcMethod+"()")

ENDCASE
```

Request.GetPhysicalPath() retrieves the name of the script, and the ATC() function is then used on the retrieved path to determine whether the current request deals with a script-mapped page. If it does, the code is routed to either ExpandTemplate() or ExpandScript(), which are fully self-contained methods that create an HTTP header and expand the pages specified in the physical path:

```
**************************************************************************
* wwFoxISAPI :: ExpandTemplate
*******************************
PROTECTED FUNCTION ExpandTemplate
LPARAMETER lcFileName

*** Default Content Type
Response.ContentTypeHeader()

*** And expand the actual template
Response.ExpandTemplate(lcFileName)

RETURN
*wwFoxISAPI :: ExpandTemplate


**************************************************************************
* wwFoxISAPI :: ExpandScript
*******************************
PROTECTED FUNCTION ExpandScript
LPARAMETER lcFileName

Response.ContentTypeHeader()
Response.ExpandScript(lcFileName,THIS.nScriptMode)

RETURN
*wwFoxISAPI :: ExpandScript
```

These methods only forward the request to the Response object, which does the dirty work of evaluating the script code. The result from these methods is an HTML string that gets stored into the Response object. The page is evaluated and parsed into plain HTML and written into the Response object. When ExpandTemplate is done parsing the script, it returns to the Process method, which can now simply access the Response object's GetOutput method to retrieve the HTML generated from the script.

```
**************************************************************************
* wwResponse :: ExpandTemplate
*******************************
***   Function: Evaluates embedded expressions inside of a page
***       Pass: lcPage    -    Full physical path of page to merge
***     Return: "" or merged text if llNoOutput = .T.
**************************************************************************
FUNCTION ExpandTemplate
LPARAMETERS lcPage,llNoOutput
LOCAL lcFileText

lcFileText = File2Var(lcPage)
IF EMPTY(lcFileText)
   RETURN THIS.Send("<h2>File " + lcPage + " not found or
empty.</h2>",llNoOutput)
ENDIF

RETURN THIS.Send( MergeText(@lcFileText),llNoOutput)
ENDFUNC
* wwResponse :: ExpandTemplate
```

```
**************************************************************************
* wwResponse :: ExpandScript
********************************
*** Function: Takes a script page and 'runs' it as a TEXTMERGE
***           document.
***      Pass: lcPage  -  Physical Path to page to expand
***            lnMode  -  1 - Interpreted (CodeBlk)
***                       2 - Compiled FXP (default)
***    Return: Nothing
**************************************************************************
FUNCTION ExpandScript
LPARAMETERS lcPage, lnMode

lnMode=IIF(EMPTY(lnMode),1,lnMode)

lcFileText = File2Var(lcPage)
IF EMPTY(lcFileText)
   RETURN THIS.Send("<h2>File " + lcPage + " not found or empty.</h2>")
ENDIF

*** Create Script Object and pass THIS HTML object to it
IF lnMode = 1    && CodeBlock
  loScript = CREATE("wwVFPScript",,THIS)
  lcVFPCode = loScript.ConvertPage(lcFileText,.t.)
  loScript.RenderPageFromVar(@lcVFPCode)
ELSE
  loScript = CREATE("wwVFPScript",lcPage,THIS)
  loScript.lRuntime = .T.
  loScript.lAlwaysUnloadScript = .T.

  *** Converts the name to FXP and tries run the page
  loScript.RenderPage()
ENDIF

ENDFUNC
* wwResponse :: ExpandScript
```

The script parsing is handled by yet another object called wwVFPScript. I described how it works above—to see the code, take a look at wwVFPScript.prg in the FoxISAPI\Classes directory.

An example application

Whew! I crammed a lot of information into the last few sections to describe some of the logic that goes into building a framework. You don't really have to understand it all to use the framework, but it helps to have a feel for how various tools are implemented when you're using it.

Let's take a look at a small application that uses the framework—a consultant register containing names of consultants to display on the Web. Consultants can be added and edited on the list if they have a valid account on the server.

Start by setting up the new application as a class, subclassed from wwFoxISAPI, in a file called Tregister:

```
*** Framework Defines
#INCLUDE WCONNECT.H

*** Web FoxISAPI and Web Connection Classes used
*** Force to be pulled into project
DO LOADFOXISAPI
DO WCONNECT


*** Application DEFINEs - change for your application
#DEFINE SITELOCATION 1

*** Must use hardcoded data paths because the application
*** doesn't know where it's loading from.
#IF SITELOCATION=1
   #DEFINE DATAPATH ".\data\"
   #DEFINE HTMLPAGEPATH "c:\webbook\foxisapi \html\"
#ENDIF

***   Notebook
#IF SITELOCATION=3
   #DEFINE DATAPATH "\\rasnote\c$\wwapps\foxisapi\data\"
   #DEFINE HTMLPAGEPATH "\\rasnote\c$\westwind\foxisapi\"
#ENDIF

#DEFINE SHOWCODEFOOTER ;
 [<HR><a
href="/foxisapi/foxisapi.dll/fidemo.Tregister.Process?Method=ShowCode&ShowMetho
d=]+;
Request.QueryString("Method")+[&PRG=TRegister.prg&">Show Code</a>]

*************************************************************
DEFINE CLASS TRegister  AS  wwFoxISAPI OLEPUBLIC
*********************************************************


lSaveRequestInfo = .T.  && Save Request for debugging


*****************************************************************************
* TRegister :: Init
*******************************
***   Function: Set up environment and startup path
*****************************************************************************
PROTECTED FUNCTION INIT

*** Call wwFoxISAPI :: Init
*** Among other things this SETs DEFAULT TO Server's path
DoDefault()

*** Add any paths you need here
DO PATH WITH ".\DATA"

*** Any SET and ON Environment setting should go here
*** See wwFoxISAPI::Init for detail of defaults set

*** For debugging let's save the Request data to
*** TEMP\TEMP.INI (Request) and TEMP.HTM (Response)
```

```
THIS.lSaveRequestInfo = .T.

ENDFUNC
* TRegister :: Init

ENDDEFINE
```

Create a new project, call it FIDemo, and add the above code to it. Then do BUILD EXE FIDemo FROM FIDemo. After you've built it, open the project and select the Server Info tab. Make sure the Server Instancing is set to Single Use. The above code makes up an empty skeleton structure for the application. The application itself starts in a list view that displays all consultant names, company names and locations as shown in **Figure 5.15**. Names are linked so users can drill down for more detail, and there's also a Remove button on the list.

Here's the very short code listing:

```
*******************************************************************
* TRegister :: ShowConsultants
*********************************
*** Function: Shows a table of users with an Edit and Remove button
*******************************************************************
FUNCTION ShowConsultants
LPARAMETER lcFilter

lcFilter=IIF(EMPTY(lcFilter),"",lcFilter)

SELECT Company,  ;
      [<A
HREF="/foxisapi/foxisapi.dll/FiDemo.TRegister.Process?Method=ShowUser&ID=]+;
      Id+[">]+ first+" "+last+ [</a>] as Name, ;
      City+", "+State+" "+Zip+" "+country as Location,;
      [<A
HREF="/foxisapi/foxisapi.dll/FiDemo.TRegister.Process?Method=KillUser&ID=]+id+;
      [">]<IMG SRC="/images/remove.gif" BORDER=0 ALIGN=CENTER></A>] AS Action;
  FROM (DATAPATH+"CRegs") ;
  ORDER BY 1,2 ;
  INTO CURSOR TQuery

Response.HTMLHeader("FoxISAPI Consultant Register",,"#FFFFFF")

Response.ShowCursor()

Response.HTMLFooter()

RETURN
* TRegister :: ShowConsultants
```

Hey, what's going on here? The entire request uses only four lines of FoxPro code! The FoxISAPI framework handles all the hard work. Everything else is wrapped up in the SQL statement. The SQL statement selects the link to the user form as well as the IMG SRC link to display the Remove button, with its link to remove a user from the list.

HTMLHeader() creates the HTTP header and header display text. The workhorse function is Response.ShowCursor(). ShowCursor renders as HTML the table or cursor open in the currently selected work area. This useful function works by using AFIELDS to retrieve information about each field and using TRANSFORM to convert it into text.

```
*********************************************************************
* wwResponse :: ShowCursor
*********************************
***   Function: Renders the currently select cursor/table as HTML.
***       Pass: llNoOutput -  If .T. returns a string. Otherwise
***                           sends directly to output.
***     Return: "" or output if llNooutput = .t.
*********************************************************************
PROTECTED FUNCTION ShowCursor
LPARAMETER llNoOutput
LOCAL lcOutput, lnFields, lcFieldname,x

lcOutput = ;
  [<TABLE BGCOLOR="#EEEEEE" Width="98%" ALIGN="CENTER" Border=1>]+CR

IF EMPTY(ALIAS())
   RETURN ""
ENDIF

lnFields = AFIELDS(laFields)

*** Build the header first
lcOutput = lcOutput + "<tr>"
FOR x=1 to lnFields
   lcfieldname=Proper(lafields[x,1])
   lcOutput = lcOutput + "<th BGCOLOR=#FFFFCC>"+lcFieldName+"</th>"
ENDFOR
lcOutput = lcOutput + "</td></tr>"

SCAN
    lcOutput = lcOutput + "<TR>"
  *** Just loop through fields and display
  FOR x=1 to lnFields
          lcfieldtype=lafields[x,2]
            lcfieldname=lafields[x,1]
          lvValue=EVAL(lcfieldname)

          DO CASE
          CASE lcFieldType = "M"
              lcOutput = lcOutput + "<TD>" + STRTRAN(lvValue,CHR(13),"<BR>") +
"</TD>"
          OTHERWISE
              lcOutput = lcOutput + "<TD>" + TRANSFORM(lvValue) + "</TD>"
          ENDCASE
  ENDFOR && x=1 to lnFieldCount

  lcOutput = lcOutput + "</TR>" + CR
ENDSCAN

RETURN THIS.Send(lcOutput + "</TABLE>",llNoOutput)
ENDFUNC
* wwResponse :: ShowCursor
```

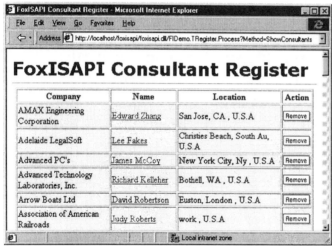

Figure 5.15. *Displaying the consultant register.*

This should give you an idea of how to build reusable code that can make short work of mundane tasks. Keep in mind that this is a minimal method—you'll likely want to elaborate on this scheme to provide a more customized view. **Figure 5.16** shows details about a particular consultant.

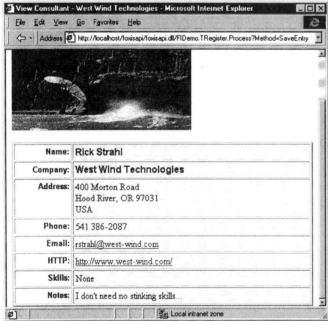

Figure 5.16. *You can display the actual consultant by using a little code and a template page stored on disk.*

To display the consultant information, use a template page with the following code:

```
PROTECTED FUNCTION ShowUser
*************************************************************************
* TRegister :: ShowUser
********************************
*** Function: Edits/adds a consultant
*************************************************************************
LPARAMETER lcUserId
LOCAL lcUserId
PRIVATE pcErrorMessage

IF EMPTY(lcUserId)
  lcUserId=Request.Form("ID")
ENDIF

IF !USED("CRegs")
   USE (DATAPATH+"CRegs") IN 0
ENDIF

SELE CRegs
LOCATE FOR ID=lcUserId
IF !FOUND()
   THIS.StandardPage("Couldn't find Consultant",;
                  "The consultant listing is no longer available...")
   RETURN Response.GetOutput()
ENDIF

THIS.ExpandTemplate(HTMLPAGEPATH+"cView.wc")

RETURN
* TRegister :: ShowUser
```

Again, only a few lines of code are needed to show the selected consultant. This time, the bulk of the work is handled by the ExpandTemplate method described earlier. **Figure 5.17** shows cView.wc, a page that was created using the visual editor of FrontPage 98.

The fields of the cRegs table are "bound" to this form using Active Server tags, as shown in the code snippet above. The tags can be either simple field values or, as above, VFP expressions embedded into the page by ExpandTemplate.

The toolbar at the top of the form also includes an Edit button. When the user clicks it, she's prompted for a login password (a generic password WebRegister for all consultants in this case—the NT account needs to exist in order for this to work). If completed, the actual edit form is displayed. The request that performs these tasks looks like this:

```
*************************************************************************
* TRegister :: ShowRegForm
********************************
*** Function: Displays the registration INPUT form.
*************************************************************************
FUNCTION ShowRegForm
LOCAL lcID, lcAuth
```

```
*** Make sure user is logged in under NT Account
lcAuth=Request.ServerVariables("Authenticated Username")
IF EMPTY(lcAuth) *** Send request for Authentication
   RETURN Response.Authenticate(Request.ServerVariables("Server Name"))
ENDIF

*** Grab the user ID - if new there isn't one
lcId=Request.GetFormVar("ID")

IF !USED("CRegs")
   USE (DATAPATH + "Cregs")
ENDIF
SELE Cregs

*** Locate on Phantom Record to display blanks (New records)
IF EMPTY(lcID)
   LOCATE FOR .F.
ELSE
   LOCATE FOR ID = lcId
ENDIF

*** Show page from disk
Response.ExpandTemplate(HTMLPAGEPATH + "cInput.wc")

RETURN
* TRegister :: ShowRegForm
```

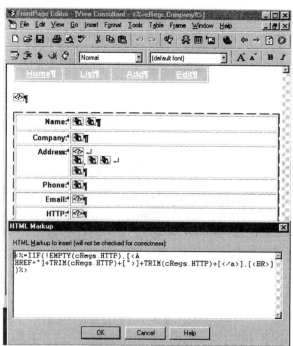

Figure 5.17. The consultant review form was designed in FrontPage using template tags to expand the field values to display.

Note that this request handles new entries or existing entries, depending on whether the ID passed to the form is available. If it isn't, the code moves to the End Of File "phantom record" (a record that contains all empty values for fields), which is the source for most of the fields on the cInput.wc form.

The input form displays a state field, which the standard form simply shows as an input field. You can add some dynamic code to the template page to show a list of states in a drop-down list, with the currently set state preselected. **Figure 5.18** shows the form with both the old state input field and the new drop-down list script code in FrontPage.

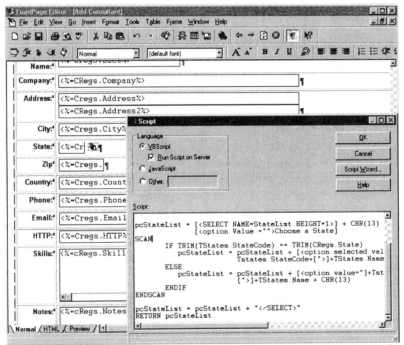

Figure 5.18. Adding script code with FrontPage using the script editor. I suggest typing your code in VFP and pasting it into the editor.

To create this drop-down list, create a new script block from the toolbar and insert the following FoxPro code (the result looks like **Figure 5.19**):

```
*** State List Popup For Registration
SELECT State as StateCode, Name from States ;
  ORDER BY Name ;
  INTO CURSOR TStates

pcStateList = [<SELECT NAME=StateList HEIGHT=1>] + CHR(13) + ;
            [<option Value ="">Choose a State]
SCAN
```

```
    IF TRIM(TStates.StateCode) == TRIM(CRegs.State)
        pcStateList = pcStateList + [<option selected value="]+;
                        Tstates.StateCode+[">]+TStates.Name + CHR(13)
    ELSE
        pcStateList = pcStateList + [<option value="]+Tstates.StateCode+;
                        [">]+TStates.Name + CHR(13)
    ENDIF
ENDSCAN

pcStateList = pcStateList + "</SELECT>"
RETURN pcStateList
```

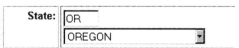

Figure 5.19. *The dynamically created State pop-up list in the final HTML document shows the preselected state.*

If you name the drop-down list with the same name as the text box, you can remove the text box. When you save the values from the form, the value (based on the StateCode field), rather than the display value, will be saved to the table.

The remaining task is to save the entry to a table. The input form can be updated by clicking the Update button, but it requires you to type the password for this entry. User-defined passwords are used to make sure that only the user who created an entry can edit it. In the demo, the passwords are the consultants' first names. Here is the code used to save an entry:

```
********************************************************************
* TRegister :: SaveEntry
*********************************
***   Function: Saves the input form values to the database. If a hidden
***             ID exists already on the form use the id and update
***             that record.
********************************************************************
FUNCTION SaveEntry

lcId=Request.Form("ID")

IF !USED("CRegs")
   USE (DATAPATH + "Cregs")
ENDIF

SELECT Cregs

lcPassword=Request.Form("Password")
IF EMPTY(lcPassword)
   THIS.StandardPage("No Password specified",;
                "You need to specify a password in order to save this
record.")
   RETURN
ENDIF
```

```
IF !EMPTY(lcID)
   LOCATE FOR ID = lcID
   IF !FOUND() and Password # TRIM(lcPassword)
      THIS.StandardPage("Invalid Password","Are you sure you know what you're
doing?")
      RETURN
   ENDIF
ENDIF

lclast=Request.Form("Last")
lcFirst=Request.Form("First")
lcCompany=Request.Form("Company")

IF EMPTY(lcLast) AND EMPTY(lcCompany)
  THIS.StandardPage("Missing information",;
                    "You must at least specify company or last name.")
  RETURN
ENDIF

*** Ok to enter or update now
IF EMPTY(lcID)
  APPEND BLANK
  REPLACE ID WITH SYS(3)
  lcId = cRegs.id
ENDIF

REPLACE ID WITH lcID,;
        last WITH lcLast,first WITH lcFirst, company WITH lcCompany,;
        address WITH Request.Form("Address"),;
        address2 WITH Request.Form("Address2"),;
        City WITH Request.Form("City"),;
        State WITH Request.Form("State"),;
        Zip WITH Request.Form("Zip"),;
        Country WITH Request.Form("Country"),;
        Phone WITH Request.Form("Phone"),;
        Email WITH Request.Form("Email"),;
        HTTP WITH Request.Form("HTTP"), ;
        Skills WITH Request.Form("Skills"),;
        Notes WITH Request.Form("Notes"),;
        Logo WITH Request.Form("Logo"),;
        Password WITH lcPassword

*** Display the information by calling the ShowUser routine
THIS.ShowUser(TRIM(lcId))

RETURN
* TRegister :: SaveEntry
```

There's nothing tricky about this code. It performs several checks to establish which user it is working with, and performs the password check. If all is well, the information is saved. Finally, the code calls the ShowUser method. This method was used previously as a direct response method, but this time around I'm passing a parameter to it directly. The method uses the following code to determine whether it needs to retrieve the ID from the Query String of the URL or whether to use a passed parameter:

```
IF EMPTY(lcUserId)
  lcUserId=Request.Form("ID")
ENDIF
```

I often build a semi-generic display routine that is called from other request methods. These methods can work either independently as direct display methods or when called from other methods within the same class. It's one way to reuse display functionality from within your application.

Other cool things you can do

I hope this simple application has given you a feel for what you can do with FoxISAPI. It's a very basic example, but I highlighted a number of important framework features and described how you can actually create working code with it. Keep in mind that I wrote very little code to build this applet—most of the display is handled by built-in routines and by using templates built with an HTML editor. Real-life applications are likely to be more complex, but the complexities are probably more related to the application logic rather than the Web/HTML-related tasks.

Now I want to show off more complex functionality that you can build into the framework. I'm not going to provide detailed explanations or code, but I'll briefly discuss how the demos work to get you thinking about the possibilities of using a framework based on pure Visual FoxPro code.

Queries against SQL Server

I suppose this is fairly obvious, but you can, of course, also run against SQL data sources with your Web applications. The sample includes a short demo that hits the SQL Server Pubs sample database and allows viewing and editing of the Author list. The little applet uses two requests: One code-based list and one that uses script page SQLAuthor.wcs. **Figure 5.20** shows the two forms in the browser.

The author list is a simple request using a custom wwSQL class to access the SQL Server database via a wrapper class around SQL Passthrough. (You could use views, but this custom class is faster to boot and includes full error handling.) The code looks like this:

```
FUNCTION SQLShowCursor
*********************************************************************
* wcDemoProcess :: SQLShowCursor
*********************************
*** Function: Retrieves some data from SQL Server
***    Assume: Assume you have a ODBC DSN called PUBS to the SQL
***            demo database (Pubs)
*********************************************************************

*** In typical situations you'll want to create a permanent property
*** on the server to hold the following reference (THIS.oCGIServer.oSQL for
example)
*** and initialize it in the server startup code
loSql = CREATE("wwSQL","DSN=pubs;uid=sa;pwd=")

lcLast = Request.QueryString("Name")
```

```
IF TYPE("loSQL") # "O"
   THIS.ErrorMsg("SQL Connection to Pubs failed",;
                "Most likely this means you need to set up an ODBC data source
to the PUBS database")
   RETURN
ENDIF

loSQL.cSQLCursor = "TQuery"
loSQL.Execute([SELECT Au_fname as First,'<A
HREF="/foxisapi/SQLAuthor.wcs?Id='+Au_id+'">'+Au_lname+'</a>' as
Last,City,Contract FROM Authors ]+;
                [ WHERE au_fname like '] +lcLast +[%' order by au_lname] )
IF loSQL.lError
   THIS.ErrorMsg("SQL Error",loSQL.cErrorMsg)
   RETURN
ENDIF

Response.HTMLHeader("Pubs SQL Server Data")

*** If we're not returning a string send output directly to output source
Response.ShowCursor()

Response.HTMLFooter(SHOWCODEFOOTER)

RETURN
ENDFUNC
* wcDemoProcess :: SQLShowCursor
```

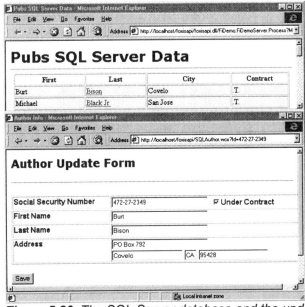

Figure 5.20. *The SQL Server database and the update form, both within the browser.*

It doesn't look much different than native VFP data access code, does it? The wwSQL class handles the connection to the data source (you need a DSN called Pubs and an account called SA with no password—otherwise change the connection string). The nice thing about the class is that it handles all errors that occur during the SQL connection/commands and gives a clean, trappable interface for handling these errors, which is more crucial in this transaction-based environment.

To display the individual author information, a script page is used:

```
<html>
<head>
<title>Author Info</title>
</head>
<body>
<%
PRIVATE lcID, loSQL
lcID = Request.QueryString("ID")
lcAction = UPPER(Request.Form("btnSubmit"))

loSQL = .NULL.
loSql = CREATE("wwSQL","dsn=pubs;uid=sa;pwd=")
IF VARTYPE(loSQL) # "O"
   Response.Write("SQL Error: Couldn't connect to server...")
   RETURN
ENDIF
IF loSQL.lError
   Response.Write("SQL Error: " + loSQL.cErrorMsg + loSQL.cErrorMsg2)

   RETURN
ENDIF

loSQL.cSQLCursor = "TQuery"

DO CASE
   CASE lcAction = "SAVE"
      lcID = Request.Form("txtAu_ID")

      loSQL.Execute([SELECT * from Authors where Au_id = ']+lcId+['])
      if reccount("Tquery") < 1
         *** New Record
      ELSE
         *** Update
         lcSQL = [Update Authors SET au_lname='] + Request.Form("txtAU_Lname")
+ [',]+;
                           [       au_fname='] + Request.Form("txtAU_fname")
+ [' ]+;
                           [ where Au_id = ']+lcId+[']

         loSQL.Execute(lcSQL)

         if loSQL.lError
            Response.Write("<b>SQL ERROR...</b><br>" + loSQL.cErrorMsg)
          RETURN
         ENDIF
      ENDIF
```

```
Response.Redirect("/foxisapi/foxisapi.dll/FiDemo.FiDemoServer.Process?Method=SQ
LShowCursor")
      RETURN
   OTHERWISE
      loSQL.cSQL = [SELECT * from Authors where Au_id = ']+lcId+[']
      loSQL.Execute()
    IF loSQL.lError
        Response.Write("<b>SQL ERROR...</b><br>" ) &&+ loSQL.cErrorMsg)
        RETURN
    ENDIF
ENDCASE
%> </p>

<p><strong><big><big><font face="Verdana">Author Update
Form</font></big></big></strong></p>

<hr>

<form align="center" METHOD="POST" ACTION="SQLAuthor.wcs">
  <table border="1" width="639">
    <tr>
      <td bgcolor="#FFF8C1" width="212" valign="top"><strong><font
face="Arial">Social Security
      Number</font></strong></td>
      <td width="415"><input type="text" name="txtAu_Id" size="28" value="<%=
Au_Id %>">  <input
      type="checkbox" name="txtContract" value="ON" <%=
IIF(Contract,[Checked],[]) %>><strong><font
      face="Arial">Under Contract</font></strong></td>
    </tr>
    <tr>
      <td bgcolor="#FFF8C1" width="212" valign="top"><strong><font
face="Arial">First Name</font></strong></td>
      <td width="415"><input type="text" name="txtAU_FNAME" size="28"
value="<%= Au_FName %>"></td>
    </tr>
    <tr>
      <td bgcolor="#FFF8C1" width="212" valign="top"><strong><font
face="Arial">Last Name</font></strong></td>
      <td width="415"><input type="text" name="txtAU_Lname" size="28"
value="<%= Au_LName %>"></td>
    </tr>
    <tr>
      <td bgcolor="#FFF8C1" width="212" valign="top"><strong><font
face="Arial">Address</font></strong></td>
      <td width="415"><input type="text" name="txtAddress" size="28" value="<%=
Address %>"> <br>
      <input type="text" name="txtCity" size="20" value="<%= City %>"> <input
type="text"
      name="txtState" size="2" value="<%= State %>"> <input type="text"
name="txtZip" size="20"
      value="<%= Zip %>"></td>
    </tr>
  </table>
  <p><input type="Submit" Name="BtnSubmit" VALUE="Save"> </p>
```

```
</form>

<hr>
<a href="/foxisapi/sqlauthor.wcs::$DATA">

<p>Show Script Code</a> </p>
</body>
</html>
```

This script consists of a big chunk of code that executes at the top of the page for handling the query for the list and the save action of the button. When you save, the data is updated in the database using the wwSQL class, and then the page is redirected to the list page. The bottom of the page contains an HTML table that holds the input fields for changing the individual entry.

Another thing that should become apparent by now is that there's no one right way to build a Web response page. You have a lot of options at your disposal. The last request could have been created by using pure code (Response.Write()), mixing code and a template page, or by using a pure script page as I did above. My inclination is to use code for business logic and templates for displaying the code whenever possible. It gives the most flexibility in terms of development, without giving up the customizability of the interface.

Creating Adobe Acrobat documents from VFP reports

I've been talking a lot about creating non-HTML HTTP output. Here's an example of how you can create output in a binary format usable by a third-party viewer—namely Adobe Acrobat. Adobe Acrobat is cool technology because it provides a portable mechanism to deliver richly formatted documents that are viewable and printable, and, with additional software, even editable. Furthermore, Adobe's PDF format is well compressed so that document size is often as small or even smaller than an equivalent HTML document.

One big issue when working with Web applications is the inability to print efficiently from a Web browser. The problem is that the Web browser has no understanding of the data on the page, and hence breaks text without concern for data groups and general layout. It's also difficult to create complex reports that display well in HTML.

It's much easier to do this with the VFP report writer. One way to create a report for viewing over the Web is to print it to an Adobe Acrobat file, which can be viewed on the client side with the Acrobat Reader. The resulting document is rendered exactly like the actual report, preserving the rich text formatting (fonts, bold/italic, colors, alignment, and so forth), paging and page numbers, and providing a searchable, editable (with the proper Adobe software) document that can be printed from the viewer.

You can download the free viewer from the Adobe Web site (www.adobe.com). Adobe also sells software that allows creation of Acrobat documents—one feature of this package is a printer driver that allows conversion of standard printer output to an Acrobat document. Unfortunately, this printer driver is not very well behaved, and the implementation for providing programmatic access is badly thought out. It can be done, but beware of some of the issues. The following class encapsulates the process into an easily accessible class. In order to use this sample, you need to have a copy of the Adobe Acrobat software. This package ($199 list) includes a printer driver that makes it possible to capture printer output into an Adobe Acrobat document.

Figure 5.21 shows what a Visual FoxPro report looks like in Adobe Acrobat. The report looks identical to the report form designed in the Visual FoxPro report writer. In fact, it's much more viewable than the VFP Report Preview! In addition, notice the buttons for printing and searching the document. That's right—you can click the Search option and the viewer will find the first occurrence for you. PDF documents are actually formatted text documents (a modified version of Postscript) so the text in the document is available in text mode.

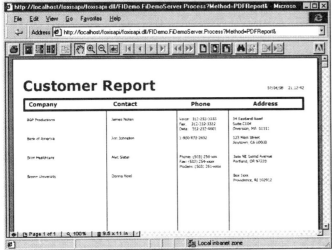

Figure 5.21. *Viewing a Visual FoxPro report with Adobe Acrobat results in a viewable, printable and searchable document. With further Adobe software you can even edit the text! This report was run with a company filter of "B" entered on a Web page.*

Unfortunately, Internet Explorer has some problems with the Adobe Acrobat Reader ActiveX control. When viewing content directly returned from a POSTed form request, the viewer sometimes fails to display content. In particular, multi-page documents cause problems. Netscape browsers do not experience this problem.

As a workaround, you can generate your reports to a file and then create a link to the file, rather than returning the output directly to the browser as the HTTP response as described below.

Neither Microsoft nor Adobe seemed to be concerned with this issue when I contacted tech support, which is a shame since this is extremely useful technology. Bug both companies' tech support people to get them to fix this problem!

How it works

The basic idea behind creating dynamic PDF documents is to use the PDFWriter software to generate a print file, and then take the contents of the printed file and return it directly to the Web browser with the appropriate content type of `application/pdf`.

To abstract the process I created a wwPDF class, which makes this process very easy. Here is the code used to print a report with this class using FoxISAPI:

```
PROTECTED FUNCTION PDFReport
****************************************************************************
* FIDemoServer :: PDFReport
********************************
*** Function: Create a report and output it as a PDF document.
***    Assume: PDFWriter is installed and configured per wwPDF.prg
****************************************************************************

lcCompany = UPPER(Request.Form("Company"))

SELECT * ;
   FROM TT_Cust ;
   WHERE UPPER(Company) = lcCompany ;
   ORDER BY Company ;
   INTO CURSOR TQuery


oPDF=CREATE("wwPDF","WINNT")

Response.ContentTypeHeader("application/pdf")

Response.Write( oPDF.PrintReportToString("custlist") )


ENDFUNC
* FIDemoServer :: PDFReport
```

The wwPDF workhorse method that accomplishes this task is the PrintReport method:

```
****************************************************************************
* wwPDF :: PrintReport
********************************
*** Function: The worker function. This method actually goes out,
***           sets the printer and prints the report. Use this
***           instead of a REPORT form command.
***      Pass: lcReport    -   Name of the FRX Report to run
***            lcOutputFile -   Filename to print the PDF output to
***            lcExtraReportClauses  - Any extra tags like FOR, WHEN etc.
***    Return: .T. or .F.
****************************************************************************
FUNCTION PrintReport
LPARAMETERS lcReport, lcOutputFile, lcExtraReportClauses

lcExtraReportClauses=IIF(EMPTY(lcExtraReportClauses),"",lcExtraReportClauses)
```

```
*** Only one report at a time - block until complete
IF !THIS.LockSemaphore()
   RETURN .F.
ENDIF

SET PRINTER TO NAME 'Acrobat PDFWriter'
REPORT FORM (lcReport) &lcExtraReportClauses TO PRINT NOCONSOLE
SET PRINTER TO

DECLARE Sleep in WIN32API INTEGER

ltStart = datetime()

*** Wait for THIS.nTimeout seconds - if not complete, fail
lnHandle=FOPEN(THIS.cTempOutputFile,0)
do while lnHandle = -1 AND DATETIME() < ltStart + THIS.nTimeout
   =sleep(200)
enddo

*** Couldn't open the PDF file so fail
if lnHandle = -1
   THIS.UnlockSemaphore()
   RETURN .F.
ENDIF

*** Get rid of an existing file
ERASE (lcOutputFile)

=FCLOSE(lnHandle)

*** Move the temp file to the actual file name by renaming
RENAME (THIS.cTempOutputFile) TO (lcOutputFile)

THIS.UnlockSemaphore()

RETURN .T.
ENDFUNC
* wwPDF :: PrintReport
```

The main purpose of this function is to change the printer to the PDFWriter and simply print the specified report. Unfortunately, it isn't quite so easy. Configuring the PDFWriter to print without dialogs requires tweaking an INI file in a non-determinate location. When creating the wwPDF options, you have to tell it where to find the INI files—WINNT and WIN95 options are used for the most likely location. If that doesn't work, you have to locate the file manually. Making the changes to the INI file to switch between interactive and non-UI operation also requires a reboot of the system. The steps to configure the PDFWriter are included in the header of the wwPDF class.

Additionally, the driver is incapable of printing more than one document at a time. If you're running more than one instance of your application, or any other application that's using the PDFWriter, the output file is determined by an INI file setting. If two clients write to the INI file simultaneously, output will get mixed up. To avoid this from the FoxISAPI application, I had to implement a Semaphore locking scheme with a table that locks a record and holds it locked until the report is printed. Any other report wanting to print at the same time has to wait for the lock to clear. The timeout for this is configurable.

All of this logic is hidden from the external interface of the class, though. PrintReport sends the report to a file on disk. The PrintReportToString method uses PrintReport to generate the report to disk, and then retrieves the disk file into a string, which is a binary image of the report. To return the document directly to the browser, just do this:

```
Response.ContentTypeHeader("application/pdf")
Response.Write( oPDF.PrintReportToString("custlist") )
```

Cool, isn't it? The ability to send back any kind of content is quite useful. You can do the same with any document that the Web browser understands. For example, you can send back a Word or Excel document and immediately open it inside the browser with this same approach.

Sending data over HTTP

I'll look a lot more closely at sending data over the wire in a later chapter, but here's a little preview. Let's say you have a Visual FoxPro form that needs to retrieve some data from your Web server. Let's say you want to run a query on the server. Earlier I introduced the wwIPStuff class, which lets you retrieve HTTP requests from a Web server.

Because you can send binary data through the HTTP request, it's easy to run a query, save the file to disk, and read it into a string. Then you can simply send the file down through the Request object and pick it up on the other end of the connection, taking the result string and storing it to a temporary table that you can work with. Here's the code needed on the server:

```
************************************************************************
* FIdemo :: HTTPCustlist
*********************************
***    Function: Runs a query based on a Filter passed on the query
***              string. The result cursor is turned into a string
***              and returned to the client.
************************************************************************
FUNCTION HTTPCustlist

lcFilter = Request.QueryString("Filter")

lcFname = SYS(2015)
SELECT Company, Careof as Name from TT_Cust ;
   &lcFilter ;
   ORDER BY Company ;
   INTO TABLE (lcFname)

IF _TALLY < 1
   USE
   RESPONSE.Write("Error: No Records")
ELSE
   *** Load the query result into a string
   USE
   lcBuffer = FileToStr(ForceExt(lcFname,"dbf"))
   Response.Write(lcBuffer)
ENDIF
```

```
*** Must delete the temp table
ERASE (ForceExt(lcFname,"dbf"))

RETURN
ENDFUNC
* FIdemo :: HTTPCustlist
```

Note that you can pass this request a filter string, which should be a valid WHERE clause, such as WHERE Company = 'B'. The client can then make a request on the server with the following URL:

```
foxisapi.dll/FIDemo.FIDemoServer.Process?Method=HTTPCustList&Filter=WHERE
Company='B'
```

Figure 5.22 demonstrates the query and the result of retrieving the file from a Visual FoxPro client application and displaying the table in a Browse window.

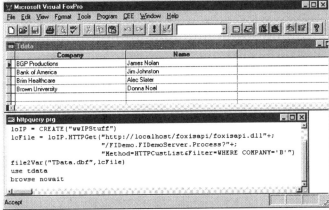

Figure 5.22. *It takes only a few lines of code to retrieve a result table from a FoxISAPI server. wwIPStuff's HTTPGet retrieves the file as a string, which is converted to a file that can be viewed in a browser window or loaded into a form.*

This code lacks error checking, but that's easy to add. I like to use the Error: prefix to denote any problems with file transfers. You can check for that and extract an error string to return.

> *Once again, this technique requires that you use the Foxisapi.dll from the Developer's Download Files at www.hentzenwerke.com, rather than the stock one that shipped in the VFP box. The original DLL truncates strings at the occurrence of the first CHR(0). Because VFP tables and other binary data can contain NULL characters, the original DLL will fail on most binary files.*

Keep in mind that the example I provided above is fairly limited. You can't send a file that has memo fields because you're no longer dealing with a single file that you can turn into a string. A little more work is required—using an encoding mechanism. I'll talk much more about using HTTP to communicate between clients and servers in the client-side programming section, and I'll show you more sophisticated ways to transfer data to and from the Web server.

This is a simple example, but it should give you an idea of what's possible. This approach makes it possible to build applications that communicate directly with a Web server from a VFP application. Because the Web server is running FoxISAPI, you can build real client-server applications with VFP on both sides of the network. In addition, this mechanism is powerful because you can access data as described, as well as execute code on the server! A request can run complex business logic in regular FoxPro code before deciding what data to actually return. Also, using wwIPStuff gives you full flexibility over the connection and security. You can run over HTTPS (secure HTTP using SSL) and use Authentication to verify user passwords if necessary. You're also not accessing the database directly as you are with tools like RDS, which can be a huge security problem—the indirect access gives hooks to make the data access bulletproof, even for open Internet applications, without giving the client full access to the database.

Rendering Visual FoxPro forms

Wouldn't it be cool if you could run your FoxPro forms over the Web? Well, guess what, you can! Now I'll show you a demo based on some tools in Web Connection, along with a general description of how they work. I haven't provided the code for the classes, although the compiled classes are available in the Developer's Download Files so you can play with them.

Check out the guest book form in **Figure 5.23**. The form displayed in the browser is rendered from a Visual FoxPro form running on the server and then being rendered as DHTML. Dynamic HTML and the absolute positioning features of cascading style sheets are used to create a form that looks very much like the original FoxPro form. Any data that the form displays before rendering will also be shown in the rendered form.

Although this looks a lot like an Active Document, it's actually pure, thin client output consisting entirely of HTML—no binaries are required on the client other than Internet Explorer 4.0 (required!). The form runs on the server and is rendered as DHTML, which is sent back to the browser to display.

The logic that handles the rendering of this form is wrapped up in an easy-to-use class. The class takes an input of a form object and has a method called ShowContainer(), which can take any Visual FoxPro container class and render it, including any nested containers inside. The entire application above requires about 100 lines of Web code—the remainder of the logic sits in the VFP form and knows nothing about the Web. The form runs as a standalone class.

Figure 5.24 shows another example, this time with page frames and grids.

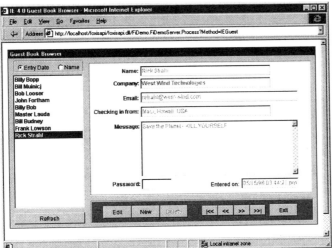

Figure 5.23. *Is it live or is it Memorex? This form was rendered from a live Visual FoxPro form, keeping intact all of the display attributes.*

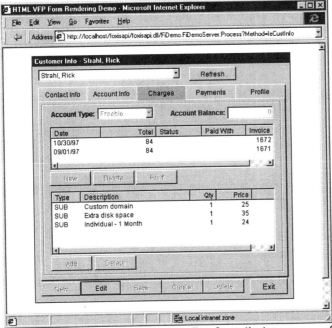

Figure 5.24. *Another Visual FoxPro form that uses pageframes and several grids. Pageframes are rendered natively with DHTML and some script code, while grids require a custom ActiveX control.*

Again, this form is an actual application that was converted to a Web interface with only minimal changes to the form. The form's logic continues to be used to update the display and actual data bound to the form. The Web code merely drives the form's methods with the following code. Here's the complete FoxISAPI request code required for this form application:

```
FUNCTION IECustInfo
************************************************************************
* wwDemoProcess :: IECustInfo
********************************
*** Function: Demonstrates a simple implementation of HTML Form.
***           Shows off use of Page Frame and data bound listbox.
************************************************************************
LPARAMETER lcFormVars, lcIniFile, lnReleaseFlag
LOCAL oGuest, lcCustId, lcAction

lcFormAction =
"/foxisapi/foxisapi.dll/FiDemo.FiDemoServer.Process?Method=IeCustInfo"

*** All buttons are *ALWAYS* tied to btnSubmit
lcAction=UPPER(Request.Form("btnSubmit"))
lcName=Request.Form("combo1")

*** Back to WC Demo Page
IF lcAction = "EXIT"
   Response.HTMLRedirect("/foxisapi/")
   RETURN
ENDIF

DO PATH WITH ".\wwdemo\custform"

DO FORM "customer.scx" NAME oCust LINKED WITH lcName NOSHOW

*** Create the rendering object
oHTMLForm=CREATEOBJECT("wwHTMLForm",oCust,Response)

IF lcAction="EDIT"
   oCust.EditMode(.T.)
ENDIF
IF lcAction="SAVE"
   oCust.Navigate("CUSTSEARCH",lcName)
   oCust.EditMode(.T.)

   *** Now update the form values
   oHTMLForm.SetValues(Request)

   *** And tell the form to save it
   oCust.SaveEntry()
ENDIF

Response.HTMLHeader(,"HTML VFP Form Rendering Demo")
Response.SendLn("<CENTER>")

oHTMLForm.lShowAsFullHTML=.F.
oHTMLForm.lShowFormCaption=.T.
oHTMLForm.lAbsolutePosition=.F.
```

```
oHTMLForm.cFormAction=lcFormAction

oHTMLForm.ShowContainer()

Response.Send([</center>])
Response.HTMLFooter(SHOWCODEFOOTER)

ENDFUNC
* wwDemoProcess :: IECustInfo
```

Surprised at how little code is involved here? Note that this form is live—you can actually view and edit entries! So what does the above code do? First it figures out which, if any, button was clicked. All button clicks route back to this single request, and the CASE statement decides what to do about the button clicks. Only Save and Edit need to be handled—all other buttons just redisplay the form. The name displayed in the combo box is retrieved and will be used as the state piece that decides which record to display.

Next, the form runs on the server. It runs with the NOSHOW clause, which minimizes resource use and makes the form run faster. The form must be modeless or your server will hang. Next, an instance of the wwHTMLForm object is instantiated, as well as a reference of the form and a reference of the Response object (Response). The class uses the Response object internally to immediately send all output to the Response output source, rather than accumulating a string. (You can also do this by not passing in a Response object—the GetOutput() method allows output retrieval then.)

When the form runs it receives a parameter of the name to display, which causes the form to call its internal mechanism by calling its Navigate method to locate and display the correct record. At this time, the invisible form displays the correct data invisibly and is ready to be rendered.

The form class just generates HTML so it's possible to create HTML at the top of the page before showing the rendered form. I didn't display any headers here, but you could call Response.HTMLHeader and add a custom header and/or any other HTML at the top or bottom of the page. I actually embedded the custom Show Code footer on the page.

Now it's time to configure the rendering object. Most of these deal with how the form is to display:

```
oHTMLForm.lShowAsFullHTML=.F.
oHTMLForm.lShowFormCaption=.T.
oHTMLForm.lAbsolutePosition=.F.
oHTMLForm.cFormAction=lcFormAction

oHTMLForm.ShowContainer()
```

 The call to ShowContainer creates the actual HTML for the request. The generated HTML is rather lengthy, especially for a form as complex as the one above. You can look at the demos included with the Developer's Download Files at www.hentzenwerke.com or go to www.west-wind.com/wconnect/ to see the HTML.

Cascading style sheets are the key to making the HTML work. These allow for absolute positioning and precise configuration of any object in an HTML document. For example, this code shows configuration of an input box and its label:

```
<DIV CLASS="TEXT" ALIGN=RIGHT
STYLE="POSITION:ABSOLUTE;Color:#000000;LEFT:22;TOP:24;WIDTH:79;HEIGHT:17;Font:n
ormal bold 9pt 'Arial'">Last Name:</DIV>

<INPUT NAME="pgfcustomer.page1.txtlast" ID="pgfcustomer.page1.txtlast" DISABLED
STYLE="POSITION:ABSOLUTE;LEFT:109;TOP:20;WIDTH:183;HEIGHT:24;Font:normal bold
9pt 'Arial';Color:#000000;BACKGROUND:#FFFFFF" VALUE="Strahl">
```

The class takes the top-level reference and then walks through the Objects (or Buttons) collection to render each object using the appropriate style tags. The class includes hooks so you can override the behaviors that are tied in by Baseclass by default. Each interface object is implemented as a separate class that has methods for HTML rendering as well as updating its display value. Each object works off an object reference to the actual interface object, and thus can read and write properties of the object directly.

The example above also deals with updating the form when the user is in Edit mode. Notice that everything is driven through methods on the form. A call to the EditMode() method makes all form fields editable. Now when the form is rendered, all HTML fields will also be editable. The save code looks like this:

```
IF lcAction="SAVE"
   oCust.Navigate("CUSTSEARCH",lcName)
   oCust.EditMode(.T.)

   *** Now update the form values
   oHTMLForm.SetValues(Request)

   *** And tell the form to save it
   oCust.SaveEntry()
ENDIF
```

To capture the result data, the form is again put into Edit mode. The wwHTMLForm also includes a method to update the form with the values captured from the HTML form. If you look at the HTML Input field above, you'll notice that the name of the field is identical to the object containership reference that the object has on the form: pgfcustomer.page1.txtlast. Based on that, the SetValues method takes a Request object input and repopulates the form with the new values from the Web form. You can optionally bind the data source as the field name, too, to directly update the data. Finally, a call to the form's SaveEntry() method actually saves the values to a file—SaveEntry here doesn't do any error checking, but this is where validation rules should be checked. Notice how the form, not the Web request, is responsible for accessing the data, totally separating the Web interface from the logic. Also notice that the wwForm class is part of Web Connection. Yet without making any changes to the class, it works in this FoxISAPI framework. It would also work easily for Active Server Pages because the object can create freestanding text output if needed. The flexibility and object-oriented features of Visual FoxPro have made it possible to build such a powerful tool. If nothing else, you can think of it as a very sophisticated WYSIWYG DHTML editor!

To quickly render a form you can also do this:

```
DO FORM Guest Name oGuest LINKED
DO wwForm with oGuest
```

Keep in mind that wwHTMLForm is mainly a rendering tool. It takes an active instance of an object and renders the full contents of that live object as HTML. The code you write is responsible for properly managing that live object, communicating the Web page events such as button clicks and selections of list boxes. The key to getting forms to work is to make sure an externally accessible interface allows a few lines of code to make the form do what it needs to to display itself correctly. In other words, wwHTMLForm doesn't run your forms on the Web—it only renders them!

This technology works by walking the containership hierarchy of user interface objects and then rendering each object as HTML. The class first looks at the top-level container and then digs into any lower-level containers to render each one. Each object has a corresponding HTML Control rendering object that takes the full object as an input and then parses the properties of that object into an HTML string. Each object then returns the generated HTML to its container, which calls GetOutput() to retrive the string and send to the Web server. Standard methods for handling properties common to most objects make these rendering objects small and fairly similar.

Although I'm not providing the code for these classes, I'm hoping that you have a good idea of how to build this kind of tool on your own if you choose not to look at Web Connection. These classes are fairly sophisticated in how they handle forms—for simpler scenarios it might be much easier to create simpler rendering tools.

Multiple instances via the pool manager

I've talked extensively about using multiple instances of your servers to simulate multi-threading. Since Visual FoxPro is single-threaded and the ISAPI interface is multi-threaded, the only way to process simultaneous requests in Visual FoxPro is to use multiple instances of your server. To do this, FoxISAPI uses a pool manager inside the ISAPI DLL that creates and manages multiple instances of your single-use EXE servers.

FoxISAPI manages an instance of each server created and keeps it loaded in memory. This group of servers is called the "pool," from which FoxISAPI selects one to process your request. **Figure 5.25** shows how FoxISAPI becomes a client to multiple instances of your server. The pool manager works on a first-come, first-called basis. Only when the first server is busy is the second one called, and only when the second is busy is the third called, etc.

So how does it work? With multiple instances of the same server, requests are served by the pool manager, which maintains a pool of servers. If the first instance is busy, the second instance will take the request. If all servers are busy and the pool of servers is exhausted, the request is queued. To use the internal pool manager, the server must be a single-use EXE.

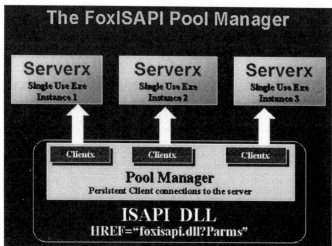

Figure 5.25. FoxISAPI Pool Manager handles instantiation and rotation of multiple servers to provide simultaneous request processing.

Multiple servers are configured via the FoxISAPI.ini startup config file:

```
[foxisapi]
busytimeout = 5
releasetimeout=13
statusurl = Status
reseturl= Reset
SingleModeModeUrl = SingleMode
MultiModeUrl = MultiMode

[wwFoxISAPI.TFoxISAPI]
wwFoxISAPI.TFoxISAPI=2
R_FoxIsapi.T_R_Foxisapi=1

[foxis.employee]
foxisr2.employee=2
foxisr1.employee=1
foxis.employee = 2
```

The first keys in the [FOXISAPI] section determine how you can manage servers. The various URL keys allow you to customize the commands used on the URL to run that command:

```
foxisapi.dll/status
foxisapi.dll/reset
foxisapi.dll/singlemode
```

The Status URL displays a list of all loaded servers. Reset releases all servers. SingleMode releases all servers but the first, so you can run maintenance operations that require EXCLUSIVE access to the data. Multimode is the default and runs multiple server instances— use this link after you're done using Singlemode.

The actual Automation servers are configured with a separate section for each ProgId in FoxISAPI.ini. The section serves as a map to translate your ClassID passed on the URL to translate to the actual ProgIds that you want to call. You can call both the same server and a local or remote server and tie it to the same ProgId that FoxISAPI can use on the query string. Because local and remote servers must have different class IDs, this mechanism allows you to transparently load the remote server with the same URL as the local server. The INI file map figures out the program ID mapping.

In the [foxis.employee] example above, FoxISAPI would first load the FoxISr2 server when starting up. Once this server gets busy, FoxISAPI would load another instance because the key value is 2. When both of these are busy, foxisr1 would load. Finally, a local copy will start, and two instances of that can run before requests start queuing.

When working with remote servers, you typically want to load the local servers first because they run faster and provide snappier response. Remote servers are more difficult to configure and take quite a bit longer to load and unload. See the DCOM section of Chapter 9 for more details.

FoxISAPI debug mode

To make it easier to debug your Automation servers, the latest version of FoxISAPI has a debug mode. When running in debug mode, FoxISAPI loads the Visual FoxPro development environment as an Automation server rather than your actual server. The VisualFoxPro.Application object is created and is called with syntax equivalent to this:

```
oServer=CREATEOBHECT("VisualFoxPro.Application")
oServer.EVAL(oDebug("Server.Class.Method('lcFormVars','lcIni',0)")
```

This causes Visual FoxPro to call a program file called oDebug—a PRG file that you have to create to respond to this request. This file must be located in your global Visual FoxPro path as set from Tools/Setting options (most likely your VFP startup path or your Utils directory) or in the Windows System directory where the server is actually starting from. The latter is the most reliable place because VFP is guaranteed to find it there.

 To make sure that the VFP runtime finds oDebug, I add a Config.fpw file to my WINNT\SYSTEM directory:

```
PATH=C:\wwapps\FoxISAPI;c:\wwapps\common
```

To put a server into debug mode, you have to modify your server entry in FoxISAPI.ini and set the number of servers to load to the special value of 0:

```
[FIDemo.FIDemoServer]
FiDemo.FiDemoServer=0
```

Once you make this change, you have to unload your servers using the FoxISAPI Reset link. If you look at the status display for the FIDemo.FIDemoserver entry, you'll see that the actual ProgId is pointing at VisualFoxPro.Application instead of FIDemo.FIDemoserver.

The next time you load your server, it brings up the Visual FoxPro development environment as an Automation object and runs oDebug.prg. In the code below I have oDebug.prg pop up the Debugger at startup so you can step through the code to see what's happening, but you can set a breakpoint anywhere once you've assured yourself that this code will work. When oDebug.prg gets control it needs to parse the parameter, which contains the full server string plus the three standard FoxISAPI parameters. Once the class and method have been parsed, you can create an instance of the class as a VFP object (rather than an Automation object) and then use EVAL() to invoke the method with the parameter returned. The code looks something like this:

```
LPARAMETER lcParameter

*** lcParameter = full OLE server string
*** FirstServer.TfirstServer.Process('Method=TestUser=Id1&Name=Rick',
                                      'fox.ini',0)

*** Make VFP Visible
_SCREEN.visible=.T.

SET STEP ON

*** Force server to go to this directory
SET DEFAULT to c:\wwapps\foxisapi

*** Load FOXISAPI framework classes
DO LoadFoxISAPI
DO WCONNECT

*** Add any other procedures/classes
SET PROCEDURE TO FIRSTSERVER ADDITIVE

*** Parse the Server string
lnDot2=AT(".",lcParameter,2)
lnBracket=AT("(",lcParameter)

lcParms=EXTRACT(lcParameter,"(",")")
lcClass=EXTRACT(lcParameter,".",".")
lcMethod=SUBSTR(lcParameter,lnDot2 +1, lnBracket - lnDot2 -1)

*** Create the parse Class name
oServer=CREATE(lcClass)

*** Now run the parsed method with the parameters
*** Return returns back to the foxisapi.dll COM client
RETURN EVAL("oServer."+lcMethod+"("+lcParms+")")
```

Notice that you need to explicitly set up your environment here, because VFP starts in your System directory. As with any Automation application, you need to set the default directory. wwFoxISAPI handles this in the Init, but you'll need to do this here first in order to be able to load the classes needed to create an instance of the class. Also, you need to load any class libraries that normally would be built into your project, because you're now calling your server class as a standard VFP class. Hence the SET PROCEDURE TO and the call to LOADFOXISAPI and WCONNECT, which load the framework classes into memory.

Once this code gets control, though, VFP is in full development environment mode. You can SET STEP ON to bring up the debugger and press CTRL-F2 to bring up a command window. Off you go to debug your server interactively.

There are a couple of serious caveats to debug mode. First, because FoxISAPI always calls oDebug, you need to customize this file for each server you debug. Paths, class libraries and procedure files need to be loaded as appropriate to set up your environment. Because it's not configurable, you'll have to manage these settings on your own, probably with backed-up copies of oDebug.prg for each configuration or #DEFINEs to bracket code for each server.

Much more serious is the problem of the VFP COM object's EVAL() method truncating parameters at 256 characters. If you submit a form that has lots of fields on it, the FoxISAPI request on VisualFoxPro.Application will always fail with a COM error. There's no workaround, which means you can't debug requests with lots of POST data and you must resort to code-based debugging, sending output to file to check values and program flow. It's not a pretty picture, but you can debug most basic requests just fine.

Summary

This chapter has taken you through the mechanics of FoxISAPI and given you some ideas of how you can employ this powerful tool to build your own flexible Web applications. There's no doubt that this tool requires a fair amount of understanding of Visual FoxPro COM objects work. At least a basic knowledge of how COM security is implemented for COM objects launched in the Web server's execution context is required to make FoxISAPI work and to understand how to handle the inevitable issues you'll run into when you start out with it. Using the wwFoxisapi class provided should ease some of that pain by providing pre-fab code for doing common operations and providing an error handler that will catch most errors before they hang your server. The bottom line is that FoxISAPI is more difficult to get started with than most other tools.

On the other hand, once you get through the initial installation issues, FoxISAPI has a lot to offer in terms of flexibility of the kinds of applications you can build with it. Because it relies exclusively on FoxPro code, you can take full advantage of the flexible language and object-oriented features as well as the data engine. With a few framework classes it's also possible to migrate forms and even reports to the Web using those visual tools to build the core logic, and using Web request handlers to simply "drive" the visual tools. The advantage of these approaches is that you get to build and test your applications separately from the Web interface.

FoxISAPI pros
- Provides a fast and efficient interface to the Web server.
- The internal FoxISAPI pool manager makes this tool the most scalable solution for Visual FoxPro code available from Microsoft.
- Flexible because it uses FoxPro code exclusively.
- Offers native data access and full access to the FoxPro language.
- Extensible with framework code that can provide sophisticated, high-level tools.

FoxISAPI cons

- Difficult first-time configuration.
- Servers can only be COM objects.
- Difficult to debug your applications due to the COM-only nature of servers.
- Unsupported by Microsoft.

Section 3
Client-Side Development

Client-side development is becoming more popular as people realize that there's more to the Internet than HTML and e-mail. The ability to use the Internet as a network is a powerful concept. It's entirely possible to have a rich Visual FoxPro client application driving a Web server on the other end of an Internet connection, allowing logic and data to be shared across the wire. Harnessing the power of the Internet in your standalone or browser-hosted applications can range from simple integration of e-mail and URLs to much more complex HTTP-based applications that use HTTP to drive applications over the Web.

Chapter 6 introduces some basic technologies that you can use to easily integrate Internet functionality into your applications. This chapter shows how to call Internet links, send e-mail, send and receive files via FTP, retrieve data from the Web via HTTP, integrate the Internet Explorer WebBrowser control, and even provide the ability to edit HTML directly from your standalone VFP applications.

Chapter 7 dives into the more advanced topic of building distributed applications using HTTP with logic on the client side and server side. In this chapter you'll find out how to have a VFP application act like a browser in order to drive a server application.

Chapter 6
Internet Enabling Your VFP
Applications

Reworking your applications to run over the Web is one way to take advantage of the Internet, but it's also an intense undertaking that requires you to completely rethink the way your applications work. In many situations, you can take advantage of Internet functionality at a much lower level simply by integrating specific functionality directly into your applications. This chapter deals with different ways to enhance your existing applications by using several quick and easy ways to plug in new functionality.

The easy way to the Internet

The Internet is a hodgepodge of protocols, which provide the connectivity features that make it so popular. The good news is that you can easily integrate much of this functionality into your own applications with a minimal amount of code. In this chapter I'll show you how to access the Web in a number of different ways, from using the powerful Shell interface to using the Internet Explorer WebBrowser control in your own applications, to using low-level HTTP requests to pull data into your applications from the Web. I'll also show you how to send Internet e-mail and how to use FTP from within your applications to send and retrieve files from an FTP server.

The focus of this chapter is on providing access to basic Internet functionality, rather than totally redesigning your application to be a true distributed application. Don't dismiss the simplicity of some of these tools and techniques—they provide useful functionality with minimal effort.

The Shell API

One of the easiest and powerful features of the Windows operating system is the Shell API. This API is not Internet specific but it provides some cool features for Internet use. It provides a mechanism for "executing" any kind of document that Windows knows about. Using this API you can "run" a Word document or an .EXE file, access a URL in your default browser, force an e-mail window to pop up, or bring up your favorite HTML editor to edit an HTML document. The interface works through a mechanism called *monikers,* which is essentially the Windows way to parse command lines. If Windows can recognize a moniker, it will attempt to execute it the same as it does when you double-click on a document with a known extension in the Windows Explorer.

The Shell API is implemented in several different ways, the simplest of which is an API call you use in your Visual FoxPro applications. To try it, create the following function:

```
FUNCTION ShellExec
LPARAMETER lcLink, lcAction, lcParms

lcAction = IIF(EMPTY(lcAction), "Open", lcAction)
lcParms = IIF(EMPTY(lcParms), "", lcParms)

DECLARE INTEGER ShellExecute ;
    IN SHELL32.dll ;
    INTEGER nWinHandle, ;
    STRING cOperation, ;
    STRING cFileName, ;
    STRING cParameters, ;
    STRING cDirectory, ;
    INTEGER nShowWindow

DECLARE INTEGER FindWindow ;
    IN WIN32API ;
    STRING cNull,STRING cWinName

RETURN ShellExecute(FindWindow(0, _SCREEN.caption), ;
                    lcAction, lcLink, ;
                    lcParms, SYS(2023), 1)
```

and then try the following links (adjust the paths as necessary):

```
ShellExec("http://www.west-wind.com/")
ShellExec("ftp://ftp.west-wind.com/")
```

You'll find that in both instances the ShellExecute API brings up the currently selected default browser (yes, this can be Netscape), and attempts to load the page you specified from the Web. You can also force your e-mail client to pop up:

```
ShellExec("mailto:billg@microsoft.com")
```

with Billy's name already entered into the To: field and the message window ready for you to start typing your latest reason for hating Windows. Although the Shell API can be used to access any link that you could use in an HTML document's HREF link, you can also access other things on your system:

```
*** Open Explorer in c:\temp
Shellexec("c:\temp\")

*** Runs VFP
ShellExec("c:\vstudio\vfp98\vfp6.exe")

*** Opens a word document
ShellExec("c:\Webbook\Chapter7\Chapter7.doc")

*** Opens a Zip file in WinZip
ShellExec("c:\downloads\southpark.zip")
```

You can also cause documents to be edited and printed, if the document type supports it:

```
*** Visual Interdev comes up
ShellExec("http://www.west-wind.com/", "Edit")
ShellExec("c:\Webbook\Chapter7\Chapter7.doc", "Print")
```

The former causes the resulting HTML from the West Wind site to be opened in your favorite HTML editor (if you have one configured), ready for editing. The latter fires up Microsoft Word and prints the requested document.

Because it has the ability to bring up a Web browser, this API is an easy way to bring people to your Web site by clicking on a button or menu option. You can easily integrate this functionality to take users to information pages, update pages, and of course, order pages to buy more stuff from you. You can even use it to display customized information, or information that's updated on a regular basis, simply by using naming conventions for the HTML pages on the server (how about a tip of the day with HTML pages, such as Tip102098.htm?). You can also cause the request to be dynamic through the URL query string by querying a dynamic server link such as an ASP page or FoxISAPI request:

```
ShellExecute("http://www.west-wind.com/wwThreads/default.asp?MsgId=_SA012344")
```

This takes you directly to the specified message on this message board application. You could conceivably display query information on the server in the same fashion.

In addition, the API makes it easy to show HTML in your applications, either from file or from a string. Here's a useful little function that uses ShellExecute to display an HTML string in the browser:

```
FUNCTION ShowHTML
LPARAMETERS lcHTML, lcFile, loWebBrowser

lcHTML = IIF(EMPTY(lcHTML), "", lcHTML)
lcFile = IIF(EMPTY(lcFile), SYS(2023) + "\_HTMLView.htm",lcFile)

STRTOFILE(lcHTML, lcFile)

IF VARTYPE(loWebBrowser) = "O"
  *** If a browser object was passed use it
  *** instead of an external browser window
  loWebBrowser.Navigate(lcFile)
ELSE
  ShellExecute(lcFile)
ENDIF
RETURN
*EOP ShowHTML
```

You can simply pass any HTML string to this function and it will render it in the browser and pop it open. If you have an existing instance of a WebBrowser object or an IE COM object (more on this later), you can render the HTML within that object instead of in the external window controlled by ShellExecute.

You can also call the Shell API's COM interface to access all sorts of interesting Windows functionality:

```
o = CREATEOBJECT("Shell.Application")
o.Open("http://www.west-wind.com/")

*** Fire up Windows Dialogs modally
o.SetTime()
o.FindFiles()
o.ShutDownWindows()
o.FileRun()
o.ControlPanelItem("Network")
```

"Open" works very much the same as the ShellExecute API call, only it always uses the Open action verb. There's no Edit or Print option, so you have to use ShellExecute for those operations. However, the Shell API also includes access to most Windows desktop operations—but keep in mind that these operations all require user intervention of some sort. These methods bring up dialogs in which the user must fill in information or click a button to continue. What does all this have to do with the Internet? Not much—but you might find these related operations useful.

What about Visual FoxPro's Hyperlink object?

Visual FoxPro 6.0 introduces a new class named Hyperlink. It's not well-named, because it's really a thin wrapper around the Internet Explorer that allows you to navigate to a specific Web page. Unlike the ShellApi calls, it doesn't work with all browsers, only Internet Explorer. Its primary purpose is to launch a new browser window from an ActiveDoc. This doesn't mean you can't use it in regular applications. The object exists so that you don't have to worry about making API calls or using a COM object, but realistically it doesn't provide much functionality—you're almost always better off using ShellExecute or the Shell COM objects directly.

The Hyperlink object is a non-visual control on which you make method calls to ask it to perform an operation. The most common thing you'll do is add it to a form, and then use it from a label, button, or other control, like this:

```
THISFORM.HyperLink1.NavigateTo("http://www.microsoft.com/")
```

In addition, you have GoBack and GoForward methods, which take you to the previous or next page.

Unfortunately, unlike ShellExecute, the NavigateTo method does not support all file types supported by the Shell—only Internet-related links. So accessing directory lists and even non-HTML files doesn't work. If you open a MailTo: link, you'll get a browser window with a failed navigation page, in addition to the opened e-mail editing window. Finally, the Hyperlink object will open a new window for every new site you access, rather than reusing an existing browser instance.

I suggest that you skip the Hyperlink object and use the Shell API or COM interfaces directly. You'll have much more control over the available functionality, and it's only slightly more difficult to use these interfaces than the built-in Hyperlink object.

The Internet protocols of wwIPStuff

wwIPStuff is a class library that provides common Internet protocols, wrapped in a single, easy-to-use class library. The class library is freely distributable for owners of this book; otherwise it's available as shareware from West Wind Technologies. The library was originally built to provide functionality that would be commonly required in the course of Web application development. It includes support for SMTP e-mail, FTP functionality, domain name lookup and reverse lookup, the ability to dial a RAS connection, and a number of other features related to driving HTTP connections through code. The HTTP features are described in great detail in the next chapter.

Sending SMTP Internet e-mail

E-mail continues to be the most popular activity on the Internet, and more and more Internet applications are taking advantage of an e-mail interface. wwIPStuff implements SMTP e-mail via a DLL interface in wwIPStuff.dll, which contains a C++ e-mail class that performs the socket operations of communicating with the mail server. The VFP code simply acts as the front end to a function with a large parameter interface that passes the information to the DLL for processing.

To install, simply make sure that you have wwIPStuff.vcx/.vct, wwUtils.prg and wwIPStuff.dll in the current path or somewhere along the Visual FoxPro SET PATH. Using the class itself is very simple. You have to set only a few relevant properties on the wwIPStuff object to send a message:

```
SET CLASSLIB TO wwIPSTUFF ADDITIVE
SET PROCEDURE TO wwUtils ADDITIVE

loIP = CREATEOBJECT("wwIPStuff")

loIP.cMailServer = "your.mailserver.com"  && or IP address
loIP.cSenderEmail = "yourname@yours.com"
loIP.cSenderName = "Jimmy Roe "

loIP.cRecipient = "jroe@roe.com "
loIP.cCCList = "jbox@com.com,ttemp@temp.com"
loIP.cBCCList = "somebody@nowhere.com"

loIP.cSubject = "wwIPStuff Test Message"
loIP.cMessage = "Test Message body" + CHR(13)

*loIP.cAttachment = "c:\temp\pkzip.exe"

*** Wait for completion
llResult = loIP.SendMail()
IF !llResult
   WAIT WINDOW loIP.cErrorMsg
```

```
ELSE
   WAIT WINDOW NOWAIT "Message sent..."
ENDIF

RETURN
```

wwIPStuff is a minimalist SMTP client that lets you use the class interface to set the e-mail properties and the SendMail method to actually submit the e-mail message. You can specify the sender's e-mail name (note that you can potentially spoof an e-mail address—that's the way SMTP happens to work) and then supply recipient lists. You can provide either a single e-mail address or a list. When using the latter, separate each primary recipient, CC and Blind CC recipient with commas. The actual e-mail message consists of a subject line and message body, which can be of any length. You can optionally attach one file to the message; files are encoded to MIME format.

E-mail messages can be sent in two different modes: Synchronous or Asynchronous. Plain SendMail() waits for completion of the Send operation, and then returns error or completion information along with a valid .T. or .F. result. If .F. is returned, you can check the cErrorMsg property for the error that occurred. SendMailAsync() sends the message without waiting for a result. The operation runs on a separate thread, so it appears to the client application that the return is instant. When running Web applications in particular, this is the preferred way to send messages, to avoid blocking the server while waiting for the mail sending operation to complete.

Note that SMTP is a server-based protocol, which means that messages sent to it are submitted but not necessarily processed immediately. This means that, even with the SendMail call that returns a good status code, there's no guarantee that the e-mail message actually got to its recipient. The only way you'll find out about an invalid e-mail address or a closed mailbox is by the returned mail error that will arrive in your inbox.

FTP transfers

wwIPStuff provides a number of FTP functions that facilitate file uploads and downloads. The FTP functions are implemented using VFP code that talks to the system WinInet.dll FTP functions. I don't have enough room here to print the source code, but it's very similar to the HTTP code for Distributed HTTP applications described in Chapter 7. The full VFP source code is also available in wwIPStuff.vcx.

To download a file via FTP, use the following code:

```
SET CLASSLIB TO wwIPStuff ADDITIVE
SET PROCEDURE TO wwUtils ADDITIVE

loFTP = CREATEOBJECT("wwFTP")

lnResult = loFTP.FTPGetFile("ftp.westwind.com", "pkunzip.exe", ;
   "c:\temp\pkunzip.exe")
IF lnResult # 0
  ? loFTP.cErrorMsg
  RETURN
ENDIF
```

FTPGetFile() is a pure synchronous call that grabs an online file and downloads it to a local file. Because it's synchronous and doesn't provide any transfer-status feedback on long files, this function might make users think that their machine has locked up.

To work around this problem, there's FTPGetEx(), which supports event-method calls to allow you to cancel a download and handle a status display. To do so, you have to either subclass wwFTP or drop it onto a form and implement the OnFTPBufferUpdate() method. The full code looks like this:

```
SET CLASSLIB TO wwIPStuff additive
SET PROCEDURE TO wwUtils additive

PUBLIC o
o = CREATEOBJECT("myFTP")
WAIT WINDOW NOWAIT "Alt-x to abort download..."
ON KEY LABEL ALT-X o.lCancelDownload = .T.

IF o.FTPConnect("ftp.west-wind.com") # 0
  ? o.nError
  ? o.cErrorMsg
  RETURN
ENDIF

IF o.FtpGetFileEx("wconnect.zip","c:\temp\wconnect.zip")  # 0
  ? o.nError
  ? o.cErrorMsg
  RETURN
ENDIF


ON KEY LABEL ALT-X
RETURN

DEFINE CLASS myFtp AS wwFTP

FUNCTION OnFTPBufferUpdate
LPARAMETER lnBytesDownloaded, lnBufferReads, lcCurrentChunk

DO CASE
CASE lnBufferReads > 0
  WAIT WINDOW "Bytes read: " + TRANSFORM(lnBytesDownloaded) NOWAIT

  *** DoEvents    && Handle a UI event like Cancel Button Click
CASE lnBufferReads = -1
  WAIT WINDOW "Download aborted..." TIMEOUT 2
ENDCASE
RETURN

ENDDEFINE
```

Here I'm using the Alt-X ON KEY LABEL command to trap an abort of the download by setting the FTP object's lCancelDownload flag to .T. When the flag is set, the FTP code aborts when the next chunk of data is to be fetched.

In order to display status information during the download, the OnFTPBufferUpdate method receives a running total of downloaded bytes. The parameters to this method hold the running total of bytes, the number of reads that have occurred so far, and the current chunk of data that was read. The last item is useful for building output incrementally for non-binary or other streamed data that can be read as it comes in. The lnBufferReads parameter contains a number greater than 0 while reading, and -1 if an error occurred or the operation was aborted (that is, lCancelDownload was set).

If you need to control other UI elements, such as a form with a Cancel button, you need to make sure that you call DoEvents in the update routine so that the UI event can fire and run.

You can also upload files in the same manner using the FTPSend and FTPSendEx methods. Here's an example of FTPSend (the SendEx version provides the same OnFTPBufferUpdate "events" as the FTPGetFileEx method):

```
o = CREATEOBJECT("wwFTP")
lnResult = o.FTPSendFile("ftp.west-wind.com", "c:\temp\pkunzip.exe", ;
                         "/pkunzip.exe", "username", "password")
IF lnResult # 0
  ? o.cErrorMsg
ENDIF
```

Note that the username and password are required only if you're uploading files to a restricted directory that doesn't allow uploads to anonymous users. This is generally the case with FTP uploads, but it's entirely up to the site administrator to set these permissions.

In addition to these functions, you can get a FTP directory listing and delete files on the server using the aFTPDir and FTPDeleteFile methods of the wwFTP object. Take a look at the class library and the included HTML Help file for more details about how to call these methods.

Using the Internet Explorer Shell COM interface

The Web browser is probably the most visible portion of the Internet today. Browsers are used everywhere and are increasingly prevalent in distributing information to users. It's only natural that there should be functionality to drive the browser programmatically to perform tasks from within your applications. The integration of Internet Explorer and Windows is a boon for developers who need to provide Web content in their applications.

In this section I'll describe how to programmatically add Web browser functionality to your applications, but keep in mind that this requires a full installation of Internet Explorer 4.0 or later. While you may argue with this point for the "fair competition" reasons that Microsoft foes have brought forth, I personally feel that this is a step in the right direction for making it possible to build sophisticated applications that use the browser programmatically. This leap forward would never have happened without the tight relationship between Internet Explorer and Windows. Let Netscape and Oracle complain—I'm stoked that we can easily build applications on top of this technology.

Earlier I demonstrated the ShellExecute API as a great way to easily access file content. This high-level API is part of the Windows Shell API, which is responsible for controlling the operation and behavior of the Windows Explorer shell. Much of that API is also exposed via several COM interfaces that allow you to drive the shell programmatically. The Windows

Shell interface includes Internet Explorer; it allows you to create an instance of the browser and control it via various navigation methods. Try this from the command window:

```
o = CREATEOBJECT("InternetExplorer.Application")
o.Top = 10
o.Left = 10
o.Width = 400
o.Height = 200
o.visible = .T.
? o.Navigate("http://www.west-wind.com/")
? o.Navigate("http://www.microsoft.com/")
? o.GoBack()
? o.LocationName              && Title of document
? o.Type                      && Document Type
```

Finding out about COM interfaces

When you're working with new COM objects, it's useful to know what functionality is actually available. The first step might be to look at the MSDN documentation, but it's incomplete for some of the system COM interfaces. To find out the real interface, look at the Type Library. To do so, use the Visual FoxPro Class Browser by selecting a Type Library (TLB) or the host .DLL directly (the Shell API lives in Shdocvw.dll in your SYSTEM directory). The Class Browser gives you a raw interface view of the type library, which is a little difficult to read, but you can see what's available with a little digging. Another choice is the Visual Studio OLEViewer utility, which provides the same information as the VFP browser but in a more visual format—it also allows you to jump from object to object. However, I think the best way to see a type library quickly is to use the Visual Basic Class Browser. Inside the VB development environment you can either add a reference to the object you want to work with, or—like the VFP Class Browser— open a DLL or TLB file directly. The advantage of VB is that the interface properly translates the types and provides cross-links to the parent classes. It also shows a much nicer view of the member properties, methods, and all the enumerated types (constants).

Although the COM ProgId for this object is InternetExplorer.Application, it's actually part of the same Shdocvw.dll that hosts the other Shell API COM functionality discussed above. If you look in the Class Browser, look for the IWebBrowser2 interface, which corresponds to the InternetExplorer.Application object.

Document availability

If you were to run the above code in a program on a fast machine, you'd run into Unspecified Error COM messages. These are caused by the fact that you can't call various document attributes until the document has finished loading. For example, the Type property isn't available until the document header has loaded into the browser. Because the browser loads the documents asynchronously, there's no guarantee that Type will be valid when your code hits it. With the COM object, your only recourse is to let the error happen, and keep retrying until it works. The Type property is a good one to use because it will always have a value—whether or not an error page is displayed.

After we discuss the WebBrowser control, you can use the DocumentComplete() event to figure out when a page has finished loading by setting a completion flag.

Capturing IE COM events

In order to do anything useful with the WebBrowser control in code, you need to be able to capture events from the COM object. Unfortunately, VFP doesn't natively support sinking COM object events (it can only sink ActiveX control events). Microsoft recently released a small utility called VFPCOMUtils that allows you to attach an event handler object to a COM object that fires events. To do this with the IE COM object, try the following (VFPComUtils is available from the Microsoft VFP Web site):

```
PUBLIC oVFPCOM, oIE, oIEEvents

oVFPCOM=CREATE('vfpcom.comutil')
oIE=CREATE('internetexplorer.application')
oIE.VISIBLE = .T.

*** Create a class of all events COM object exports
*** including method headers with parameters
*oVFPCOM.exportevents(y,'c:\temp\ieevents.prg')

oIEEvents=CREATE("IEEvents")

*** Let IEEvents handle events for IE COM obj
oVFPCOM.bindevents(oIE,oIEEvents)

oIE.navigate("http://localhost/default.asp")
```

If you run the commented-out Exportevents code above and return, the utility will create a PRG file that is a skeleton object containing all event methods that the interface exposes, sans the implementation code. Input parameters are provided for you so you can get started quickly filling in the blanks. Take this code and append it to the original PRG file above (trimmed):

```
DEFINE CLASS IEEvents AS CUSTOM

PROCEDURE StatusTextChange(TEXT)
SET MESSAGE TO TEXT
ENDPROC

PROCEDURE DownloadComplete()
ACTI SCREEN
 ? "Download Complete"
ENDPROC

PROCEDURE TitleChange(TEXT)
ACTI SCREEN
 ? "TitleChange "+Text
```

```
ENDPROC

PROCEDURE
BeforeNavigate2(pDisp,URL,Flags,TargetFrameName,PostData,Headers,CANCEL)
ACTI SCREEN
  ? "BeforeNavigate"
ENDPROC

ENDDEFINE
```

With all this code in place, you can now capture events for the IE COM object reference. It's important to capture events, especially the DocumentComplete and NavigateComplete2 events, which are required hooks to let you know that the document is in place and ready for navigation and programmatic access. I'll talk more about this with the WebBrowser control in the next section.

The WebBrowser ActiveX control

The IE WebBrowser control and the IE COM object share much of the same object model. In fact, the actual HTML document interface is identical because both use the same MSHTML engine. Internet Explorer itself is just a thin EXE shell that uses the HTML document container, which is rather similar in all of Microsoft's implementations of it. Even the external interface is similar to the WebBrowser control, exposing more functionality for your programs to work with. Keep in mind as you read that much of the WebBrowser control's programmatic functionality also applies to the IE COM object. The main difference is that the ActiveX control supports events directly so that you can capture them in the ActiveX control's event functions. With the COM object, you have to manually attach the VFPComUtils object to capture the events and write a separate class to handle the events. In most cases you'll want to use the ActiveX control, since it's easier to control, but you have the option to choose either one almost interchangeably with respect to the object model.

> **❗ Distributing the WebBrowser control**
> The WebBrowser control is part of a **full** Internet Explorer installation. Microsoft allows you to redistribute Internet Explorer as a part of your application by signing up for a free redistribution agreement—or you can simply ask users to download and install it if they don't already have it. The WebBrowser control is probably the best example of why Microsoft is coupling IE so closely with the operating system. It gives your applications the power to totally control the browser through application code, making it become part of the application.

Here's an example of how to use the IE WebBrowser control on a form—try building a desktop browser that can be left active at all times as your VFP desktop background. **Figure 6.1** demonstrates the results.

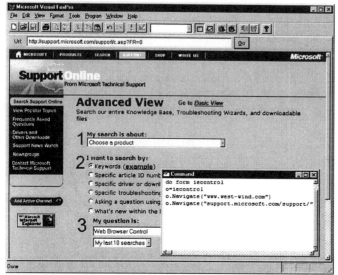

Figure 6.1. *This form demonstrates a good use of the WebBrowser control as a VFP desktop backdrop by using the new VFP 6.0 AlwaysOnBottom form property. Notice that the command window (and any other forms you open up) runs on top of the browser desktop. The form navigation is driven through VFP and the form's Navigate method.*

Follow these steps to create this "Active Desktop" for VFP:

1. Create a form and add the Microsoft WebBrowser control to it. Name the control *oBrowser*.

2. In the browser's Refresh method, add a single line with NODEFAULT. This is required whenever you use the control; otherwise you'll receive an "Unspecified Error" the first time you run the browser.

    In StatusTextChange add:

    ```
    LPARAMETERS text
    SET MESSAGE TO text
    ```

    In NavigateComplete2 add:

    ```
    LPARAMETERS pdisp, url
    THISFORM.txtUrl.value = URL:
    ```

3. In the form, add a method called Navigate and have it do the following:

    ```
    LPARAMETER lcUrl
    THISFORM.oBrowser.Navigate(TRIM(lcUrl))
    ```

4.   Add a textbox and button, named *txtURL* and *btnGo*, respectively. Add the following to the button's code:

```
THISFORM.Navigate(TRIM(THISFORM.txtUrl.Value))
```

5.   Finally, set up the form with the following properties: Titlebar = .F., WindowState to Maximized, and AlwaysOnBottom = .T. The last property allows the browser to sit below any other form in the Fox desktop to give the illusion of a desktop application. (You also could use this for a seamless HTML document in an application! This document could then drive your help, company links, and so on.) The form also has some resize code to force the browser form to maximize. See the code for details.

To test the form:

```
DO FORM IEControl NAME oD LINKED
```

You can use it interactively to type in a URL or you can use a reference to the form to control it programmatically (this is the primary reason I added the Navigate() method to the form). So you can do this:

```
oD.Navigate("www.universalthread.com")
```

You now have a desktop browser that you can leave active while you work. Note that this is a standard VFP form, so if you need the real desktop you can simply call oD.Hide() and oD.Show() as needed.

The major difference between the IE control and the COM object is that the control exposes events that you can capture and respond to. In the above code I captured the StatusTextChanged event, for example, to set the VFP status bar and the NavigateComplete2 event to update the URL with the current location. There are a number of relatively self-explanatory events that you can play with.

The NavigateComplete2 and BeforeNavigate2 events are especially important. These events allow you to capture operations occurring inside the HTML document to allow or disallow requests to complete.

It's not just for Web content

The WebBrowser control has many uses that go way beyond the Web. HTML is not a good tool for everything, but it's nice for certain applications that require a rich graphical experience. Sometimes it's just easier to display information as HTML—sometimes it's a good idea to build output dynamically with VFP code into HTML format and use the browser control as the preview mechanism to see what it will actually look like.

Here's an example of how I've used the WebBrowser control in an application. I've built a tool that helps to build HTML Help. HTML Help is by its very nature built with HTML. Rather than building all topics by creating HTML documents directly, I store the help content in a database. The content is a bit structured but contains only minimal formatting and a few HTML markup tags that enhance plain text—like bold, italic, list and a few style tags.

(Anything can be embedded, but generally markup beyond body text is light.) The help information is stored in a VFP table that contains various fields that categorize each help topic. The input fields are entered in plain text and exitboxes, stored in the table. The field values are then generated dynamically into HTML in preview and final output modes. By doing it this way I'm not closely tied to Microsoft's Help strategy (which seems to be changing frequently), and I get more flexibility in building my help topics to boot because I can manipulate the topic content separately from its presentation via HTML. For example, it's easy to auto-generate help topics for, say, a class library for developer documentation by importing a VFP class library.

The idea is simple: The data is stored in a database, but the final output is displayed as HTML. Chapter 5 discussed a template-parsing engine that can easily generate FoxPro code and expressions into a text document using Active Server-like script tags. I actually use this same engine (wwVFPScript) to generate each topic on the fly to embed the actual help-file data into an HTML template. The result is an interface that can display each topic as it will look in its final form as HTML Help. **Figure 6.2** demonstrates what the Visual FoxPro application looks like. When the record pointer is moved in the TreeView, a new HTML document is generated (in this case as a file) and reloaded into the WebBrowser control. The pseudo-code for the Refresh operation looks something like this:

```
lcHTML = oHelp.RenderTopic()
STRTOFILE(lcHTML, ProjectPath + "_preview.htm")
THISFORM.oBrowser.Navigate("file://" + ProjectPath + "_preview.htm")
```

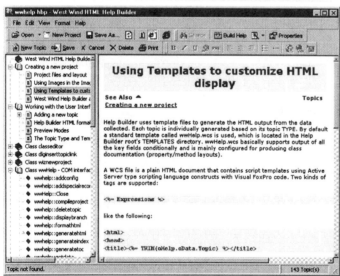

Figure 6.2. This form displays data from a database as HTML in a browser control. As the help record is changed via the TreeView, each topic is generated on the fly as HTML and displayed in the browser. This gives you the ability to use HTML features like cross-links, images, and rich text display that would be otherwise difficult to achieve in a VFP form.

In this application I chose to redisplay the entire page every time, by generating a document to disk and then refreshing the browser with the disk file by doing this:

```
THISFORM.oBrowser.Navigate(SYS(2023) + "\_Preview.htm").
```

The Internet Explorer document model

In the Help Builder application I chose to regenerate the help topic as a whole each time. But it's also possible to update the existing HTML document directly by accessing the Internet Explorer document model. The MSHTML engine used by Internet Explorer and the WebBrowser control exposes its entire document object model (DOM) programmatically. The object model is set up in such a way that you can access every tag of a loaded HTML document directly, and manipulate each one through its methods and attributes. At first this can be confusing because the sheer number of object types and the different attributes exposed by each seem overwhelming. But the model is fairly consistent, so once you learn a few of the common tags, it gets easier to pick up the others.

> ### HTML object model documentation
> *It's important to have good documentation, and I primarily use the Visual Basic Object Browser to look up each object type. To do this, open a project and add a project reference to Mshtml.dll in your SYSTEM directory or find the Microsoft HTML Object Library entry from the list of existing objects. Then go to the HTMLDocument object and drill down into the different tag types available. Once I find the proper objects, I use MSDN to look up the actual types and parameters needed to work with the interfaces.*

Manipulating the document through code

The ability to manipulate the document from the container application is extremely powerful. To run the following examples from the command window, you can do the following:

```
DO FORM IEControl NAME oForm LINKED

*** for space store the browser in o
o = oForm.oBrowser
```

Note that the following will work with any reference to a WebBrowser control, as well as a reference to the IE COM object, assuming a document is loaded. For example, once you have a document loaded, you can access and manipulate the HTML content with code like this:

```
*** Return HTML minus the header
? o.Document.Body.InnerHTML

*** Return text without HTML tags
? o.Document.Body.InnerText
```

Both commands access the HTML Document object of the browser, which allows reading and writing HTML directly from and to the browser window. The Body object encapsulates all of the HTML between the <body> and </body> tags in the document, and the InnerHTML property returns all of that HTML text. InnerText retrieves the same text with all HTML formatting removed. You can also get the OuterHTML, which includes the actual <body></body> tags, while InnerHTML does not:

```
*** Return HTML minus the header
? o.Document.Body.OuterHTML
```

InnerHTML and OuterHTML are supported by most objects in the Document object. In addition to reading, you can write to the document, which allows you to dynamically change the HTML of a document:

```
o.Document.Body.InnerHTML = "<h1>Welcome to Visual FoxPro</h1>"
```

The HTML on the right replaces the previously loaded document *body,* effectively giving the appearance of a new document. Note that you can't replace the entire HTML document, but only the *body* of the document. You can modify individual header tags using the various header collections, but there's no way to retrieve and set the full HTML document. The largest single string you can get is with the <body> tag. (This behavior is to change with IE 5 and beyond, where you will be able to grab and update the entire HTML document.)

This explains why I used file output in my HTML Help project above, because the user could customize the output template, including the headers, which include complex style sheets. While the document exposes the headers as separate objects that can be modified, it gets a lot more complicated than simply replacing the entire document text. Because the templates have extensive style sheets, meta tags and other header elements, I opted to go the simpler route of simply writing to file. You might think writing to file is slow, but the difference between writing the file and changing the document is not noticeable for anything but the smallest documents.

Tag collections

Your access is not limited to the entire document as a whole, but you can directly manipulate any portion thereof. All HTML tags in a document are accessible via collections that allow iterating through all instances of each tag. For example, if you wanted to get all the bold text in a document, you could do this:

```
FOR EACH loTag IN o.Document.All
   IF UPPER(loTag.Tagname) == "B"
      ? loTag.InnerHTML
   ENDIF
ENDFOR
```

Document.All is the master collection that allows you to go through every single tag in the document—which is exactly what the code above does. It runs through every tag and checks to see whether it's a bold tag, and if so, retrieves it for display.

There are a number of other predefined collections, such as Forms, Anchors, Images, Frames and Scripts. (For a full list, see MSDN or use the Object Browser on the MSHTML object.) To retrieve all HREF links in a page, use the following:

```
FOR EACH loLink IN o.Document.Links
   ? loLink.Href
ENDFOR
```

If you've ever wanted to build a Web spider, this should make your job rather easy!

Custom ID tags

Internet Explorer also supports the concept of custom ID tags, which are used by the HTML object model to parse the HTML text. For example, take a look at the following HTML code:

```
Visual FoxPro Version: <b ID="VFPVersion">n/a</b>

<form method="POST" action="CustomBrowserTags.htm">
  <p>Name: <input type="text" name="txtName" ID="txtName" size="20"></p>
  <p>Company: <input type="text" name="txtCompany" ID="txtCompany"
size="20"></p>
  <p><input type="submit" value="Save" name="btnSubmit"><input type="reset"
value="Reset"
  name="BtnClear"></p>
</form>
```

Notice the ID tags VFPVersion, txtName and txtCompany in the document. With this document loaded in the browser, you can easily get at these tags. Notice that the original document has *n/a* as the version number. To insert the real VFP version number from your code, do this:

```
o.Document.all.VFPVersion.innertext = Version()
```

When you do, *n/a* changes to the VFP version number in the HTML document! Think about this for a second—this mechanism allows you to build very easy data binding from a VFP host container into an HTML document if necessary, simply by delimiting every piece of dynamic data in the HTML page with its own custom ID tag. Using Assign methods on your objects you can have an HTML document update whenever a property is changed, for example.

Using a custom ID tag is an easy way to "bookmark" any area of the HTML document. All you need is Document.all.IDTag, and you get back an object reference to that tag. Once you have a reference, you can read and write the content and call methods on the object. The type of the object and the functionality available to it will vary based on the type of HTML object being referenced. The above code demonstrates how you can easily update an HTML form in a form's Refresh event with values from the currently selected record in a table. This is more impressive with the HTML form above. From VFP you can now do this:

```
*** Retrieve the HTML form variable
lcName = o.Document.all.txtName.value
lcCompany = o.Document.all.txtCompany.value

*** Set the HTML form variable
o.Document.all.txtName.value = "Rick Strahl"
o.Document.all.txtCompany.value = "West Wind Technologies"
```

This allows you to read and write values inside the HTML form! Using this mechanism, you can essentially bind Fox data directly to an HTML document displayed through your application. While I don't think this is the right way to go for everything (after all, why use a browser inside VFP to display data?), there are many occasions when HTML is simply a better way to display output. A good example is dynamic data that changes drastically in size and possibly even layout from record to record. Nested relations (such as many-to-many) are also sometimes easier to handle with a streamable output source like HTML, rather than a fixed-field-based format like input fields and grids.

To find out what type of object you're dealing with, you can always use the following:

```
? o.Document.All.txtName.ID
? o.Document.All.txtName.classname
? o.Document.All.txtName.tagname
```

although the classname often is not set. You should also get into the habit of checking for types before actually accessing these objects. If something is mistyped in your document or can't be found, or if you have a duplicate tag entry, you can get unexpected results. Trying to access an invalid object will result in a COM exception, so the up-front check will save you from having to catch those errors later. Use the TYPE() function to check for type "O."

DIV and SPAN tags for blocks of HTML

You can also mark entire sections of HTML with an ID. Above I used the ID attribute on a <b> (bold) tag. ID tags can be applied to any HTML element on a page. This includes range tags like DIV and SPAN, which are used to delimit blocks of HTML.

```
<DIV ID="Detail" Style="display:none">
Some HTML text goes here…
</DIV>
```

This HTML snippet won't be visible when first loaded, but you can access that range with:

```
o.Document.All.Detail.display = ""
```

To hide the text again:

```
o.Document.All.Detail.display = "none"
```

You can also use this mechanism to build HTML into a string via your own code and then assign the code directly to the DIV tag area.

```
lcHTML = loHelp.RenderTopic()
o.Document.All.Detail.innerHTML = lcHTML
```

You'll probably use DIV tags extensively in dynamic documents that show and hide data frequently, and in documents into which you want to embed generated HTML.

DIV is a block-based tag, while SPAN is a paragraph-based tag. If you want to delimit some text within a paragraph, use the SPAN tag. SPAN will not cause an HTML line break to occur, while DIV does. Otherwise the concept of SPAN tags is identical to DIV.

Selections and text ranges

It's also possible to get at selected text inside the HTML document. For example, the user could be looking at a large text document and highlight an article that needs to be imported into a specific field of the database. You could do:

```
REPLACE kb.article WITH o.Document.Selection.CreateRange.htmlText
```

The Selection object (IHTMLSelectionObject) is not the most intuitive—you explicitly have to create a range (IHTMLtxtRange) of selected text. If you pass no parameters to CreateRange, the default selected text is used from the HTML document. Once you have a reference to the selected text, the HTMLText property retrieves the actual text.

To replace text in a selection, use this:

```
? o.Document.Selection.createrange.PasteHTML("My HTML Text here")
```

Capturing navigation events

Web applications are all about hyperlinks and navigation from one location to another, and the WebBrowser control allows you to control navigation with various navigation events that fire in the control. The most important of these is the BeforeNavigate2 event, which occurs as soon as the user clicks on a link or submits a form—anything that causes the browser to display a new document. The event fires *before* the browser actually navigates to the new page, which gives you a hook to capture the request for navigation and change it as you see fit. Here you can also cancel navigation altogether, so that code can run without navigation taking place, which allows you to run some Fox operation instead of a browser navigate.

One use for this might be to capture any links that go outside your company by checking the URL parameter for the appropriate domain names or IP addresses. You can also capture any link and change it. For example, you could check to see if any link to the Netscape site is accessed and automatically change that link to go to the Microsoft site instead. That's a silly example, but there might be very legitimate uses for URL redirection at the application level.

For stand-alone applications it's even more important to capture navigation events. Rather than going out to the Internet, applications typically must perform operations before displaying data. For example, in Help Builder I want to capture a cross-link the user clicks on, and then treat it like just another page generation for displaying a new help topic. This is all controlled via VFP logic that retrieves the data from the database and renders it as HTML. I handle this code using a script hook in the BeforeNavigate2 event. All links that I want my application to handle look like this:

```
Vfps://EventId/Parameter1/Parameter2/
```

The following code in BeforeNavigate2 can then retrieve these event IDs and parameters:

```
*** ActiveX Control Event ***
LPARAMETERS pdisp, url, flags, targetframename, ;
            postdata, headers, CANCEL

DO CASE

*** HANDLE any URL's that have VFPS
CASE LEFT(UPPER(url),7) = "VFPS://"
   lcCommand = UPPER(EXTRACT(url, "//", "/"))
   DO CASE
   *** Order Id key - show that order
   CASE lcCommand = "TOPIC"
      lcTopic = SUBSTR(url, RAT("/",url) + 1)
      THISFORM.ShowInvoiceForm(lcOrderid)
      *** Don't want to actually show URL
      CANCEL = .T.
   CASE lcCommand = "HELP"
      THISFORM.ShowHelp()
      CANCEL = .T.
ENDCASE
```

BeforeNavigate2 receives many parameters but they are mostly self-explanatory. The most important ones are URL and Cancel. The URL contains the HREF link or Form Action that the user came from, which is usually the key that you can check for a specific action to happen. The Cancel flag is passed in by reference; when you set this value to .T., it prevents IE from navigating to the requested page. If your application handles the request and performs an action that causes the browser display to update on its own, you'll want to Cancel. If you want some action to occur but still want the browser to go to the requested URL, leave Cancel alone or set it to .F.

The above code works by assuming that any captured links start with a protocol ID of VFPS, so processing occurs only on links with that prefix. (You can make up your own scheme, of course—VFPS was originated by Ken Levy and stands for VFPScript. The term has come to mean any code that is handled by VFP.) Extract() is a function in wwUtils that extracts strings from within another string—in this case it looks for the double forward slash (//) and the single slash (/) that should contain the event ID. Depending on the type of ID returned, you can then grab additional parameters by parsing the string as needed.

Note that VFPS is an invalid browser protocol, so unless you set Cancel = .T. you'll get a browser error, unless you change the URL to some valid value or link.

Accessing HTML script from your VFP code
Not only can you manipulate the document, but you can also cause things to *happen* in the HTML page. Once you get an object reference to an object, you can call any of its methods and cause it to do something. For example, you can get a reference to a button and call its Click method:

```
o.Document.all.btnClear.Click()
```

You can also call any script code directly using the document's Script object. Assume you have a method called ValidateInput() inside the HTML document as VBScript or JavaScript. You can cause that to fire with the following code:

```
o.Document.Script.ValidateInput("parameter")
```

This essentially allows you to control an HTML application through code fired from a VFP host application. Note that any script code must be in the HTML document's header to be accessible through Document.Script. If you have multiple blocks of code in script tags, only the first block is recognized, so keep it organized in one place when creating pages accessed from VFP.

Passing an object

It also works the other way around, but it's a little more tricky. Because you can call methods inside the HTML document page, it's also possible for you to pass parameters to the script function or object method—including object references! You could, for example, pass an object reference to the calling form down to VBScript. To do this you need a global object that can accept the object reference and hold it inside the HTML document, and a method that sets it. See the following client-side HTML:

```
<body>
<script LANGUAGE="VBSCRIPT">
DIM oVFP   'public variable!

Function SetVFPObject(loVFP)
   Set oVFP = loVFP 'assign to public
End Function
Function MoveParent()
   oVFP.Top = 0
   oVFP.Left = 0
End Function
</script>
<form method="POST" action="CustomBrowserTags.htm">
   <p>Name: <input type="text" name="txtName" ID="txtName" size="20"></p>
   <p>Company: <input type="text" name="txtCompany" ID="txtCompany"
size="20"></p>
   <p><input type="submit" value="Save" name="btnSubmit"><input type="reset"
value="Reset"
   name="BtnClear" ID="btnClear"><input type="button" value="Move Parent Form to
0"
   onclick="MoveParent()"></p>
</form>
</body>
```

The global variable oVFP will receive the object reference that is set by the function call to SetVFPObject. Inside Visual FoxPro you can pass the reference down like this:

```
o.Document.Script.SetVFPObject(THISFORM)
```

The above HTML form has a button that calls the MoveParent script function which, in turn, uses the object reference set by the previous call. When you click it inside the browser, the form that hosts the browser window will move.

This is an obvious mechanism that you can use to capture nonstandard and control-level events inside the browser and pass them back to your Visual FoxPro application. You can use any object, not just a form. You could, for example, pass in a complex business object that could validate input directly inside the HTML script.

While this is very cool, it's important not to lose sight of what you want to accomplish. It might simply be easier at times to generate HTML pages with the data already embedded, rather than to manipulate an existing page through extensive script code with VFP object references. Simply put, using the browser to store logic can make applications more difficult because the logic is split up in multiple places. But there are also good uses for it, especially when the interface requires a Web front end that must run with DHTML, or when the display features of HTML provide clear advantages over form-based output.

Keep in mind that DHTML is Microsoft's future form interface, so these techniques will allow you to get a head start with interactive DHTML. Also, with DCOM over HTTP making its appearance in the near future, you'll be able to directly manipulate VFP objects over an Internet connection. This very same mechanism of passing object references can be used to access these objects over the Internet.

There's always the question of whether to use an inside-out or outside-in approach for cross-application objects. I've shown the outside-in approach that uses VFP to drive the browser. You could just as well use DHTML as your primary interface and simply use a VFP COM object created from within VBScript to access the business logic. Knowing when to use which is the tricky part—you have to figure that out on your own.

Things to watch out for with the Document object
It's important to understand that the object model is available only after a page has been loaded! If you try to access the control document before your first call to Navigate(), you will receive an error. For this reason it's a good idea to always initialize the WebBrowser control with a blank page by doing this:

```
oBrowser.Navigate("about:blank")
```

This generates a blank page that still has a document structure in place. This page is internal so it loads fast, too. You'll see how important this is in a second.

IE loads documents asynchronously. This means after you call Navigate(), control returns to you immediately, but the document may not yet be in place. This is especially critical if you're loading data off the Internet, but can also be a problem when you load long documents from disk or locally. When you access document properties, first check to see if the document is complete. You can use the DocumentComplete() or ProgressChanged() methods to set a flag to let the form know whether the document is ready for use:

```
FUNCTION ProgressChanged
LPARAMETER progress, progressmax
IF progress = -1
  THISFORM.lDocLoaded = .T.
endif
ENDFUNC
```

You should set lDocLoaded to .F. just before calling the Navigate() method on the browser (this is why I almost always wrap the browser's Navigate() method with a form-level Navigate() method). ProgressChanged with a progress value of -1 is more reliable than DocumentComplete, especially if you're accessing or calling script code in the page (see the example below).

Or you can add a special set of ID tags to the end of the document, before the </body> tag:

```
<span ID="EndOfDocument"></span>
```

Then check with TYPE("o.Document.All.EndOfDocument") = "O" to see whether that text has arrived yet. The latter will work only with documents of your own creation, but it's the easiest and most reliable way to check for completion (DocumentComplete doesn't always fire correctly).

Realize that running in a loop, waiting for completion, does not work well. VFP seems to lose events when running in a loop, causing neither the DocumentComplete nor ProgressChanged events to fire reliably. You'll need to handle these events directly, rather than running stall code and waiting for certain flags to get set.

Getting this right can be tricky—I've had mixed results with the IE 4 WebBrowser control, but I see stable results with the IE 5 control. An example of the technique that works is listed below.

A Web Browser example
Here's a simple example form that demonstrates some of these concepts in the context of a customer browser for the TasTrade database. **Figure 6.3** illustrates a Visual FoxPro form that uses the WebBrowser control to display its data.

This form uses several classes and utilities that were introduced in Chapter 5, including the wwResponse object for HTML rendering and the Web Connection scripting features used to actually render the page with embedded code. The HTML page displayed in the browser is generated by an HTML template that mixes FoxPro expressions and HTML. It is then "evaluated" by the wwEval object. The code is too complex to show here in its entirety, but in essence you see things like this in the document created with FrontPage:

```
<td height="23"><input name="txtCompany" value="<%= customer.company %>"></TD>
```

The <%= %> tag delimits any valid Visual FoxPro expression that is inserted into the document. The actual list of invoices is generated with Visual FoxPro code as a string and embedded into the HTML document with a single PRIVATE string variable. The code in VFP is in a form method called ShowInvoices(),which returns the string using the following code:

```
LOCAL lnCounter
PRIVATE pcInvoiceList

pcInvoiceList = THISFORM.ShowInvoices(customer.cust_id)
SELECT Customer

lcPage = THISFORM.cHTMLPagePath + "customer.wcs"
lcHTML = MergeText(FileToStr(lcPage))
StrToFile(lcHTML,"_preview.htm")

THISFORM.cNavigateTo = "SHOWRECORD"
THISFORM.oBrowser.Navigate(CURDIR() + "_Preview.htm")
```

The HTML page then embeds the pcInvoiceList string into the document with:

```
<span ID="InvoiceTableBody"><%= pcInvoiceList %> </span>
```

The entire HTML document is generated on the fly based on the HTML template page Customer.wcs. The MergeText function (in wwUtils.prg) is used to evaluate the page. The function returns a string that is then saved to a temporary file using STRTOFILE(). Once the file is saved to disk, I then use the browser's Navigate method to actually load the page into the browser window.

Notice the cNavigateTo assignment. I want to pass a form reference to the IE page, and I use the ProgressChanged event of the browser to assign it:

```
LPARAMETERS progress, progressmax
IF progress = -1
    IF THISFORM.cNavigateTo == "SHOWRECORD"
      THIS.document.script.SetRef(THISFORM)
      THISFORM.cNavigateTo = ""
    ENDIF
ENDIF
```

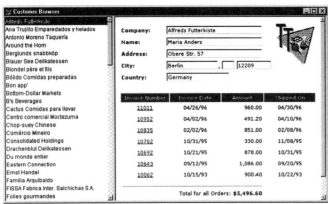

Figure 6.3. This form demonstrates a number of different ways to control the WebBrowser control from your VFP application: HTML rendering, capturing hyperlink clicks, and capturing edit events inside the browser.

The ProgressChanged event is the most reliable to capture the end of the document loading. "-1" means the document is fully loaded and the document is ready to be accessed.

Once loaded, the code sends a reference of the VFP form down to the script page:

```
THISFORM.oBrowser.document.script.SetRef(THISFORM)
```

And the following HTML script code accepts this call:

```
<script LANGUAGE="VBScript">
Dim goForm

Sub SetRef(ByVal loForm)
  Set goForm = loForm
End Sub

Sub Window_OnBeforeUnload
  Set goForm = nothing
End Sub
</script>
```

This code creates a public variable named goForm, which is set in SetRef(). Because I pass down the reference to the parent form, this gives the VBScript code the opportunity to make callbacks into the VFP form. The sample form uses this for field updates—if you change a value in the customer information fields, code like this will fire:

```
Sub txtCompany_onchange()
  goForm.UpdateField "customer.company", me.value
End Sub
```

The VFP form's UpdateField() method can handle automatically propagating the changes from the form into the database.

```
* UpdateField - generic field update routine
LPARAMETER lcField, lcValue
replace &lcField with lcValue
```

Note that this method could be called from anywhere in the VBScript page and would allow manual assignment of values to fields. Because any object can be passed down to the script page, imagine some VBScript code calling functions like `goForm.Application.Eval("Version()")` to retrieve information from VFP generically. There's nothing to stop the code from running a SQL command or using cool functions like STRTRAN that don't exist in VBScript.

This is not quite as trivial as direct data binding of VFP data, but it at least gives you the ability to hook into VFP code from within VBScript. You can capture any events in the IE form and make callbacks into the form to handle them as needed.

The generated invoice list consists of HREF links that all point to VFPS:// script links. These are handled in the WebBrowser control's BeforeNavigate2 event:

```
LPARAMETERS pdisp, url, flags, targetframename, postdata, headers, CANCEL

DO CASE
*** HANDLE any URL's that have VFPS
CASE LEFT(UPPER(url),7) = "VFPS://"
  lcCommand = UPPER(EXTRACT(url,"//","/"))
  DO CASE
  *** Order Id key - show that order
  CASE lcCommand = "ORDERID"
    lcOrderId = SUBSTR(url,RAT("/",url)+1)
    THISFORM.ShowInvoiceForm(lcOrderid)
    *** don't want to actually show URL
    CANCEL = .T.
  CASE lcCommand = "SHOWINVOICELIST"
    THISFORM.ShowRecord()
    *** don't want to actually show URL
    CANCEL = .T.
  ENDCASE
ENDCASE
```

Here I handle only two event IDs—one to display an invoice and one to display an invoice list. All other links that might be embedded are just passed along their merry way.

The Invoice form is a bit more complex and uses the Web Connection Scripting engine, also described in the FoxISAPI chapter. The invoice form actually runs extensive code inside the HTML page. Driving this is some fairly simple Fox code that uses the wwVFPScript object:

```
PARAMETER lcOrderId

lcOrderId = UrlDecode(lcOrderId)   && in wwUtils.prg

SELE Orders
LOCATE FOR Order_id = lcOrderId

loScript = CREATE("wwVFPScript")
lcScriptPage = FILETOSTR(THISFORM.cHTMLPagePath + "invoice.wcs")
lcVFPCode = loScript.ConvertPage(lcScriptPage, .T.)
lcHTML = loScript.RenderPageFromVar(@lcVFPCode, .T.)

STRTOFILE(lcHTML, "_preview.htm")

THISFORM.oBrowser.Navigate(SYS(5) + CURDIR() + "_preview.htm")
```

The HTML code bears more of the logic, so most of the logic is invisible in the Fox code and is moved into the HTML page. Here's the loop that displays the line items:

```
<% lnGrandTotal=0.00
lnTotal=0.00
lcId = Order_ID
SELECT ordItems
SCAN FOR Order_id = lcOrderId
    SELE Products
    LOCATE FOR Product_id = OrdItems.Product_id
```

```
      SELE OrdItems
      lnUnitPrice = Products.Unit_Price
      lnQty = OrdItems.Quantity
      lnTotal = lnQty * lnUnitPrice
      lnGrandTotal = lnGrandTotal + lnTotal
%>
<tr><td align="CENTER"><%= Product_ID %></td>
    <td><%= Products.Prod_Name %></td>
    <td align="CENTER"><%= Quantity %></td>
    <td align="RIGHT"><%= TRANSFORM(products.Unit_Price,"999,999.99") %></td>
    <td align="RIGHT"><%= TRANSFORM(lnTotal,"999,999.99") %></td>
</tr>
<% ENDSCAN %>
```

Scripted HTML is very powerful, especially when dealing with local applications, because the user can customize the look and feel as well as the basic logic of the application without recompiling any code.

This example is geared toward showing a variety of features that you can use to create local HTML-based applications, rather than showing a truly useful implementation of an HTML interface. Obviously there's little benefit to building this interface as HTML, as opposed to a VFP form-based interface. It looks modern and provides a nice way to display lists of varying lengths as HREF links, but beyond that it doesn't add much value. But many applications, especially those that require a rich visual interface or extensive user customization, can provide a much more flexible interface than you can provide with static forms. In other cases HTML is a requirement, as is the case for my HTML Help Builder product.

As I mentioned above, it's important to keep sight of what's important in your application. Using HTML in the application is something that should be carefully considered. It can be a big advantage if you need to build applications that need to run both on the local machine and over the Web. Both Web and standalone apps can potentially share logic that is used to create the HTML interface.

Editing HTML

Okay, so now you can easily display and even control the HTML interface, but many applications also require you to *edit* HTML. Once you start using HTML as a mechanism for your users to customize their user interface, or as the content for text data, it's important to simplify the process of creating HTML.

Unfortunately, the tools for accomplishing this are scarce. I've been taking two approaches: Using a VFP text box and a special method that allows insertion of common HTML markup tags, and using the Microsoft DHTML Edit Control.

One of the simplest ways to add HTML editing capability is to add a method to an EditBox that causes user selections to be replaced by HTML based on hotkeys or toolbar clicks for formatting text as bold, italic, and so on. The following is a truncated version of InsertHTML() in the wwHTMLEditbox class:

```
LPARAMETERS lcAction
LOCAL lcSelText

*** Markup tag string
lcLTag = THIS.cLTag  && <
lcRTag = THIS.cRTag  && >

*** Get the selected text and position
lcText = ""
lcSelText = THIS.SelText

DO CASE
CASE lcAction = "BOLD"
  lcText = lcLTag + "b" + lcRTag + lcSelText + lcLTag + "/b" + lcRTag
CASE lcAction = "ITALIC"
  lcText = lcLTag + "i" + lcRTag + lcSelText + lcLTag + "/i" + lcRTag
CASE lcAction = "LIST"
  lcText = lcSelText
  lcText = STRTRAN(lcText, CHR(13) + CHR(10), CHR(13))
  lcText = STRTRAN(lcText, CHR(13) + CHR(13), CHR(13))
  lcText = STRTRAN(lcText, CHR(13), CHR(13) + lcLTag + "li" + lcRTag + " ")
  lcText = lcLTag + "ul" + lcRTag + CHR(13) + lcLTag + "li" + lcRTag + " " + ;
    lcText + CHR(13) + lcLTag + "/ul" + lcRTag
CASE lcAction = "HREF"
  pcURL = lcSelText
  pcText = lcSelText
  plCancel = .F.
  loForm = CREATEOBJECT("wwHRefDialog",pcUrl,pcText)
  loForm.Show()
  goHelp.Closable = .T.
  IF !plCancel
    lcText = lcLTag + [a href="] + pcURL + ["] + lcRTag + ;
      pcText + lcLTag + [/a] + lcRTag
  ENDIF
CASE lcAction = "SETFONT"
  lcFont = GetFont()     &&"Arial",10,"N"
  IF EMPTY(lcFont)
    RETURN
  ENDIF

  lnColor = GetColor()

  lcFontTag = lcLTag + [span style="Font:]
  DIMENSION laFont[1]
  IF AparseString(@laFont,lcFont,",") = 3
    DO CASE
    CASE laFont[3] = "B"
      lcFontTag = lcFontTag + "Normal Bold "
    CASE laFont[3] = "BI"
      lcFontTag = lcFontTag + "Italic Bold"
    CASE laFont[3] = "NI"
      lcFontTag = lcFontTag + "Italic Normal"
    CASE laFont[3] = "N"
      lcFontTag = lcFontTag + "Normal "
    ENDCASE
```

```
  lcFontTag = lcFontTag + laFont[2] + "pt "

  IF lnColor >= 0
    lcFontTag = lcFontTag + laFont[1] + [;Color:] + HTMLColor(lnColor)
  ENDIF
ENDIF

lcFontTag = lcFontTag + ["] + lcRTag

lcText = lcFontTag + lcSelText + lcLTag + "/span" + lcRTag
ENDCASE

IF !EMPTY(lcText)
  THIS.SelText = lcText
ENDIF
```

This code grabs the current selection of the EditBox and then replaces it with the marked-up HTML text. You can do simple markups, like the bold and italic example above, or more complex ones that pop up dialogs to get additional information. For example, you might pop up a dialog to insert a hyperlink—it might ask for the target link as well as its caption. You can call this code from a toolbar button with:

```
THISFORM.oHTMLEdit.InsertHTML("BOLD")
```

You can also call this code from a menu option or from KeyPress events for specific keystrokes so that Ctrl-B will invoke the bold function. To add this functionality to a menu, use the following:

```
_SCREEN.ActiveForm.oEditHTML.InsertHTML("BOLD")
```

This will automatically convert the currently selected text to bold.

HTML markup formatting problems

Another problem with text stored as HTML is that pure HTML is not easy to type. HTML doesn't respect plain line breaks, for example, requiring <br> and <p> tags to break lines. It also requires special handling of characters such as spaces, quotes, and pound signs. To get around this issue, I typically use what I call *formatted HTML* for HTML data entry. Formatted HTML automatically formats plain text in such a way that it displays well as HTML. Line breaks are automatically converted into the appropriate HTML tags, as are special characters. When the user enters text, the HTML of the actual field value is unformatted, and it's reformatted into HTML when saved.

Actual HTML markup can also be a problem. For example, if you type text containing < or >, these characters are interpreted as HTML resulting in missing text. The same goes for script tags such as {}, which are used by JavaScript, and (again) those special characters that HTML interprets when rendering. This can be a problem if you're editing code.

To get around this problem, it's a good idea to use special characters for HTML markup, rather than native HTML markup tags. For example, in Help Builder I use <<tag>> instead of the <tag> format of native HTML. This way I can always convert any HTML displayed as text using ">" and "<" (which are HTML markup tags for displaying < and > symbols as text rather than tags). The following function converts user-entered, "formatted" HTML into the final HTML to be displayed in the browser:

```
*************************************************************************
* wwHelp :: FormatHTML
*********************************
***   Function: Fixes a message that has no formatting. Convert
***             <> and quotes and {}.
***       Pass:
***     Return: Old Setting
*************************************************************************
LPARAMETER lcHTML

*** Convert 'code tags' to extended chars
lcHTML = STRTRAN(lcHTML, THIS.cLTag, CHR(254))
lcHTML = STRTRAN(lcHTML, THIS.cRTag, CHR(253))

*** Convert HTML to plain text with &gt &lt
lcHTML = STRTRAN(lcHTML, "<", "&lt;")
lcHTML = STRTRAN(lcHTML, ">", "&gt;")
lcHTML = STRTRAN(lcHTML, '"', '"')

*** Convert extended chars back to HTML tags
lcHTML = CHRTRAN(lcHTML, CHR(254), "<")
lcHTML = CHRTRAN(lcHTML, CHR(253), ">")


lcHTML = STRTRAN(lcHTML, CHR(13) + CHR(10), CHR(13) )
lcHTML = STRTRAN(lcHTML, CHR(13) + CHR(13), "<p>")
lcHTML = STRTRAN(lcHTML, CHR(13) + CHR(13), "<p>")
lcHTML = STRTRAN(lcHTML, CHR(13), "<br>")

RETURN lcHTML
```

Using the DHTML Edit Control

Microsoft recently introduced a new control for editing HTML visually. The DHTML Edit Control is essentially an enhanced version of the IE WebBrowser control that handles keypress events. It allows you to edit HTML in full WYSIWYG mode that's 100% accurate for display in Internet Explorer.

You can download the DHTML control from the Microsoft Web site at http://microsoft.com/workshop/author/dhtml/edit/default.asp. The binary distribution is relatively small (250K) and requires just two files out of the installation BIN directory.

Once you've installed the control, you can add it to a form by following these steps:

1. Insert an OLE Container control.
2. Use the Create New option and select DHTML Script Control. (Note: don't use the Safe for Scripting version, which is more limited and doesn't let you load and save files locally!)

You can also dynamically add the control to a form using THISFORM.AddObject("oHTMLEdit"," DHTMLEdit.DHTMLEdit").

Because the control is actually an enhanced IE control, the entire Document object I described above for the WebBrowser control is available for programmatic manipulation—it's possible to select text and manipulate selected text using various events of the control. However, for the Edit Control, the Document object is accessible only through its *DOM* property, rather than through the Document property of the WebBrowser control. The Edit Control also exposes common hotkeys for text manipulation, like Ctrl-B for bold, Ctrl-I for italic, Ctrl-L for hyperlinks, and so on (see the DHTML control's HTML Help document for other hotkeys). Selections work as you would expect with full editing capabilities of the HTML text. This makes this control immediately useful for editing existing HTML documents.

The key method is: LoadUrl() to load a file or link from the Internet into the DHTML Edit Control. Once the document is loaded, you can edit it visually. Set the SourceCodePreservation flag to avoid reformatting any existing HTML code. Then edit the document by simply typing into it and using the control's various hotkeys. If you want to add custom markup beyond the built-in tags, you can add menu options that pick up the current document's selection and modify it as needed—similar to the wwHTMLEditBox code above. Instead of using SelText you'd use THISFORM.DOM.Selection.CreateRange.HTMLText() to read and PasteHTML() to paste text directly into the HTML source. You can save changes by grabbing the DocumentHTML property's value, STRTOFILE(), to save the HTML text to either the same file or a different one.

Another noteworthy feature of the Edit Control is its ability to handle special markup of things that are normally invisible in HTML text output. For example, embedded script tags are invisible to the HTML display, but are obviously contained in the HTML source. If you happen to delete text that includes the script tags, you'll inadvertently delete the code. You can use the ShowDetails property to have the control display *glyphs* in the document. The glyphs are placeholders for any invisible HTML elements and show up as graphical stars in the document. You should always leave ShowDetails set to .T. to make sure users of the control do not delete the invisible text. One problem with any markup text is that the control actually converts script tags into comments. To see what I mean, highlight some text and try the following steps in the DHTMLEdit Sample:

1. DO FORM DHTMLEdit and click the Go button to load the sample template page.
2. Select some text that includes some marked-up text (indicated by stars).
3. Click the Selection button, which prints the HTML of the selection to the VFP desktop.

You'll see that all of the Active Server tags (<%= %>) have been converted to comments. When you save or get the DocumentHTML property value, these comments are converted back into their proper tags, but this makes it very difficult to replace any tags efficiently. Script markup is very tricky to do, which is one reason I haven't used this control more often.

While the control is easy to use for displaying existing HTML, it's not quite so easy if you need to create HTML from scratch because you have to insert or at least pre-create HTML. There's no easy way to create the header section of an HTML document via the control, although you can of course preload an HTML file with the header already in place. (Headers include the title, META tags, style sheets, and so on.)

I won't go into great detail here, because I don't think this control is mature enough to use for real work yet. It definitely feels like a first cut in terms of its provided functionality. The visual editing features are adequate, but the control interfaces aren't quite there yet especially in regards to embedded script code. If you need HTML editing in your applications, I recommend that you check out this technology. Keep an eye on it as the technology evolves because it's an exciting prospect for allowing your users to work with HTML as their primary data input.

Summary

I hope this chapter has given you some ideas about how to extend your existing applications—and new ones to come—with Internet functionality. Most of the things I described take only a few lines of code to integrate and can provide great functional enhancements to your applications. Keep in mind that I've shown only a few of the more common things you can do. A number of third-party Internet ActiveX controls provide functionality for just about any Internet protocol available. If you need to add it to your apps, you can probably find a control to use.

Integration of the browser into applications is going to become ever more prominent. Even if you don't plan to use a browser in your own apps just yet, try to familiarize yourself with the object model. It's going to become the primary interface for desktop applications over the next few years because Microsoft has long promised a DHTML-based forms package capable of plugging into all of its development tools. Microsoft itself uses the browser and DHTML editing controls extensively today, so you can get an idea of how to put it to work in your own apps. Keep in mind that the browser is not just for Web content, but also for displaying your own application output.

Chapter 7
Building Distributed Applications
over HTTP

HTTP is much more than just a protocol used by the Web browser for transmitting HTML. In this chapter I'll show you how to use HTTP generically from a Visual FoxPro client application to execute logic on a Web server that is also running Visual FoxPro. You'll see how to retrieve content and data over HTTP, fire logic on the server and handle bidirectional transfer of data using familiar SQL commands over HTTP. This approach allows you to build rich GUI applications that take advantage of the distributed nature of the Internet without having to conform to a limited HTML interface. Using the techniques described here, you can extend the reach of existing applications across the Internet with minimal amounts of code—using all native Visual FoxPro code.

Hyper thinking

The Web has opened a whole new area of development for building truly distributed applications that can run over widely distributed networks. It has made it possible to build public-access applications at relatively minor cost compared to the infrastructure that was previously required to build this type of distributed application. Much of this has occurred through the use of the Hyper Text Transfer Protocol or HTTP.

Unfortunately, this new medium requires an entirely new approach to application development that focuses heavily on a limited user interface presented in HTML. HTML is a text-based markup language that is essentially line-based and produces output much in the way that ancient word processors like WordStar and WordPerfect of the DOS days did. Compared to typical rich Windows UI applications, even the new 4.0 versions of browsers have a lot of catching up to do in ease of use and usability of the form user interface used for data entry, which is typical for database applications. A lot of things can be done with HTML if you're imaginative, but the end result still leaves a lot to be desired in usability.

The good news is that you *don't have to* build distributed Web applications with HTML. It is absolutely possible to build an application using a rich UI and use the Web simply as a database interface to communicate. The key to making this work is HTTP.

HTTP is based on a client/server model. Typically, the Web browser is the client that requests data from the Web server. The browser is the display mechanism that shows the content served up by the Web server. The server is nothing more than a way station that figures out what type of content to provide to the client. HTTP is the underlying messaging protocol used for all transactions on the World Wide Web. Although the primary use of the protocol is to power the World Wide Web and HTML-based applications, it can do a lot more than plain HTML. Essentially, you can use HTTP to transport any kind of data over the Web, including binary data and even database files!

What if you could build an application using Visual FoxPro on the client side talking to a Web server on the other end of the connection that is also a Visual FoxPro application? Rather than using clumsy HTML you could take advantage of the power of VFP's user interface and ease of data access to build a truly user-friendly application and still get the distributed features promised by HTML-based Web applications.

Microsoft has provided high-level support for various Internet protocols in a system library called WinInet. This library supports relatively simple API interfaces for accessing HTTP, FTP, Gopher and WinSock. I showed the basics of this interface in the last chapter; in this chapter I'll look in much more detail at the HTTP functions that WinInet provides. Microsoft endowed it with a familiar file-based architecture where you can open a connection and then read and write to it directly. This wrapper on top of the WinSock API makes it possible for high-level languages such as Visual FoxPro to directly access the functionality in this system interface.

How can you use HTTP in your applications?

Here's a look at the implications of direct data access over HTTP. The ability to send and receive data in any format you choose gives you the capability to implement your own client/server architecture that can communicate over *any* Internet connection. Here are some useful applications that stand out:

- Any real-time data connection that updates a form from data found on the Web—stock charts or weather information, for example—can simply access an HTTP link and download the data. If you provide timely data to your clients (whether it's financial data or an image captured from your back yard), you can make the data available directly from within a VFP application.

- Software or data updates lend themselves immediately to this technology. Subscription-based services might provide data updates over the Internet using HTTP to download files. The same mechanism can be used to update your actual application files, downloading the update and then running an update program. Technology like this is already in use in many commercial products that prompt you to download updates—your applications easily can do the same.

- Offline applications. Distributed applications often involve taking data offline for processing. The common traveling sales rep example works here: Rep downloads the latest product data for a meeting, goes offline and takes one or multiple orders during the course of the day. At the end of the day the collected data is sent back to the office. Instead of using the internal network via dialup, the tools described here allow this to occur over the Web with a custom application using the Internet as a network.

- Interactive applications that need to communicate with remote Web servers, but don't want to use HTML. Basically any application that runs on the Web could be written with a GUI front end and controlled through these HTTP functions. Some applications simply require a more robust user interface than is possible with HTML today.

- Controlling Web pages from within a client application. For example, it's possible to use search engines from within your applications simply by emulating a browser with native HTTP calls. You can retrieve the result and parse the resulting data into meaningful content. There's tons of information on the Web—it's just a matter of tapping into it. A simple example might be a software registration form—you can feed the values of the form directly to the Web server instead of using an HTML form.

One thing you should keep in mind: Although this approach does not use HTML to display the output, you still need a back-end Web server application to actually provide the data. In the examples here I'll use FoxISAPI as the back end, talking to Microsoft Internet Information Server and providing the logic and data back to the client, but you can talk to any Web server on the Web and use any software on the server that is capable of returning HTTP content.

WinInet with Visual FoxPro

In order to use WinInet you need WinInet.dll in your Windows System directory. This DLL is installed with all recent builds of Windows (SP3 for NT, Win98 and Win95 OSR2) and most of Microsoft's latest Internet tools—if you have Internet Explorer 3.0 or later installed, you have it. Note that you can't simply copy the DLL—at least not the 4.0 version of it—because there are dependencies, and only a full install really works.

> *If you can't rely on people having IE installed, you can use an old version of WinInet.dll that shipped with versions prior to IE 4.0. You can download a copy that's been tested for standalone use from www.west-wind.com/files/wininet.zip. This older file works, with the exception of several features such as proxy support, large HTTPS buffers and using ports other than 80.*

In the following sections I'll introduce the wwIPStuff class, which wraps the WinInet HTTP functionality into an easily accessible interface for application code. The class also provides FTP, SMTP e-mail, domain lookup and a few other features, some of which were discussed in the last chapter. The following code snippets from the class are slightly simplified and edited for length, listing only a few key properties and the relevant snippets used in the examples.

 For more detailed code listings and descriptions, see the wwIPStuff.vcx class with the Class Browser, included with the Developer's Download Files at www.hentzenwerke.com.

The easiest way to get started is with the HTTPGet method, which is a simple way to retrieve Web content into a string with a single method call. To use it you can simply do:

```
SET CLASSLIB TO wwIPStuff ADDITIVE
o = CREATE("wwIPStuff")
lcHTML = o.HTTPGet("http://www.west-wind.com/")
```

This retrieves the entire content of the Web page into a string.

The wwIPStuff class implements both a simple HTTPGet interface and a more low-level interface that actually makes the connections with separate method calls, then loads the page and closes the connection. The latter has more flexibility and allows posting data, while the former is a single method call with a single parameter (actually, an optional second parameter specifies the buffer size) that can only retrieve data. Let's have a first look at coding WinInet from Visual FoxPro by looking at the implementation of HTTPGet:

```
***********************************************************
DEFINE CLASS wwIPStuff AS CUSTOM
***********************************************************
PROTECTED cDLLPath, hHTTPSession, hIPSession, cPostbuffer

*** Custom Properties
cDLLPath = ""

*** Last Error Code
nError = 0
cErrorMsg = ""

*** HTTP Internet Handles
hHTTPSession = 0
hIPSession = 0

cUsername = ""
cPassword = ""


***********************************************************
* wwIPStuff :: HTTPGet
*******************************
***    Function: Retrieves an HTTP request from the
***              network and returns a string. Read an
***              HTML or data file across the network.
***      Assume: Blocking call - waits for completion
***              before returning. Only plain HTTP GETs
***              are supported. No passwords. Untested
***              with Proxy Servers - requires Port 80
***              access
***        Pass: tcURL       -  The full URL to retrieve
***                              Only HTTP requests!!!
***              tnBufferSize -  size of the result(16k)
***      Return: Result string or "" on error
***********************************************************
FUNCTION HTTPGet
LPARAMETERS tcUrl, tnBufferSize

tnBufferSize = IIF(!EMPTY(tnBufferSize),;
               tnBufferSize,16384)


DECLARE INTEGER InternetCloseHandle ;
   IN WININET.DLL INTEGER

DECLARE INTEGER GetLastError IN WIN32API

DECLARE INTEGER InternetOpen ;
```

```
   IN WININET.DLL ;
   STRING, INTEGER, STRING, STRING, INTEGER

hInetConnection = ;
   InternetOpen("West Wind Web Connection 2.7",;
   INTERNET_OPEN_TYPE_DIRECT, NULL,NULL,0)

IF hInetConnection = 0
   THIS.nError = GetLastError()
   THIS.cErrorMsg = THIS.GetSystemErrorMsg(THIS.nError)
   RETURN ""
ENDIF

THIS.hIPSession = hInetConnection
THIS.WinInetSetTimeout()

SzHead = "Accept: */*" + CR + CR

DECLARE INTEGER InternetOpenUrl ;
   IN WININET.DLL ;
   INTEGER, STRING, STRING, INTEGER,;
   INTEGER,INTEGER

hHTTPResult = InternetOpenUrl(hInetConnection, ;
   tcUrl, szHead,;
   LEN(szHead), INTERNET_FLAG_RELOAD,0);

IF hHTTPResult = 0
   THIS.nError = GetLastError()
   THIS.cErrorMsg = THIS.GetSystemErrorMsg(THIS.nError)
   RETURN ""
ENDIF

DECLARE INTEGER InternetReadFile ;
   IN WININET.DLL ;
   INTEGER, STRING @cBuffer,;
   INTEGER nBuffer, INTEGER @nSizeRead

lcBuffer = SPACE(tnBufferSize)
lnSize = LEN(lcBuffer)

llRetVal = InternetReadFile( ;
   hHTTPResult, @lcBuffer,;
   LEN(lcBuffer), @lnSize)

IF llRetVal = 0
   THIS.nError = GetLastError()
   THIS.cErrorMsg = THIS.GetSystemErrorMsg(THIS.nError)
   RETURN ""
ENDIF

InternetCloseHandle(hHTTPResult)
InternetCloseHandle(hInetConnection)

RETURN (IIF(lnSize > 1, SUBSTR(lcBuffer,1,lnSize),""))
* EOF HTTPGet
```

WinInet works in typical WinAPI style by using handles to connections. A typical connection requires three handles. You first open a handle to your Internet Session, which initializes WinInet and a connection for you. You then use the handle to connect to an actual site, which returns a second handle. The third and final handle is specific to the file or page you want to open and is used to make the read against the open connection. HTTPGet is a high-level function that combines several calls into one for convenience—I'll explain the manual steps further on.

The important thing to remember about handles is that once you create them, you need to get rid of them or you'll incur a handle leak, which will make you run out of handles eventually and leak a small amount of memory for each handle. The wwIPStuff class manages the persistent handles to an extent by using properties and a few simple methods to close them down properly. But always make sure you close a connection before establishing a new one with the same object reference. A good way to make sure of that is to create a new instance of the class for each connection because the Destroy method properly disposes of any open handles.

Time to put this puppy to use. Start with retrieving a simple Web page to a string as shown in **Figure 7.1**. Create a form and add edtHTML and txtUrl fields to the form. Then add a button to load a URL from the Web and add the following code:

```
SET PROCEDURE TO wwIPStuff ADDITIVE
o = CREATE("wwIPStuff")
THISFORM.edtHTML.Value = o.HTTPGet(TRIM(THISFORM.txtUrl.Value),100000)
```

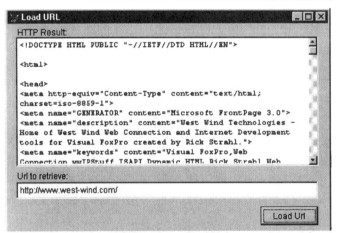

Figure 7.1. *Using WinInet to pull a Web page to a string takes only two lines of code using the wwIPStuff class.*

It's important that the URL you type into txtUrl is fully qualified, including the "http://" protocol prefix. The second parameter specifies the maximum size of the buffer returned to you. The buffer is pre-created and passed to InternetReadFile(), which fills it with the result. The default is 16K, which is enough for typical Web pages, but you can use smaller or larger values as necessary. Small values are useful if you only want to "ping" Web pages to see if they're still running without pulling down a huge Web page. The smaller buffer forces WinInet to read only a small amount of data from the open connection, which makes the request run much faster than a full document buffer returned.

In the example, when you click the button, HTTPGet goes out to the Web page specified and pulls it down into the edit box for viewing.

At first thought it might seem silly to pull down just a Web page—after all, you can use a browser to actually view the data, and you could even view that data in your own form using the WebBrowser control. Using WinInet is much more resource friendly than IE and is a non-UI operation that doesn't need a form and doesn't use COM, but rather optimized API calls. The simple interface is also easier to use than IE and is not subject to timing issues as IE is.

Once you have the data as a string, you can strip the page of all HTML tags and use it as plain text, using a function called StripHTML(). This useful function is part of wwUtils, which is included in this project.

For example, the above Web page includes a page counter that shows the number of hits. I could use the following code to extract this information from the Web page:

```
SET classlib TO wwIPStuff ADDITIVE
SET PROCEDURE TO wwUtils ADDITIVE

o = CREATE("wwIPStuff")
lcHTML = o.HTTPGet("http://www.west-wind.com",100000)

lcHTML = StripHTML(lcHTML)   && Remove HTML tags
lcCount = Extract(lcHTML,;
                "This page has been visited",;
                "times")
IF !EMPTY(lcCount)
  lnCount = VAL(lcCount)
ENDIF
```

StripHTML() and Extract() are a couple of useful functions for parsing data out of strings. They can be found in the wwUtils procedure file available with the Developer's Download Files at www.hentzenwerke.com. I've used similar code to download data from the National Weather Service to retrieve wind information for placement on maps. There's lots of data out there in raw form. If you can get at it via an HTTP request, you can probably put that data to use in your programs. These functions should help.

Retrieving plain HTML can also be useful for checking up on a site to determine whether it's still running, for building a stress tester that continually hammers a site, or using a Web spider that crawls links in a page to collect information for you. Or you can pull Web pages into database memo fields and then display them at a later time with the Web browser control.

Doing data over HTTP

HTML is okay, but it lacks the precision of database data. In the ASP and FoxISAPI server chapters you learned how to build Web request servers that can send HTTP results back to the browser. In most cases you sent back HTML, but of course it's also possible to send back data. **Figure 7.2** shows a form that downloads a customer list based on a name typed in the text box.

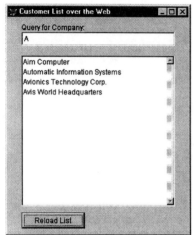

Figure 7.2. *Downloading FoxPro table data over the Web involves sending the file as a string from server to client.*

This code goes in the Reload button's Click() event:

```
o = CREATE("wwIPStuff")

*** Retrieve all companies in the txtQueryCompany Field
lcText = o.HTTPGet(;
   "http://localhost/foxisapi/foxisapi.dll?http~CustList1~"+;
   TRIM(THISFORM.txtQueryCompany.value),100000)

IF EMPTY(lcText) OR lcText="FAILED"
   WAIT WINDOW "Invalid HTTP Response..." NOWAIT
   RETURN
ENDIF

tcFilename = SYS(3) + ".txt"
lnHandle = FCREATE(tcFileName)

=FWRITE(lnHandle,lcText)
=FCLOSE(lnHandle)

THISFORM.lstCustList.RowSourceType = 0

CREATE CURSOR TCustList ;
(  CUSTNO     C (8),;
   COMPANY    C (30),;
   CAREOF     C (30) )

APPEND FROM (tcFileName) DELIMITED
ERASE (tcFileName)

THISFORM.lstCustList.RowSourceType = 2
THISFORM.lstCustList.RowSource = "tCustList.company, careof"
THISFORM.lstCustList.Requery
```

This search dialog makes a request against a FoxISAPI Web server back end, requesting the specified customers. The server obliges by sending a list of comma-delimited records as a text string. To quickly see what the server sends, try this URL in the browser:

```
http://localhost/foxisapi/foxisapi.dll/fidemo.httpdemo.process?
                             method=CustList1&Company=B
```

You'll see the comma-delimited list of records in the browser, minus the line breaks. The server sends this string and the client code simply takes the string, dumps it to a file and then imports it into a temporary cursor. The list box then is assigned a Rowsource pointing at this cursor and displays it in the list.

I implemented the server piece using FoxISAPI because it offers the greatest flexibility when dealing with native FoxPro table data.

> *Before running any of these demos, make sure you've created the servers in Chapter 5, or at least read through how to build a new FoxISAPI server using the wwFoxISAPI class. The classes shown here were compiled as part of the FIDemo server, and the source code can be found in <InstallPath>\FoxISAPI\http.*

The server class that contains the demos is called HTTPDemo in HTTP.prg in the Developer's Download Files at www.hentzenwerke.com. You need to manually add the HTTP.prg file to the FiDemo project and recompile the project. Remember to set the server to SingleUse once you've compiled the project, and then recompile. You must use the updated FoxISAPI.dll from www.hentzenwerke.com in order for the binary transfers (described later in this chapter) to work. If you ran the FoxISAPI examples in Chapter 5 you won't have to do anything further since the HTTP files were already compiled into the server. If you haven't run the Chapter 5 samples, you will have to read through the sections that explain how to compile and configure the FoxISAPI servers.

The FoxISAPI server code for the customer list looks like this (additional server methods in this chapter will be inserted into this class later):

```
***************************************************************
DEFINE CLASS HTTPDemo AS wwFoxISAPI OLEPUBLIC
***************************************************************


*********************************************************
* HTTPDemo :: CustList1
********************************
***  Function: Returns a customer list based on the URL
***            'parameter' passed. Delimited returned.
*********************************************************
FUNCTION CustList1

lcCustToFind = Request.QueryString("Company")

lcFile = SYS(3) + ".TXT"

SELECT custno,Company, Careof ;
   FROM (DATAPATH + "TT_Cust") ;
```

```
        WHERE Company = lcCustToFind ;
        ORDER BY Company ;
        INTO CURSOR TQuery

COPY TO (lcFile) TYPE DELIMITED

*** Send the Delimited string over the wire
Response.Write(FileToString(lcFile))

ERASE (lcFile)

USE IN TQuery
IF USED("TT_CUST")
   USE IN TT_Cust
ENDIF

ENDFUNC
* CustList1

ENDDEFINE
```

The server code is straightforward: It retrieves the Query String parameter we passed on the URL as Company=B to use as a filter in the SELECT statement that retrieves the actual customer records. The result is copied to a temporary file in delimited form. The file is read back into a string and then simply sent as-is into the HTTP output stream with Response.Write().

Instead of a comma-delimited list, you can also send a file directly. You can simply use FILETOSTR(lcDBFName) and send that down the HTTP stream! On the other end you pull in the resulting string and dump it back to the file with STRTOFILE(lcResult,lcTempDBFName), which you can then attach to the list box to view or import into the cursor as shown above.

Real data over HTTP
Comma-delimited files and files wrapped up as strings are only a start. The problem is that the DBF file format consists of more than one file to contain both the standard data and memo fields. Neither approach shown in the last section works with files that contain memo fields because you actually need to send two files. To get around this problem, you need to use an encoding scheme that knows about Visual FoxPro data. Here are a couple of functions found in wwIPStuff that do just that:

```
************************************************************
* wwIPStuff :: EncodeDBF
********************************
***   Function: This function encodes a DBF file ready to
***             be sent up to a server using HTTPGetEx in
***             the POST buffer. The file will be URL
***             encoded.
***     Assume: Note you can send a ZIP file here, too!
***             100 byte header on top of file contains
***             5 byte ID (wwDBF) filename (40 bytes) and
***             size(10 bytes) for each
***             file
```

```
***        Pass: lcDBF     - Full DBF filename w/ ext
***              llHasMemo - .t. or (.f.)
***      Return: Encoded Buffer or "" on failure
**********************************************************
LPARAMETERS lcDBF, llHasMemo
LOCAL lcBuffer1, lcBuffer2

lcDBF = IIF(TYPE("lcDBF") = "C",UPPER(lcDBF),"")

IF !FILE(lcDBF)
   RETURN ""
ENDIF

lcBuffer1 = File2Var(lcDBF)
lcHeader = "wwDBF" + PADR(justfname(lcDBF),40) + ;
           STR(LEN(lcBuffer1),10)
IF !llHasMemo
  lcHeader = lcHeader + SPACE(50)   && Pad out header
  RETURN lcHeader + lcBuffer1
ENDIF

lcFPT = STRTRAN(LOWER(lcDBF),".dbf",".fpt")

lcBuffer2 = File2Var(lcFPT)
lcHeader = lcHeader + PADR(JUSTFNAME(lcFPT),40) + ;
          STR(LEN(lcBuffer2),10)

RETURN lcHeader + lcBuffer1 + lcBuffer2

**********************************************************
* wwIPStuff :: DecodeDBF
********************************
***   Function: Decodes a buffer that has been encoded
***             with EncodeDBF
***     Assume: The inbound buffer should *NOT* be
***             URLEncoded since the result from an
***             HTTPGET operation will already have been
***             decoded for you!
***       Pass: lcBuffer - String that contains the file
***             lcDBF    - Full Name of DBF to create
***     Return: .t. or .f.
**********************************************************

LPARAMETERS lcBuffer,lcDBF
LOCAL lnSeparator

IF LEN(lcBuffer) < 105
   RETURN .F.
ENDIF

lcHeader = SUBSTR(lcBuffer,1,105)
lcFname = TRIM(SUBSTR(lcBuffer,6,40))
lnSize1 = VAL(SUBSTR(lcBuffer,46,10))
lnSize2 = VAL(SUBSTR(lcBuffer,96,10))
```

```
*** Use parm or the filename specified in the header
lcDBF = IIF(EMPTY(lcDBF),lcFname,UPPER(lcDBF))

IF lcHeader # "wwDBF"
   WAIT WINDOW NOWAIT "Invalid Decode File Header"
   RETURN .f.
ENDIF


lcFile1 = ""
lcFile2 = ""

IF lnSize1 > 0
   lcFile1 = SUBSTR(lcBuffer,106,lnSize1)
   IF LEN(lcFile1) < lnSize1
      WAIT WINDOW NOWAIT "Invalid File Size: " + ;
               STR(LEN(lcFile1)) + " of " + STR(lnSize1)
      RETURN .F.
   ENDIF
ENDIF
IF lnSize2 > 0
   lcFile2 = SUBSTR(lcBuffer,106 + lnSize1, lnSize2)
   lnSizex = LEN(lcFile2)
   IF LEN(lcFile2) < lnSize2 - 1
      WAIT WINDOW NOWAIT "Invalid Memo File Size: " +;
               STR(LEN(lcFile2)) + " of " + STR(lnSize2)
      RETURN .F.
   ENDIF
ENDIF

=File2Var(lcDBF,lcFile1)

IF !EMPTY(lcFile2)
   =File2Var(STRTRAN(lcDBF,".DBF",".FPT"),lcFile2)
ENDIF

RETURN .T.
```

These functions work by taking an input file and adding a header that describes what's contained in the file. The header includes a size for each component and a file name so that the decoding party can figure out the name of the file encoded. The additional benefit of this header is that it's an easy way to tell whether the entire file has been retrieved, by checking the file sizes and comparing them against the decoded strings. If the size doesn't match, an error occurred during the download or the file was incorrectly encoded.

With this code in place, you can send memo data when sending data on the server:

```
**********************************************************
* HTTPDemo :: CustList2
*********************************
***   Function: Returns a customer list based on the URL
***             'parameter' passed. This time as file!
***     Assume: wc.dll?http~CustList1~CompanySearchString
**********************************************************
```

```
FUNCTION CustList2

lcCustToFind = Request.QueryString("Company")

lcFile = SYS(3) + ".DBF"

*** This query includes Memos
SELECT custno,Company, Careof, Address, phone ;
   FROM TT_Cust ;
   WHERE UPPER(Company) = UPPER(lcCustToFind) ;
   ORDER BY Company ;
   INTO DBF (lcFile)
USE

o = CREATE("wwIPStuff")

*** Encode with Memo File
lcText = o.EncodeDBF(lcFile,.T.)

*** Send the binary File string over the wire
Response.Write(lcText)

ERASE (lcFile)

USE IN TT_Cust

ENDFUNC
* CustList1
```

Both client and server use wwIPStuff to handle the encoding on the server and decoding on the client. EncodeDBF() simply takes a file name as input and creates a string from the file. If the llMemo parameter is true, the DBF and FPT are packaged together. On the client side, use DecodeDBF() to unpack the file into DBF and/or Memo files:

```
*** Retrieve all companies starting with "A"
lcText = o.HTTPGet(;
    "http://localhost/foxisapi/foxisapi.dll/fidemo.httpdemo.process?";
    " Method=CustList2&Company=A")

*** Creates the file including Memo
IF !o.DecodeDBF(lcText,"TCustList.dbf")
   RETURN   && DecodeDBF will display nowait WAIT win
ENDIF

*** Do something with the file
USE TCustList
BROWSE
USE

*** Clear out the temporary files
ERASE TCustList.dbf
ERASE TCustList.FPT

RETURN
```

Cool, isn't it? Fewer than 20 lines of code for both the client and server! With this basic technology you can very easily update data over the Web. To make this even more efficient, you could add third-party ZIP control to the Encode and Decode functions and zip the data on the fly once it gets over a certain size, cutting down on the size of the text traveling over the wire.

You can use a standard GUI VFP application to access information that is retrieved on a remote server. This can be a polling-type link that might use a timer to occasionally update data you see in a form, or a by-request operation where the user requests the update from a button click.

Sending data with HTTP POST

Up to now we've only *requested* data from the server, but your application might also need to *update* data on the server. For example, you might have a salesperson log on to the Web and send the sales data she collected over the course of the day back to the home office. To do this, you need a mechanism to send data *to* the Web server from your VFP application.

HTTP has a built-in mechanism for sending data to the server called a POST request (there are several ways to do so, but POST is most commonly used). The most common use of POST requests occurs when you submit an HTML input form on a Web page. The data is encoded (the format is known as URLEncoded) and sent up to the server via the HTTP request initiated by the browser. A typical Web back-end application can then query the posted data to retrieve the form variables as part of the server data sent to the back end. With FoxISAPI and the wwFoxISAPI class I'm using here, the retrieval mechanism is Request.Form().

Typically, only small amounts of data are sent via POST fields, but here again, as with the results returned from an HTTP GET operation, you can send *any* kind and size of data. Although an HTTP POST sends data to the server, POST operations are typically piggybacked on a regular HTTP request so you can also return an HTTP result as part of the same request. In other words, you could post data to simulate an HTML input form *and* retrieve the result page or response that tells whether the request succeeded. The server then has the option of using the input to perform additional logic before creating a result to send back to the client. This two-way communication allows you to build sophisticated server communications with HTTP POST requests.

When I showed the HTTPGet() method, I used the simplified WinInet function *InternetOpenUrl,* which handles most of the opening, loading and retrieving results. When running a POST request, however, you need to use lower-level WinInet functions to add the additional settings required to send a buffer. This means calling three separate methods in the wwIPStuff class: HTTPConnect() to connect to a server, HTTPGetEx() to actually retrieve and/or send the data, and HTTPClose() to shut down the connection. The actual API code also has to take a few extra steps, making a few additional low-level connections through WinInet—in all, it's quite a jumble of DECLARE – API definitions. But the low-level mechanism pays off by providing many other options, such as allowing access to authentication of username and password, secure connections via Secure Sockets Layer (SSL), the HTTP headers and, most importantly, the POST buffer. Here's the code for the three methods:

```
**********************************************************
* wwIPStuff :: HTTPConnect
*******************************
*** Function: Connect to an HTTP server.
***    Assume: Sets two handle values in this class. Each
***            instance of this class can only manage
***            one HTTP session at a time. Use this low
***            level function for quick repeated access
***            to HTTP pages.
***      Pass: lcServer   - Server name
***            lcUsername - Optional Username
***            lcPassword - Optional Password
***            llHTTPS    - .T. for secure connections
***    Return: 0 on success or WinAPI Errorcode
**********************************************************
LPARAMETER lcServer, lcUsername, lcPassword, llHTTPS
LOCAL lhIP, lhHTTP, lnError, lnHTTPPort

lcServer = IIF(!EMPTY(lcServer), lcServer, THIS.cServer)
lcUsername = TRIM(IIF(!EMPTY(lcUsername), lcUsername, THIS.cUsername))
lcPassword = TRIM(IIF(!EMPTY(lcPassword), lcPassword, THIS.cPassword))

*** Assign Default Ports
IF THIS.nHTTPPort = 0
   lnHTTPPort =   IIF(llHTTPS,INTERNET_DEFAULT_HTTPS_PORT,;
                         INTERNET_DEFAULT_HTTP_PORT)
ELSE
   lnHTTPPort = THIS.nHTTPPort
ENDIF

THIS.lSecureLink = llHTTPS OR THIS.lSecureLink

THIS.cServer = lcServer

THIS.nError = 0
THIS.cErrorMsg = ""

DECLARE INTEGER InternetCloseHandle ;
   IN WinInet.DLL ;
   INTEGER

DECLARE INTEGER GetLastError;
   IN WIN32API

DECLARE INTEGER InternetOpen ;
   IN WININET.DLL ;
   STRING,;
   INTEGER,;
   STRING, STRING, INTEGER

hInetConnection = ;
   InternetOpen("West Wind Web Connection 3.00",;
   THIS.nHTTPConnectType,;
   NULL,NULL,0)
```

```
IF hInetConnection = 0
   THIS.nError = GetLastError()
   THIS.cErrorMsg = THIS.GetSystemErrorMsg(THIS.nError)
   RETURN THIS.nError
ENDIF

THIS.hIPSession = hInetConnection
THIS.WinInetSetTimeout()

DECLARE INTEGER InternetConnect ;
   IN WININET.DLL ;
   INTEGER hIPHandle,;
   STRING lpzServer,;
   INTEGER dwPort, ;
   STRING lpzUserName,;
   STRING lpzPassword,;
   INTEGER dwServiceFlags,;
   INTEGER dwReserved,;
   INTEGER dwReserved


lhHTTPSession=;
    InternetConnect(hInetConnection,;
    lcServer,;
    lnHTTPPort,;
    lcUsername,;
    lcPassword,;
    INTERNET_SERVICE_HTTP,;
    0,0)


IF (lhHTTPSession = 0)
   =InternetCloseHandle(hInetConnection)
   THIS.nError = GetLastError()
   THIS.cErrorMsg = THIS.GetSystemErrorMsg()
   RETURN THIS.nError
ENDIF


THIS.hIPSession = hInetConnection
THIS.hHTTPSession = lhHTTPSession

RETURN 0

**********************************************************
* wwIPStuff :: HTTPGetEx
*********************************
*** Function: Retrieves an HTTP request from the
***           network and returns a string. Read an
***           HTML or data file across the net.
***    Assume: Blocking call - waits for completion
***           before returning. Use AddPostKey
***           to post data to server.
***           Must call HTTPConnect/HTTPClose to
***           manage connection to Server.
***      Pass: tcURL      - URL to retrieve
```

```
***              tcBuffer     - HTTP result (by Reference)
***              tnBufferSize - Size of the buffer (ref)
***              tcHeaders    - HTTP Headers sent from
***                             client request. Separate
***                             key:value pairs with CR
***    Return: WinAPI Error Code (check THIS.cErrorMsg)
********************************************************
LPARAMETERS tcPage, tcBuffer, tnBufferSize, tcHeaders
LOCAL hHTTPResult, lcOldAlias

tcPage = IIF(EMPTY(tcPage),THIS.cLink,tcPage)
tnBufferSize = IIF(TYPE("tnBufferSize") = "N",;
                tnBufferSize,0)

lcOldAlias = ALIAS()

THIS.cLink = tcPage

IF USED("wwPostBuffer")
   SELECT wwPostBuffer
   tnPostSize = LEN(wwPostBuffer.cPostBuffer)
   lcPostBuffer = IIF(tnPostSize > 0, wwPostBuffer.cPostBuffer, NULL)
ELSE
   tnPostSize = 0
   lcPostBuffer = NULL
ENDIF

IF USED(lcOldAlias)
   SELECT (lcOldAlias)
ENDIF

THIS.nError = 0
THIS.cErrorMsg = ""

DECLARE INTEGER HttpOpenRequest ;
   IN WININET.DLL ;
   INTEGER hHTTPHandle,;
   STRING lpzReqMethod,;
   STRING lpzPage,;
   STRING lpzVersion,;
   STRING lpzReferer,;
   STRING lpzAcceptTypes,;
   INTEGER dwFlags,;
   INTEGER dwContext

HHTTPResult = HttpOpenRequest(THIS.hHTTPSession,;
   IIF( tnPostSize > 0, "POST","GET"),;
   tcPage,;
   NULL,NULL,NULL,;
   INTERNET_FLAG_RELOAD + IIF(THIS.lSecureLink,INTERNET_FLAG_SECURE,0),0)

IF (hHTTPResult = 0)
   THIS.nError = GetLastError()
   THIS.cErrorMsg = THIS.GetSystemErrorMsg()
   RETURN THIS.nError
ENDIF
```

```
THIS.hHTTPSession = hHTTPResult

*** HTTPSendRequest actually goes out and gets the data
*** Note the buffer may not be completely downloaded
*** when you start reading the data below
DECLARE INTEGER HttpSendRequest ;
   IN WININET.DLL ;
   INTEGER hHTTPHandle,;
   STRING lpzHeaders,;
   INTEGER cbHeaders,;
   STRING lpzPost,;
   INTEGER cbPost

IF tnPostSize > 0
  tcHeaders = "Content-Type: application/x-www-form-urlencoded" +;
              IIF(!EMPTY(tcHeaders),CR + tcHeaders,"")
ELSE
  tcHeaders =  IIF(!EMPTY(tcHeaders),tcHeaders,"")
ENDIF

lnRetval = 0
lnRetval = HttpSendRequest(hHTTPResult,;
   tcHeaders,LEN(tcHeaders),;
   lcPostBuffer,tnPostSize)

IF lnRetval = 0
   THIS.nError = GetLastError()
   THIS.cErrorMsg = THIS.GetSystemErrorMsg()
   =InternetCloseHandle(hHTTPResult)
   RETURN THIS.nError
ENDIF


*** Retrieve the HTTP Header
DECLARE INTEGER HttpQueryInfo ;
   IN WININET.DLL ;
   INTEGER hHTTPHandle,;
   INTEGER nType,;
   STRING @cHeaders,;
   INTEGER @cbHeaderSize,;
   STRING cNULL

lcHeaders = SPACE(1024)
lnHeaderSize = 1024
lnRetval = HttpQueryInfo(hHTTPResult,;
                        HTTP_QUERY_RAW_HEADERS_CRLF,;
                        @lcHeaders,@lnHeaderSize,NULL)
THIS.cHTTPHeaders = TRIM(STRTRAN(lcHeaders,CHR(0),""))

*** Call HTTP Event method - 0 means the header is sent
THIS.OnHTTPBufferUpdate(0,0,THIS.cHTTPHeaders)

*** Now Read the actual result data
DECLARE INTEGER InternetReadFile ;
   IN WININET.DLL ;
   INTEGER hHTTPHandle,;
```

```
   STRING @lcBuffer,;
   INTEGER cbBuffer,;
   INTEGER @cbBuffer

IF tnBufferSize > 0
   *** Use Fixed Buffer Size
  tcBuffer = SPACE(tnBufferSize)
  lnBufferSize = tnBufferSize
  lnRetval = InternetReadFile(hHTTPResult,;
     @tcBuffer,;
     tnBufferSize,;
     @tnBufferSize)
ELSE
   *** Build the buffer dynamically
   tcBuffer = ""
   tnSize = 0
   lnRetVal = 0
   lnBytesRead = 1
   lnBufferReads = 0
   DO WHILE .T.
        lcReadBuffer = SPACE(THIS.nHTTPWorkBufferSize)
        lnBytesRead = 0
        lnSize = LEN(lcReadBuffer)

      lnRetval = InternetReadFile(hHTTPResult,;
         @lcReadBuffer,;
         lnSize,;
         @lnBytesRead)

      IF lnRetVal = 1 AND lnBytesRead > 0
         *** Update the input parameters - result buffer and size of buffer
         tcBuffer = tcBuffer + lcReadBuffer
         tnBufferSize = tnBufferSize + lnBytesRead
         lnBufferReads = lnBufferReads + 1
         THIS.OnHTTPBufferUpdate(tnBufferSize,lnBufferReads,@lcReadBuffer)
      ENDIF
       IF (lnRetVal = 1 AND lnBytesRead = 0) OR (lnRetVal = 0)
          EXIT
       ENDIF
     ENDDO
     lnBufferSize = tnBufferSize
ENDIF

IF lnRetval = 0
   THIS.nError = GetLastError()
   THIS.cErrorMsg = THIS.GetSystemErrorMsg()
ENDIF

=InternetCloseHandle(hHTTPResult);

tcBuffer = (IIF(tnBufferSize > 1 AND tnBufferSize <= lnBuffersize, ;
  SUBSTR(tcBuffer,1,tnBufferSize),""))

RETURN THIS.nError
```

```
**********************************************************
* wwIPStuff :: HTTPClose
*******************************
*** Function: Closes an HTTP Session.
***    Return: nothing
**********************************************************

DECLARE INTEGER InternetCloseHandle ;
   IN WININET.DLL ;
   INTEGER hIPSession

=InternetCloseHandle(THIS.hHTTPSession)
=InternetCloseHandle(THIS.hIPSession)

THIS.hHTTPSession = 0
THIS.hIPSession = 0
RETURN


**********************************************************
* wwIPStuff :: AddPostKey
*******************************
*** Function: Adds a key to the post string
***     Pass: tcKey   - Key to add (or RESET to clear)
***           tcValue -  The value to set it to
***    Return: nothing
**********************************************************
LPARAMETERS tcKey, tcValue
LOCAL lcOldAlias
tcKey=IIF(TYPE("tcKey") = "C",tcKey,"")
tcValue=IIF(TYPE("tcValue") = "C",tcValue,"")

lcOldAlias=Alias()

IF !USED("wwPostBuffer")
   *** Use a cursor so we can hold very large buffers
   CREATE CURSOR wwPostBuffer ;
      ( cPostBuffer M)
   APPEND BLANK
ENDIF

SELECT wwPostBuffer

IF tcKey = "RESET"
  REPLACE wwPostBuffer.cPostbuffer WITH ""
  RETURN
ENDIF

IF !EMPTY(tcKey)
   * THIS.cPostBuffer= && No good for buffers over 1meg
  REPLACE wwPostBuffer.cPostBuffer WITH wwPostBuffer.cPostBuffer + tcKey + ;
                "=" + URLEncode(tcValue) + "&"
ENDIF

IF USED(lcOldAlias)
   SELECT (lcOldAlias)
ENDIF
```

These low-level functions take advantage of a number of customization options for the HTTP request by checking various class properties and parameter values. There is support for security (HTTPS and authentication with username and password), attaching custom HTTP headers to the request (tcHeaders input parameter), the ability to retrieve the HTTP header (cHTTPHeader) from a request in addition to the content, and, most importantly, the ability to send information and data to the Web server by using the POST buffer.

POST data is attached to the request through a special method called AddPostKey. You call this method by supplying a key/value pair:

```
oIP.AddPostKey("Name","Rick Strahl")
```

AddPostKey() properly encodes the variable data and formats it to simulate an HTML form submission. POSTed data must be in URLEncoded format, which strips out all "unsafe" characters and converts the input into a plain ASCII string. *Safe* characters in this context include A-Z, a-z and 0-9—all other characters are converted into their hexadecimal ASCII codes: %0D for a carriage return (CHR(13)), for example. This process can be very slow, especially if you do it with Visual FoxPro code on a very large binary file (remember our goal is to send binary file images of DBF files). The URLEncode function (in wwutils.prg) handles the conversion of the string. To make this slow process a lot faster on large strings, the wwIPStuff.dll file contains a routine that does it with C code when the buffer is greater than a couple of thousand bytes.

```
************************************************************
PROCEDURE URLEncode
*******************
***   Function: Encodes a string in URL encoded format
***             for use on URL strings or when passing a
***             POST buffer to wwIPStuff::HTTPGetEx
***      Pass: tcValue   -   String to encode
***    Return: URLEncoded string or ""
************************************************************
LPARAMETER tcValue
LOCAL lcResult, lcChar, lnSize, x

*** Large Buffers use the wwIPStuff function
*** for quicker response
IF LEN(tcValue) > 2048
   LnSize = LEN(tcValue)
   TcValue = PADR(tcValue,lnSize * 3)

   DECLARE INTEGER VFPURLEncode ;
      IN WWIPSTUFF ;
      STRING @cText,;
      INTEGER cInputTextSize

   LnSize = VFPUrlEncode(@tcValue,lnSize)

   IF lnSize > 0
      RETURN SUBSTR(TRIM(tcValue),1,lnSize)
   ENDIF
```

```
      RETURN ""
ENDIF

*** Do it in VFP Code
lcResult = ""

FOR x = 1 TO len(tcValue)
   lcChar = SUBSTR(tcValue,x,1)
   IF ATC(lcChar,"ABCDEFGHIJKLMNOPQRSTUVWXYZ0123456789") > 0
      lcResult = lcResult + lcChar
      LOOP
   ENDIF
   IF lcChar = " "
      lcResult = lcResult + "+"
      LOOP
   ENDIF
   *** Convert others to Hex equivalents
   lcResult = lcResult + "%" + RIGHT(TRANSFORM(ASC(lcChar),"@0"),2)
ENDFOR && x = 1 to len(tcValue)

RETURN lcResult
* EOF URLEncode
```

Posting application data

With this wwIPStuff framework code in place, you can send data to the server. The simplest thing you can do is to create a Visual FoxPro form that simulates a Web page. Let's build a short data entry form that allows you to enter new customer information into a database by extending the customer list display sample we used originally. **Figure 7.3** shows the customer entry form that you can access by clicking on a customer in the list or by clicking the New button on the list form.

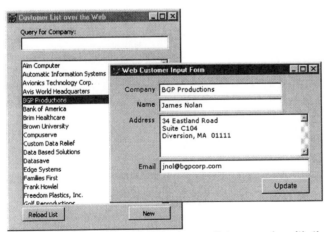

Figure 7.3. *Extending the customer list example with the ability to update data on the Web server using HTTP POST to submit the data.*

First bring up the CustList.scx file used in the first data example and add the following code to the list box Valid event to allow viewing specific customer information:

```
DO FORM custinput with TCustList.CustNo
```

Pass down the customer ID so that the customer form can retrieve the entire record from the Web site by using this ID as a parameter. In the CustInput form's Init event you'll find the code responsible for pulling the customer data from the server:

```
* CustInput::Init
LPARAMETER lcCustNo

SET PROCEDURE TO wwUtils ADDITIVE
SET CLASSLIB TO wwIPStuff ADDITIVE

IF !EMPTY(lcCustNo)
   *** Retrieve the full record
   loIP = CREATE("wwIPStuff")
   lcFile =    loIP.HTTPGet(;
"http://localhost/foxisapi/foxisapi.dll/fidemo.httpdemo.Process?";
"Method=GetCust&Custno="+Alltrim(lcCustno),20000)

   IF UPPER(lcFile) = "ERROR"
      WAIT WINDOW NOWAIT lcFile
      RETURN
   ENDIF

   IF loIP.DecodeDbf(lcFile,"TCust.dbf")
      SELECT 0
      USE TCust
      THISFORM.txtCustNo.VALUE = TCust.Custno
      THISFORM.txtCompany.VALUE = TCust.Company
      THISFORM.txtCareof.VALUE = TCust.Careof
      THISFORM.edtADdress.VALUE = TCust.Address
      THISFORM.edtEmail.VALUE = TCust.Email

      USE IN TCust
      ERASE TCust.DBF
      ERASE TCust.FPT
   ELSE
      WAIT WINDOW "Couldn't load Customer " + lcCustNo
      RETURN
   ENDIF
   THISFORM.btnInsert.caption = "Update"
ENDIF
```

If a customer ID was passed in, the code pulls the customer record from the server by downloading the record as a file and storing it to Tcust.dbf/fpt. The `&Custno=" +` `ALLTRIM(lcCustno)` portion of the URL lets the server know which record to retrieve. The server packages up the file using EncodeDBF() and then sends it down to the client, which uses DecodeDBF() to convert the file back into a DBF called Tcust. The values from this file are then stuffed into the form fields for display. Note that there's some minimal error handling in this code, which requires checking the result HTTP buffer for error string results. The scheme I use typically returns "OK" when all is well, or "Error: Error string" if something didn't work. You also need to check for a blank string, which means an error occurred in the connection. More on error handling later.

The form can also be updated. If you have a new customer, the txtCustno field will be empty, otherwise it'll contain the existing customer ID. Based on this, the server knows whether to INSERT a new record or UPDATE an existing one. The client-side code that posts the fields to the server looks like this:

```
oIP = CREATE("wwIPStuff")

oIP.HTTPConnect("localhost")

lcOutput = ""
lnSize = 0

oIP.AddPostKey("Company", THISFORM.txtCompany.value)
oIP.AddPostKey("Name", THISFORM.txtCareof.value)
oIP.AddPostKey("Address", THISFORM.edtAddress.value)
oIP.AddPostKey("Email", THISFORM.edtEmail.value)
oIP.AddPostKey("CustId", THISFORM.txtCustNo.Value)

lnResult = oIP.HTTPGetEx(;
"/foxisapi/foxisapi.dll/FiDemo.HTTPDemo.Process?Method=UpdateCust",;
@lcOutput,@lnSize)

*** Check for connection error
IF lnResult # 0
  WAIT WINDOW oIP.cErrorMsg NOWAIT
  RETURN
ENDIF

*** All is well
IF lcOutput = "OK"
   WAIT WINDOW NOWAIT "Customer Info Inserted..."
   RELEASE THISFORM
   RETURN
ENDIF

*** We have an error to display
MESSAGEBOX(lcOutput,48,"Update Error")
```

The key to this request is the AddPostKey() method calls, which are responsible for making the field values available to the Web server. The values are posted through the call to HTTPGetEx(), which also returns a result. Notice how HTTPGetEx() is called by passing in a buffer and size variable by reference:

```
lcOutput = ""
lnSize = 0
lnResult = oIP.HTTPGetEx("...foxisapi.dll...?Method=UpdateCust", @lcOutput,
@lnSize)
```

Here I assign a null string to the buffer, which lets HTTPGetEx() dynamically size the buffer. When HTTPGetEx() returns, it returns an error code (0 if all went well or else an API error). You can check the cErrorMsg property in that case to see the error, or use the GetSystemErrorMessage() method to retrieve the raw API error. HTTPGetEx() also fills the buffer passed in (lcOutput) with the result data, similar to the way HTTPGet does. lnSize receives the size of the actual result string.

Once the result has been received, it's easy to check for OK or ERROR to see whether the request succeeded or failed. Note here that an update is happening in this request so no significant result is returned, but you could certainly have the Web server return a result data set or an HTML page. That's up to your application implementation.

On the FoxISAPI server side, the code to insert or update the record is also very straightforward (GetCust is listed here, too, for the sake of completeness):

```
************************************************************
* HTTPDemo :: GetCust
*********************************
FUNCTION GetCust

lcCustno = PADL(ALLTRIM(Request.QueryString("CustNo")),8)

lcFileName = Sys(2015) + ".dbf"
SELECT * From (DATAPATH + "TT_CUST") WHERE CustNo = lcCustNo ;
       INTO DBF (lcFileName)
USE
IF _TALLY = 0
   Response.Write("Error: Invalid Customer number" + lcCustNo)
   RETURN
ENDIF

loIP = CREATE("wwIPStuff")
lcFile = loIP.EncodeDBF(lcFileName,.T.)

Response.Write(lcFile)

ERASE lcFileName
ERASE ForceExt(lcFileName,"FPT")

RETURN


************************************************************
* HTTPDemo :: UpdateCust
********************************
FUNCTION UpdateCust

lcCustId = Request.Form("CustId")

lcCompany = Request.Form("Company")
IF EMPTY(lcCompany)
   Response.Write("Error: Company Field cannot be blank...")
   RETURN
ENDIF
```

```
IF EMPTY(lcCustId)
   INSERT INTO (DATAPATH + "TT_CUST") ;
            (Company, careof, email, address, custno) ;
            VALUES ( lcCompany,;
                      Request.Form("Name"),;
                      Request.Form("Email"),;
                      Request.Form("Address"),;
                      SYS(3))
   Response.Write("OK - Insert")
ELSE
  IF !USED("TT_Cust")
     USE (DATAPATH + "TT_CUST") IN 0
  ENDIF
  SELECT TT_Cust
  LOCATE FOR custno = lcCustID
  IF FOUND()
     REPLACE Company WITH lcCompany,;
             Careof WITH  Request.Form("Name"),;
             Email WITH Request.Form("Email"),;
             Address WITH Request.Form("Address")
     Response.Write("OK - Update")
  ELSE
      Response.Write("Error: Customer not found. Not updated")
      RETURN
  ENDIF
ENDIF

Response.Write("OK")

RETURN
```

The update code checks to see if a customer ID was passed—if not, a new record is added with INSERT—otherwise the data updates an existing customer. Request.Form() is used to retrieve all form variables posted. This is really no different from how you would treat input from an HTML page.

There's no error handling here. In a real application you'd probably do some additional checks for valid data and empty field values before inserting them into the database. In this example, the error message should be sent back with a message like this:

```
Response.Write("Error: Invalid Fieldx Value")
```

The client handles this with a MessageBox() if "ERROR" is returned as part of the response.

Hey, Mr. Postman, bring me some data
The previous example showed how you can use a Visual FoxPro client application to essentially mimic a browser without using an HTML interface. For many simple operations, or those that can run both on the Web and from within an application, this is probably fine but it requires a fair amount of code. Because you're using Visual FoxPro on both ends of the connection, it's much easier to deal with files passed back and forth. The advantage of this approach is that you can use Visual FoxPro's data binding features rather than having to deal with the data by hand on a field-by-field basis.

Figure 7.4 shows a form containing a grid into which you can type a company, name and message. The idea is that you can dynamically create the table to be sent to the server. Type some data into the grid, and then click Send File to Server to actually POST the data by sending the file as a POST variable called *CustFile*.

The server receives the data and decodes the file back into its DBF form. It then inserts a new record into the table ("Hey there from the server"), re-encodes the file, and sends it back to your VFP form on the client side, which then displays the result in the lower grid.

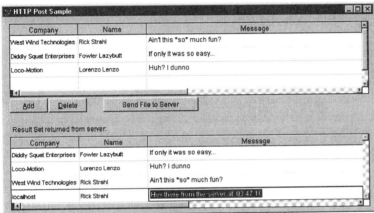

Figure 7.4. Sending and receiving data files over HTTP is easy. This form allows entering of data to send to the server, which adds a record and then returns the full result for display in the lower grid.

Here's the relevant code that goes into the Send button's Click event:

```
o = CREATE("wwIPStuff")

wait window nowait "Selecting data to send..."

*** Clear the result file and the result grid
SELECT TGetDownload
ZAP
THISFORM.Grid2.refresh

*** Select all items from the input cursor
SELECT Company, Name, Message FROM TPostTest ;
    ORDER BY Company, Name ;
    INTO DBF TEMPFILE
USE  && Must close before reading

WAIT WINDOW NOWAIT "Encoding data..."

*** Encode the file and memo
lcFileText = o.EncodeDBF("TempFile.dbf",.T.)

*** Create the Post Buffer
o.AddPostKey("CustFile",lcFileText)
```

```
*** Init vars that need to be passed by reference
lcBuffer = ""
lnSize = 0

WAIT WINDOW NOWAIT "Connecting to site..."

lnResult = o.HTTPConnect("localhost")
IF lnResult # 0
   WAIT WINDOW "HTTPConnect error: " + o.cErrorMsg
   RETURN
ENDIF

WAIT WINDOW NOWAIT "Sending data and retrieving result file..."
lnResult =
o.HTTPGetEx("foxisapi/foxisapi.dll/fidemo.httpdemo.process?method=SendCustList"
, ;
         @lcBuffer,@lnSize)
IF lnResult # 0
   WAIT WINDOW "HTTPGetEx error: " + o.cErrorMsg
   RETURN
ENDIF

*** Decoding result file from server
lcFileText = o.DecodeDBF(lcBuffer,"TempFile.dbf")

SELECT TGetDownload
ZAP
APPEND FROM TempFile
GO BOTTOM
THISFORM.Grid2.refresh

ERASE TEMPFILE.DBF
ERASE TEMPFILE.FPT

WAIT CLEAR

o.HTTPClose()

RETURN
```

The key to this routine is the following lines of code:

```
*** Encode the file and memo
lcFileText = o.EncodeDBF("TempFile.dbf",.T.)

*** Create the Post Buffer
o.AddPostKey("CustFile",lcFileText)
```

The first line encodes the result from the SELECT statement into a string. The resulting string is then added to the POST request buffer. The file is now transferred to the server as a form variable when HTTPGetEx runs. Simple, huh? You could also send multiple files in a single pass using this mechanism. Simply assign each packaged file to a separate post variable with AddPostKey().

Once the server gets the request, it turns the file back into a string using Request.Form("CustFile") and then uses DecodeDBF() to turn the string back into a DBF/FPT file. Once the file is on disk, the server uses the table, adds a new record to it, then repackages the result with EncodeDBF() and simply sends it back to the client with Response.Write():

```
************************************
* HTTPDemo :: SendCustList
************************************
FUNCTION SendCustList

lcFileBuffer = Request.Form("CustFile")

o = CREATE("wwIPStuff")
IF !o.DecodeDBF(lcFileBuffer,"TTempFile.dbf")
   Response.Write("Error: Invalid File info")
   RETURN
ENDIF

USE TTempFile

INSERT INTO TTempFile(Company, Name, Message) ;
    VALUES (Request.GetServerName(),"Rick Strahl",;
            "Hey there from the server at: "+TIME())

*** Close the file and delete it!
USE In TTempFile

lcFileText = o.EncodeDBF("TTempFile.dbf",.T.)

Response.Write(lcFileText)

ERASE TTempFile.DBF
ERASE TTempFile.FPT

RETURN
ENDFUNC
```

The client then unpacks the file with DecodeDBF() and shows the result in the bottom grid.

This is not a practical example, but it does demonstrate the whole range of using DBF files for messaging between client and server. Keep in mind that this code is simplified and lacks solid error handling, which I'll discuss further on.

Building in even more functionality!

The framework code I've described above reduces the overhead required to send and receive data files over HTTP to a few lines of code. You'll find that the physical aspects of data transfers are very easy to implement on both the client and server sides. The wwIPStuff class encapsulates so much of the logic that a few lines of code will do the trick. But let's practice our incremental development skills and take this approach one step further.

The wwIPStuff class library contains another class called wwHTTPData, which is derived from aHTTPData. This class wraps up much of the code involved in transferring files and running queries over the Web into a single class that can run a SQL statement over the Web with a single method call. To make this work you need to build two pieces that depend on each other: a server component and a client component, which are implemented as methods of the wwHTTPData class.

Figure 7.5 shows the HTTPSQL sample form. This form lets you run a SQL statement over HTTP against your Web server using various options, including running over HTTPS and zipping the result cursor for transfer.

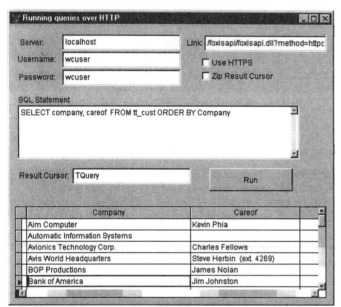

Figure 7.5. The wwHTTPData class allows running SQL statements over the Web from a client application. This form demonstrates most of the options available via class properties.

I'll start with the client-side code. I want to achieve a SQLPassthrough-type syntax for using the class and method. So to run a query over HTTP the code looks like this:

```
o = CREATE("wwHTTPData")

o.cServername = THISFORM.txtServer.value
o.cHTTPLink = THISFORM.txtLink.value
o.cUserName = THISFORM.txtUserName.value
o.cPassWord = THISFORM.txtPassword.value
o.lIsZipped = THISFORM.chkZipping.value
o.lSecure = THISFORM.chkHTTPS.Value

o.cSQLCursor = TRIM(THISFORM.txtSQLCursor.Value)

*** Run the request!
o.Execute(THISFORM.edtSQL.Value)

IF o.lError
```

```
      MESSAGEBOX(o.cErrorMsg,48,THISFORM.Caption)
ELSE
      THISFORM.grdResult.RecordSource = THISFORM.txtSQLCursor.Value
ENDIF
```

The idea is to set a few properties on an object and then run SQL statements against it. The first group of property assignments configures the object more or less generically. Once the properties are set, you run multiple Execute calls. Execute itself takes a SQL statement as a parameter (or you can set the cSQL property and not pass a parameter at all) and is responsible for actually calling the server. Here's how it works:

```
************************************
* wwHTTPData::Execute   && Client
************************************
LPARAMETER lcSQL
LOCAL lnSize, lnBuffer, lnResult

THIS.lError = .F.

lcSQL = IIF(TYPE("lcSQL") = "C",lcSQL,THIS.cSQL)

THIS.lError = .F.

IF !INLIST(LOWER(lcSQL),"select","create")
   llNoResultSet = .T.
ELSE
   llNoResultSet = .F.
ENDIF

lnResult = THIS.oHTTP.HTTPConnect(THIS.cServerName, THIS.cUsername, ;
   THIS.cPassWord, THIS.lSecure)
IF lnResult # 0
   THIS.cErrorMsg = THIS.oHTTP.cErrorMsg
   THIS.nError = lnResult
   THIS.lError = .T.
   RETURN .F.
ENDIF

THIS.oHTTP.AddPostKey("txtSQL",lcSQL)
THIS.oHTTP.AddPostKey("txtMaxBufferSize",LTRIM(STR(THIS.nMaxBufferSize)))
IF THIS.lIsZipped
   THIS.oHTTP.AddPostKey("IsZipped","True")
ENDIF

lcbuffer = SPACE(THIS.nMaxBufferSize)
lnSize = THIS.nMaxBufferSize

lnResult = THIS.oHTTP.HTTPGetEx(THIS.cHTTPLink, @lcBUffer, @lnSize)
IF lnResult # 0
   THIS.cErrorMsg = THIS.oHTTP.cErrorMsg
   THIS.nError = lnResult
   THIS.lError = .T.
   RETURN .F.
ENDIF
```

```
IF llNoResultSet
   IF EMPTY(lcBuffer)
      RETURN .T.
   ENDIF
ELSE
   IF EMPTY(lcBuffer)
     THIS.cErrorMsg = "No data was returned from this request..."
     THIS.nError = -1
     THIS.lError = .T.
     RETURN .F.
   ENDIF
ENDIF


IF lcBuffer = "Error"
   THIS.cErrorMsg = lcBuffer
   THIS.nError = -1
   THIS.lError = .T.
   RETURN .F.
ENDIF


IF llNoResultSet
   RETURN .T.
ENDIF


*** Retrieve the file name from the buffer
lcFileName = FORCEEXT(ADDBS(SYS(2023)) + TRIM( SUBSTR(lcBuffer,6,40) ),"dbf")


IF !THIS.oHTTP.DecodeDbf( lcBUffer,
IIF(THIS.lIsZipped,ForceExt(lcFileName,"zip"),lcFileName) )
   THIS.cErrorMsg = "Error: Error Decoding the downloaded file"
   IF AT("401",lcBuffer) > 0 AND ATC("Unauthorized",lcBuffer) > 0
      THIS.cErrorMsg = "Error: Unauthorized access. Check username/password"
   ENDIF
   THIS.nError = -1
   THIS.lError = .T.
   RETURN .F.
ENDIF


IF THIS.lIsZipped
   IF THIS.oHTTP.UnzipFiles(ForceExt(lcFileName,"zip"), ADDBS(SYS(2023))  ) # 0
      ERASE (ForceExt(lcFileName,"*"))
     THIS.cErrorMsg = "Error: Unzipping failed. Most likely you selected too
many messages to download..."
      THIS.nError = -1
      THIS.lError = .T.
       RETURN .T.
   ENDIF
ENDIF


USE (lcFileName) ALIAS THTTPImport
SELECT * FROM THTTPImport WHERE .T. into cursor ( THIS.cSQLCursor )
USE IN THTTPImport
ERASE (forceext(lcFileName,"*"))


RETURN .T.
```

Because you're communicating with a server object of your own design, this code can make a number of assumptions about the data being returned. Thus the error messages are formatted so that errors are caught and assigned to the cErrorMsg property. Notice also that the code checks for empty output—it might actually be okay to not return anything when running a SQL command that doesn't return data, such as anINSERT. Execute handles all packaging and formatting of the SQL statement and unpacks the result cursor that comes back from the server. The result is converted into a cursor by reselecting the data into Cursor and then deleting the temporary download file.

The server component, called S_Execute(), is implemented as another method of the same object. S_Execute takes as input a Web Connection Process object, which can be easily emulated by a wwFoxIsapi class by adding oHTML and oCGI properties that map to Response and Request objects. The idea is that S_Execute() is a self-contained method that can retrieve the input parameters for the SQL statement and return the output of the result cursor directly into the HTTP output stream. S_Execute is called as follows from a wwFoxISAPI request:

```
*** At the Class Definition level (Required for wwHTTPData!!!)
oCGI=.NULL.
oHTML=.NULL.


************************************************************************
* httpDemo :: HTTPData
*******************************
*** Check for validation here
*** Authentication is optional
*** Supported values in the INI -
***  Any         - Any Authorized user
***    Username   - A specific user - must match Authenticated User
***    ""         - None - no Authentication
lcAuthUser = "wcuser"  && THIS.GetAppIniVar("AuthUser","wwHTTPData")

THIS.oCGI = Request      && This code is required for wwFoxISAPI classes
THIS.oHTML = Response    && Add oCGI and oHTML as properties to your object

*** Create Data Object and call Server Side Execute method
***(wrapper for Process Method)
loData = CREATE("wwHTTPData")
loData.S_Execute(THIS, lcAuthUser)
```

Huh? Only five lines of code? Yup—S_Execute() acts as a fully self-contained request handler that sends output directly to the HTTP output stream so no additional Response.Write() calls are necessary.

Note the code to set a username for authentication. This is optional, but highly recommended to provide some added protection for your data. Because you can run SQL statements directly using this class, any VFP client application potentially has access to your server. The authentication can provide added protection to force users to log in prior to accessing data on the server. The request must send the authentication with the cUsername and cPassword properties. This information is then mapped against an NT username. If a username is not found, the command will not be executed. You can also use "", which means "Let everyone on," or "Any", which means "Allow any validated server user account."

You can see how the authentication is handled in S_Execute() among other things:

```
**************************************************************************
* Server side Execute
*******************************
*** Function: Generic Execute request handler routine that can
***            be used to pull data from the wire.
***            Typically called from a wwHTTPData client in VFP
***     Assume: Requires Web Connection server request (loProcess)
***       Pass: loProess    -    wwProcess object
***             lcAuthUser   -    User name allowed access (user,"ANY","")
**************************************************************************
LPARAMETER loProcess, lcAuthUser
LOCAL lcResultAlias, loEval, lcFileText, lnMaxLength, lcSQL, llUseZip, loHTML,
lcUserName

THIS.lError = .F.
THIS.cErrorMsg = ""

IF !THIS.Authorize(lcAuthUser, loProcess)
   RETURN
ENDIF

loHTML = loProcess.oHTML

lcFullSQL = loProcess.oCGI.GetFormVar("txtSQL")
lcSQL = LOWER(lcFullSQL,10))
llUseZip = !EMPTY(loProcess.oCGI.GetFormVar("IsZipped"))
lnMaxLength = VAL(loProcess.oCGI.GetFormVar("txtMaxBufferSize"))

IF EMPTY(lcSQL)
   loHTML.Send("Error: No SQL statement to process.")
   RETURN
ENDIF

lcOrigAlias = "wwd_" + SYS(2015)
lcOrigFileName = ADDBS(SYS(2023)) + lcOrigAlias

IF lcSQL = "select"
   lcFullSQL = lcFullSQL + " INTO TABLE " + lcOrigFilename
ENDIF

IF lcSQL # "select" AND lcSQL # "insert" AND lcSQL # "update" AND ;
   lcSQL # "delete" AND lcSQL # "create"
   loHTML.Send("Error: Only SQL commands are allowed.")
   RETURN
ENDIF

*** Turn off user interface functions so any error dialogs
*** will cause an error in the wwEval::Execute() call
*** In particular this will avoid File Open Dialogs
#IF  WWVFPVERSION > 5
  SYS(2335,0)
#ENDIF
```

```
loEval = CREATE("wwEval")
loEval.Execute(lcFullSQL)
IF loEval.lError
   loHTML.Send("Error: SQL statement caused an error." + CHR(13) + lcFullSQL)
   RETURN
ENDIF

#IF  WWVFPVERSION > 5
  SYS(2335,1)
#ENDIF

IF lcSQL # "select" AND lcSQL # "create"
   *** If no cursor is returned nothing needs to be returned
   RETURN
ENDIF

*** Otherwise encode the result file
lcResultAlias = Alias()

lcFileName = ADDBS(SYS(2023)) + "wwd_" + SYS(3) + ".dbf"

*** Now select the result into another cursor that we know by name
*** (CREATED TABLES WE MAY NOT)
SELECT * FROM (lcOrigAlias) INTO DBF (lcFileName)
USE
USE IN (lcResultAlias)

loIP = CREATE("wwIPStuff")

IF llUseZip
   IF loIP.ZipFiles(ForceExt(lcFilename,"zip"),;
                    ForceExt(lcFileName,"*"),9 ) # 0
      Response.Send("Error - unable to zip the file")
      RETURN
   ENDIF
   lcFileText = loIP.EncodeDBF(ForceExt(lcFilename,"zip") )
ELSE
   lcFileText = loIP.EncodeDBF(lcFileName,.T.)
ENDIF

IF EMPTY(lcFileText)
   loProcess.oHTML.Send("Error: File not encoded.")
   ERASE (ForceExt(lcFilename,"*"))
   ERASE (ForceExt(lcOrigFilename,"*"))
   RETURN
ENDIF

IF LEN(lcFileText) >= lnMaxLength
   loProcess.oHTML.Send("Error File is too large to send.")
   ERASE (ForceExt(lcFilename,"*"))
   ERASE (ForceExt(lcOrigFilename,"*"))
   RETURN
ENDIF

loProcess.oHTML.Send(lcFileText)
```

```
ERASE (ForceExt(lcFilename,"*"))
ERASE (ForceExt(lcOrigFilename,"*"))
```

The majority of this code deals with formatting and running the SQL statement. The wwEval class is used to safely execute the SQL statement. If an error occurs, the wwEval class's Error method captures the error and passes it back to the calling code without causing any other error handlers to kick off and bail out of the code or generate a runtime error. Also, note the call to SYS(2335), which turns off all user interface functions in a COM object. If a UI operation like a File Open dialog occurs, an error is generated rather than bringing up the dreaded File Open dialog, which could lock your server. This is new in VFP 6.0 and allows getting around some nasty hangup problems that previously couldn't be captured.

The query runs and is dumped to a predetermined temp file. The file is encoded with EncodeDBF() and, if okay, it is sent down the HTTP pipe. The result table can optionally be zipped on the fly (if the third-party DynaZip DLLs are available on the system). Because some commands won't return a result set, their code bypasses all the packaging and they simply return without result output.

Now a word of warning! This class can be very dangerous if not used in a controlled application environment. Because you have full access to the data on your server, a single `DELETE FROM <your favorite table here>` can wipe out all data in a single stroke. To protect yourself, you have two lines of defense: Hide the URL that you're hitting in your code to make the link non-obvious, and require authentication before allowing access even through your application. But even with these precautions in place, somebody in the know, like a disgruntled employee, might still have access to the data directly. Consider these issues very carefully before you generically implement a SQL request handler. The safest solution is to use embedded code that wraps the request in question with program logic—check the URLs that requests are coming from if necessary, or explicitly ask for authentication from users.

Putting it all together

You now have all the pieces to build an application that can run over the Internet as a client/server application using a totally open, non-proprietary protocol that can access your remote server from any Internet connection. You have full flexibility at the protocol level, and best of all, you can do it all with Visual FoxPro on both the client and server. Think of the flexibility you get with this approach! Whether you want to build offline applications like message readers, or applications that have a more sophisticated front end than HTML can provide, this simple client/server architecture makes it possible to build distributed applications with the tools you already know—and with very little code.

To review, a typical application that runs over HTTP can take advantage of the HTTP connections in the following ways:

- Sending "commands" via the URL's command line to trigger some operation on the server. For example: foxisapi.dll?method=ShowCustData&UserId= DA1111, where DA1111 might be a parameter sent to the server to let it know to work on Customer ID DA1111.

- Retrieving data *from* an HTTP link via HTTPGet() or HTTPGetEx().

- Sending data *to* the server via POSTing data using HTTPGetEx(). Remember that HTTPGetEx() can do both POST and GET operations on a single request, as demonstrated in the last example.

- Simulating a Web browser with a VFP front-end application by simply posting variables to a server.

- Transferring raw data over HTTP and running full-blown SQL statements across the wire if both ends are running Visual FoxPro.

Let's come back to the message board example on my Web site I cited at the beginning of this chapter. My site hosts a message board that is used to post messages for support of Web Connection and general Web programming issues. People access the Web site to view information online, but I recently built an offline reader (see Figure 7.6a) that allows these visitors to use a local VFP application to view that same data. Rather than browsing the Web site, the users can download messages via HTTP and merge them into an existing local file. At the same time, any messages that users want to post can be sent up to the server and merged into the online file for updating. Messages are posted and visible on the Web site as well as available for download.

The motivation for this operation is clear: You can build a vastly more efficient UI with a VFP application than on the Web, and the access to the data is much faster. A onetime download, which usually takes only a few seconds, can bring down the data for the entire day immediately, while viewing the messages online can take much more time depending on your connection. Rather than downloading new HTML every time, you load the message content only once—and in compressed format to boot.

In addition to the speed, the client has a lot more flexibility with the data. Users can see unread messages because a local file can flag messages as read. This is impossible online because there's no easy way to attach user information to the online message file, such as which users have read which messages. Locally, it's a simple True/False flag that you can easily query and display with a special image in the Treeview. **Figure 7.6a** (top) shows the GUI version, while **Figure 7.6b** (bottom) shows the Web version.

Here's a look at some key code elements of this application. The following code is a real-world example including error checking, showing how you can put this technology to work:

```
* Form method that handles file downloads
* Pass qualified WHERE clause for the SELECT statement
* Filter must be time zone adjusted (in Download form)
FUNCTION DownLoadMessages
LPARAMETER lcDownLoadFilter

loIP = CREATE("wwIPStuff")

*** Add the Download Filter as a POST key
loIP.AddPostKey("Filter",lcDownLoadFilter)
```

```
THISFORM.StatusMessage("Downloading Messages...",,1)

lnResult = loIP.HTTPConnect(wwt_cfg.server)
IF lnResult # 0
   THISFORM.StatusMessage("Error: " + loIP.cErrorMsg)
   RETURN -1
ENDIF

*** Presize the result buffer - only want 500k at a time
lcBUffer = SPACE(500000)
lnSize = LEN(lcBUffer)
lnStartTime = SECONDS()

lnResult = loIP.HTTPGetEx(;
      "/wconnect/wc.dll?wwthreads~Downloadmessages",;
      @lcBUffer,@lnSize)
IF lnResult # 0
   THISFORM.StatusMessage("Error: " + loIP.cErrorMsg)
   RETURN -1
ENDIF

IF lcBUffer = "ERROR - No Records"
   THISFORM.StatusMessage("No messages to download")
   RETURN -1
ENDIF

IF EMPTY(lcBUffer)
   THISFORM.StatusMessage(;
     "Error: No data was returned by the server...")
   RETURN -1
ENDIF

IF !loIP.DecodeDbf(lcBUffer, "TImport.dbf")
   THIS.StatusMessage("Error: File Import failed. "+;
                      "Too many messages!")
   RETURN -1
ENDIF

*** All went well - Now import the messages
lnReccount = 0

SELE 0
USE TImport
SCAN
   SELECT wwThreads
   LOCATE FOR Msgid = TImport.Msgid
   IF !FOUND()
      SELECT TImport
      SCATTER MEMO MEMVAR
      SELECT wwThreads
      APPEND BLANK
      GATHER MEMO MEMVAR
      lnReccount = lnReccount + 1
   ENDIF
ENDSCAN
```

```
USE IN TImport
ERASE TImport.*
*** Refresh the form with the new data
THISFORM.BuildTree()
THISFORM.StatusMessage("Downloaded " + LTRIM(STR(lnReccount)) + ;
  " message(s) in " + STR(SECONDS() - lnStartTime,2) + " seconds")


RETURN lnReccount
```

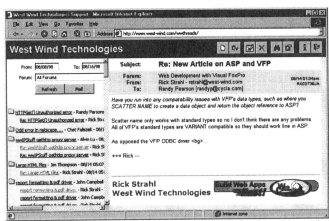

Figures 7.6a and 7.6b. *Which user interface do you think is easier to use? The rich GUI version (top) allows the message views to be configurable to the user so he can see unread messages and threads as flagged. The Web version (bottom) is generic and not customized for each user.*

There are a couple of notable issues here. This code works by sending a request to the server with a POST variable called FILTER, which is a complete WHERE clause to a SELECT statement. Typically the filter contains a date range that is adjusted for time zones, but this code can also be used from a search dialog, simply by passing the appropriate search parameters in the filter expression to provide a Web-based search. This makes this method reusable for all download operations required by the application.

Note that the HTTP download buffer is allocated to a whopping 500K in order to make sure that I can capture a reasonably large file. Even so, 500K will only allow retrieval of approximately three weeks' worth of data—anything more and the download will fail. Because I have a rough idea of traffic, I give the user a warning dialog if he's trying to download more than three weeks of data at once.

Next, notice all the error handling. With these file downloads it's extremely important to check every call that is returned from WinInet. If an error occurs, back out gracefully with a message to the user. You need to decide on the server end what to return in case of an error. In this case the request returns a file, so the code checks for an empty string and then for proper size as specified by the encoding header (this happens in DecodeDBF()).

On the Web Connection server end (almost identical to the wwFoxISAPI code) the code looks like this:

```
* HTTPProcess :: DownloadMessages
FUNCTION DownLoadMessages
LOCAL lcFilter, lcToDate, lcFromDate, lcForum

lcFilter = Request.GetFormVar("Filter")

IF EMPTY(lcFilter)
   lcForum = Request.GetFormVar("Forum")
   lcFromDate = Request.GetFormVar("FromDate")
   lcToDate = Request.GetFormVar("ToDate")

   lcFilter = "Forum='" + PADR(lcForum,30) +"' AND " +;
           "timestamp >= {" + lcFromDate +"} AND "+;
           "timestamp <= {" + lcToDate + "} + 1"
ENDIF

lcFile = SYS(3)
SELECT ThreadId, Msgid, Subject, Message, FromName, FromEmail, To,Forum,;
      TimeStamp ;
      FROM (DATAPATH + "wwThreads") ;
      WHERE &lcFilter ;
      INTO DBF (lcFile)

IF _TALLY < 1
   Response.Send("ERROR - No Records")
   USE
   ERASE (lcFile + ".*")
   RETURN
ENDIF
USE

loIP = CREATE("wwIPStuff")

lcFileText = loIP.EncodeDBF(lcFile + ".dbf",.T.)

IF EMPTY(lcFileText)
   Response.Send("ERROR - File not encoded.")
```

```
      ERASE (lcFile + ".*")
      RETURN
ENDIF

IF LEN(lcFileText) >= 500000
   Response.Send("ERROR - File is too large to send.")
   ERASE (lcFile + ".*")
   RETURN
ENDIF

*** This is the actual FILE Send operation!
Response.Send(lcFileText)

ERASE (lcFile + ".*")

ENDFUNC
* DownLoadMsgs
```

Note the sending of the error messages in the appropriate places. The error messages can be retrieved on the client side and can provide meaningful display in the status bar of the reader. Note, in particular, the size check for the 500K response size. If the encoded file is greater than 500K, a message is sent back rather than attempting (and failing) to send a file that's too large. The client and server sides need to agree on these sizes for this to work properly.

For good measure, here's the client code for uploading messages to the server:

```
FUNCTION UploadMessages

LoIP = CREATE("wwIPStuff")

THISFORM.StatusMessage("Uploading Messages...",,1)

SELECT * FROM wwThreads ;
   WHERE Post AND !DELETED() ;
   INTO DBF TExport

IF _TALLY < 1
   USE
   ERASE TEXPORT.DBF
   ERASE TEXPORT.FPT
   THISFORM.StatusMessage("No messages to upload...")
   LoAPI = CREATE("wwAPI")
   loAPI.Sleep(2000)
ENDIF

THISFORM.StatusMessage("Uploading " + LTRIM(STR(_Tally)) + " Messages...",,1)

USE
lcFileText = loIP.EncodeDBF("TExport.dbf",.T.)

ERASE TEXPORT.DBF
ERASE TEXPORT.FPT
```

```
IF EMPTY(lcFileText)
   THISFORM.StatusMessage("Invalid File Info - not uploaded")
   RETURN
ENDIF


loIP.AddPostKey("FileText",lcFileText)

lnResult = loIP.HTTPConnect(wwt_cfg.server)
IF lnResult # 0
   THISFORM.StatusMessage("Error: "+loIP.cErrorMsg)
   RETURN
ENDIF

lcBUffer = SPACE(500000)
lnSize = LEN(lcBuffer)

lnResult = loIP.HTTPGetEx("/wconnect/wc.dll?wwthreads~UploadMessages",;
                         @lcBuffer,@lnSize)

IF lnResult # 0
   THISFORM.StatusMessage("Error: "+loIP.cErrorMsg)
   RETURN
ENDIF

*** Must check if the Upload went Ok
if lcBuffer # "OK"
   *** No - don't delete messages to post
   THISFORM.StatusMessage("File Upload Failed")
   RETURN
ENDIF

THISFORM.StatusMessage("Deleting Posted Messages...",,1)
DELETE FROM wwThreads WHERE Post

THISFORM.StatusMessage()

RETURN
```

Here the result from the POST operation simply returns OK or an error code, which is irrelevant—it either worked or it didn't.

Don't forget about security!
Sending data over the wire, especially over an open Internet connection, can be dangerous. Remember that it's possible to intercept the data traveling over the Net with a packet analyzer and potentially hijack sensitive information. Your first line of defense is to use HTTPS (Secure HTTP or SSL) to transmit your data to and from the Web server. HTTPS requires a secure certificate on the Web server (see Chapter 10's Security section). Once installed, all communication using HTTPS is encrypted. Unfortunately, the encryption process noticeably slows down communications and you'll want to use it only on requests where security is really required—all others should continue non-secure. The wwIPStuff class supports HTTPS using the low-level HTTP functions by specifying the fourth parameter of .T. for HTTPConnect() or the lSecure property to establish a secure link:

```
FUNCTION HTTPConnect
LPARAMETER lcServer, lcUsername, lcPassword, llSecure
```

Another simple way to protect yourself from unauthorized access is to use passwords. WinInet supports security via standard Web-based *Basic Authentication* or *NT Challenge Response* that uses NT domain security for permissions. You can connect to the server using a specific security context, which exists only while connected to the server over the HTTP connection. wwIPStuff supports this with the second and third parameters to the call to HTTPConnect(). With wwFoxISAPI, you can force a request to password-validate a user with the following code:

```
*** See whether user is already Authenticated
lcUser = Request.GetAuthenticatedUser()

IF EMPTY(lcUser)
   *** Nope - force Login dialog
   Response. Authenticate()
   RETURN
ENDIF
```

Authenticate() is a method in the FoxISAPI wwResponse class that requests authentication from the Web server via an HTTP header that is returned as a result. The HTTP result looks like this:

```
HTTP/1.0 401 Not Authorized
WWW-Authenticate: basic realm = "localhost"

<HTML><h2>Gotta enter your password to get in!</h2></HTML>
```

WinInet supports navigating this request and sending the username/password to the server and essentially logging the user in. The server request runs again, and this time the user is authenticated and the request can proceed. The client end is automatic with the call to HTTPConnect(). On the server you have to implement the above code to enforce the authentication check.

Another security issue to keep in mind is that links that download data can also be accessed by a browser directly. Although users will likely never see the actual link that is called, it's possible to access the same data link you might use to retrieve data directly via the Location URL line in the browser if a user can guess the URL. Nothing like somebody figuring out your file upload link, and sending you continuous uploads that will fill up and crash your server's hard disk. Consider your URL names carefully and use authentication where applicable to avoid these problems.

Note that both Secure HTTP and authentication don't work with the plain HTTPGet. If you only want to retrieve data securely, you have to use HTTPConnect() and HTTPGetEx().

What about other server tools?

I've used FoxISAPI as the Web server back end in the previous examples. For these examples to work, you need to use the Foxisapi.dll provided with the Developer's Download Files at www.hentzenwerke.com because the update fixes problems with sending binary output to the client. The wwIPStuff code originated from the Web Connection libraries, so it also works safely with Web Connection. If you use another tool such as Active Server Pages, you need to make a few adjustments. I haven't checked out tools like FoxWeb or X-Works—check with the authors to determine whether they support binary output.

With Active Server Pages, the problem is more complicated. VBScript uses double-byte Variants internally, which can cause several problems with binary data. Variant strings are null terminated so when you send a binary string to output they terminate at the NULL. You can get around this problem by using the Response object's BinaryWrite method instead of the basic Write. This method outputs any text string (or Byte Array as the docs call it) as-is, without first converting it to VB's double-byte, wide-character formatting. This will work fine if you create your binary data inside the VBScript code or with one of the built-in objects.

Unfortunately, I've been unable to send binary data created inside Visual FoxPro through an Active Server Page. The problem is that ASP converts the result from a VFP COM object into a Variant, which truncates the result at any NULLs that are encountered. Because VFP cannot return a typed string result (as you can from C, Delphi or VB-created COM objects), the result string is always a double-byte Variant. Sending this Variant with BinaryWrite results in actually sending two bytes per character back to the client, while Write will truncate at NULLs. This limitation means you have to confine yourself to sending non-binary data (like comma-delimited strings or URLEncoded strings) from any VFP COM object.

As a workaround you can use a VFP COM object to send the output. You can pass in the Response object to the method, then use BinaryWrite() from within the Fox object to send the output:

```
Function ASPResponseMethod
LPARAMETER loResponse

lcBinary = FunctionThatReturnsBinary()
loResponse.BinaryWrite(lcBinary)
RETURN
```

This is the only way I've been able to pass binary data back through the ASP engine from VFP. Sorry, but ASP is not a good platform for HTTP messaging with VFP COM objects.

WinInet issues
You should be aware of some issues related to using WinInet's HTTP functions in the context of creating HTTP transfer operations.

Although the wwIPStuff class contains support for connection, receive, and send timeouts (*WinInetSetTimeout()*), a request that hangs in the middle of a connection will not time out according to these values. Instead, a Windows Sockets system default (typically 30-40 seconds) is applied by WinInet. This can be a problem because the WinInet functions don't provide any feedback while in process, and the user might think the request hung. Microsoft calls this "by design" because Web servers typically handle timeouts based on the Web server specified timeout value to allow large requests to complete. I suggest you carefully test your requests under various connection environments to see exactly how your application might be affected by lost or unavailable connections.

Sending huge files in either direction is probably not a good idea unless you have a speedy Internet connection. Bandwidth is always critical, but you also need to think of the system limitations. The process of URLEncoding a string to be sent to the server is slow, especially when using FoxPro code to do the encoding. This is why the online version switches to DLL functions for faster encoding operation. The latest version of wwIPStuff also supports a mechanism of sending data in Multipart Form format, which requires no encoding. This is a brand-new feature which you can read up on in the provided documentation for wwIPStuff. This mechanism can drastically reduce the size of uploaded form data.

Web servers also have a timeout—if you're sending a huge amount of data to the server over a slow link, the server might disconnect you when it's timeout is up, even though data might still be transferring.

The examples in this chapter use fully synchronous access to the Web server, which means you connect, start downloading, and then wait for completion of the request without any feedback. The latest version of wwIPStuff provides an asynchronous version of the HTTP functions that can help, but it's a bit more work to get the result data because you now have to deal with events for download completion, errors, and so on. wwIPStuff implements some workarounds by spying the HTTP header and then using event hooks to let your code know when a new chunk is retrieved, but it's beyond the scope of this discussion. You can examine the cHTTPHeader property and the OnHTTPBufferUpdate() method in the wwIPStuff documentation for more information about how to retrieve status information while transferring data.

In addition to data size, keep in mind that when *sending* data to the server, the URLEncoding process also makes your data much larger—up to three times as big as the original (%0D, for example, for a Carriage Return (Chr(13))). You can get around the size limitations and feedback issues by "chunking" your downloads—break them into smaller files and then request the remaining files successively. It requires some logic and state-keeping to work efficiently.

You can also get some size relief by using a third-party zip control such as DynaZip. DBF data is a prime candidate for compression, yielding 80 percent compression or better for typical VFP tables. The message board uses DynaZip to perform compression, which has resulted in tremendous improvements in transfer times (for example, bringing down 200+ messages over 28.8k in under a minute). But zipped files also tend to be binary content, so although the data might get 80 percent smaller, it becomes more prone to require extensive encoding, which might boost the size back up.

Unrelated to file transfers, I've had a few problems with WinInet when accessing a lot of *different* sites in quick succession. For example, using wwIPStuff to build a Web crawler or to verify site links, you might fire off various requests in quick succession. WinInet handles some operations in the background on separate execution threads. Sometimes when quickly connecting and disconnecting from different sites, some threads don't clean up properly, leaking handles. Furthermore, accessing a link that redirects to another page causes WinInet to leak three handles because the connection is never properly closed—regardless of whether you release the IP handles. Make sure you check typical operation with WinInet to see whether your code is affected by these problems. I expect these to get fixed by Microsoft as WinInet use becomes more prevalent. Neither of these issues should be a problem if you're implementing applications that always connect to the same server.

Summary

Realize that this architecture is *not* meant to replace HTML front-end applications. By using this approach you are requiring all clients to have Win95/NT and the Visual FoxPro runtime, so all the cross-platform and thin-client advantages that HTML brings to the party don't apply. Plain and simple—you're dealing with Fat Client technology by running VFP on the client. But you do gain the ability to take advantage of the Web's distributed environment to make your application reach out and communicate with users everywhere.

If you're building corporate or shrink-wrapped applications that need to communicate from widely spread locations, this is an easy way to link applications to a home site. Whether you're pulling occasional data updates or querying real-time data over the Web, you get the distributed aspect of Web applications without having to bite the HTML bullet.

The big benefit is that you can take advantage of VFP's rich UI features to provide a productive work environment and still provide the distributed, plug-in-from-anywhere connectivity. I use this front end for a number of maintenance operations, from downloading orders from my Web site directly into my Point of Sale application, to checking my error logs on various sites by downloading them to the local machine. In all cases, this VFP front end is only an extension to existing Web applications that are running a full HTML interface. The possibilities are endless, and many companies and popular software packages are already taking advantage of this type of interface. You can do the same from your Visual FoxPro applications!

Pros
- Use a rich user interface instead of limited HTML.
- Use VFP data locally, including data-binding.
- Continue to take advantage of VFP's data access and language features on both ends of the connection.
- Full application environment—not a limited "script-safe" environment that a browser requires.
- Can be used as a data access mechanism for Active Document applications.

Cons
- Fat Client—Visual FoxPro required on the client.
- Potential security issues.

Chapter 8
Remote Data Service

In the last chapter I introduced you to the concept of data transfer over HTTP using your own custom implementation of a data service provider through FoxPro classes that can pack and unpack data on both ends of a connection. More recently Microsoft has introduced Remote Data Service (RDS), which provides the same kind of functionality wrapped up in a system service provided as part of ActiveX Data Objects (ADO). With RDS you can ask for an ADO recordset over the Internet from a Web server and use that data on any client that supports ActiveX controls, including Internet Explorer. Furthermore, Internet Explorer supports direct data binding to RDS recordsets, which, although limited, can provide an easy way to display data in tables. Unfortunately, this technology is very rough, especially when used with Visual FoxPro data, but it bears discussion here because it's very promising for the future.

In addition to data, RDS allows access to COM objects over HTTP. Yes, through the intermediate services that RDS provides it's possible for you to instantiate an object over the Internet and call methods on it. The methods can return values or an ADO recordset as a result, which makes it a powerful mechanism to mix code and data.

Direct data access over the Internet is a feature of particular interest to database developers. Until recently, and usually today, when people think of Web applications they're mostly thinking about server-side applications that use tools such as Active Server Pages and FoxISAPI to handle all application logic (even multiple tiers) on the server. In the last chapter I introduced you to the concept of distributed applications, where part of the application runs on the client and part on the server. Data access is a logical extension of that concept and one that simplifies the process of moving logic to the client side of an Internet connection. The WinInet tools I introduced for data access work well if your client is Visual FoxPro—they give you full control over both sides of the connection and even the actual "system" code because it's all implemented in FoxPro code.

I built the WinInet data access tools quite a while back, and RDS is an official Microsoft system version of those data access concepts, legitimizing the concept of data access across the Internet through integrating it as part of the Microsoft Data Access Components and more precisely as an extension of ADO.

I have to warn you, though—I've used this technology only in testing. I rarely write about topics that I haven't used for real applications, but I think it's worthwhile to make an exception here. The reason that I haven't used it yet is a simple one: I don't believe these tools are ready for production work. But I think it will be a significant part of Microsoft's future database access strategy and that it's worthwhile to take the time to explore it now, to understand the current problems and to bug Microsoft to fix them. RDS is very exciting for bringing easier data access over the Internet down to your FoxPro and Internet Explorer client applications.

How RDS works

RDS accomplishes a very important feat: It gives the client application the impression that you are directly accessing a database on the server over the Internet. Think of it as a stripped-down, remote version of ADO that works with disconnected recordset objects that can be reconnected to their original data source after updating them locally.

RDS is implemented as an ActiveX control, which is used on the client side. The ActiveX control serves several purposes:

- Handles the communication with a Web server to marshal data from client to server.
- Exposes the result data via ADO to the client.
- Allows updating the original data from changes made on the client.

Figure 8.1 describes the flow of data over an RDS connection. The client code essentially establishes a connection with a data source on the server, which must be a running Internet Information Server. To use the ActiveX control, you set a handful of properties that determine the server to which the query will be sent and the SQL statement to run on the server. The ActiveX control forwards these property settings to the specified Web server. An ISAPI extension on the server picks out the query properties and fires up a data-processing COM object (Advanced.DataFactory by default) to process the command. The client can override this COM object from the client side and point at a custom component that implements the specific data-handling interface required (very similar to an ADO DataProvider). The COM object performs the requested query and creates an ADO recordset. The recordset is sent back as a return value from the COM method call. The ISAPI extension then regains control and packages the recordset into a format suitable to be sent over HTTP back to the client. The ActiveX control on the client retrieves this packaged ADO recordset, reassembles it on the other end, and makes it available to the client application through its recordset property. Note that the data must first be downloaded and, depending on the flags set on the control, the request might have to wait for the data to complete downloading.

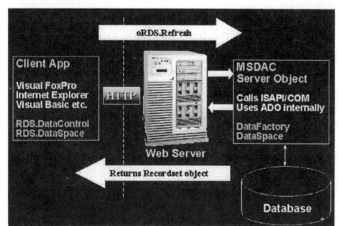

Figure 8.1. RDS works by marshaling an ADO recordset over HTTP. The server is a Web server component that runs the query and sends a recordset to the client.

Once on the client, the recordset object can be used to access and update the data. While using the recordset, the data is offline, meaning any changes made are not immediately updated on the server. You can change, delete and add data in offline mode. A special method called SubmitChanges() allows the client recordset to update the original data set on the server. RDS marshals the data back up to the server and tries to update the data. If there are update-contention issues, RDS will throw an exception that you can respond to—it's supposed to be an all-or-nothing process, although the current functionality causes incomplete updates to happen even on the row level. (I'll talk more about these problems toward the end of this chapter.)

All this requires the data to travel back and forth across the wire. The server fetches data as needed with the Refresh() method and then sends it back with SubmitChanges(), causing a fair amount of network traffic. You'll want to be very selective (pun intended) to pull only the data you really need on the client side.

An example using Internet Explorer

In this example I'll use Internet Explorer as the client, because I think that this is likely to be a common scenario for Web sites that provide interactive database access. RDS is client-side technology that accesses data via a Web server on the server end. Keep in mind that RDS must have an ActiveX control to work properly, so for now at least, this technology is limited to Internet Explorer—it won't work with Netscape or any other browser. Because this code is IE-specific, I borrowed the user interface from one of the examples in Chapter 5. **Figure 8.2** shows the output from the guest application using RDS to retrieve and update data on the server.

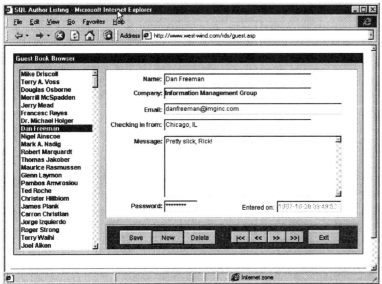

Figure 8.2. This guest book example downloads the existing list of guests up front, and then allows browsing the list to add and edit guest information. Once the data is downloaded, all data access is local.

Make sure RDS is installed on your server. Open the Windows registry to see if you have these keys under HKLM\SYSTEM\CurrentControlSet\ Services\W3SVC\Parameters\ADCLaunch:

RDSServer.DataFactory
AdvancedDataFactory

If these keys don't exist, go back to your IIS setup on the NT Option Pack disk and select Remote Data Service from the IIS setup options.

 Let's discuss how the application shown in Figure 8.2 is put together by looking at the highlights. To set up the sample from the Developer's Download Files at www.hentzenwerke.com, follow these steps:

1. Copy the RDS directory to your hard drive.
2. Add the new directory as a virtual directory to IIS, making sure Execute rights are set.
3. Copy the data files to another directory.
4. Set up a System DSN in the ODBC Driver Manager using the VFP ODBC Driver to point at the above data path. Call it *VFPGuest*.

Then take a look at the Guest.asp page. The first and most important part of this page is the RDS ActiveX control that is embedded into the page with the following object tag:

```
<head>
<object classid="clsid:BD96C556-65A3-11D0-983A-00C04FC29E33"
        ID="oRDS" WIDTH="1" HEIGHT="1">
  <param name="SERVER" value="http://<%=
Request.ServerVariables("SERVER_NAME")%>/">
</object>
<title>RDS Guest Book</title>
</head>
```

Notice that there's an Active Server tag in there. The actual page loaded from the server is an ASP page. The ASP doesn't do anything other than provide the dynamic server name, which is important if this page will be used on different servers (say localhost for testing and www.west-wind.com online). With High or Medium security set on the browser, the server must always point at the same server as the page that is running. So, when the page loads from www.west-wind.com, the data access must also occur on that server or the call to Refresh() to get the data will fail.

The next thing that happens is that the HTML page loads and binds the data retrieved in the page's Load event into the data-bound controls. I'll come back to the HTML and field data binding in a second. For now, look at how the data gets loaded. The following code fires in the document's Load event and causes the data to be downloaded from the server:

```
<script language="VBScript"><!--

'---- enum Values ----
Const adcExecSync = 1
Const adcExecAsync = 2

'---- enum Values ----
Const adcFetchUpFront = 1
Const adcFetchBackground = 2
Const adcFetchAsync = 3

Const adEditAdd = 2

Sub Load
   'Change the asynchronous options such that execution is synchronous
   'and Fetching can occur in the background
   oRDS.ExecuteOptions = adcExecSync
   oRDS.FetchOptions = adcFetchBackground


   oRDS.Connect = "dsn=VFPGuest"          ' Server DSN

   oRDS.SQL = "Select custid,Name,Company,email,entered,message,location," +_
              "phone,heardfrom,password  from Guest"

   oRDS.Refresh           'Download the data

   oRDS.Sort = "NAME"     'Sort order
   FillListBox()          'listbox can'tbe data bound so fill manually

   oRDS.Recordset.MoveFirst  'show first item
End Sub
...
</script>
```

The key code elements are the Connect and SQL properties and the Refresh() method, which cause the ActiveX control to download the data from the server. The Connect property can point to any valid connection string on the server. Keep in mind this will be a DSN or plain connection string *on the server*, not the client. In this case I used a DSN on the server, but you can also access a file directly on the server using the following syntax (and this is very, very scary security wise! More on this later):

```
oRDS.Connect = "driver=Microsoft Visual FoxPro Driver;" & _
               "Exclusive=No;SourceType=DBF;" & _
               "SourceDB=d:\wwapps\wc2\wwdemo;uid=;pwd="
```

The SQL property allows you to execute SQL commands on the server. Make sure you minimize the data that comes down by specifying only the fields you actually need. The call to Refresh() actually causes RDS to retrieve data. Now, depending on how much data you're downloading, the rest of the page waits for the data download to complete. Once the data has come down, I use the FillListBox() method to get data into the listbox. This requires some script code because listboxes can't be data-bound in Internet Explorer:

```
Sub FillListBox()
   Set rs = oRDS.RecordSet
   lnCount = rs.RecordCount
   rs.MoveFirst

   ' Clear the list first - manual again
   For x = 0 to document.all.lstGuests.length -1
      'msgbox document.all.lstGuests.Options(0).text
      document.all.lstGuests.Options.remove(0)
   Next

   ' Fill the actual data into the list - set display and value
   For x = 1 to lnCount
      Set loOption = document.createElement("OPTION")
      loOption.Text = rs("Name")
      loOption.Value = rs("CustId")
      document.all.lstGuests.add(loOption)
      rs.MoveNext
   Next
End Sub
```

I use the recordset object to loop through the records and populate the listbox using the Add() method of the list box (lstGuests). First the list must be cleared but there's no built-in method, so it has to be done manually with a few lines of code. If you remember the ASP chapter you'll remember that the syntax for accessing the individual fields of the recordset is `rs("FieldName")`. In the code, note also that both a value and display text are assigned with the listbox's Value and Text properties, respectively. The former makes lookups easier in order to refresh the form—because the listbox isn't data-bound, the translation between a listbox item and the data display must be done manually using the ShowRecord() function shown below.

After loading the listbox, the record pointer is reset to the first record in the set with `oRDS.Recordset.MoveFirst()`. The actual display of all fields in the HTML form is handled via IE data binding. Fields are bound using the Dynamic HTML *DataSrc* and *DataFld* tags:

```
<INPUT NAME="txtname" datasrc="#oRDS" DataFld="Name" ID="txtname"
STYLE="POSITION:ABSOLUTE;LEFT:293;TOP:20;WIDTH:288;HEIGHT:23;"
"Font:normal normal 9pt 'Arial';Color:#000000;BACKGROUND:#FFFFFF" >
```

Each field on the form has the datasrc set to #oRDS, which is the object name of the ActiveX control in the document preceded by a pound sign (#). DataFld describes the RDS field name in the recordset that should be displayed.

The bound controls refresh automatically when the record pointer is moved, so it's easy to implement the navigation buttons of the guest form. For example, the Move Next button simply embeds the MoveNext() call to the recordset object directly into the Input tag:

```
<INPUT NAME="btnSubmit" ID="btnSubmit" TYPE="SUBMIT" VALUE=">>"
         onclick="oRDS.RecordSet.MoveNext">
```

While I took the simple route here, it's usually a better idea to use a separate function in order to perform extra processing such as checking for beginning or end of file.

When navigating through the listbox, navigation is based on a guest ID, which requires two methods:

```
Sub lstGuests_OnChange
   ShowRecord(lstGuests.Value)
End Sub

Sub ShowRecord(lcCustId)
   Set rs = oRDS.RecordSet
   lnCount = rs.RecordCount
   rs.MoveFirst
   For x = 1 to lnCount
      If rs("CustId") = lcCustId  Then
         Exit For
      End If
      rs.MoveNext
   Next
End Sub
```

The listbox isn't data bound, so when you move the record pointer or click on an entry, ShowRecord() must be called to move the record pointer. Because ADO doesn't support searching a result set, you have to do this manually by searching manually through the recordset. Note that this can be very slow. I ran the guest book with 350 records and the search on the end of the list took upwards of five seconds to refresh the record. Because ADO is all COM and every line of code in VBScript is interpreted, this is no speed demon unless you keep your recordsets small. ADO does support the Filter property, which lets you quickly get to a specific record:

```
rs.Filter = "CustId = '" & lcCustId & "'"
```

But unfortunately that code filters the entire recordset, so once the filter is set you can't use MoveNext() and MovePrevious() anymore. You can reset the filter with rs.filter = "", but there's no way to hang on to the current record pointer location when you do. These are just some of the seemingly simple issues you run into with ADO in general and RDS specifically that make database development very difficult—the lack of basic features like searching and requerying a result set is tough to overcome.

You can also update data. Because the input fields are bound to the data, any updates you make affect the underlying recordset. The changes are made as soon as you type in new data. Remember that you're working with the data offline—the data doesn't go to the server until you call SubmitChanges(). In the sample, you have to click the Save button when saving a new entry or making changes to an existing record:

```
Sub btnSave_OnClick()
   oRDS.SubmitChanges
   FillListBox()
End Sub
```

To add new records you can use the RDS AddNew() method:

```
Sub btnNew_OnClick()
   oRDS.Recordset.AddNew()

   '*** Make sure all get initialized to non-null values
   oRDS.Recordset("CustId") =  LEFT(Timer(),8)
   oRDS.Recordset("Entered") = now
   oRDS.Recordset("Phone") = ""
   oRDS.Recordset("HeardFrom")=""
   oRDS.Recordset("Location")=""
   oRDS.Recordset("Password")=""
End Sub
```

Note the initialization here. If you don't do this initialization you can run into problems with NULL values. The VFP ODBC driver has problems with the NULL formatting that ODBC assigns to all non-provided values in INSERTS, so this is a constant concern. Initializing each field you're working with beforehand makes sure the fields aren't NULL to start with.

Table-based data binding with RDS
Data binding is a powerful feature that makes it easy to get data to the client, especially if you're dealing with read-only data or in scenarios where simple data entry or modification needs to occur. For a little variety I used the SQL Server Pubs database here, but you could use a Fox table or database in its place. The following example simply pulls all the records from the SQL Server sample Pubs database and displays them for simple data editing in a table. **Figure 8.3** shows this simple form.

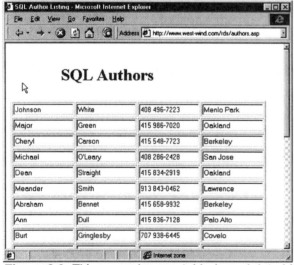

Figure 8.3. This example uses table-based data binding against an RDS recordset retrieved from SQL Server. This updateable "grid" of fields takes practically no code— the data binding provides all the display and input field handling of the table.

What's cool about this example is how little code it takes using the IE data binding features. As in the example above, the Load event handles loading the data:

```
Sub Load
  oRDS.ExecuteOptions = adcExecSync
  oRDS.FetchOptions = adcFetchBackground

  oRDS.SQL = "Select au_FName, au_LName, Phone, city from authors"


  oRDS.Connect = "dsn=pubs;UID=sa;PWD=;" ' System DSN must be installed on this
system
  ' oRDS.Connect = "DRIVER={SQL
Server};server=(local);uid=sa;pwd=;database=Pubs"

  oRDS.Refresh
End Sub
```

The real time saver is the way that data binding to an HTML table is implemented:

```
<table border="1" datasrc="#oRDS">
<tdbody>
  <tr>
    <td width="50"><input datafld="au_fName" size="15" id="first"
name="first"></td>
    <td width="50"><input datafld="au_lName" size="15" id="last"
name="last"></td>
    <td width="50"><input datafld="Phone" size="15" id="last"
name="Phone"></td>
    <td width="50"><input datafld="City" size="15" id="City" name="City"></td>
  </tr>
</tdbody>
</table>
```

A *DataSrc* tag can be tied directly to an HTML table. Each row of the table causes IE to fetch additional data, much in the same way a SCAN/ENDSCAN works in FoxPro. Fields for display or data entry need only add the *DataFld* tag to specify which field is to be displayed from the currently active recordset.

Not only does it take only a few lines of code to create this table with remote data, but it's also quite efficient. You see, data binding to a table allows IE to render the table as the data comes in, adding rows dynamically to the table as more data becomes available, rather than waiting for the data up front. This is efficient both from a data perspective as well as from table rendering. Normally tables cannot display before the data is in place (it's too bad this dynamic rendering doesn't work with plain non-data tables—you can look for this feature in Internet Explorer 5.0).

The bottom of the form also includes an Update button that takes any changes made to the displayed data and propagates them back up to the server. The code is simple:

```
Sub btnUpdate_OnClick()
  oRDS.SubmitChanges
End Sub
```

That's it! What you have here is a form that is bound to data on the server, but running offline with the ability to go back online at any time using SubmitChanges(). Note that there's almost no code involved with this form. The only real code deals with setting up the SQL query and actually pulling the data down.

Using RDS inside VFP

RDS is implemented as an ActiveX control so you can also use it inside VFP. However, the ActiveX control is a lightweight, IE-style control, which can't be hosted as a control inside a Visual FoxPro form. The RDS.DataControl can only be instantiated via code. The code to run a query over the Internet with RDS looks something like this, using the same guest book example data from before:

```
lcConnStr = "dsn=VFPGuest"
lcSQL = "select name,company,Message from guest"

oRDS = CREATEOBJECT("RDS.DataControl")

oRDS.SERVER = "http://Localhost/"
oRDS.CONNECT = lcConnStr

oRDS.FetchOptions = 1    && adcFetchUpFront
oRDS.ExecuteOptions = 1    && adcExecSync

oRDS.SQL = lcSQL

*** Wrap Execute command into 'safe exec' object
*** so we can trap any errors
oEval = CREATEOBJECT ("wwEval")
lnResult = oEval.Evaluate( "oRDS.Refresh()")
IF oEval.lError
   ? oEval.cErrorMessage
   RETURN .NULL.
ENDIF

*** Convert the RecordSet into a DBF file
rs2DBF(oRDS.recordset,"TQuery")

BROWSE

RETURN oRDS
```

A couple of things are done a little differently here than in the Internet Explorer code. Because we're running inside VFP it makes sense to run our query synchronously by waiting for completion of the query. To do so, set the following two settings:

```
oRDS.FetchOptions = 1    && adcFetchUpFront
oRDS.ExecuteOptions = 1    && adcExecSync
```

The default is 2 and 2, which runs asynchronously and fires events instead. Handling these events is a bit tricky so you'll usually want to use synchronous operation.

> ❗ *You can use asynchronous operation with the control if you are willing to do a little more work. You can use the new VFPCOMUtils COM object from the Microsoft Web site to capture the OnReadyStateChanged and OnError events. VFPCOMUtils:*

```
*** In order to capture events we need to bind them
oRDS = CREATEOBJECT ("RDS.DataControl")
oVFPCOM = CREATEOBJECT ("vfpcom.comutil")
oRDSEvents = CREATEOBJECT ("RDSEvents")

oVFPCOM.BindEvents(oRDS,oRDSEvents)
… remaining RDS code goes here

DEFINE CLASS RDSEvents AS CUSTOM
  lError = .F.
  nError = 0
  cErrorMsg = ""

  PROCEDURE onreadystatechange()
    * Add user code here
    ACTIVATE SCREEN
    ? "On ReadyStateChange"
  ENDPROC

  PROCEDURE onerror(SCode,DESCRIPTION,SOURCE,CancelDisplay)
    * Add user code here
    ACTIVATE SCREEN
    ? "On Error" + DESCRIPTION
    THIS.lError = .T.
    THIS.nError = SCode
    THIS.cErrorMsg = DESCRIPTION
  ENDPROC
ENDDEFINE
```

Bindevents() allows another Fox object to handle the events for a particular COM object instance. VFP doesn't support COM events natively, so this COM utility allows an extension interface to make it possible to respond to the events via this secondary object instance. The code in the secondary object can implement any of the object methods that the COM object exposes. To have an object skeleton created for you, use the following method call:

```
oRDSEvents.ExportEvents(oRDS,CURDIR()+"RDSEvents.prg")
```

This creates a PRG file with a class that contains all the event methods of the object in question.

Error handling
The other issue is error handling. If you're running in synchronous mode, error handling works like any other COM object in VFP—it throws exceptions. The most common problem occurs when you call the oRDS.Refresh() method, which runs the query. Refresh() sends the query to the server and lets the server execute it. The server will return error information to the ActiveX

control, which in turn throws a regular COM exception if an error occurred. The error information is returned as an ODBC or OLE DB-type error (similar to errors coming from SQLEXECUTE()). For an invalid field in the SQL query, an error message would look something like this:

OLE IDispatch exception code 0 from Microsoft OLE DB Provider for ODBC Drivers: [Microsoft][ODBC Visual FoxPro Driver]SQL: Column 'ZIPCODE' is not found...

You can capture errors like this easily enough with global error handlers, but with online applications there are a lot of things that aren't easily handled by generic handlers, so I prefer capturing the error at the source. To do so I use a safe execution class called wwEval (a full version is included in this chapter's code and discussed in Chapter 5). Its purpose is to wrap an EVALUATE() or macro command into a class so that the class's error handler can capture any errors that occur and pass it forward without causing an error in the calling function or method. When the call returns, the lError property can be checked and the cErrorMsg property can be retrieved to decide what to do about the error (exit, in this case).

```
*** Wrap Execute command into 'safe exec' object
*** so we can trap any errors
oEval=create("wwEval")
lnResult = oEval.Evaluate( "oRDS.Refresh()")
IF oEval.lError
   ? oEval.cErrorMessage
   RETURN .NULL.
ENDIF
```

The core of wwEval looks like this:

```
DEFINE CLASS wwEval as CUSTOM

lError = .F.
nError = 0
cErrorMessage = ""
vErrorResult = ""

FUNCTION Evaluate
LPARAMETERS lcEvalString

THIS.lError=.F.

THIS.Result = EVALUATE(lcEvalString)

IF THIS.lError
   THIS.lError = .T.
   THIS.cErrorMessage=Message()+ " - " + Message(1)
   RETURN THIS.vErrorResult
ENDIF

RETURN THIS.Result
ENDFUNC
```

```
FUNCTION ExecuteCommand
LPARAMETERS lcEvalString

THIS.lError = .F.

&lcEvalString

IF THIS.lError
  THIS.lError = .T.
  THIS.cErrorMessage = Message()+ CR + "Code: " + lcEvalString
  RETURN THIS.vErrorResult
ENDIF
ENDFUNC

FUNCTION ERROR
LPARAMETER nError, cMethod, nLine

THIS.lError = .T.
THIS.nError = nError
THIS.nErrorLine = nLine
THIS.cErrorMessage = MESSAGE()

ENDFUNC
ENDDEFINE
```

When using the Evaluate() or ExecuteCommand() methods, any variable references that you use must be in scope inside the class. In the above example, oRDS must be a PRIVATE variable—if it were LOCAL, oRDS wouldn't be in scope in the Evaluate() or Execute() methods because LOCAL is in scope only on the current call stack level. If used in classes, THIS from the calling method won't be in scope so you have to assign it to a PRIVATE variable and then use it instead of THIS.

 This class comes in very handy when dealing with situations where you know errors might occur frequently and need to be handled immediately. The wwEval class is included with the Developer's Download Files at www.hentzenwerke.com and provides a number of other features, including the ability to evaluate Active Server script syntax with VFP code from strings.

Using RDS results in your code
Once Refresh() has returned successfully, you have a recordset object to work with. You have a couple of choices about how to access and manipulate the data that came down from the server. You can use the RDS data directly or you can convert it to DBF format and use VFP's data engine to work with it. The approach depends on whether you plan to update the data.

The first and most logical approach is to simply use the ADO recordset directly in your FoxPro application. You can manipulate the recordset as an object and even bind it to data controls by using the object as the data source. **Figure 8.4** shows the guest application running as a VFP form talking to the Web server using the RDS.DataControl object.

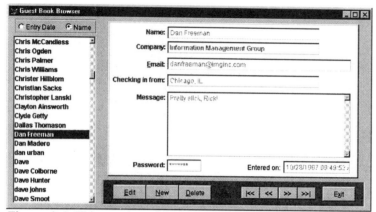

Figure 8.4. This version of the guest book uses the RDS.DataControl from VFP to download and manipulate data. The form is data bound by using the recordset directly as the data source for the input fields.

The form uses nearly the same approach that was used in the Internet Explorer example: it downloads the entire data set and then allows the set to be browsed locally. Any updates made to the data are sent back to the server. The input fields on the form are bound to the recordset's fields by setting the data source to `THISFORM.oRDS.Recordset.Fields("Name").value`. This allows the value to be read by the control as well as updates the data in the disconnected ADO recordset. Any changes made can then be updated with a simple call to SubmitChanges(). Here's a closer look at some of the key features. In the Init() event of the form, the following code establishes the recordset:

```
SET PROCEDURE TO wwEval ADDITIVE

THISFORM.oRDS = CREATE("RDS.DataControl")

oRDS = THISFORM.oRDS
oRDS.InternetTimeout = 5000

oRDS.Server = "http://localhost/"
oRDS.Connect = "dsn=VFPGuest"

oRDS.FetchOptions = 1      && adcFetchUpFront
oRDS.ExecuteOptions = 1    && adcExecSync

oRDS.SQL = "SELECT * FROM Guest ORDER BY Entered DESC"

WAIT WINDOW NOWAIT "Hang on - loading entries from the server..."

*** Wrap Execute command into 'safe exec' object
*** so we can trap any errors
oEval = CREATEOBJECT("wwEval")
lnResult = oEval.Evaluate( "oRDS.Refresh()")
```

```
IF oEval.lError = .T.
   MESSAGEBOX (oEval.cErrorMessage)
   RETURN
ENDIF

WAIT CLEAR

WITH THISFORM
  .FillListBox()
  .oRds.Recordset.MoveFirst
  .txtName.ControlSource     = "THISFORM.oRDS.RecordSet.Fields('Name').value"
  .txtCompany.ControlSource  =
"THISFORM.oRDS.RecordSet.Fields('Company').value"
  .txtEmail.ControlSource    = "THISFORM.oRDS.RecordSet.Fields('Email').value"
  .txtLocation.ControlSource =
"THISFORM.oRDS.RecordSet.Fields('Location').value"
  .edtMessage.ControlSource  =
"THISFORM.oRDS.RecordSet.Fields('Message').value"
  .txtPassword.ControlSource =
"THISFORM.oRDS.RecordSet.Fields('Password').value"
  .txtEntered.ControlSource  =
"THISFORM.oRDS.RecordSet.Fields('Entered').value"
  .txtCustId.ControlSource   = "THISFORM.oRDS.RecordSet.Fields('CustId').value"
ENDWITH
```

Most of this code should look familiar from the IE example of loading the actual data from the server. If, for whatever reason, the recordset can't be loaded, the form will not load; instead it will abort with an error message. Again, note the use of the safe evaluation code to allow checking for this problem right away.

Notice that all the ControlSource values for the input fields must be assigned manually. Because the RDS control can't be dropped onto the form natively and must be created in code, the data binding doesn't work until the RDS object is initialized and has data in it. Because the form fields initialize before the form Init, this doesn't work. If you want to use data binding directly, you can use the form's Load event, but then there's no clear way to abort if the recordset doesn't load. The code above works well but is decidedly non-visual, requiring binding to be handled in code.

To fill the listbox on the form, you have to manually add items to the list because you can't bind the list directly to the recordset:

```
* FillListBox
rs = THISFORM.oRDS.RecordSet

oList = THISFORM.lstGuests
oList.Clear()

rs.MoveFirst()
DO WHILE NOT rs.EOF
  oList.addItem(rs.Fields("Name").value)
  rs.MoveNext()
ENDDO
```

Because the listbox isn't data-bound and the recordset doesn't support searching, responding to a click uses some really old-fashioned code. The following code looks for an entry by comparing the recordset name to the actual display value:

```
* Listbox :: When
rs = THISFORM.oRDS.Recordset
rs.MoveFirst()

DO WHILE !rs.EOF
  IF TRIM(rs.fields("NAME").value) == TRIM(THIS.DisplayValue)
    THISFORM.Refresh()
    RETURN
  ENDIF

  rs.MoveNext()
ENDDO
```

Fortunately, this code is much faster in VFP than it is with VBScript running inside the browser. You'll still see hesitation on some of the last records, but it's nothing like the VBScript code. The rest of the form code deals with basic manipulation of the recordset through methods of the form. When data is updated it's sent back up to the server with the following code:

```
* Form :: Save
oRDS = THISFORM.oRDS
oEval = CREATE("wwEval")
oEval.Evaluate("oRDS.SubmitChanges()")
IF oEval.lError
  MESSAGEBOX("Server Update Failed" + CHR(13) + oEval.cErrorMessage, 48,"RDS
Sample")
  RETURN
ENDIF

loButton = THISFORM.btnEdit

*** Do nothing. In HTML we have to show the form
*** located on the appropriate record, then wwForm::SetValues
loButton.Caption = "\<Edit"

*** Show Form in View Mode
THISFORM.ShowForm(1)
```

Notice again the use of the oEval object for SubmitChanges(). SubmitChanges() will report any errors that occur during the update process, including any update conflicts. You can capture the errors here and decide how to proceed. As you might expect, dealing with concurrency can be a very thorny issue because you have very little control over checking what was updated and when with RDS. There's no equivalent to CURVAL() and OLDVAL() as you have in VFP. Figuring out where the conflict occurred means parsing the error message. Hence it's a good idea to make any updates as atomic as possible—use row-level updates rather than table-level updates.

The remainder of the code in the form is fairly straightforward in its manipulation of the recordset object. Check out the code in the Guest.scx file for more detail.

Problems, problems, problems with RDS data access

Keep in mind that the preceding examples are very simple, yet even on those I ran into a multitude of problems that required workarounds. Some issues I couldn't resolve. Some of these are RDS limitations; others are bugs in the VFP ODBC driver. Yet others are problems with the IE scripting engine. All of these add up so that developing stable RDS applications involves a lot of trial and error, a lot of workarounds and sometimes insurmountable problems that might even cause you to scrap this approach.

ODBC problems with Visual FoxPro

The first problems you're likely to run into with RDS data access have to do with the Visual FoxPro ODBC driver. In particular, empty values—and what RDS thinks are null values—cause an RDS download to fail. For example, I originally tried my samples against a small test file. I then decided to test the same code on my Web server against real data that users had entered. Guess what, it didn't work! After some lengthy investigation, it turned out that RDS couldn't handle empty memo fields. This might be fixed by the time you read this, but it took me hours to figure out what was causing the error.

Along the same lines, updating data that has empty values causes ODBC to assume NULL rather than VFP-type empty values. If your table doesn't support NULL values, any updates will fail when you call SubmitChanges().

Speaking of SubmitChanges(), there's an extremely serious bug: If you update data and the update fails for whatever reason, partial data gets written. For example, if you append a new record and you leave a field blank, you'll get a null-related error. However, if you check the updated VFP table you'll see that a new record was added anyway, with only partial data filled in. This might also be fixed by the time you read this.

RDS problems

While testing I ran into other weird problems. For example, I had some problems with one of my SQL commands that caused Refresh() to fail. After it failed a few times legitimately, I reset the SQL statement to a valid one (SELECT * FROM GUEST) and that didn't work, either. I tried changing the data source. It still failed. I tried another page using a totally different database running on SQL Server and that failed, too. In essence, RDS became corrupted to the point that nothing worked. But I didn't realize that right away, of course, which caused me to change all sorts of code before discovering that RDS was bonked. Finally, I had to restart the Web server to get things to work again.

Internet Explorer data binding problems

Wait, we're not done yet. Internet Explorer also has problems with data binding and data input. In the guest book examples, fields are bound directly to data, so making a change to the field automatically sends the data back to the underlying recordset. But there are issues in how IE deals with field input. The most annoying bug can be reproduced by going to any input field, typing a space, and then tabbing off. It doesn't matter whether or not other data follows the space—you'll get an *Invalid Type* error. IE also can't display NULL values, so if your tables contain NULLs or if ODBC/OLE DB translates empty values to NULLs you can have problems with the display in IE.

These problems make it unacceptable to bind data directly to input fields. The workaround is to manually update and collect field values and forego the data binding on input fields. It's much like the SCATTER/GATHER approach used by many developers in the Fox 2.x days to "bind" data to fields and allow updating. This approach has the additional advantage that you have a chance to prevalidate the data before it goes back into the recordset. Data binding is a direct field-to-recordset binding mechanism, so there are no formatting checks or error events that fire at the time of update. You have to wait until you submit the changes so that any possible database rules fire or an invalid input type is captured.

Summary

As I pointed out in the beginning, I think the plain data-handling technology has too many problems to be used for real applications at this time. Still, it's exciting technology and something that you should take a look at. Microsoft is bound to correct the problems (even though many of the issues have been around for over a year and a half) because RDS figures prominently in their Web data-access strategy. We can only hope Microsoft looks closely at the problems sooner rather than later. Isn't it great to wait for somebody else to fix software problems?

Accessing objects over HTTP with the RDS.DataSpace control

Object access across RDS provides a more interesting and possibly more usable approach today. With the RDS.Dataspace object you can instantiate a COM object on the Web server and call methods on it. The COM object runs on the server, and you can return either a simple type return value (no objects—only IDispatch/Variant compatible types) or an ADO recordset. If you return an ADO recordset from the server, the Recordset property of the RDS control is set in much the same way as with the RDS.DataControl. This is very powerful, because rather than simply pulling data down, you can cause Visual FoxPro code to run on the server and *then* optionally send data down to display, using the same RDS code that you used when accessing the data via the DataControl.

How it works

The DataSpace control works in a similar fashion to the RDS control. Think of the RDS control as a generic DataSpace object that allows direct access to data. The DataSpace control captures calls to its internal CreateObject() method and passes that object-creation request to the Web server over HTTP. The server component creates an instance of the object and creates a handle that identifies it.

Every time a method call is made, the object is created and the method is called. The return value is captured and the object on the server is immediately unloaded. The return value is then sent back to the client over HTTP. The return value can be only a simple type or an ADO recordset.

It should be obvious from this description that your object must be stateless in order to work with RDS; you shouldn't keep any information in properties except what's required for a particular method call. In fact, remote RDS objects do not support property access over the HTTP connection at all, which makes sense because the object is stateless. Because the object is loaded and unloaded between each method call, you'll also want to minimize the amount of method calls that you make on the object, preferably passing in many parameters at once to avoid server round trips. **Figure 8.5** shows how object access over HTTP works.

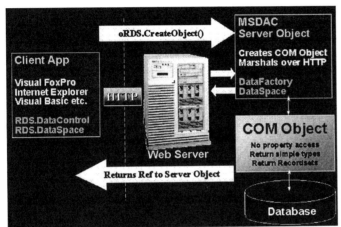

Figure 8.5. The RDS.DataSpace object allows you to access objects on the server indirectly. The MSDAC server component manages the object connection of your client to the server through stateless operation, which causes the object to be loaded and unloaded on every request.

An example—a generic server object

Let's look at an example by creating a COM object to call over the HTTP connection. You can find the code for these examples in RDSServer.prg for the server code and RDSObject.prg for the client. The goal for the server object is to build a few generic methods that'll allow running remote FoxPro queries and commands on the server to essentially plug VFP logic into a client over the Web. The base object with a simple test method looks like this:

```
****************************************************************
DEFINE CLASS rdsServer as Custom OLEPUBLIC                .
****************************************************************
***   Function: Demonstrates RDS Dataspace functionality
***             Access over HTTP
****************************************************************
cAppBasePath = ""
lError = .f.
cErrorMsg = ""


*******************************************************************************
* rdsServer :: Init
*******************************
```

```
FUNCTION Init

SYS(2335 ,0)    && Turn off all UI ops

SET EXCLUSIVE OFF
SET DELETED ON
SET EXACT OFF
_VFP.Autoyield = .F.

*** Add start path to the path
THIS.cAppBasePath = GetAppStartpath()
DO PATH WITH THIS.cAppBasePath

RETURN

*****************************************************************************
* rdsServer :: HelloWorld
*********************************
FUNCTION HelloWorld
RETURN "Hello World from Server " + SYS(0)

*****************************************************************************
* rdsServer :: Error
*********************************
***   Function: Error Method. Capture errors here in a string that
***             you can read from the ASP page to check for errors.
*****************************************************************************
FUNCTION ERROR
LPARAMETER nError, cMethod, nLine
THIS.cErrorMsg = THIS.cErrorMsg + "<BR>Error No: " + STR(nError) + ;
  "<BR>  Method: " + cMethod + "<BR>  LineNo: " +STR(nLine) + ;
  "<BR>  Message: "+ message() + Message(1) + "<HR>"

ENDDEFINE
```

This should look familiar by now from the ASP and FoxISAPI chapters—the base object functionality includes an error handler that lets you avoid hanging the server. Note that you'll never be able to read the cErrorMsg parameter when running over HTTP. Because the object is stateless, the error clears on every access of the server but nothing is stopping you from checking the error in your method code and handling it accordingly.

To call the simple HelloWorld() method from the client over the Web, do the following:

```
CLEAR

lcHost = "http://localhost/"
oRDSDataSpace = CREATEOBJECT("RDS.DataSpace")
oServer = oRDSDataSpace.CreateObject("rdsServer.rdsServer", lcHost)

? oServer.HelloWorld()

RETURN
```

As you can see, the entire process isn't much more complicated than using CreateObject() with native VFP code. To return a recordset from the server, add the following method to the server:

```
*******************************************************************
* rdsServer :: ReturnGuestRs
*******************************
*** Function: Runs a SQL query and returns a result recordset
*******************************************************************
FUNCTION ReturnGuestRs
LPARAMETER lcWhere

lcWhere = IIF(EMPTY(lcWhere), "", lcWhere)

SELECT * FROM "Guest" ;
   &lcWhere ;
   INTO Cursor TQuery

rs = DBF2Rs()

USE IN Tquery

RETURN rs
```

Then try the following:

```
rs = ReturnGuestRs("WHERE UPPER(Name)= 'B'")
? rs.Fields("Name").Value
```

The recordset is marshaled from your custom query and can be used on the client side. The DBF2RS utility (courtesy of Ken Levy), which is included with the Developer's Download Files at www.hentzenwerke.com, takes a VFP cursor and converts it to an ADO recordset (RS2DBF is also provided). The recordset can then be returned from the method call and accessed on the client side.

Because you can call a server object, it becomes fairly easy to tie in Visual FoxPro code to your server. Even better is the fact that you can create a few generic methods that allow you to run VFP code on the server without having to recompile. The following methods should give you some ideas. Most of the features were discussed in the FoxISAPI chapter, including ShowCursor() and the ability of wwEval to execute full code blocks of Visual FoxPro code at runtime.

```
*******************************************************************
* rdsServer :: ReturnSQL
*******************************
*** Function: Generic routine that returns the result from a
***           SQL command as a recordset to the client
*******************************************************************
```

```
FUNCTION ReturnSQL
LPARAMETER lcSQL

&lcSQL ;
  INTO CURSOR TQuery

rs = DBF2Rs()

USE IN Tquery

RETURN rs

************************************************************************
* rdsServer :: ReturnSqlTable
********************************
***   Function: Function runs a SQL query then returns the
***             result as an HTML string
************************************************************************
FUNCTION ReturnSQLTable
LPARAMETER lcSQL

&lcSQL ;
  INTO CURSOR TQuery

*** Create HTML table from data
lcHTML = THIS.ShowCursor()

USE IN Tquery

RETURN lcHTML


************************************************************************
* rdsServer :: Evaluate
********************************
***   Function: Evaluates an expression, function or method call
***       Pass: lcCode   -   Expression to Eval
***     Return: Result from expression
************************************************************************
FUNCTION Evaluate
LPARAMETERS lcCode
loeval = CREATEOBJECT("wwEval")
RETURN loEval.Evaluate(lcCode)
ENDFUNC
* rdsServer :: Evaluate


************************************************************************
* rdsServer :: ExecuteCode
********************************
***   Function: Generically executes some code on the server
***     Assume: Uses Randy Pearson's CodeBlock
***       Pass: lcCode -  block of VFP code
***     Return: Result from Execution
************************************************************************
```

```
FUNCTION ExecuteCode
LPARAMETERS lcCode

lcCode = IIF(EMPTY(lcCode), "", lcCode)

set step on
loEval = CREATEOBJECT ("wwEval")
RETURN loEval.Execute(lcCode)

ENDFUNC
* rdsServer :: ExecuteCode
```

To use some of these functions, look at the following snippets of code:

```
lcHost = "http://localhost/"
oRDSDataSpace = CREATEOBJECT("RDS.DataSpace")
oServer = oRDSDataSpace.CreateObject("rdsServer.rdsServer", lcHost)

*** Return results from any query as an HTML table
SET PROCEDURE TO wwUtils ADDITIVE
ShowHTML( oServer.ReturnSQLTable("SELECT * FROM GUEST") )

*** Generically execute code and return a value
lcCode = ;
  "Select company,name from guest into cursor TQuery" + CHR(13) + CHR(10) + ;
  "rs = dbf2rs()"+ CHR(13) + CHR(10)+ ;
  "RETURN rs"

rs = oServer.ExecuteCode(lcCode)
? rs.Fields("Name").value
```

You can also return a recordset object and assign it to a DataControl object:

```
oRDS = CREATEOBJECT ("RDS.DataControl")
oRDSDataSpace("RDS.DataSpace")

oServer = oRDSDataSpace.CreateObject(…)
…
rs = oServer.ExecuteCode(lcCode)

*** Bind the returned recordset to the RDS Datacontrol
oRDS.SourceRecordSet = rs

*** Make a change to the data
rs.Fields("Name").value = "Ricky Strahl"

*** Marshal changes back to server
oRDS.SubmitChanges()
```

Summary
The RDS DataSpace object is very powerful, as you can see, but it's crucially important that you understand how the architecture works. In essence you're calling a remote object on the server, which functionally has the same implications as calling a FoxISAPI server or an ASP

COM component—hang it and your app dies. But the idea of controlling the server directly from the client, rather than using the server to do all of the work, is very appealing. However, it also exposes some security holes I'll discuss in the next section.

You'll also run into the same scalability issues faced by pure server applications—your component might have huge numbers of simultaneously connected users. Because RDS loads and then unloads the object on each method call, there's a fair amount of overhead involved. If you're running the initial release of Visual FoxPro 6.0, you'll run into blocking issues because only a single method call on the server can execute at one time. A forthcoming Service Pack of Visual FoxPro 6.0 addresses this by allowing multiple instances of objects to process methods concurrently on multiple threads (see Chapter 9 for more information about this update).

Beware of security issues!

While I've been demonstrating these examples you might have noticed that the way RDS works can be a huge security problem. This is because the *client* can basically dictate how to access the data or object on the server. Because the client code can be created in any client application, like Visual FoxPro or Visual Basic or even Internet Explorer scripting code, *anybody* has access to your back-end data or RDS object.

Data security

As you might expect, this is a serious security issue. Look at what's possible with the RDS data control. Earlier I told you that you can connect to the server with:

```
oRDS.Connect = "driver=Microsoft Visual FoxPro Driver;" & _
               "Exclusive=No;SourceType=DBF;" & _
               "SourceDB=d:\wwcode\wc2\wwdemo;uid=;pwd="
```

Well, nothing is stopping the crafty IE VBscript coder from accessing another directory. Even if you hide your SourceDB in a DSN, the client can possibly still guess directories on your server and access data directly. It requires some knowledge about what files are available, but if that knowledge is in place (perhaps an ex-employee?) all data is at risk to be retrieved and even manipulated without the client having rights on that server. That's right—it doesn't matter if client X doesn't have rights, because the data is accessed through the Web server and the impersonation account that RDS runs. The RDS server piece runs in an Admin or System account and has full rights on the server.

Even a secure data source like SQL Server can be compromised. If RDS is installed and you have a DSN to access your SQL server, RDS can be scripted from the client side. Somebody with inside information could gain access to a database and issue DELETE FROM <YourMostImportantTableHere> to wipe out all of your data!

Scary, ain't it? Once a user has figured out what data is available, he's free to issue a SQL command of DELETE FROM GUEST. Worse, if you're using Internet Explorer it's easy to figure out how data is accessed. Take a look at the Guest.asp example—the DSN is visible directly if you view the HTML source. You can gain better protection by using a fat client application, or wrapping the data access logic in an ActiveX control that handles the server connection without exposing any information about the data. Still, even with that approach you're open to somebody guessing where your data sits—it's unlikely, but definitely possible, especially for people inside the company.

To make things even worse, RDS is installed through the IIS 4.0 install program, which doesn't warn you about any security issues. If you choose to install Remote Data Service (which is the default!) during the IIS 4.0 installation process, you're opening up your system to this behavior, possibly without even knowing what the security issues are. To check this out, look in the IIS Admin console for the MSADC virtual directory. If it's there, RDS has been installed. There's no direct way to uninstall RDS, either—you have to make some changes in the server's registry (or you can remove the MSADC virtual directory). RDS determines what it has access to through the following registry key:

`HKLM\SYSTEM\CurrentControlSet\Services\W3SVC\Parameters\ADCLaunch`

Any of the servers listed here are those that can be invoked through the RDS.DataSpace's CreateObject() method. Here are the two default keys that RDS installs:

- **RDSServer.DataFactory**
  RDS uses this generic data service when you use the RDS.DataControl to access data on the server. If you remove this key, direct RDS data access will no longer work. This is probably the biggest security risk.

- **AdvancedDataFactory**
  This object is used to create new instances of objects on the server using DataSpace.CreateObject(). Remove this key to disallow remote object instantiation.

In addition to the default keys, you can add entries for your own objects. Any objects you create to be called through DataSpace.CreateObject() must be registered here by creating a key with the ProgId of the server.

Object security

Data access is the most vulnerable security issue because of the way that RDS allows the client side to directly access a remote data source via an ODBC/OLE DB connect string. Using Dataspace objects allows a little more security because you can essentially hide the database connection issues in code that runs on the server. But that still leaves your remote object open to access from the client. This, however, could be a little more difficult to hack because you need to know the interface to the object.

Again, the biggest issue is the fact that IE Scripting is wide open for anyone to examine. If you use a remote Dataspace object and it's scripted through IE, viewing the HTML source will expose the code required to hit the server. Any method calls made can be misused. Say you have a method called DeleteRec to delete the current order displayed. From this information it wouldn't be hard to figure out other order numbers and start deleting those as well.

Some workarounds

RDS is inherently insecure, precisely because the client security is not checked. There are some ways around this, however:

- **Hiding code in ActiveX controls**
  The biggest problem is that using IE Scripting makes code visible on the client side. You can work around this by putting your code into binary modules like ActiveX controls (VB or VC++) instead of VBScript. That way the data access code is not visible to the client.

- **Using authentication for object access**
  This type of authentication would have to work through a Web server application that can log users in. You can obviously limit access to the actual pages that contain the scripted RDS code. You can use an authentication scheme to force users to log in first and then use the authentication information in the Web page through ASP scripting (by using `<%= Request.ServerVariables("Remote_User") %>` and embedding this into a method call). Along the same lines, you could validate the user and then pass down a unique cookie on each hit. The cookie can be retrieved on the client side and passed down to the server on each method call. This would ensure that users go through the proper paths to get to the desired page.

  However, this approach will not guard against internal sabotage. People who have legitimate access could still hack into the system by accessing the server directly and guessing at functionality to which they might not have direct access (RDSDemo.RDSServer for example).

- **Fat client**
  Fat client applications written in VFP, VB, and so on offer a lot more security because the connect and access information is not visible to the actual user. This provides protection from client eyes, but it doesn't protect you from somebody in the know who's hacking in and making the same calls on the server.

Controlling security for applications that have client-side logic and server access services is always problematic because the nature of the beast requires the client to have generic access. With that flexibility comes the power both to build cool applications and to abuse security rights. I demonstrated similar issues with the WinInet data transfer code, but there, at least, you had control over the process so you could use your own authentication schemes and build them directly into the "protocol" level. No such luck with RDS because it's generically packaged by Microsoft.

If you want to use data or objects on the server that can be accessed by a wide Internet audience, you're opening up a security hole because anybody who knows how can get at the data logically. However, levels of security vary, and RDS is very bad at this because it doesn't offer *any* security options from the client side. Even if you want to build a tightly controlled Internet application that allows access only to certain users, user verification is difficult. You're still taking the risk of allowing access to anyone who has knowledge of the data or object interface.

DCOM over HTTP

Another option for object access that's coming with NT 5 (Windows 2000) and COM+ is DCOM over HTTP. DCOM provides similar capabilities to the RDS DataSpace object, but with direct access to server objects. The advantage of DCOM is that security is configurable at the component level so you can lock out unauthorized users. For wide-audience applications, though, you'll run into the same issues as with RDS. DCOM's security model also requires clients to be configured to access a server over the network—something that RDS does not require. For wide-audience apps this would be a major problem, but one that could be addressed with an ActiveX wrapper module.

Regardless of the route you take, you should start thinking along the lines of building ActiveX controls for server-access code from browser-based or fat client applications. It's really the only safe way to deal with remote objects at this time.

Summary

RDS is exciting technology, but I have a lot of reservations about at this time. The ability to access data directly over HTTP should be a very exciting prospect to most database developers, and RDS makes this process reasonably easy. It works from within Internet Explorer so you can build pure browser-based data access applications. Object access over HTTP allows you to run any COM object on the Web server, providing a simple mechanism to share logic between the client and server sides.

The biggest problems with RDS have to do with the many little glitches you'll run into as you use it. From full-on failures of RDS to minor things like the IE data-binding controls not accepting fields with leading spaces, it can be a frustrating experience to build your first app that uses RDS. I spent a lot of time building even the simple examples in this chapter. The bottom line is that RDS works, but it takes some doing to make it work *right*. I hope Microsoft improves this tool in the future, but it seems much of RDS has remained stagnant since its original introduction.

The other issue is security. RDS has no security model, and using any of the RDS technologies exposes your server to serious security issues. Essentially, RDS allows open access to any data sources on the server and any objects that are registered to be used with RDS. Anybody who knows where and how to get at the data can access these tools to perform damaging operations on the server without proper authorization.

Pros
- Easy data access over HTTP.
- Compatible with ADO.
- Works from IE Scripting model, Visual FoxPro and all COM clients.
- Remote object access is extremely powerful.

Cons
- Many problems with VFP ODBC driver, IE data binding, and stability.
- RDS client data object is very limited for data manipulation.
- Lack of a security model makes this technology very dangerous.
- Browser support includes only Internet Explorer.

Section 4
Enterprise Development

Web development is inherently different from developing standalone or even traditional client/server applications. Server-based applications tend to run on a single or a small number of servers and might be accessed by tens of thousands of users simultaneously. In order to provide smoothly running applications, developers must take care to manage the resource use of these servers against the incoming transaction load. Scaling applications and load-balancing resources against available resources is a critical piece of any commercial Web application.

There are many interrelated factors involved in building large-scale applications. Section 4 introduces these concepts and demonstrates how they relate to Visual FoxPro. However, while the actual application and Visual FoxPro are crucial, many additional factors such as servers, network hardware, security, and proper configuration of the operating system are just as important. It's vital to understand the interdependencies of the various pieces and to be able to put together a team of people that can handle all aspects of a Web application—much of this goes far beyond just the application development aspect that you may be used to from standalone applications.

This section introduces these concepts by starting with a discussion of how the Visual FoxPro COM model fits into this server-based environment. Chapter 9 discusses issues like multi-threading and Active Server Pages COM calling interfaces as well as using Microsoft Transaction Server with VFP. Chapter 10 discusses scalability issues in great detail, outlining the concepts and specific examples of what to look at when putting an application together. Topics include performance tuning, data access method comparisons, load balancing, stress testing, running applications across multiple machines, and how security affects the application. Chapter 11 deals with the development process and discusses the people requirements for building a large-scale Web application.

While many of these topics may seem like overkill for smaller applications, the very same issues apply—albeit on a smaller scale. It pays to think about growth issues from the start, rather than having to re-engineer applications later. Take the time to review the content of this section even if you don't think you'll be creating 'large-scale' applications.

Chapter 9
Visual FoxPro and COM

Microsoft's focus has been on extending functionality of all aspects of Windows and the Internet through COM. All the new technologies pouring out of Microsoft are becoming accessible through the use of COM as soon as they become available in the operating system and the development tools. Visual FoxPro provides the functionality to act as both a COM client and COM server to allow you to take advantage of the COM programming model in VFP's familiar environment.

You've already seen how COM is used extensively with Active Server Pages and FoxISAPI, as well as some client-side technologies. The basics of COM are simple enough to understand and implement, but things get trickier once you go beyond these basics and need to scale COM applications (or any kind of application, for that matter) to large transaction volumes. In relation to scalability, I'll discuss how Visual FoxPro implements its COM threading model and how this relates to the Web technologies already discussed, as well as its role for using Microsoft Transaction Server with VFP. I'll also discuss the basics of DCOM and how running COM objects on remote machines can help spread the load of your applications across the network.

COM scalability and Visual FoxPro 6.0

COM provides the gateway to hook in Visual FoxPro functionality from Web applications and other server applications. When you run an app in a server environment, application rules change quite drastically. You're no longer dealing with "applications," but rather with "servers" that provide specific functionality to clients. On the Web and in other high-volume operations, this means that your COM objects can have large numbers of clients that are more or less simultaneously accessing your server components. The key to building applications that work well in this environment is being able to handle many simultaneous requests to provide good responsiveness to the user, without overloading the machine's resources. In addition, it's important to minimize contention for resources between different components accessing these resources. This extends to concurrency of objects loaded into a process (IIS in Web applications), data access and lock issues, as well as hardware resources like the CPU.

Visual FoxPro has been a COM client since version 3.0 and became capable of building COM servers with version 5.0. Visual FoxPro 6.0 adds support for Apartment Model Threading (AMT) in order to provide better performance and scalability to its server implementation. However, the initial release of VFP 6.0 has some serious limitations in terms of scalability. VFP 6.0 implements AMT, but it's forcing server access to be synchronized and causing simultaneous method calls to wait for completion of another request before continuing. In essence, the blocking issues are such that only one method call at a time can execute on any given server.

The good news is that Microsoft has been working on this issue. The problem will be addressed in a shortly forthcoming interim release that provides a new multi-threaded runtime (Microsoft's term). At the time of this writing, there was no official announcement of when this update will ship. However, it has been demonstrated in public by Microsoft and I have been running a very early beta version for testing with this book, which confirms that the multi-threaded runtime works as expected. I would expect this new update to be released in the first quarter of '99, but that's my estimate and not Microsoft's (the latest is that it will be in Visual Studio SP3). If you are doing COM development, this update is significant enough that you'll definitely want to get your hands on it as soon as it's released.

Let's start this chapter by reviewing how COM accesses objects.

What is Apartment Model Threading and why should you care?

You've probably heard the term Apartment Model Threading before. It's a crucial mechanism that allows the COM subsystem to run multiple, essentially single-threaded applications/components at the same time, giving a simulation of multi-threading.

AMT works by allowing multiple, simultaneous instances of your COM component to be created on separate threads. The operation is transparent and the logistics for the threading model are built into the Windows COM subsystem, with Visual FoxPro 6.0 complying to the Apartment Threading Model. Although COM, through this mechanism, makes it possible to run your COM servers as multi-threaded objects that can operate concurrently, your program has little control over the multi-threading environment. In other words, the system controls the threading model and your application behaves just as a standalone application running in a multi-user environment—the COM system determines how many instances (threads) are active at any point of activity on your server.

Contrast this with a "real" multi-threaded object created with C++, which can be reentrant (enter the same binary in memory code multiple times simultaneously) and serve multiple requests simultaneously from a single instance. Because high-level tools like VFP and VB aren't reentrant, multiple separate instances are created on separate threads, each with its own global data stored in Thread Local Storage. Each instance is independent (no data sharing!), which eliminates the need for synchronizing access to object data, as a true multi-threaded C++ object would have to do. COM performs a slick sleight of hand to enable applications like VFP to run in a multi-threaded environment! The downside is that each instance must duplicate certain data and its environment, which takes up a significant amount of memory. (With the new multi-threaded runtime, a minimal server takes about 700 KB—with the old VFP 6 runtime it was closer to 1.5 MB.) Hence memory is used and load time is comparatively slow because an environment block and local storage must be set up for each server.

To take advantage of Apartment Model Threading in VFP, simply create an in-process component (build a multi-threaded COM server (.dll)) in the Project Manager, making sure each OLEPUBLIC class is marked for multi-use operation) and then instantiate your component via CreateObject/CoCreateInstance or an equivalent function call from any COM-compliant client. If the client is multi-threaded like IIS, it can take advantage of the scheduling magic that COM performs to allow your server to be called on multiple, simultaneously operating threads. In the case of Active Server Pages, the client is Internet Information Server using an ASP page that has created an object reference of your component via the Server.CreateObject() method.

Regardless of how you create your object, COM always invokes your object on a specific thread, and guarantees that it's always called on this same thread for the duration of its reference lifetime. In Microsoft-speak, this thread context is known as an *apartment*. The COM subsystem in Windows handles the logistics of marshaling requests on your component to the appropriate thread if necessary. If the thread calling your component is already the correct thread, no marshaling takes place. Marshaling becomes an issue only if objects are persisted across multiple threads or, in terms of IIS, across multiple requests. In ASP this manifests itself as objects tied to the Session or Application objects. If you're using FoxISAPI, the object references to your server need to be marshaled on each request, from the incoming ISAPI thread to the originally pooled thread that created the COM object.

If you're curious, marshaling is a process that affects how quickly COM method calls and parameter passing takes place over cross-apartment or cross-process threads. COM provides a mechanism for communicating across these boundaries through a proxy and stub object that duplicates the COM interface of your COM object, providing a sort of store-and-forward mechanism of any requests. The proxy and stub objects are used for the communication layer that is abstracted at the COM level to allow communication over the most efficient protocol available. Because of the way the proxy/stub architecture works, COM can provide a consistent interface to your server regardless of whether the object runs in the same process, out of process, or even on another machine. For each of these scenarios, the proxy/stub objects will know the correct mechanism to marshal the calls from client to server.

With cross-apartment marshaling, a thread has to potentially wait for the required apartment thread to free up. Once it does, COM switches context to this thread, which involves copying the thread-specific data block to the existing thread. With Apartment Model Threading, threads often don't have to switch context because the calling thread is already the correct one, and the call can be quite fast. At other times—most likely when the server becomes very busy—thread marshaling must take place because the client holds multiple simultaneous references on various threads. In this case, COM needs to spend the extra overhead to switch context and potentially wait for threads to clear up.

Marshaling is always used when calling out-of-process Automation servers (including in-process objects running in an MTS process), where threads need to be marshaled from the client process to the server process. This is the main reason why in-process components run faster. But keep in mind that marshaling issues affect only performance of the actual method call interface and parameter passing—*not the actual operation of your Visual FoxPro server code*! For instance, a call to a method that takes two seconds to process won't be noticeably faster than an in-process method compared to an out-of-process one, because the overhead of the call is tiny compared to the two-second operation that takes place. But a short method call that makes maybe two VFP function calls that take a hundredth of a second, running in a tight loop called 100 times in a row, will be much slower—sometimes as much as a few hundred times slower!

Apartment Model Threading is available only to DLL/in-process COM objects. EXE/out-of-process servers must be managed manually in thread pools to allow concurrent method calls. Note that in-process servers in Visual FoxPro 6.0 can no longer have any user interface—this means no message boxes, no error dialogs, and no File Open dialogs. Even WAIT WINDOW and INKEY() are not allowed! All access to any UI will generate a VFP exception in your COM server. (You can still "run" forms in VFP without generating an error, but the UI is not visible. It's equivalent to DO FORM NOSHOW.)

Problems with the initial release of VFP 6.0

VFP 6.0, unlike VFP 5.0, *does* support Apartment Model Threading, but *it blocks access to the same server while another call to that same server is executing.* The server is blocked at the component level, which means that the components start up on a new thread but have to wait for a blocking lock to clear before they can enter the processing code. This means that if two users hit a page that uses the same COM server (remember, a server can contain multiple objects), the requests will queue up one after the other. If there is a 10-second request followed by a one-second request, the one-second request might have to wait up to 11 seconds for its returned result. That's very limiting for an Active Server Page, or any other multi-threaded client, on a busy Web server that might have hundreds or even thousands of simultaneously active users!

An interim release to the rescue

This blocking behavior is addressed in a forthcoming Service Pack of Visual Studio (release date unknown at this time, but expected in early 1999). See **Figure 9.1**. This release provides a new multi-threaded runtime that handles thread isolation and does not block simultaneous method calls. I'm currently using an early beta version of this release, which allows me to fire up unlimited, simultaneous instances of my server.

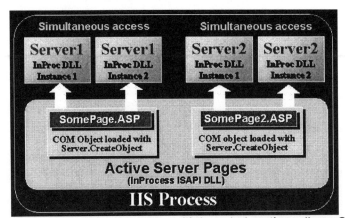

Figure 9.1. Using the new multi-threaded runtime allows COM components to execute requests concurrently. Any number of object calls and server instances can be accessed at any time, given server resources to process these requests. This behavior requires the forthcoming interim release of Visual FoxPro 6.0 and will not behave this way with the original version of VFP 6.0.

It's ironic that this important functionality took so long to get into Visual FoxPro, but the Fox team did a tremendous job of accomplishing this difficult task with such a huge product and existing code base. The multi-threaded behavior is a vital requirement for building server applications that must deal with requests of different execution times. With this code in place, short requests can execute immediately without having to wait for long requests to complete. For a hands-on example, take a look at "ASP Scalability" section in Chapter 4, where the behavior of Visual FoxPro with either the multi-threaded or single-threaded runtime is demonstrated with a detailed sample.

Another obvious application that requires multi-threading support is Microsoft Transaction Server. As with ASP, the updated multi-threaded runtime allows multiple objects to run simultaneously inside MTS, whereas the original version of VFP 6.0 did not. This issue is even more crucial for MTS because the MTS package wraps all access from any application process on the system to a component. The new multi-threaded runtime offers a solution to these problems, allowing Visual FoxPro to finally be a fully viable part of the Microsoft Enterprise Platform.

In my early testing, I've found that the multi-threaded runtime is very efficient and can take advantage of multiple processors at over 85% utilization rates for multiple processors. With two processors, processing efficiency reached close to 190% of a single processor, and with four processors 330% of a single processor was achieved. Since overhead exists in processor context switches at the OS level, these numbers are excellent.

Using the new multi-threaded runtime

To support the new runtime, Microsoft introduced a new runtime file called Vfpt.dll, which is used instead of the old Vfpr.dll file for the single-threaded runtime. When you install the VFP update, both runtimes are added to your system and new compile options in the project's Build option allow you to route your server to the appropriate runtime. To build your servers with the multi-threaded runtime, use the following syntax:

```
BUILD MTDLL aspDemos FROM aspDemos
```

You'll also find a new Build option to build a multi-threaded COM server, as shown in **Figure 9.2**.

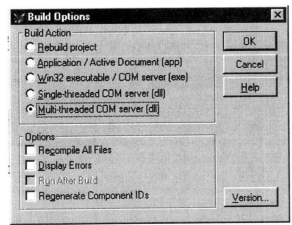

Figure 9.2. Using the project's Build dialog to create a COM DLL with proper multi-threaded support enabled.

The new version of the runtime strips some functionality from the full VFP runtime (menu support, reports, old @say..get statements, and so on, which is subject to change at this time) so it is more lightweight, but you might want to check your code to make sure you don't run into some of the missing features. Additionally, Microsoft suggests that the multi-threaded runtime might be slightly slower than the regular runtime because it has to access memory using thread-specific local thread storage, which is slower than direct-memory access. In my first tests I didn't experience any performance drops, so new optimizations in the runtime in general may have offset some of the possible losses. Overall, any minor performance loss should be a fair tradeoff for the added scalability of the new multi-threaded runtime.

Multi-threading is not a magic bullet

Although it's great news that VFP supports true multi-threaded COM access, realize that this will not automatically solve all of your scalability problems. In fact, it might introduce new ones. Visual FoxPro can now create new instances of your object whenever you make an instance request. However, there are no controls on how many objects can be created. You might find that all of a sudden you have too much of a good thing, with too many instances firing up simultaneously, causing your server to become overloaded.

For example, think of an application that runs a long query that takes 30 seconds to run. While running this query, VFP uses a fair amount of CPU cycles. Now imagine 100 users on a Web site all running this query simultaneously. COM will create 100 instances of your object—all of which attempt to use a single CPU (or possibly even multiple machines). The likely result is that none of those requests will return in time because the combined load brings the server to its knees. Furthermore, this situation might cause the server to get so backed up with other requests, or even more of the same slow requests, that it never recovers—the server becomes busy processing requests that are already timed out.

A slow request like this should probably be offloaded to another machine or a SQL Server for processing so that the Web server is not responsible for processing the load simultaneously. In some instances this will cause the load to migrate to another machine, but hopefully other options will exist for splitting up the load between different machines and processes.

Incidentally, there's a way to limit how many servers are loaded by using Microsoft Transaction Server. This new feature is available with NT Service Pack 4 or later. By default, MTS will create a maximum of 100 apartment threads (per package) for client work. These threads are used for actual processing of each request to your COM object, which means you can have 100 simultaneously processing requests but many more active object references. If the pool of active objects is exhausted, requests start queuing, which is what you'd like to have happen in order to avoid server overload. You can change the value by editing the following registry key for your MTS component:

```
HKLM/Software/Microsoft/Transaction Server/Package/{your package GUID}
```

Add a new DWORD value key named ThreadPoolMax and enter a numeric value for the number of thread as appropriate. I suggest that you should never have more than a few instances of your component in call at any given point in time—typically two or three per processor if all processing is local, but more if you're processing data remotely on a SQL back end or using DCOM to offload processing to other machines. Anything more can result in unacceptable system slow-downs. If you use packages with multiple components, you'll have to carefully evaluate your object counts and come up with a number that works for you. The key is to balance the server's resources against the amount of work it is asked to do without running the processor into the 85-90%+ range.

Microsoft Transaction Server

There's been a lot of hype around Microsoft Transaction Server, but until Service Pack 3 with the multi-threaded runtime support ships, Visual FoxPro is not a good client to MTS. Although the original VFP 6.0 release runs in MTS, it cannot process simultaneous requests on any server. MTS relies heavily on loading multiple instances of your COM object (one for each client reference) into its own address space regardless of the calling application process, which necessitates running and calling simultaneous instances. The new runtime fixes these issues and lets VFP be a good MTS citizen.

MTS is somewhat misnamed—although it provides transactional features, it also provides a number of other useful COM system services, including:

• **Resource management of COM objects—Just In Time Activation (JITA)**
  COM objects loaded through MTS can be automatically unloaded and reloaded. MTS caches the VFP runtime, so load and reload is very fast. MTS may also cache COM references of your object, so if objects are loaded in quick cycles your servers are never unloaded/reloaded even though your client code releases references. MTS handles all of this through its own abstraction layer, saving resources on the server. But there is a cost: COM operation through MTS is slower than calling COM objects directly. Note: JITA is *not* a pool manager—objects are unloaded with each request or method call, which is very inefficient!

• **Role-based security**
  MTS implements a new security model that allows you to configure roles for a component. The roles are configured at the component level and mapped to NT users. Your code can then query for the roles under which the component is running, rather than using the much more complex NT Security model and functions to figure out user identity. Roles are also useful for deployment because they can be packaged with the component and can be automatically installed on other machines if the necessary accounts exist.

• **Packaging technology**
  MTS includes a packaging mechanism that allows taking a *package* (an MTS word for an application or group of objects), which might contain multiple COM objects, and packing it up into a distribution file. The distribution file contains all binary files (DLLs, type libraries and support files) as well as all information about the registry and the security settings of the component. This package can be installed on another machine for instant uptime.

- **Transactional features**
  This is where MTS gets its name. MTS allows database-independent management of transactions spanning multiple data sources and multiple COM objects. Essentially MTS can wrap operations into its own transactional monitor, which works through the Distributed Transaction Controller (DTC), causing any database operations to be monitored. Components can call transactional functions to complete or abort operations, at which time MTS—rather than the application—causes the data sources to commit or revert. Data sources must be DTC compliant, which means SQL Server or Oracle at this time. (This may also apply to other data sources with third-party drivers.) Visual FoxPro data is not DTC compliant. The key feature of this technology is that transactions have been abstracted to the COM layer; rather than coding transactional SQL syntax, you can use code-based logic to deal with transactions. The transactions are SQL back-end independent (as long as the back end is DTC capable). Transactions can also span multiple servers and even across servers running different SQL back ends, such as SQL Server and Oracle. A single transaction could wrap data access that writes to both.

- **Context management**
  MTS includes a static data store object similar to ASP's Application object to allow components to store data for state-keeping and inter-component communication.

Do you need Microsoft Transaction Server?

Before you decide to use MTS you should ask yourself whether you need its functionality. If you don't need any of its specialty features like role-based security or multi-phase commit of database transactions, there might be no good reason to bother with it. Even when running the new multi-threaded VFP runtime, MTS is not much more than a wrapper around your COM object. This out-of-process COM object wrapper in turn acts as a proxy and hosts all access to your component via passthrough. All object access occurs through an out-of-process COM call, and there's the additional overhead of passing the data through two interface layers. The result is that running components inside MTS tends to be slower than running them as plain in-process COM objects, without gaining any scalability benefits.

MTS hosts your COM objects inside a package, which is an out-of-process component you can see on the Processes tab of the Task Manager running as Mtx.exe. Each package uses its own Mtx.exe host to encapsulate its objects. When an MTS component is installed into MTS, the ClassIds and ProgIds get mapped to the package, which in turn knows how to pass on any interface calls directly to the actual objects. The end result is that a client application never has a direct connection to your COM object, but always has a proxy reference to the MTS package, which passes through all interface calls.

Through some registry mapping, an instance of this object is instantiated when you issue CREATEOBJECT. The package then creates your object and calls the methods in typical passthrough fashion. Any method calls made to the component hit the package container's proxy object first, and then are passed down to your internal COM object. **Figure 9.3** shows how objects are called from an ASP page. Note that if multiple simultaneous requests are made on your component, multiple instances start up and run inside the MTS package. If you're using the new multi-threaded runtime, you'll be able to get simultaneous method calls with the original version of VFP 6.0. The standard runtime calls to your component will block, essentially allowing only a single method call to occur at a time in a given package.

The wrapper package provides component services I mentioned earlier, as well as isolates your component from the client process. (Hey, that's not really a feature since you can do that with out-of-process components on your own—but that's marketing for you.)

Out-of-process packages are the norm, but MTS also supports in-process packages. These work the same as out-of-process packages but run inside the client process. However, I've seen problems with this approach, and it seems Microsoft provided this feature more for its own system services (like IIS virtual applications) than anything else. Running components in in-process packages has resulted in many weird and unexplainable crashes and lockups in my tests, where the out-of-process packages of the same exact configuration work fine. Your mileage might vary. In-process packages are slightly faster, but they also void the process-isolation features that protect the client process from a crashing component in your package. You might not be able to restart in-process packages, and they often require the calling process to shut down before refreshing or updating the components.

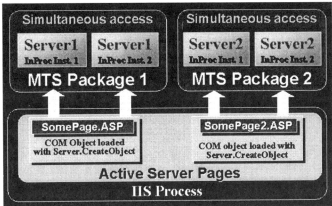

Figure 9.3. When running through MTS, your components are accessed indirectly through an MTS package, which provides a pass-through interface.

The state of the stateless

MTS provides some cool features, but it doesn't do much for scalability. Still, even if you decide you don't need MTS, you should consider building objects that are compatible with it. You can accomplish the best performance with MTS and any other COM client by using stateless objects. Stateless objects are objects that don't rely on property values to maintain their "state" or context between method calls. These objects make no assumptions about any values for themselves or other "global" aspects of the system. They reestablish themselves when they start up, by using parameters or values stored in a database or establishing state from scratch.

If you're going to build an effective component for use with MTS, it should be stateless. For MTS this means that when a method call completes it should be able to release the object and hand you a brand-new copy on the next request. In order for this to work, your component cannot rely on non-default property settings used by multiple consecutive method calls.

If the object is stateless, MTS can take the existing object reference and recycle it to pass on to another client. That's the theory, anyway, but in reality MTS destroys your object after each call to SetComplete() and then totally re-creates it when you make another method call, rather than simply caching existing references. Object pooling likely will be provided in later versions of MTS, but the current behavior provides a safe environment for legacy (non-MTS) components by always guaranteeing startup state to a stateless component that is not the optimal way to cache objects.

The key functionality to building an MTS component deals with establishing and then releasing the state of the object or its *Object Context*. To do so, you have to reference the MTXAS.AppServer object and use its GetObjectContext(), SetComplete() and SetAbort() methods.

To demonstrate how MTS works, I'll build a small functional sample that uses the same logic that I used to demonstrate the multi-threaded behavior of the new multi-threaded runtime. I'll recycle the same SlowHit() code that demonstrates multi-threaded access to the component and adjust it so it works within the confines of MTS. To start, create the basic server code:

```
DEFINE CLASS MTSDemo AS Custom OLEPUBLIC

oMTS = .NULL.
hFile = 0

FUNCTION Init
  THIS.WriteOutput("Init Fired")
  THIS.oMTS = CREATEOBJECT("MTXAS.AppServer.1")
ENDFUNC

FUNCTION Destroy
  THIS.WriteOutput("Destroy Fired")
  IF THIS.hFile > 0
    FCLOSE(THIS.hFile)
  ENDIF
ENDFUNC

****************************************************************************
* MTSDemo :: SlowHit
*******************************
***   Function: Allows you to simulate a long request. Pass number of
***             seconds. Used to demonstrate blocking issues with
***             VFP COM objects.
****************************************************************************
FUNCTION SlowHit
LPARAMETER lnSecs
LOCAL loMTS, loContext, x

THIS.Writeoutput("SlowHit Fired" + TRANSFORM(lnSecs))
loContext = THIS.oMTS.GetObjectContext()

lnSecs = IIF(EMPTY(lnSecs), 0, lnSecs)

DECLARE Sleep IN Win32API INTEGER
FOR x = 1 TO lnSecs
```

```
  FOR x = 1 TO lnSecs
     Sleep(1000)
  ENDFOR
ENDFOR

DECLARE INTEGER GetCurrentThreadId IN Win32API

IF !ISNULL(loContext)
   loContext.SetComplete()
ENDIF

RETURN GetCurrentThreadId()
ENDFUNC


FUNCTION WriteOutput
LPARAMETER lcString
IF THIS.hFile = 0
   Declare INTEGER GetCurrentThreadId IN Win32API
   THIS.hFile = FCREATE(Sys(2023) + "\MTSDemo" +SYS(2015) + ".txt")
ENDIF
IF THIS.hFile # -1
  FWRITE(THIS.hFile, lcString + CHR(13) + CHR(10))
ENDIF

ENDFUNC
ENDDEFINE
```

A few optional pieces in this code deal with logging information to disk—I'll discuss these later. The key feature of a COM object built for use in MTS is that it can retrieve an object reference to the MTXAS.AppServer.1 object, which is the MTS base object. To retrieve the context within MTS for the currently active request, use its GetObjectContext() method and store it to a variable:

```
THIS.oMTS = CREATEOBJECT("MTXAS.AppServer.1")
loContext = THIS.oMTS.GetObjectContext()
```

I stuck the CreateObject() call into the Init event of the class so I don't have to retype the code that has to run in each call method. As you'll see in a minute, the Init of your server fires every time a method call is made to your object, so this is no more efficient than directly calling the same code in each method. However, it saves some typing and centralizes the code.

The only thing left to do in your server method code is to call either SetComplete() or SetAbort()—it doesn't matter which one you call, since this component isn't participating in any MTS transactions. To tell MTS that it's okay to release resources on the object, use:

```
IF !ISNULL(loContext)
   loContext.SetComplete()
ENDIF
```

MTS components outside of MTS
*I explicitly check for the existence of the object before calling
SetComplete(), which allows you to test the server's operation without
running inside MTS. You can always create the MTXAS object (even when you're
not running inside MTS), but the GetObjectContext() method returns NULL if not
called from within an MTS object. If you trap for this state, you can write
standalone components or those that work as part of MTS.*

Now create a project and add a PRG file (or VCX if you choose to go that route) named
MTSServer. Now compile this server into a COM object:

```
BUILD MTDLL MTSServer FROM MTSServer
```

If you don't have the multi-threaded runtime, just use BUILD DLL instead—but realize your
server will block simultaneous client requests.

Before dumping the server into MTS, use the following code to test it:

```
o = CREATEOBJECT("MTSServer.MTSDemo")
? o.SlowHit(5)
```

This should run the server, wait for five seconds, and then spit out a thread ID number. If that
works, move this component into MTS by following these steps:
1. Start the Microsoft Management Console.
2. In the treeview, select Microsoft Transaction Server, then My Computer, then Packages
    Installed.
3. Click the New icon on the toolbar and create an empty package named *MTS Book Demo*.
4. Select the new package, press the right mouse button, and click Properties.
5. Click the Identity tab and notice that the default is set to Interactive User, which is the
    currently logged-in account. If your component runs prior to login, the SYSTEM account
    will be used. Here you can also change the user account to a specific user account. Note:
    This setting determines the user context and the rights for what resources your component
    can access, regardless of the client. Save and exit this dialog.
6. Go down one more level to Components and click the New icon.
7. Click Install New Components and select Mtsserver.dll. If you aren't using the new multi-
    threaded runtime, also add the TLB file. Click OK.
8. In the component's Properties, set its Transaction options. If you don't use distributed
    transactions through DTC, set the "Does not support Transactions" option, which will
    result in slightly faster performance than the other options. Use "Supports Transactions" if
    you have a mixed-request load. **Figure 9.4** shows how the installed component should
    look inside MTS.

Once the component is registered with MTS, nothing changes in the way the client calls
the object, so re-run the previous code but bump the timeout to a higher number:

```
o = CREATEOBJECT("MTSServer.MTSDemo")
? o.SlowHit(15)
```

Run this code from VFP and then switch back to the Transaction Server Manager. You'll notice that the icon for your object is now spinning, which means it is active and "in call" or in context. Click the detail view and you'll see one active object and one in-call object while your server continues to wait for completion. Once the method completes and the code executes the SetComplete() method call on the Context object, the in-call counter goes down by one, leaving you with one active object reference and no objects that are in call. This status display is quite useful when figuring out how MTS works.

If you create another object in your VFP application like this:

```
o2 = CREATEOBJECT("MTSServer.MTSDemo")
```

the active object count will go up by one. Because Visual FoxPro is single threaded, you can't run two simultaneous instances from the VFP client. But you can simulate the process by firing up another copy of VFP, loading instances from there, and running several SlowHit calls simultaneously. These, too, will show up as active instances and stick around. If you now run a SlowHit request in each instance of Visual FoxPro, MTS will show two active in-call objects. You can simulate the same scenario by creating a pair of ASP pages, using Server.CreateObject() to create instances of your servers, and then running them simultaneously—you'll see them show up as in-call objects while processing. In short, all your object instantiations run through MTS regardless of which process (IIS, VFP) created the object. (See the scalability example in Chapter 4.)

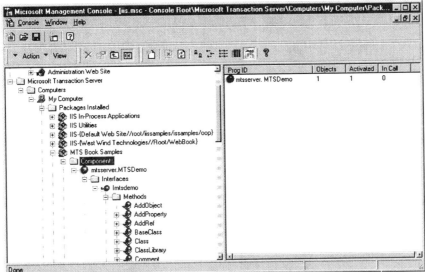

Figure 9.4. The MTSServer component loaded into Microsoft Transaction Server. The package is the "host" container that can host multiple separate objects. When objects are in call, you can view basic transaction statistics on the active object, which is signified by a spinning icon.

Understanding JITA

Notice that if you create an object from the command window, it will immediately show as activated. Once you make the SlowHit method call and it completes, the object is no longer shown as activated! Yet, if you go back and re-run SlowHit on your existing object reference, it works just fine. What's going on here?

That's Just In Time Activation in action. The above code creates an object, but doesn't call SetComplete() immediately after creating the object in the Init. Until you do, the object is assumed to have state and cannot be released. As soon as you call SetComplete(), MTS is free to unload your object. The VFP client app, however, doesn't know that the object was unloaded and assumes it is still active with the app still holding a reference. But the actual reference is to the MTX proxy, rather than the real object, which the package has unloaded. When you make the next interface call on the object, MTS re-creates that object and services the request from this new instance.

As you can see, this requires your object to be stateless. If state was maintained between method calls, all properties would clear, and only the startup properties would be provided. If you have to keep state from one method call to another, be sure *not* to call SetComplete() or SetAbort() in the client code, in which case the object will not be unloaded by MTS. The object stays loaded and dedicated to your client, showing as activated but not in call while between method calls.

Let's look a little closer at what's happening behind the scenes here. To do so, we need to use the WriteOutput() method in the code above. When called, WriteOutput()sends output to a temporary file; the purpose of this exercise is to see how MTS loads objects. Run the following example code against the object:

```
o = CREATEOBJECT("MTSServer.MTSDemo")
? o.SlowHit(1)
WAIT WINDOW
? o.SlowHit(2)
WAIT WINDOW
? o.SlowHit(3)
```

The Write method creates a new file with a SYS(2015)-generated tag to keep the files separate. It does so once per object instance creation by using the hFile file handle at the object level. For hFile to be valid, it has to maintain state—otherwise a new file will be created. After running these four lines of code, you'll find that three temporary files were created in your TEMP directory. Each file contains the following information:

```
Init Fired
SlowHit Fired3
Destroy Fired
```

This demonstrates clearly that MTS does not actually cache object references, but rather re-creates your object from scratch on each method call! This means Init and Destroy fire on each method call that uses SetComplete() and SetAbort(). In addition to being stateless, your object also has to be lightweight in terms of how it instantiates and destroys, in order to be efficient.

If you have lots of Init code or many properties that are initialized when the object is created, you'll incur a significant amount of overhead on each call to the MTS-controlled object.

Remember, Just In Time Activation unloads objects after the method call completes and a call to SetComplete() or SetAbort() is made in the method. If you now take out the call to SetComplete() from the SlowHit() method, the object will stick around. Your Write method will create the following output for the three method calls above:

```
Init Fired
SlowHit Fired1
SlowHit Fired2
SlowHit Fired3
Destroy Fired
```

I consider this unloading/reloading to be extremely inefficient behavior, even for lightweight objects. Rather than re-creating objects on each hit, these object references should be pooled and reused, especially if objects are truly stateless. But that's not how MTS currently works, so you'll have to put up with the extra overhead it imposes.

MTS security
There are two kinds of security to set up with MTS: *package security* as configured by the identity of the package and *role-based* security for actual security-checking from within the code. The package identity determines which user account is impersonated when the components in the package run. In other words, the package has access to all resources that the specified user has access to. You can choose either Interactive User, which is a good choice for standalone applications and even most Web applications, or a specific user account.

One of the nicest features of MTS is its ability to check for security via roles, independent of a user's login ID. MTS allows you to map users to an MTS role and lets you easily check for this role through code. The user in question will be the client that is calling your application, typically the Interactive User in standalone applications, or the IUSR_ account when calling from a Web application. Client applications can check who is accessing them by configuring roles for specific users and then checking for the role with the IsCallerInRole method:

```
IF loContext.IsCallerInRole("BookReader")
   THIS.WriteOutput("Caller is in role")
ENDIF
```

To add roles, use the management controls to add a role and then add users to the role as needed. **Figure 9.5** shows the setup of BookReader users.

Role-based security comes in very handy when you need to check user identities closely inside a component. For Web applications, most requests come in as generic users on the IUSR_ account, but through Authentication (basic Authentication or NT Passthrough security) it's possible to pass user account information down to components to be checked by roles.

Figure 9.5. You can create roles by adding NT users to a specific role. From within your code, using IsCallerInRole and the Security object, you can easily check the roles for clients of your objects.

MTS summary

I've only scratched the surface of Microsoft Transaction Server functionality here; I don't have enough space to cover it in more detail. You can find an excellent article on MTS functionality with VFP by Randy Brown on the Visual FoxPro Web site, which will give you a functional overview of some non-scalability-related features of MTS.

As far as scalability is concerned, only a few features are of any consequence—in particular, Just In Time Activation and using the SetComplete() and SetAbort() methods of the MTS Context object to control state-keeping. I feel that these features on their own provide very little value at this time. Lack of a true pool manager that can reuse existing object references, rather than re-creating objects constantly—and the fact that MTS incurs a fair amount of overhead to COM calls through its passthrough interfaces—make it a downgrade, rather than an upgrade for VFP components. I'm hard pressed to find any real plus points for this technology in its current state.

MTS provides a good feature set, but this technology appears misbundled. The transactional features of MTS don't belong with the state management and scalability features—these should have been totally separate components to help focus this product better.

However, if you need some of the transaction-server features such as the security options, distributed transaction management, the shared property manager (a global context store much like the ASP application object), then MTS is a real boon. Distributed transactions in particular are extremely difficult to deal with; MTS makes these operations much easier by wrapping the DTC logic into the transaction interfaces. This functionality can save you a lot of manual work.

MTS still feels like it needs another revision before it becomes the tool it was meant to be—judging from some features that are implemented only as inactive stubs, it looks as if the next version, probably incorporated into the new COM+ architecture, will deliver a better solution for scalability issues.

Although I think MTS doesn't provide much value, you should consider writing code to be MTS-ready. MTS is strategic for Microsoft and will be integrated directly into the COM+ architecture, so all components will have the ability to access MTS's feature set without the extra registration steps. To work toward this architecture, consider building stateless components that don't rely on internal resources of keeping context between calls. It will make for better standalone components as well as those that might later need to run in MTS.

Pool managers in FoxISAPI/Web Connection

In light of Visual FoxPro's early problems with COM scalability, other ways were found early on to scale COM applications through application logic. In a way this demonstrates exactly why tools like MTS have a place in the market, because they can potentially eliminate the need to build custom code to handle scalable applications. The following tools do just that.

Pool managers are common in high-transaction applications where resources cannot be assigned and created for each client. Rather than giving each user a dedicated resource (objects, in this case), a small number of resources are shared among a large number of clients by handing references to those that need them, and then handing the references back to the pool on completion. The resource is handed back with uncertain state, which is why objects must be stateless in order to be part of a resource pool. With COM objects, this means objects are created and references are added to the pool. Once created, the objects stay loaded at all times and are passed to the client that's next in line to receive a reference. If all pooled objects are busy, requests start to queue, waiting for instances to free up.

FoxISAPI, and also West Wind Web Connection, implement their own pool managers in order to manage multiple objects for simultaneous access. These pool managers are built to work with any kind of COM object, but they work more completely with out-of-process components. Out-of-process components have some very useful points that relate to object management. Unlike in-process servers, EXE servers can be fully unloaded from IIS's process, forcibly if necessary. This means that a misbehaved object can be killed under program control, allowing the server to recover from an exception, another fatal error or even a timeout, all without locking up the Web server. The pool manager also supports use of in-process objects, but for tools like FoxISAPI and Web Connection, out-of-process components are the preferred route to take because of their object-management capabilities and the fact that these tools use a single COM object call per request to call the VFP server. The overhead for the single call is minimal and not worth the limitations and complications imposed by in-process servers. See **Figure 9.6**.

Pool of single-use EXE servers or in-process DLL servers

For scalable Web applications, the pool managers built into these tools provide much better control over the load placed on a machine by allowing a pool of objects to be created and references to be passed out of that pool. The benefit is that the servers are already loaded and only direct method calls occur. Unlike servers loaded through Microsoft Transaction Server, the references kept by FoxISAPI do not reload on each hit. On the first hit, servers start up and are managed by the pool. When a request finishes, the reference is returned to the pool and made available for the next incoming request. Both tools also allow you to specify how many objects you would like to start up and on which machine they should run. It's even possible to run the same component on the local and a remote machine.

The preferred mechanism is to use EXE servers for stability and to control the server object more tightly. EXE servers can be shut down remotely and, if something goes wrong and the server hangs, can be forcibly killed by terminating the process through program control. This allows you to reset and reload hung servers, servers that caused an exception, servers that timed out on a request, servers that crashed in Fox code, or those that accidentally caused a dialog to pop up. None of these things can be handled in DLL servers because it's impossible to terminate an in-process COM object that is hung. While the object is in call, releasing all client references has no effect.

The tools use ISAPI C++ code to manage custom pool managers directly through code built into the ISAPI extension. The pool is also managed and kept to a predetermined size to prevent overloading your machine with too many simultaneously running servers that would kill the server on CPU load. When the server pool is completely in use, pending requests are queued until servers become available.

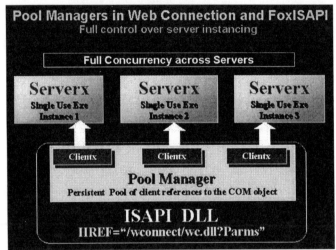

Figure 9.6. The pool managers in FoxISAPI and Web Connection provide full concurrency for the servers running in the pool. Because they are implemented as part of the ISAPI extension, the pool managers also can control instantiation by limiting object counts and killing servers when errors or timeouts occur.

Full administrative control over servers

Since the ISAPI extension controls the pool manager, it's possible to control the pool through its built-in management interface. The pool manager allows limiting the number of objects to load into the pool and how objects are accessed. Both FoxISAPI and Web Connection provide the ability to unload and reload servers and to enter maintenance mode that allows a single server to run for EXCLUSIVE data access. Web Connection also allows online binary code updates ("hot swapping"), automatic restarting of individual hung or timed servers, recovery from VFP server exceptions, and the ability to run in full admin mode—which blocks all server access except for the logged-in administrator— all without taking the site down.

These features might sound exotic, but once you start running a high-volume site you'll realize that taking a site down just to replace a COM component is a major issue. The same is true if you have to perform maintenance operations, and these functions automate the process of getting servers into maintenance mode. The integration of the COM loader code and pool manager give you tight control of these processes while tying them directly to Web interfaces.

Not generic

Pool managers can be very efficient, because in most situations they must be hand-coded at the system level. With FoxISAPI and Web Connection, the pool manager is implemented in the ISAPI extension itself, so the pool manager can be directly tied to the ISAPI application interface (including its administration functionality). But this also means that the pool manager is not generic, and it's a complex task to build a stable and efficient pool manager (if you're interested you can check out the source code for FoxISAPI since it ships with Visual FoxPro).

I hope this is one area that MTS can help in the future. MTS promises to provide a generic pool manager that can make this type of functionality available to any multi-threaded application. While it won't be as efficient as custom-coded implementations, it still will go a long way toward providing scalability out of the box for any multi-threaded client—without you having to worry about writing your own pool managers.

Reaching out over the network with DCOM

In order to scale applications beyond a single machine, COM supports a mechanism for instantiating objects on other network machines. Distributed COM uses a proxy/stub mechanism, not unlike the MTS model, to allow a client to call an object on another machine over the network. The client gets a local proxy object, which communicates with a stub object. The proxy and stub support the interface of the object you are calling and allow the client to act as if that object were local. The proxy and stub know how to pass data (parameters and property settings) back and forth, a process known as *call context marshaling*. This gets tricky and complex for object properties and parameters, because in some cases entire object memory images must be transferred across the network in some cases.

The beauty of DCOM is that it completely hides all the ugly details, allowing the COM client to call the object like any other COM object. A few special rules apply to objects that run over DCOM:

- The object must be out-of-process.
- The object must implement the IDispatch interface.
- All parameters and properties must be compatible with IDispatch.

Objects that run over DCOM must follow these rules—they cannot load into the client's process because they run on another machine across the network. There's one exception to this rule: You can build in-process objects that run in an MTS package. Because the MTS package is an out-of-process object, it can work over DCOM while your component inside the package runs as an in-process object on the server.

The IDispatch requirement is moot for FoxPro servers because FoxPro objects are always IDispatch implementations and support only variant datatypes and parameters. This is significant for C++ developers, however, who cannot call custom COM interfaces and can't pass pointers.

Direct instantiation via CREATEOBJECTEX()

To make an object run over COM, simply compile it into an EXE file and register it on the server by using YourServer.exe/regserver. To call the server from a client VFP machine, you can simply do this:

```
o = CREATEOBJECTEX("visualfoxpro.application","www.west-wind.com")
? o.Eval("Sys(0)")
```

This code instantiates Visual FoxPro as a COM object on my Web server machine and returns the name of that machine by using the Eval() method of the VFP application object. (Note: I can do this because I'm a valid user—you, on the other hand, won't be able to do this, at least not on my server.) CREATEOBJECTEX() is a new command for Visual FoxPro 6.0, and it's also available in VB and VBA with optional parameters of the CreateObject() function.

Keep in mind that the object—or at least its type library—must be registered on the client machine. The ClassId and Interface DispIDs are retrieved locally for performance reasons, so no round trip to the server is required for each lookup. If you're distributing an application for use with DCOM, you can simply copy the type library and have the Setup Wizard register it. Once you've done this, you should be able to call the remote object. Note that if the interface changes on the server, the type library (or the full server) must also be updated on the client.

Remote objects without CREATEOBJECTEX()

Unfortunately, the equivalent of CREATEOBJECTEX() is not available in all COM clients. In particular, Active Server Pages does not support this functionality directly. There are a couple of ways that you can still create remote objects from ASP:

- **Call the remote object from a local object.**
  It might be useful to take this approach if you have both local and remote application services. For example, it's a good idea to isolate specific tasks on other machines. You could have the Credit Card Validation object running on a dedicated machine, and the Product Information database running on another server. The local VFP client COM object would make the required remote DCOM calls only when needed, using CREATEOBJECTEX(). The disadvantage is that resources are tied up on the local machine while it waits for the remote machine to complete operation.

- **Use DCOMCNFG to force components to load on a remote machine.**
  COM supports another routing mechanism that's stored in the registry. You can configure an object to start up on a remote machine rather than locally. When you configure an object in this fashion, you can no longer run the object locally because it will always instantiate on the remote machine. When using this approach, the type library for the object must be registered on the local machine. You can do this with the Clireg32.exe utility (which uses the VBR file generated when you build a COM object) or by simply registering the full object locally.

To configure a server for remote instantiation, use the NT Dcomcnfg.exe utility, which you can run from the Windows NT Run window. **Figure 9.7** shows the Location tab where you can specify the computer on which to run the component.

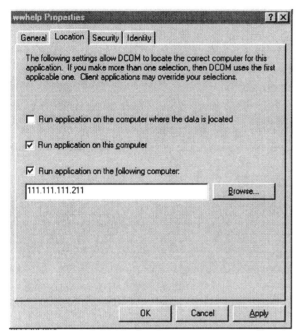

Figure 9.7. DCOMCnfg allows you to specify where a server is to run.
The server or its type library must be registered locally. The Location tab
allows you to specify the network computer on which the component should
run. This can be a TCP/IP or Netbios name.

Notice that I'm using an IP address for the machine name. It is possible to run DCOM over the Internet, although it's rather slow for making the connection to the server. Once connected, though, performance can be okay.

Beating the beast: DCOM security

The ability to instantiate objects over the network opens up the issue of security. As demonstrated above, if access was open there'd be a huge hole in security because anybody could start up VisualFoxPro.Application on my Web site and start using oVFP.DOCMD("ERASE *.*") to wipe out my System directory.

Security is a thorny issue for DCOM. It's difficult to configure because multiple levels of security are involved, both at the system and component levels. The key to running DCOM servers successfully starts with setting server access rights. You can do this generically for all objects or for specific servers. I prefer the latter because it gives you more control. **Figure 9.8** shows the Security tab for configuring access and launch permissions.

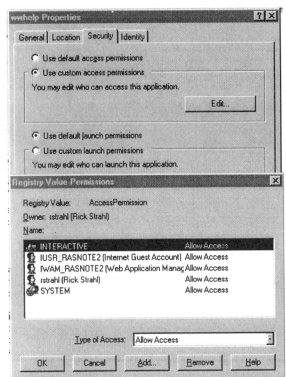

Figure 9.8. The Security tab allows you to specify which users can load and call your object. You need to set both access and launch permissions, which are required to make method calls and to access properties. If you're using Web applications that call your COM object, be sure to add IUSR_.

Finally, you can control under which user context the server runs. Impersonation changes the user context while the component is running, and then reverts back to the original setting. (See **Figure 9.9**.) This is crucial to allow components to temporarily achieve rights that the component client would not otherwise have. For example, suppose that an ASP page user runs under the IUSR_ account and hits your site. Now in order to access data in your data directory, IUSR_ must impersonate a user account that can access files in your data directory.

Usually you'll want to set the user account to "The interactive user," which means the currently logged-on user or the SYSTEM account if nobody is logged on. This works well for FoxISAPI, for example, and allows access to the desktop; if your server has a user interface, it will be visible.

For remote operation, it's best to use an admin user account that exists on both the client and server machines. The server must have the client account installed as a local account unless the client is connecting over a local network that can validate a domain name from both ends of the connection.

For a thorough discussion of DCOM security, see the "1998 NT Enterprise Development" issue of *Visual Basic Programmer's Journal.*

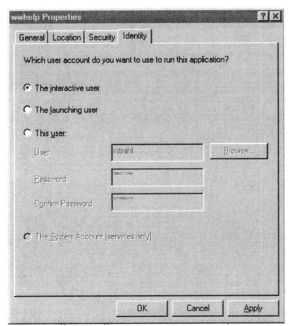

Figure 9.9. Impersonation determines the user account that's used while
your server is running a method. This user should have access rights to
all resources (such as directories) that contain data files; the user should
also exist on the remote server as a local account.

Security and the IIS client

It's tricky to get these security settings right, especially when you're dealing with IIS as a
client. The problem is that the IUSR_ account is anonymous and not easily duplicated across
machines. But the IUSR_ account on the local machine is the client, and the account must exist
on the remote server in order to launch the server there. To do this, you must follow these
messy steps:

1. On the local machine, open User Manager and find the IUSR_ account.
2. Change the password to something you can remember. By default this value is random,
    but you'll need to create the IUSR_ account on the remote machine and use this same
    password.
3. Go into the IIS Console, change the Anonymous user to IUSR_, and type the new
    password.
4. On the remote server, create the IUSR_LocalServer account (same as on the client IIS
    machine) and the password to match.
5. Bring up DCOMCNFG and select the server on the remote machine.
6. Click the Security tab and add the IUSR_LocalServer account to the launch and access
    rights.

Fun, eh? Now the IUSR_ account from the IIS machine has the right to load the server on the remote machine.

Performance and network issues
DCOM works over the network—and with this slow connection come performance concerns. As I pointed out before, a local type library is used to minimize round trips to the server to retrieve type, method and classID information. But all other server access requires potentially large amounts of data to be passed back and forth.

Keep in mind that DCOM, when running over a network, must send all data between client and server, while when executing on local objects it can simply access local memory. For example, if you use ADO to create a recordset and you pass the reference to a DCOM object, the entire recordset contents will copy, while on the local machine the reference would simply reference the existing ADO object. Objects require the entire memory footprint to travel over the wire so that the stub on the server can re-create the full environment that the proxy sees on the client. It's a beauty how this complex system functionality works, but expect it to be slow if you have complex or data-intensive objects.

Take care to avoid passing complex, nested objects, and try to pass as much information as possible in single method calls, rather than repeatedly calling methods or properties. Each method call and property access requires a network round trip, so having one method that passes 10 parameters will be much more efficient than making nine property assignments and one method call.

Also, keep in mind that net connections can be very slow, especially over the Internet. In addition to network latency there are issues with disconnects that cause your object to fail in the middle of a method call and, worse, lose its connection to the server so that the object is no longer valid. You can trap for these errors by capturing COM exceptions, which are generated by the local proxy. However, knowing what went wrong on the server or where exactly the server failed might not be possible when the connection is dropped. For this reason you should make sure that object methods are granular enough to be easily undone on failures. As you can see, there are some complex tradeoffs to be made between performance and reliability.

DCOM conclusion
DCOM holds a lot of promise. It delivers the ability to take advantage of the network and even the Internet to connect to COM objects on other machines. It's relatively easy to do, and performance is decent. Unfortunately, running DCOM requires a fair amount of client configuration and settings that must be frequently updated. These settings are not intuitive; they're easy to mess up, causing objects to fail with very little indication of where the problem lies on the client or the server. Worse, they're not easily configured with install programs—most of the configuration is manual and requires administrator rights.

This is one area that MTS addresses well. MTS allows you to export packages that contain all security information. The package can be moved and installed on a new machine, and in most cases it will run as-is without any further settings.

COM summary

COM is Microsoft's focus for application development. If you're building server applications, you'll be using COM for the foreseeable future. And VFP is an excellent tool for building components, both at the middle and server tiers.

COM with Visual FoxPro, however, is a double-edged sword. On the one hand it's easy to build servers, but on the other, VFP's COM implementation has a few problems. These will be addressed in the next service pack, which will bring true multi-threaded COM runtime support to the product. This important fix will allow VFP to be a good match for any multi-threaded client, including ASP and MTS.

COM is evolving, and new technologies like MTS are getting a lot of press these days. The technology is not always all it's cracked up to be, so take the time to examine the tools and how they work with Visual FoxPro. Make sure there is a good reason to use MTS, other than "Microsoft says you should." On the other hand, MTS introduces new concepts and, while the model isn't fully developed, it is a good one. It's a good idea to program for the new model— that is, building stateless from the start and thinking about transaction functionality in your components. You can also add MTS functionality now, even if you're not running in MTS. That way your components will be ready for MTS in the future.

In this chapter I've dug into a few COM topics, but I've only scratched the surface of the complexities that underlie this model. The beauty is that COM hides complexity from the client, and it's is as easy as using CreateObject() and calling a method. I've found that, in order to understand how COM works and how your VFP objects can take advantage of it, it's important to learn as much about COM as possible. A couple of good books on the subject are *Inside COM* (Microsoft Press), and the much more technical *Essentials COM* (Addison Wesley) by Don Box, which is sort of the COM bible. Most books on Active Template Library (ATL) COM programming also have decent introductions to the COM model. *Visual Basic Programmer's Journal* frequently runs COM architecture articles that are appropriate for Visual FoxPro developers as well. It's well worth the effort to dig into COM technology.

Chapter 10
Building Large-Scale
Web Applications

Web development brings with it special challenges that you might not encounter with stand-alone applications. Web applications, especially publicly accessible ones, are subject to large numbers of users in unpredictable numbers at any time of day or night. Web apps tend to be online 24 hours a day, seven days a week, and often cannot afford downtime. The transaction volume on public sites is often unpredictable and in many situations grows rapidly from small numbers of users to an onslaught of traffic that can be difficult for your network infrastructure, your Web server and your applications to handle. In order to build effective applications for this environment, it's important to understand what's possible with the tools you are using and how to effectively measure, project and finally prepare for increasing load on your servers. Understand up front that there is no magic bullet for this process, regardless of which server and development platform you end up using (NT vs. Unix, VFP vs. C++, ASP vs. ISAPI, and so on)—they all have limitations. Proper integration is the key to smooth Web operation. For example, I've seen 100 CPU Unix servers bogging down at much less load than a single dual-processor NT box. It all comes down to proper tuning and interoperability of all the pieces in these complex applications.

Building an application that can handle large volume requires proper planning and a solid understanding of the infrastructure and its possibilities. It's also likely that it will require you to work with and understand a number of varying technologies—from server hardware and software, to network and administration tools and issues, to software development with multiple tools that are right for the job. This job might be divided among various groups in the company or it might fall into a single person's (yours?) lap to administer. I'll examine the development process and people issues in the next chapter.

In this chapter I'll discuss the issues involved with building applications that will experience large volumes of transactions on the Internet. There's more to it than simply looking at the resources available and the horsepower of the machine on which the applications run. Being able to handle large loads requires balancing hardware, software and development skills to bring about a balanced and scalable environment that can grow as your applications get busier.

Visual FoxPro is ready for the server!

People often have serious concerns when it comes to using Visual FoxPro on a Web server. The main reason seems to stem from the fact that Visual FoxPro is not commonly mentioned as a development tool meant for server-side development. However, the fact is that Visual FoxPro is an excellent tool for building server-side application components precisely because of its extremely flexible data manipulation language (DML), mixed with an easily accessible and complete object-oriented implementation and the fastest local, Windows-based database engine built into a development product. As you've seen in the server-side and even the client-side chapters of this book, there's very little that you cannot accomplish with Visual FoxPro code. Although it might not seem obvious, these features—especially performance—are very important to building applications that scale well.

Aside from its language features and performance, VFP is also fully capable of providing the basis for building scalable Web and server applications. With version 6.0 and a forthcoming Service Pack, which addresses several shortcomings in VFP 6.0's original threading model, Visual FoxPro has the ability to scale well in a high-transaction environment. You can use many Visual FoxPro servers simultaneously on the same machine, as well as scaling servers to other machines over DCOM to extend scalability beyond the limitations of a single machine. Coupled with Visual FoxPro's data-access performance, string manipulation, and general data-manipulation speed, this makes for a capable tool that can efficiently take advantage of whatever system resources (in the form of multiple CPUs or servers) you are willing to give it.

I've been building Visual FoxPro Web applications for a number of years now, and I've seen a lot of different implementations, including some very large-scale apps serving hundreds of thousands of server hits a day. I've seen applications coming down from large Unix boxes to a Visual FoxPro platform, and I've seen Visual FoxPro applications being moved away from Windows to Unix. In all of this comparative observation, I've found that Visual FoxPro in combination with Windows NT and IIS is one of the best platforms you can use for Web development in terms of performance, scalability and development productivity.

One site in particular that I've been involved with, Surplus Direct, has gone through the whole cycle—from a mainframe solution down to NT, and back up to a Unix environment. Powered by Visual FoxPro, the site has recently peaked at 750,000 back-end Visual FoxPro server hits per day, with peaks of almost 100,000 hits an hour—and with no sign of running out of steam. Mind you, these are all database and application logic hits, not just static page hits, running on four Windows NT dual-processor boxes. This particular application can scale up to any type of load, simply by adding more machines into the server pool, which provides nearly limitless scalability (given network bandwidth and database server resources).

The point is that with proper design and configuration, Visual FoxPro applications can be used to serve up any kind of load you might want to throw at them. At the same time, keep in mind that building scalable applications requires a difficult process of coordination among the operating system, system tools, the network and your application. Regardless of which tools you use—from Visual FoxPro to Visual Basic to Visual C++—most of these issues will apply because they deal with the infrastructure. In this chapter I'll talk about infrastructure issues as well as those specific to Visual FoxPro.

What is a large-scale application?

When I talk about *large-scale* Web development, realize that this is a relative term that depends on your particular environment and how you approach an application. In general I evaluate whether an app is large-scale based on two particular issues:

- Web site operation
- Development process

If a site is heavily used, it can fall into the large-scale bucket based on its sheer transaction volume and load issues. Other applications involve a complex business environment that requires the sheer size of the application to be large scale. Some applications have both. In this chapter I'll address the Web site operation issues: tuning, measuring, deployment and management. In the process, I'll look at various issues of how Visual FoxPro fits into the Windows NT and COM architecture and how this affects your development of components built with Visual FoxPro. The next chapter deals with the human aspect of the development process and interrelationships of its different tasks.

Web site operation

When judging the "size" of a Web application, many people consider its *operational aspects*. Operational aspects address questions relating to the volume of traffic, the number of hits received by certain pages, the number of back-end hits, or the number of records added to the database each day. These issues are extremely critical for server-based applications because they must be carefully balanced against the capacity of the systems that are running the application. If you overload the system you'll lock up the Web site, which can lead to disastrous results and loss of money. The operational aspects can be broken down into several areas:

- **Performance**
  Performance is an important aspect of any application. In Web applications, it's even more critical because it can affect not only the responsiveness that the user sees but also the scalability. The faster a request can be served, the lighter the load on the server and the quicker another can be processed.

- **Scalability**
  Speed is nice, but in Web applications there's the additional factor of many users accessing a site at the same time. Scalability deals with utilizing and balancing the load that the traffic incurs with the hardware on which it's running. This can be a daunting task, especially if your needs go beyond a single server machine.

- **Data volume**
  Many large-scale Web sites also generate huge data volumes. Dealing with extremely high transaction volumes on the data server is a critical issue when designing applications, because contention and locking issues are much more likely to occur in Web apps than in typical stand-alone business applications. Data volume can be the downfall of the application as the SQL back end becomes a bottleneck that cannot be scaled as easily as other aspects of the Web application. This involves volume/size scalability as well as data-server bandwidth and computing power. Data management also becomes a serious issue because it becomes increasingly difficult to store and move the information being captured. For example, one site I work with generates log entries for every hit incurred

and every visitor, along with every order placed. A typical day can generate close to 1 million new records in the database; storing and moving this data is difficult, especially when there's "no good time for maintenance" on the server.

- **Site administration issues**
  Adding new software or hardware can put serious strain on a busy, live application. Web sites are expected to be up 24 hours a day, seven days a week, and any glitch can result in a loss of valuable customers. There are also software issues with site administration, such as how to update code seamlessly in a distributed environment, how to handle errors and logging, and so on.

Performance

As you might expect, performance is extremely critical in high-transaction environments; it's also the most visible aspect that you might be familiar with from standard applications. Any application needs to run as fast as it possibly can, but for high-transaction environments it's crucial to tune code to make sure it runs at its optimum—slow requests can tie up valuable resources that might be needed by the next request in line. In a server environment, performance is significantly affected by other system elements, in particular load on the server's resources (CPU, disk, and possibly the SQL back end). While tuning your code to run as fast as possible is crucial, realize that tuning won't help if you're running the CPUs on your server at a maxed-out 90% CPU load. Nevertheless, treat performance as a top priority right from the start when you design your applications. Performance bottlenecks typically don't show up right away, but rather as applications experience rapid growth or spurts of huge traffic loads, which is a common scenario for successful Internet commerce applications.

When looking at performance, it's important to examine more than just the immediate application. Tuning your Fox code is definitely worthwhile, but tuning the operating system and maybe even the layout of your Web site can dramatically change the dynamics of how much load is incurred on your server.

Data optimization

Since we're dealing with database applications here, data optimization is the most important piece of the puzzle. Database operations tend to be the slowest operations in any Web application and also the most resource intensive, so optimizing them can bring the biggest benefits. On any given request in my applications, around 80% of the request processing time is spent with data access. Data access is, of course, one aspect at which Visual FoxPro excels, regardless of whether you're using local data against DBF files or remote connections to SQL Servers.

The following are a few general tips and guidelines to consider. Some are basic common sense, but it's a good idea to be reminded and maybe encouraged to review your existing code for them:

- **Optimize your queries.**
  If you're using local data, make sure that all of your queries take full advantage of Rushmore. Make sure you set up indexes to match your queries and make sure the queries

match the indexes *exactly*. Also, make sure you have tags on DELETED() if you're running with SET DELETED ON. Take the time to review performance and SQL optimization with VFP's ShowPlan function SYS(3054). If you're using a remote SQL Server, use the server's optimization tracing functions to review SQL commands in the same fashion. SQL Server 7.0's new Query Analyzer is a great way to optimize queries more easily than in previous versions.

- **Pull only data you need.**
  When using local data it's often easier and more convenient to simply run SELECT * queries and perform further filtering in secondary queries. However, pulling that extra data takes time and requires server resources, especially if you're using remote SQL Servers. Make sure queries bring down only the data you really need!

- **Avoid updateable views for queries.**
  Updateable views tend to be quite a bit slower than read-only views because VFP needs to track the changes you make and then synchronize them with the SQL back end. If you're running data queries that use the same views as some update routines, consider creating separate views for the query update to localize the overhead of the updateable view to the operation that really needs it. For the fastest performance, you can use VFP's SQL Passthrough to talk to the remote database directly—although the gains are not that big. Personally, I like SQL Passthrough because it offers me extra control and allows for much easier error trapping than remote views allow, but it's more work to code.

- **VFP data access is much faster than SQL back ends.**
  Many Web applications are moved to SQL right from the start, even when they use Visual FoxPro code on the back end. Make sure you evaluate carefully whether you need a SQL back end and whether it's worth the tradeoff in performance. Local Visual FoxPro data access is likely to be two to three times faster than SQL Server data access (SQL 6.5) in most situations. It's one-and-a-half to two times faster with file data on a remote server. I'll talk more about the advantages and tradeoffs in the following section.

- **Minimize or offload long requests.**
  Transaction-based systems work best with short requests. Long requests can tie up valuable resources and load up CPUs, which can very quickly bring a server to its knees. Try to break up lengthy requests into multiple smaller requests if possible. If that's not an option, consider off-loading long-running requests to other servers (perhaps a special maintenance server) or possibly a SQL Server. Keep in mind that any resource-draining operation has the potential to lock up your site because serious slowdowns and CPU load problems are self-perpetuating. As the server can't keep up, new requests pile up more quickly than the server can handle, resulting in an endless cycle of catching up.

To SQL or not to SQL

The question of whether to migrate an application to a SQL back end invariably comes up when dealing with high-performance server applications. When you think about back-end data, keep in mind that VFP has an amazingly fast data engine—if speed is what you're after, VFP is likely to be the best choice, while SQL Servers provide security and data stability.

Using Visual FoxPro data

There are good reasons to migrate to a SQL back end, but many applications may not have a need for them. FoxPro works well even against very large data sets, so take the time to test performance. Don't blindly jump to a SQL back end! Consider the following points:

- **Native data is great for server back ends.**
  For server applications, it's appropriate to use Visual FoxPro as a local data source because only a small number of simultaneous VFP clients access the data at once. Data is usually local to the machine on which the server is running—or it's on a fast, low-volume network. Unlike many standalone network applications, in a Web application a data connection is not from the user to the database, but from the Web server to the data. The execution environment is also very controlled because data access occurs from a server rather than from end-user client machines. Many data-integrity issues that can crop up in typical network applications—with large numbers of clients stemming from configuration and client problems—are not an issue with server applications.

- **VFP performance is much better than SQL.**
  Keep in mind that VFP has an amazingly fast data engine. If speed is what you're after, VFP may be the best choice. I worked on one application that, when I converted from local VFP data to a SQL back end, data access ran between two and three times *slower* for short requests and five to 10 times slower for complex queries and administrative tasks. Proper tuning of SQL Server (which took several outside consultants several weeks) brought this down a little, but still left SQL Server running nearly twice as slow on average. Where performance counts, Fox data is an excellent choice. Even if you are using SQL Server data, take advantage of the Fox engine by downloading and caching static data in local cursors to save round trips to the server.

- **VFP can handle large data volumes.**
  I worked on one high-volume commerce site where VFP back-end data was used with servers peaking close to 750,000 back-end hits a day on a single, four-processor NT box. The actual day-to-day operations of running an online shopping site ran flawlessly.

- **VFP has problems *only* with batch updates against heavily used, live data.**
  So, why switch to SQL if all is rosy? There are a few problems with VFP data access on operations that should normally be left to EXCLUSIVE use. On this project, there were issues dealing with the frequent data updates that performed large imports into live, online databases. Many of these operations could have been performed with EXCLUSIVE operation, but this wasn't possible due to the time these import operations were taking.

With multiple active servers, these update operations running against live online databases would occasionally corrupt the database and the indexes. Operations that turned up these problems were APPEND FROM and DELETE on large groups of records, while other instances of Visual FoxPro were actively using these same tables. (Note: These issues could have been worked out, but a management decision at the time forced the move to a SQL back end anyway. The moral of the story is that you can get around these issues if you can recognize the problem when it occurs.)

Using a SQL Server back end
Fox data is fast, but SQL Server provides a number of features that are simply impossible to accomplish with FoxPro data. In many situations, the tradeoff for performance can be worth it. The advantages of a SQL back end are:

- **Improved stability**
  The main reason for the move to SQL at the above site was for better stability. Getting away from the DBF/CDX file structure has resulted in significantly improved up time. The environment and nature of online batch updates mandated this move to get around data consistency problems encountered with native VFP data. The biggest problem with native data wasn't the fact that it got corrupted, which happened only on very few occasions—it's that it went undetected for quite a while, causing inconsistent but not easily traceable problems on the live site. As you might expect, those kinds of problems are almost more serious than outright failures that are immediately visible. With the SQL back end, data corruption has never occurred, albeit at the cost of very lengthy and slow updates that often lock out users while the operations run.

- **50+% performance loss (SQL and Internet overhead)**
  Overall, application throughput dropped by more than 50% when the move to SQL Server occurred. If you're moving from Fox data to SQL Server you'll almost certainly face a similar performance hit.

- **Lightened CPU load on Web server**
  SQL Server was installed on a dedicated server machine and migrated much of the data processing load to the SQL Server box, away from the Web server/VFP machines. Running a complex query on a VFP front end won't cripple the Web server because the CPU-intensive query now runs on the SQL Server. The idle CPU power can then serve other requests and more connections. The flip side is that SQL Server is now bearing the majority of processing load, with the majority of CPU power focused on the data access layer. This has potentially expensive implications if the SQL back end must be upgraded. Scaling a SQL Server beyond a single machine is difficult and expensive as well.

- **More complex data access issues**
  The move to SQL also brought difficult issues in terms of data administration. SQL servers are hard to deal with for large update commands and purges that occur on heavily used data. Locking issues can make it impossible to update data that's being operated on—extensive use of stored procedures and sectioned processing is often required to

accomplish tasks such as clearing out log files. This was one reason for moving to SQL on the Surplus site, and as it turned out, these issues were not addressed, resulting in update operations that would at times take more than 10 minutes, compared to 30 seconds or so in native Fox data. General administration of SQL Server is also more difficult: Tuning the server, managing security, maintaining data partitions, and monitoring backup and performance are not trivial tasks. They require personnel with previous experience or training, or outside consultants who specialize in SQL administration. SQL Server 7.0 makes this process somewhat easier through improved self-tuning logic in the server and much improved administrative interfaces, but knowing what to tune when the time comes still remains an important aspect of any SQL Server application. If you don't have the in-house resources, be sure to budget outside help—tuning a SQL Server is one of the most important aspects of a successful SQL application.

- **Was it worth it? Yes!**
  In retrospect, was it worth it to give up the huge performance benefit of local Fox data? In this case, most definitely yes! Stability of the application went way up, and the site experienced fewer problems getting locked or stuck with data-corruption issues. Centralized data access and management through SQL Server has also made the administration process more centralized and allows automating some of the heavy data-maintenance tasks in the middle of the night. The tradeoff was performance, which was addressed by bringing more concurrency to the front ends by adding additional machines to take requests from the Web server.

Weigh the advantages and disadvantages of VFP and SQL Server carefully. SQL Server 7.0 presumably improves performance considerably and eases some of the locking issues that continue to be the biggest problem in the batch update process. Fox data can go a long way for you, so compare your options and requirements to what you can accomplish.

Code optimization
If you're using Fox middle-tier and server components, you'll have the opportunity to optimize the code. The following tips are mostly common sense, but they point at common problems found in performance reviews of server applications:

- **Set up timing requests and logging.**
  The first step is to determine where bottlenecks lie. If you use any sort of Web tool, log your Web requests and their request times to get a rough idea of where the slowest hits come from. If you're using FoxISAPI, it's easy to log request times to a file by simply hooking your entry point routine and writing the elapsed time to a log file. This is more difficult with other tools like ASP because they may not have a central entry point that can be easily logged. In that case you'll have to create timing code for each request manually.

- **Profile your code.**
  Once you've isolated a bottleneck, examine the code and trace it down to the individual block of code. Can the code be simplified? VFP has many ways to accomplish some

tasks—is there a way to use different commands that might be faster? Are you calling functions or methods repeatedly that could run inline? Are you creating objects that might be better served as function calls? (Stand-alone functions run much faster.) Server applications often require performance over function in the tight spots.

- **Use the new Coverage Analyzer.**
  VFP 6.0's new Coverage Analyzer can help you determine bottlenecks in your code. The analyzer summarizes the data captured by SET COVERAGE ON and lets you easily see what's taking the most time to run.

- **Decide whether to use a generic framework vs. hand-optimized code.**
  If you're using a framework that helps you with HTML generation, realize that some powerful functions might not be the fastest way to accomplish things. Most of these functions have to be generic and thus have to test the environment, so they often work on dynamic determination of types. In other words, framework code is almost always slower than hand-optimized code. For example, in Chapter 5, several routines can dynamically create HTML displays of VFP table/cursor data. The code has to check the type of every field and then decide how to display it based on that type. Compare that to simply saying lcOutput = lcOutput + Tquery.Company. It is no surprise that the straight code will run as much as twice as fast.

  Understand the tradeoff between hand coding and framework code. Sometimes the functionality, readability, and reusability benefits will outweigh the performance, but if your request needs to run faster and everything else fails, hand-coding some generic routine might be the boost you need. Again, profiling will help in this determination.

- **Take advantage of VFP 6.0's new string speed.**
  Visual FoxPro 6.0 has drastically improved string operations that involve concatenation. Repeatedly calling commands such as lcOutput = lcOutput + lcString on large strings can run *several hundred times* faster than in VFP 5. String operations also work with object properties; as long as the variable on the left and the first expression on the right are the same (i.e. lcOutput or THIS.cOutput), they can be optimized. Even with this improved string handling, creating large strings as a file with TEXTMERGE or the low-level file functions—and then reading the file back to a string with FILETOSTR()—continues to be the fastest way to create large amounts of output.

- **Control class instantiation.**
  Class instantiation is still one of the slowest operations in VFP, even though VFP 6.0 has slightly improved performance. Consider creating objects and keeping them around for reuse rather than recreating them all the time, especially if objects perform complex instantiation code. In light of stateless programming, this is extremely important because instantiation of your object can occur much more frequently when objects are running under Microsoft Transaction Server. The smallest and quickest loading class in VFP continues to be the non-visual RELATION class. The fastest loading visual class is CUSTOM. If you're building COM objects of your classes, go through the class properties

and methods and make any that you don't want to expose PROTECTED—this will avoid creating the type interfaces for the COM class which reduces load and call interface access time and provides a leaner COM server that's easier to work with in the VBA environment with Intellisense.

- **Stay away from macros and EVALUATE().**
  This one's pretty obvious, but it bears bringing up. This is somewhat related to the "generic" framework code, which often has to rely on EVALUATE()s in order to dynamically determine field or object names. EVALUATE() and macros are extremely powerful, but try to avoid them as much as possible.

Web site optimization

Getting your Web application to run optimally from a code perspective should be familiar to you—it's not much different from tuning any other kind of application for optimum performance. However, Web applications require tuning in other areas as well. In particular, the Web interface itself can make a big difference on how your application "feels. Here is a list of tips to help you optimize your Web site:

- **Optimize your home page.**
  The home page of a busy commercial Web site probably gets upwards of 70% of all traffic, so it's fairly important to optimize this page as much as possible. Many people hit the home page and immediately drop off, sometimes because it's not what they were looking for, sometimes because they didn't want to wait, or sometimes simply because they were curious. Regardless of the intent, those hits, whether intentional or not, require server resources. If your home page can be static, by all means make it so. If it's mildly dynamic (captures the referring link, assigns a user ID, etc.), consider using an ASP page and storing the information in a cookie. Try to avoid database access on your home page or otherwise calling a back-end server.

  Also important is HTML and image size—keep it to a minimum to avoid clogging the network. Remember that even non-data requests put a strain on the Web server if it's busy enough.

- **Optimize site flow to minimize hits.**
  If a site is laid out well, it takes fewer steps to go where you need to and get the job done. Fewer steps means fewer hits, which means less load on the site. Try to avoid intermediate menus, and try to use clear flow—possibly combining multiple steps of functionality on a single page. If you can take one page out of a five-step procedure, you're potentially saving 20% of your process load. Think of how you can use that extra horsepower more effectively!

- **Use ASP or HTML for non-data logic pages.**
  If you're using a Web scripting back end like FoxISAPI or Web Connection that talks directly to a server, try to avoid calling that server for non-data pages. Use HTML or even

ASP pages when no data access is required. For example, my site includes a number of user-tracking and UI logic code issues, all of which are handled with ASP pages that perform no data access.

- **Can you use generated static pages?**
  We're all database people here—but sometimes it's better not to think in terms of data retrieved from a database. Really. A lot of CPU cycles can be saved if pages that rarely change are pre-generated as static pages and then simply read from disk by the Web server instead of being dynamically generated. A category list in an online store is a good example. Proper design would dictate that the data is generated from the database each time the page is accessed. However, this data might change rarely—only one new category might be added per month. Rather than generating the page each time a user wants to see the list, a standard routine could create a plain HTML file with a pre-generated list. This could save several thousand back-end hits a day.

- **Minimize maintenance operations.**
  Maintenance operations are killers that can tie up servers for long periods of time. These operations put extreme loads on the back-end server, so the best thing to do is to isolate them and have them run at night or offload them to process on other machines.

Web server optimization

Following are a few suggestions for improving performance on IIS 4.0. These can be important for heavily loaded sites:

- **Reduce connection timeouts.**
  By default, IIS sets a connection timeout of 900 seconds. IIS 4.0 uses HTTP 1.1 by default, which enables keep-alive connections at the protocol level. Keep-alives maintain live connections for the duration of the timeout, which can quickly eat up system resources if maintained for 15 minutes. It's a good idea to reduce this timeout to a lower value, but make sure you allow enough time for your longest running request. If you set the value too short and your maintenance request exceeds this timeout, the Web server will return an error.

- **Limit connections for busy sites.**
  By default, IIS starts up with service for 100,000 simultaneous connections. While this might be a reasonable number for pure static page requests, this number is much too high for dynamic applications on a single server. On a busy site it makes sense to set this value to a number of connections that can realistically be handled by your server at any given time. The number varies, but I've used 5,000 on various commerce sites—right around 5,000 client connections happened to be the breaking point where the site started bogging down dangerously and CPU load would top 90%. Your mileage will vary depending on the application and hardware its running on.

If you bogged down the site even further, you'd lose performance so drastically that nobody would be served well. Rather than doing this, the connection limitation will refuse new connections, giving the familiar (if you've visited the Microsoft site often) "Server Too Busy" message to new connections, but at least allowing those with existing connections to go on.

Obviously this setting affects only sites that are operating at the top end of their resource spectrum. If you're in this position, you likely need to address the real issues at hand with more hardware or multiple machines.

- **Set ASP options.**
  Active Server Pages incurs a number of resource hits that you can disable if you don't use them. If you don't use ASP at all, there's no sense in paying the penalty for these features.
  - **Turn off ASP Sessions if not used.**
    If you're not using ASP or you're using ASP but not ASP Sessions, turn them off! Sessions cause significant overhead on the Web server and assign cookies to clients on every ASP page hit entirely on their own. There's overhead in the cookies and even more overhead in tracking the session buffers on each hit.
  - **Turn on page buffering.**
    If you are using ASP, turn on page buffering. Page buffering builds pages in their entirety in memory or cache prior to dumping the output back to the Web server. This is typically much faster than the direct WriteClient() approach that ASP normally uses. It also gives you more flexibility: Only with buffering can you easily modify the HTTP header and cookies after some text has already been output. This buffers all output in memory—if you have truly large pages, consider using Response.Flush() to occasionally stuff accumulated page content down the pipe.
  - **Limit threads created by IIS.**
    IIS creates new threads for each ISAPI request—if one or more requests hang, it's very easy for IIS to quickly generate a huge number of threads. If your system runs with too many threads, it starts to slow down drastically. You can set a registry option to prevent this from happening by telling IIS to limit the number of threads it creates. I suggest no more than 50 threads per processor. Note: IIS uses 24 threads internally, so add that value to the count. Set this in IIS 4 or IIS 3 with this registry key:

    ```
    HKEY_LOCAL_MACHINE\SYSTEM\
    CurrentControlSet\Services\InetInfo\Parameters\PoolThreadlimit
    ```

    ```
    HKEY_LOCAL_MACHINE\SYSTEM\
    CurrentControlSet\Services\InetInfo\Parameters\ThreadTimeout
    ```

    Both values are DWORDs. Set the timeout to 15 minutes (900 seconds) or so.

- **Consider Internet connections.**
  Not all Internet connections are created equal! You might have noticed that some sites display content much faster than others. Just because you have a dedicated T1 line does not mean you get the same access performance of, say, a Netscape or Microsoft site. Your

service provider's access speed to the actual Internet backbone can vary depending on how far removed the server's routers are from the backbone in terms of router hops. High-speed routers can also improve performance. You can roughly check these things out by using the Windows TraceRt utility to see how many hops it takes to get from your IP address to a remote link. You'll find that the big portal sites are usually two hops removed from the backbone, while most other sites typically take four to six or more. In general, the fewer hops the faster your access. Bandwidth of the provider is also important—many ISPs sell T1 access, but you're really buying access to a shared T1 connection, not a dedicated T1 line. Phone companies do the same to ISPs, and so it escalates. Oversold connections can result in bad access performance, especially during peak hours. Make sure you understand how your Internet pipe access is structured.

Visual FoxPro and multithreading

One crucial aspect of performance and scalability is a product's ability to run multiple operations simultaneously. Unlike stand-alone applications, which usually don't require simultaneous operations, servers sit and respond to requests from large numbers of clients. If the server is unable to process requests simultaneously, any long-running request will block other requests that try to access that same server. Blocking is a serious problem that can quickly cause servers to back up to a point of no recovery, where the backlog of requests is larger than the capacity to service them before timeouts. As you might expect, blocking is not an option for server-based applications.

IIS and ISAPI are multithreaded, but VFP is not!

IIS and ISAPI run in a multithreaded environment that allows many simultaneous requests to happen concurrently. On the other hand, Visual FoxPro applications are single-threaded and must therefore simulate multithreading in order to run without blocking.

There are a number of ways to accomplish this task. It comes down to running Visual FoxPro as a server application that stays loaded in memory and services requests as needed. Multiple instances of VFP are required to service multiple simultaneous requests.

This can be accomplished in a number of different ways:

- **Using in-process COM objects**
  This is the "standard" Microsoft way of building scalable COM applications. Apartment model threading allows for multiple instances of an object to be instantiated. In theory you should be able to instantiate multiple objects and have them run simultaneously. However, the original release of VFP 6.0 didn't work this way because it blocked simultaneous method calls on the same server. This issue will be addressed in a shortly forthcoming Service Pack for Visual FoxPro/Visual Studio. Operation of in-process COM objects was discussed in detail in the previous chapter.

- **Creating multiple out-of-process COM objects using a pool manager**
  Prior to the multithreaded update of VFP 6.0, in-process servers could not be scaled well. Tools like FoxISAPI and Web Connection implemented their own versions of a pool manager to allow multiple instances of out-of-process components to be available to

process requests. A pool of pre-created COM objects wait for requests and the pool manager hands off incoming requests to one of the already loaded and reusable instances. These pool managers were built primarily to bypass the COM blocking issues of in-process components, but they work efficiently with out-of-process and in-process components.

- **Running multiple copies of a stand-alone application**
A server application doesn't necessarily need to be a COM object. A server application can implement a TCP/IP service or even an HTTP server directly and wait for requests. If this application is a plain EXE file, you can run multiple copies of it to service multiple requests simultaneously. As an example, my Web Connection framework provides a development mode that employs file-based messaging between the Web server and the Visual FoxPro EXE that responds to requests. Message files are sent back and forth between the server and VFP, allowing multiple separate EXE files to service those messages as needed. Most CGI-based or ISAPI-based tools use this type of approach to communicate between the Fox server and the Web server. The mechanism can vary from file-based messaging to DDE to using Windows events and Named Pipes. These polling mechanisms tend to be less efficient than COM, but they do have the advantage of being able to run interactively so they can be easily debugged. Because they're normal Fox programs, you can run them inside VFP and fire up the debugger to set break points— something you can't do with a compiled VFP COM object.

Understanding CPU load and speed

All scalability scenarios depend heavily on the environment in which the servers run and how the servers affect that environment. When examining load on a site, it's crucial to understand how the application is performing on a given machine. When I say *load* I'm mostly referring to the CPU load incurred by the application. This load is affected by all system components such as disk and memory, but shows itself most consistently in the level of CPU usage in Performance Monitor or even in Task Manager. As disks get saturated, queries slow down and require more CPU power to get to data. As memory runs out, more data is stored on disk rather than in memory cache, and you get more CPU load to access the data.

When trying to make sense of this information, consider the following:

- **How many requests can you handle over a given period?**
Load is determined by looking at a given number of hits over a given period of time. The load incurred on the machine can be measured by the CPU usage that's incurred for this traffic. In rough terms, this means a site that's running 1,000 10-second requests an hour is loaded about the same as a site that's running 20,000 half-second requests, assuming the sites are running similar pieces of software and hardware. Actually, this isn't completely accurate because the site running the 10-second requests is probably running higher CPU loads for the queries that are processing. So there's no easy way to judge an application's load, but as a rough guideline use requests over time by request length.

- **Based on your number of CPUs, what is your processor speed and request processing time?**
  Load is affected by the horsepower of the machine. Two CPUs can almost double performance (an 80-90% increase is more accurate). Faster disks and increased memory also can improve load capability. Most of the time, the slower a request runs, the more load it incurs on a server. While running, the request uses up CPU cycles and disk bandwidth. There are exceptions to this rule, however: If you're off-loading processing to other machines such as a SQL back end or a remote server accessed via DCOM, you might leave request handlers running at close to 0% CPU load while the remote machines chug away at the heavy loads. In these cases, local load can be light while remote load is heavy. The advantage is that you often can distribute that load more easily across multiple machines, which is a key feature for building scalable apps.

- **Additional instances help responsiveness, but not load on CPU.**
  I've talked about running multiple instances and multithreading in order to achieve better scalability. Remember that multithreading is not a silver bullet. It will not give you better performance, only better responsiveness.

  For example: A request taking 10 seconds and a request taking one second can run at the same time, so the client waiting for the one-second request won't have to wait 11 seconds. The one-second request might run a little slower than it would normally, because the 10-second request is already running, so it might actually take two seconds. The 10-second request also slows down a little because of the increased load on the CPU and might take 12 seconds. You've provided better responsiveness to the user of the site, but you've actually increased the total processing time by three seconds because the total now takes 14 seconds instead of 11. You've actually increased the load on the server by running these requests simultaneously, while providing better responsiveness to the users.

  Running multiple simultaneous requests will actually reduce overall performance as the operating system incurs processor overhead for thread scheduling—hence the need to limit the number of simultaneously running operations. The more simultaneous operations that are running, the slower they get. Multiple processors can help in this scenario, but the same rules apply as long as more instances than processors are running.

- **Test your expected load!**
  The most important issue in relation to load is to be ready for it. If you're running a growing Web site, you'll probably run into a situation at some point where the resource requirements of your configuration outrun your application or hardware. You'll want to avoid this as much as possible by testing your load capability in advance and knowing how much you'll be able to handle.

  At Surplus Direct we've had three occasions where we hit the wall with hardware and software. Twice the hardware couldn't take the load, resulting in locked servers running at solid 100% CPU loads and two 100% maxed T1s (the full bandwidth available at the time). The other time, the traffic was so large that the back-end servers simply could not keep up. The only way to get the site running again was to limit connections to 5000 at a time to allow at least some of the traffic to succeed. This is something you should avoid at all costs! Test your expected load and be ready to add more hardware if necessary. It seems obvious, but this is a common problem with growing Web applications that are running their first big promotions! Too much of a good thing can be a bad thing.

- **WebHammer**
  This cheap and simple tool can be used to repeatedly "hammer" your site with HTTP hits. You can set up as many as 32 simultaneous threads kicking out requests, and you can run multiple instances on multiple machines to create a variety of different requests. Download the tool at http://www.serverobjects.com/products.htm#WebHammer. There are more sophisticated tools costing thousands of dollars that provide more control and logging facilities, but for down-and-dirty load testing, WebHammer is excellent.

Scalability

With Internet commerce growing at over 100% each year, it's likely that a commercial Web site will run into growing pains. Scalability issues come to the forefront when running applications that outrun the single Visual FoxPro server, and even more so when running more than a single-server machine in order to handle the volume.

Multiple instances of VFP required

As previously discussed, Visual FoxPro is limited to single-threaded operation and requires multiple simultaneous instances (either in-process or out-of-process) in order to handle concurrent request processing. Apartment model threading and the FoxISAPI/Web Connection pool managers allow you to work around this issue by loading multiple concurrent instances of the object and reusing its resources.

Best scalability achieved with multiple processors on a single box

When it's time to throw more hardware resources at the application, the best way to scale is to add more processors to the local box. Each processor gives about an 85-90% performance increase for CPU processing. IIS is multithreaded and can take advantage of multiple processors through the NT Symmetric Multi-Processing (SMP) architecture. **Figure 10.1** shows the single-machine scenario with one Web server loading multiple instances of the application objects.

Visual FoxPro can run concurrently on multiple-processor systems, with multithreaded components running on separate processors as well as out-of-process components, which are scheduled on a particular processor at startup. Because out-of-process components are essentially separate applications with their own process and address space, NT can throw processing on one or the other processor. NT handles the details of thread scheduling and balances the load between the processors without requiring any change of code.

You might want to play with the Control Panel's System settings for performance, and decide whether to give the foreground or background tasks more priority. IIS is a system service and falls into the background-processing bucket. Any in-process VFP components loaded into IIS via ASP or directly off an ISAPI extension also run in the system context. Out-of-process components fall into the foreground-task category because these objects tend to impersonate a specific user account or the Interactive User.

The best load factor seems to be two VFP sessions per processor, with IIS sharing the processors, but that can vary based on your load application is generating and whether your processing occurs on the local machine or a remote server. The longer requests take and the more resource intensive they are, the more CPU power is required to make them work.

Figure 10.1. A single server allows us to load multiple simultaneous VFP instances and run concurrent requests. The best overall performance can be achieved by using multiple processors to improve load handling.

Use network machines to spread load

When one machine is no longer enough, the next step is to move out to the network to spread the processing load across multiple machines. See **Figure 10.2**. Plain NT currently supports four processors—eight processors are planned for NT 5 (Windows 2000)—which can handle a significant load. However, some applications will simply outrun a single box, whether it's the application or the Web server. Some sites are so busy (like the Microsoft site, for example) that multiple machines are required just to display a small set of static home pages. When a single machine won't do, the network allows you to spread the load to other machines. You can add additional machines that are accessible to the Web server to handle application or data tasks.

Several routes are available for spreading processing over the network. The most common first step to off-loading processing is to move to a SQL back end that handles data access onto a separate server. This frees the local application and the Web server from a big chunk of CPU access. Although I mentioned earlier that using a SQL back end can incur a significant performance hit from local VFP data access, it addresses the issue of data access load incurred by local data and offloads that load to another machine. VFP accessing native VFP data processes the data access on the same machine that runs the code. Even if the data is on another machine, VFP data access load is always incurred on the same box that is running the code. With a SQL Server, the entire load can be moved to a different machine. Keep in mind that VFP still incurs a fair amount of load for remote SQL requests incurred by invoking the ODBC connections and actually retrieving the SQL results. It takes between .15 and .25

seconds for a SQL connection to drop the CPU load to idle on long queries. Hence short requests may not benefit as much from data offloading as you might expect. The other reason to use a SQL Server in this scenario is that once multiple machines are involved, it becomes important to have a localized data store.

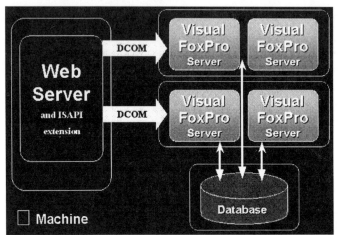

Figure 10.2. *It's possible to off-load processing load to other machines by using a remote SQL Server, or by running components on remote machines via DCOM. By off-loading to other machines, the Web server—the most crucial link to the outside world—can remain free to process requests without getting bogged down under heavy load.*

You can also offload application logic to other machines using Distributed COM. DCOM is a relatively new Microsoft technology, introduced with NT 4.0, that allows out-of-process COM objects to be accessed on remote machines as if they were local. You can make the same COM method calls as you can with a local object. To make this work, objects must be registered to run on separate machines via a separate registration utility that directs the local registry to run the server remotely. You can also use the equivalent of VFP's CREATEOBJECTEX() (utilizing the CoCreateInstanceEx API), which allows you to create remote objects directly without local registration. However, this requires your COM client to support this mechanism. Active Server does not. Web Connection supports it via a special server-load syntax, as does any COM client built in C++ that can use CoCreateInstanceEx() directly. The direct approach is much better because it allows more flexibility—the indirect approach requires the registry to be properly configured and allows a specific object to run only on a particular machine—the local machine can only instantiate objects in one location. With CoCreateInstanceEx(), multiple copies of the same object can be loaded on different machines simultaneously, including the local machine.

For applications like FoxISAPI and Web Connection, this means you can run a pool of servers of the same object that runs both locally on the Web server as well as on one or more remote machines. You can also offload processing more distinctly by calling specific business objects on other application servers. You might have a product information database sitting on one machine, a ship-rate calculation engine sitting on another, and the order-processing server on yet another. For the main Web engine you might have two local instances and two more running on another server.

The drawbacks to this approach are complexity and performance. Configuring components so they correctly share data and application paths—when those components run both locally and on remote machines—can be very complex. It also can be difficult to register them on another machine. VFP's CREATEOBJECTEX(), allows direct instantiation of objects on remote machines without having to configure the server locally. But realize that ASP does not support this command directly from an ASP page. You might be able to create a VFP object locally and then instantiate the object remotely. It's also tricky to move such an application. With DCOM there might be a lot of configuration options buried in various configuration utilities, from DCOMCNFG to the registry, and possibly hacked ClassIds to let multiple objects run simultaneously. Security is a huge issue with DCOM operation and one that's not documented well anywhere, primarily because there are so many possible combinations of security and access controls that can be applied. Calling DCOM from an IIS context poses additional issues because of the limited security rights of the IUSR_ account. Components must be configured correctly so they can run on the local machine and have rights to run under your local account on the remote machine. The security issues alone on this configuration could fill a whole chapter.

Finally, DCOM components are problematic when something goes wrong. If the remote connection fails or the remote server is rebooted while the local server is still active, you'll hang up the clients trying to connect to it. Because COM calls from high-level clients like VFP and VB are blocking, you have to wait for them to complete. If the object is not available, COM takes at least 30 seconds trying to locate it. (This is configurable in some COM clients like VFP, but not in others like ASP.) Think about what needs to happen if a remote component is not available; the answers are not always simple. Again, NT 5 and COM+ promise help in this area with load-balancing tools that can check for object availability before routing calls to remote objects.

Performance is also an issue. Remote objects take a lot longer to load, and calling methods in the remote server is comparatively slow because parameters and return values have to travel over the network. When calling remote objects, you want to minimize the number of round trips made to the server. It helps to bunch multiple method calls into single calls with more parameters if necessary. If you're sharing common data that isn't in a SQL back end, there's also the issue of accessing that data across the network often with UNC pathing, which can be very slow.

This approach has another potential problem: There's still a bottleneck of a single Web server servicing requests! If you get to a point where a single Web server can't take the incoming requests, there's no easy way to scale up.

In spite of the drawbacks, using DCOM over the network can provide significant improvements in scalability as you are off-loading large amounts of functionality to other machines. All but the heaviest usage sites on the Web can probably make do with a single Web server that routes requests to separate application servers.

IP Routing/Dispatch Manager

So, where do you go when a single Web server isn't enough? The solution lies in using multiple server machines simultaneously by employing either a hardware or software solution to route IP requests from DNS to multiple servers. It's like splitting up a single IP address among multiple servers (see **Figure 10.3**). Either a hardware router or specialty IP routing software can be used to accept an incoming IP request and route it to one of the available Web servers, which are configured to service requests for this IP address. The routing mechanism knows the "real" IP address for each of the servers in the pool and routes requests from the "virtual" IP address to these actual IP addresses. Each of the servers is configured identically, running IIS and the back-end software. In this case the back end is West Wind Web Connection, but it would work equally well using Active Server Pages (with some limitations on some of the built-in objects like sessions).

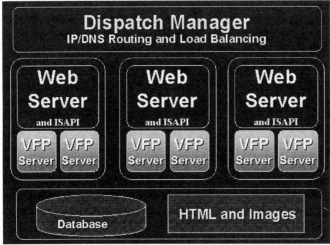

Figure 10.3. Using an IP routing scheme allows multiple Web servers to service a single IP address. Each server contains a full copy of the Web server and the Web application and provides full redundancy, making it possible to drop and add servers on the fly without affecting operation. In this example, data access is centralized to a single SQL Server box, which can become the potential bottleneck.

The simplest of these mechanisms is DNS round-robin routing, which is supported by most DNS servers. A router or DNS server can be configured to take an incoming IP address request and re-route it to a set of IP addresses in round-robin fashion, going simply from one address to the next for each incoming request. This mechanism can be implemented at the router or your DNS server. Round-robin routing works, but it is essentially a "dumb" solution. If a server in the pool goes down, these schemes will continue to send requests to the downed server, resulting in errors. These can be hard to catch because they'll be mixed in with good requests from the other, still working, servers. It's also a bit of work to change the configuration if you need to drop servers in and out of the pool frequently. Assuming you have a stable application, though, it's an easy and cheap way to distribute incoming traffic.

Hardware solutions involve routers that have built-in support for this job at the hardware level. These routers are also smart enough to see if a machine is down so it can skip its sequence in the routing loop. But routers can rely only on hardware to determine the down status. Removing servers from the pool is not quite straightforward and often requires modifying the router or router configuration files directly, which is not what you want to do in an emergency.

More sophisticated solutions involve dedicated software that monitors the incoming IP traffic as well as the servers that run in a server pool. The servers in the pool can be monitored for CPU load, number of connections and a number of other things to determine where the next request is to be sent. Servers can be managed and easily dropped in and out of the pool of active servers.

One of these software packages that I've been involved with is called Resonate (see **Figure 10.4**). The software communication pieces are Java-based with client software running on each of the servers and a "monitor" piece that runs on its own dedicated machine to monitor IP traffic. It is also very expensive, as all of the high-end solutions appear to be in this hardware area.

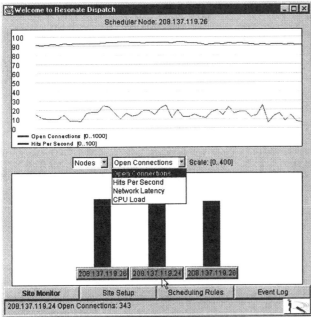

Figure 10.4. *Resonate's Monitor interface allows you to view real-time statistics about the entire pool as well as individual machines in the pool. It's possible to see CPU load on each machine or, as in this example, open connections. The monitor also allows administration of the pool for adding and removing nodes.*

A dedicated machine serves as a dispatch manager and receives all incoming TCP/IP traffic for a certain IP address. The individual servers also run a piece of software that monitors the state of the current machine (connections, CPU load, and so on) and makes that information available to the Dispatch Manager. The Manager uses this information to route requests to the servers that are the least busy, allowing fully loaded servers to catch up. Based on this information, the Dispatch Manager schedules TCP/IP requests to the least-busy servers and actually balances the load. Because this is a software solution it's easy to move servers in and out of the pool—simply bring up the client software piece and tell it to remove itself from the pool.

Expensive or not, this solution has made it possible for the site to grow at staggering rates. There is no longer any worry about the Web server or the FoxPro applications being bottlenecks because each server has full redundancy and new machines can be added at any time for relatively little cost. Each server contains a fully self-contained configuration of the Web server and the Web application; taking down any one of these servers does not compromise the site in any way. Along the same lines, adding a new machine to the pool requires configuration of the machine (installing the Web server, Resonate client and the Web application) and then simply dropping it into the pool. Machines can be added whenever load requires, giving virtually unlimited scalability.

I expect more solutions to become available for IP routing that will bring the cost down for these types of tools. The software is not all that sophisticated, but it's serving the high-end market where high prices are expected. Hopefully more mainstream vendors, possibly even Microsoft, will fill this gap in the future.

Note: As I'm doing my final edits, Microsoft has released a new Windows Load Balancing Service tool on its Web site. This tool works with the Enterprise edition of NT Server and allows functionality (according to the product info) similar to what I've described here about Resonate. I haven't had a chance to look at it, but you can find out more at http://www.microsoft.com/ntserver/nts/downloads/winfeatures/WLBS/default.asp.

ASP Sessions won't work across machines

Keep in mind that solutions involving multiple Web servers affect ASP applications directly. In particular, Session and Application objects will not work when requests span multiple servers. Because of the way IP routing works, there's no guarantee that two consecutive requests by the same user will be serviced by the same machine. In fact, even the same page might not be served from the same server: The HTML might load from one server while images load from another. Since requests can be routed to any server, the ASP Session and Application objects won't work because they are in memory on the single server on which they are running. So in order to keep state with ASP in a multi-server environment, you need to manage state on your own with cookies and a record in a database that is accessible to all servers. You can safely disable ASP session state in the IIS Admin Console for ASP options.

Data becomes the bottleneck

The IP routing scheme can provide nearly unlimited scalability to your Web server and application logic, but you have to be careful to not forget your data back end. In the application I've been describing, it looks like the SQL back end is actually going to become the bottleneck. Data access will all go to a single back-end machine, which puts serious load on that single server. The only solution for this problem is bigger hardware—possibly moving to a SQL Server running on a high-end Alpha machine with multiple processors. For now the application has not reached these limits on the SQL back end, but that time will come. This may really be the key point of scalability to consider.

Scalability summary

This section has described a number of ways that you can take an application to the next level of scalability. As you've seen, the solutions involve a lot more than Visual FoxPro. When you get to the point where everything can't run on a single box, you are moving into areas of network administration, hardware architecture and system configuration. Take advantage of experts for these various areas, rather than trying to handle everything on your own—it pays to get the various pieces right. Any part of an incorrectly implemented architecture can have disastrous results on all other components in these complex scenarios. For example, a misconfigured SQL Server can cause your applications to back up waiting for requests, which in turn can cause IIS to get overloaded with unprocessed HTTP requests. It might not be immediately apparent what's causing the problem—is it the SQL Server, or IIS, or the Web application?—because all are posting awful performance at that point. Getting things right from the start is more important in the complex server environment than with any other application.

Making changes to an installed complex architecture becomes increasingly difficult because the system relies heavily on interdependencies. Redundancy is key here—making sure you have backups that can take the place of a downed server or one that must be taken out for maintenance or system failure.

Finally, plan ahead. Take the time to build realistic simulation scenarios to see what you can actually handle. Vendors make many claims that don't hold up in live environments. Take the time to test your application before taking it online to see what you can expect as your load grows. It's not easy, and it might not even be 100% accurate, but it will give you a much better idea of your breaking points in relative terms. If you know the breaking point, you can reduce or postpone the impact by making business decisions that might delay traffic coming to your site, or by limiting access to pre-determined levels.

The bottom line is that you can certainly build large-scale applications with Visual FoxPro as well as you can with other tools. Just keep in mind that many other tools and technologies are involved. Use what works best for the job—and remember that VFP is a good choice for much of the code. The job is not trivial, but that's the nature of complex systems.

Site application administration

An often overlooked aspect of commercial Web sites is the management and administration of the site. It deals with physical site operation as well as performing maintenance operations on the application itself. This includes things like importing and exporting data, data file updates, updating application files and performing typical administrative operations on the database. I've found that the majority of Web site development actually goes into these back-end features as opposed to the public user interface.

Commercial applications tend to run 24/7, and interruption of service can be costly to the business operation. Site administration tasks are often structured to minimize downtime and must be specifically designed to deal with the online environment.

Decisions, decisions—online or offline data

When designing data access for a Web site, you have to make a choice between using data directly from existing line-of-business application database systems or running the application independently so that it interacts with existing systems through imports and exports. The decision to run data in online or offline form directly affects the level of administration required, because offline data requires synchronization tasks.

In my experience, most commerce applications run as offline applications for a variety of reasons. The main reason tends to be security—if the data runs offline there's no chance that the mainline business data will be compromised, either via security leaks or bad data being written directly to the business system. Additionally, offline data stores tend to be more efficient because they are more specific to the Web both in size and operational tuning. If your company sells 100,000 products but only a few hundred are available on the Web, it's quicker to retrieve the required items from the smaller database. The data can also be fine-tuned directly for the online operation as opposed to offline business systems, which often must perform a much wider range of services on the data. Performance of an in-house point-of-sale application that serves fewer than 100 sales associates on the phone is unlikely to be fast enough for an online commerce site that gets several thousand orders and several hundred thousand data accesses a day. Sometimes offline data is the only way to go if the business applications run in formats that aren't directly updateable via data access mechanisms such as ODBC and OLE DB, or if they run on completely different platforms.

On the downside, offline data requires that data be imported and exported frequently. On busy commerce sites this can take substantial resources. For example, when running an online store, inventory must be synched up with actual stock on hand. If that data isn't available directly, the inventory data must be updated frequently and padded to avoid running out of stock.

For offline data sites, updates can occur online without taking the site down. Whenever possible, update operations should pull data in and out independently of the Web site through separate administration applications, as to not affect the Web server's load. This might not always be possible, but it should be a goal to isolate processing intensive tasks. Admin tasks tend to be resource intensive, so there's still going to be an impact on the database server in terms of CPU load incurred.

A final issue with offline systems is a security hedge against fraud and inaccurately entered data from online users. Online fraud and inaccuracy is rampant, and the ability to capture the data into a separate data store prior to importing into the main business system can provide an additional layer of security. While some of these precautions can be handled during online validation, this can often be time consuming. For example, online credit-card validations can take 20 to 40 seconds, tying up valuable resources at the time of purchase. It might be useful to delay the validation process for a later time and importing the data from using a non-Web-driven application.

Online data, on the other hand, sidesteps much of the maintenance requirements because updates occur directly against live business systems. The problems here are possible performance and contention issues. Business systems might be in heavy use internally, which could cause delays on the Web site. While phone operators might be used to saying, "Our computers are slow today" to their customers, Web users tend to be an impatient bunch and are much more likely to leave the site if things are slow. The traffic a Web site incurs could also interfere adversely with the business application itself. There might be 100 phone operators answering phones, but maybe 5000 people browsing on the Web site at any point. Was the business application designed to take that kind of volume? Most likely the answer is no.

The other issue is maintenance. Web applications need to be up all the time, so if a business application has scheduled downtime, the Web site will have to be taken offline at the same time. A Web application suggests that users are accessing the back end data all the time. Maintenance and updates can't occur unless all users are off the system.

In general, offline apps seem to make more sense, but that decision must be based on your business process. If you're designing applications entirely from scratch, or applications that are Web-only right from the start, online operations might make more sense. But if you're interfacing with existing software and applications, the load of a Web site might be too much for an existing system to handle.

Remote application administration

A big chunk of the development of many commercial Web sites goes into the back-end functions that are not directly visible to the user. You have a choice of how you want to implement these back-end services. In my experience it pays to hook the majority of the maintenance functionality to a Web back end in order to allow personnel to access the this functionality from anywhere.

Another choice to make is whether administrative functionality is built right into the online application or whether the functionality is offloaded to special administration servers in order to minimize the Web site processing overhead. For example, you might have a special administration site such as admin.surplusdirect.com instead of www.surplusdirect.com to handle the processor-intensive processing tasks.

At Surplus Direct, maintenance operations were directly built into the Web application, but the actual maintenance operations ran on a separate, dedicated server that was part of an IP routing pool. Operations on the administrative pages included operations to import and export inventory and order information, maintain special deals, configure rotating banners, display current visitor information, and export that data to other systems that could analyze it in summarized form. These tasks and many others allowed various users to attend to their tasks through the Web interface. Areas of the administrative pages were restricted, depending on which users were asking for access.

Detailed site and user statistics

In addition to performing operations specific to the application, most sites provide usage information that is tracked as part of the application. My sites include hit logging of each request as well as visitor (or session) logs that write information about the user to a dedicated file that can be summarized at a later time. **Figure 10.5** shows a typical display that gives a quick, real-time view of daily site activity. The data is simply summarized from various application logs.

The site tracks detailed information about individual hits and shopper information in order to determine traffic patterns. Shoppers are tracked through the site anonymously, and valuable information about where they came from and how much traffic they generate is tracked into a Shoppers table. The information can be displayed at a glance in online graphs or exported for more detailed daily reports that are run and presented in Excel. The daily data is then summarized in weekly and monthly statistics that provide valuable marketing information.

Some of the information includes referring links and "Source Codes" that are captured from various advertising partner sites. These source codes give information about how effectively advertising is working on various gateway sites. This information is kept in the shopper table and visitors are optionally tagged with a cookie that maps to a user ID key in a database. This record contains cumulative purchase totals, visits, and a number of other useful bits of information that can be used to customize the user's shopping experience in the future.

Any history data is cookie-based, which means it is not reliable as is, and can only be used in context of other similarly adjusted values. This is because some people refuse to accept a cookie or because people switch browsers, and so on. Hence the percentages remain roughly the same, so the data can be compared from month to month, but the actual numbers might not be fully accurate and might understate the true values.

Should you use cookies?

Most large-scale commerce sites don't rely on cookies to track users, both because of the controversy and because a large percentage (10 to 15%) of users are using cookie-incapable browsers.

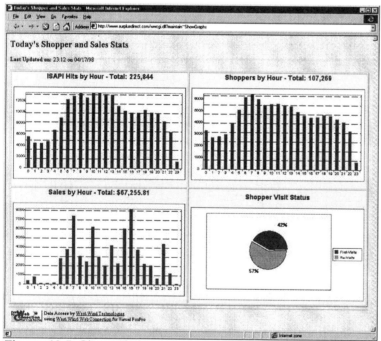

Figure 10.5. Site statistics pulled from application logs can provide real-time views of site activity. Because this data is summarized from a database, it's much easier to manipulate than Web server log files extracted from typical site-analysis programs. It also gives you much more control over what you log.

For this reason, most sites continue to use URL string-based user ID schemes. If you browse a shopping site you'll frequently see horrible URLs that have long ID strings embedded into them. These IDs are used to pass forward the current visitor's session from one page to the next, in the absence of cookies. This ID is used to reestablish the user's "session" on each hit, so you can keep track of items that have been dropped into a shopping basket, for example. These IDs work on any browser and are safe, but it is considerably more work to implement IDs rather than cookies. IDs have to be embedded in *every* URL the user accesses. One missed URL on the site and the user session is lost.

Large commerce sites probably have to go that route since 10 to 20% of the audience is too large a chunk to lose. Smaller sites, or those that attract high-end users, may be more likely to use cookies on the site. If you do use cookies, make sure you check for failed cookie assignments and explain to the user why she should accept the cookie or upgrade to a more modern browser. Using cookies definitely reduces logic required on the server to manipulate IDs, and the real security risk of cookies is no higher than IDs. The result is really the same— to keep track of users as they browse through a site.

COM server management
Finally, it's also important to deal with code maintenance. Code needs to be updated, and databases need to be maintained. When working with Visual FoxPro code, you'll most likely be working with COM objects. One key requirement is the ability to load and unload servers according to site load. The busier the site, the more servers are loaded into the pool—with optimum performance at around 2-3 servers per processor on the machine on which they run.

Depending on whether your application uses an ISAPI/CGI-type approach like FoxISAPI or Web Connection, or a scripting engine like ASP, there are different approaches to unloading and managing COM objects.

With the ISAPI approach it's possible to tightly control the lifetime of objects. With FoxISAPI and Web Connection, the ISAPI extension creates the COM objects and thus holds a reference that can be easily unloaded by the extension. Hence FoxISAPI gives some control over COM server loading and unloading, including the SingleMode option that unloads servers in the pool manager and leaves only a single instance running so it can get EXCLUSIVE access to data. Web Connection steps this up one additional level by allowing servers to automatically unload and then reload if they hang or time out—built-in crash protection. Web Connection also allows for live code updates without taking the server down by employing a built-in flag to hold requests. The ISAPI extension actually manages unloading all COM references, then updating the application files, then reloading servers, with the entire process taking under 20 seconds. With ISAPI, the flexibility can be built into the extension.

Active Server Pages is much less flexible for COM server administration. Basically ASP locks COM objects into memory. There's no way to programmatically unload COM objects as IIS caches the references. The only way to unload these cached references is to shut down the Web server or set up your virtual directory as a "Separate Memory Space" application (see Chapter 4 for details). These IIS "applications" run as MTS components that can be unloaded from within the IIS service manager and by using the IIS Admin objects programmatically. Unfortunately, that doesn't do much good on a busy site. If you unload your object while the site is busy, it'll immediately reload, never giving you a chance to copy in the new versions. The only reliable way to do this is by shutting down the Web service, and manually updating components as needed. This, in my opinion, is a major shortcoming of Active Server Pages, especially in dynamic environments where code changes are made frequently and many objects are involved.

Security on the Web

When building database Web applications, security is important because confidential data might be traveling over the wire. You wouldn't want to capture orders online, including credit card numbers, and then have somebody hijack the entire order/customer file with that sensitive information. Security comes in many flavors and applies to different aspects of a Web site. Is the information passed over the Web safe? Are the resources on your server secure from outside access? How do you keep people from accessing certain parts of your application? Are passwords kept secure across the network?

Windows NT provides excellent, though somewhat complex, security features that should address the majority of your security needs. NT allows configuration of files at the file level as well as the directory level. NT Security is extended to Web applications through NT Challenge Response (file-level access security) and Basic Authentication (HTTP application security, controllable via code).

NT uses a special account called IUSR_MachineName (where *MachineName* is your computer's name) to identify anonymous users to the Web site, and rights must be given to this user for any public areas. Public areas include your Web root and any virtual directories that are accessed through the Web. The basic configuration is handled directly through the IIS service manager, which assigns the appropriate NT file rights without you having to mess with directory rights.

In all other places, make sure you remove any IUSR_ references and the Everyone account (which shouldn't be there in the first place) to disallow unchallenged access to these non-private areas. If a user tries to access any of these restricted areas over TCP/IP or the Web, a password dialog will pop up, which allows authentication through NT Security just like you'd get through local access from the server.

The IUSR_ account is key to Web security, so be careful when changing the rights of the IUSR_ account in the User Manager. While developing applications with IIS and COM, it's easy to give the IUSR_ account Admin rights to get some security issues resolved while debugging applications. That's fine for debugging, but in an online environment an IUSR_ account with Admin rights lets anybody get at all aspects of your site. Don't forget to set your IUSR_ account as a guest account before you put your site online.

Keep data in an unmapped path

Web applications typically break into multiple parts—the Web pages, the application code (if it's extended via COM or plain Fox code) and the data. If you keep sensitive data on your Web server, make sure that the data is not accessible via a relative path over the Web. Ideally the data should reside in an off-limits area away from the Web site in an unmapped path. If the data can sit on another machine and be accessed over a non-TCP/IP network connection, you can just about eliminate your risk for data piracy (at the cost of overhead for the network access). Of course if you use a SQL Server, either locally or on a remote machine, this won't be an issue as the built-in security will control access to the data. The same goes for code, if you keep it on the same box as the server.

NT Challenge Response—directory and file security

Use NTFS partitions on your hard drives if you want to set rights on directories and files directly. FAT partitions are a lot more difficult to configure for security because you have to set up shares. FAT is also slower.

If you must have data in a Web-relative path so that the data can be updated online via FTP, make sure you set the proper password rights on these directories to disallow anonymous access by Web users. Web and FTP access rights work through NT security, so you can set them directly from Explorer by right-clicking and using the Directory or File Security dialogs. Note that Web directories typically have Read and Execute rights set (Special), and all publicly accessible directories include the IUSR_ account. Any private directories should remove the IUSR_ and Everyone accounts, and add only those users or groups that should have access.

NT supports NT Challenge Response for access to files, which means that if you're accessing a page and IUSR_ doesn't have rights, NT will try to validate your user account through the local machine or domain if you have IIS configured to run through a specific domain server. If you are a user of the local network, you might not be prompted for a password. If you aren't, NT will request a login dialog and validate you against the server's local machine or domain accounts (depending on how you have IIS configured—by default, only local server machine accounts are used for login validation). If you type the correct password, you're allowed access. This type of security works both at the directory level (which really just delegates down to the file level) and the file level.

Basic Authentication for your applications

NT Challenge Response works through directory rights, much the same way it works when accessing files locally. For applications that must validate user access, it's possible to force users to log in before continuing. This process is known as Basic Authentication and is part of the HTTP protocol.

Authentication occurs as part of the HTTP header passed back to the Web server/browser, which interprets the header and pops up a validation box. There are two steps to make this happen:

1. On the password-protected request, verify that the user is authenticated by checking for the REMOTE_USER (ASP) or Authenticated Username (Web Connection/FoxISAPI) server variable. If it's empty, the user is not validated.

2. If the user is not validated, send back an Authentication request that pops up the dialog. If the dialog's response is successful, the request from step 1 repeats. This time the user will be authenticated and should be allowed access.

Here's a simple example from Chapter 5:

```
FUNCTION Authenticate

lcUserName = Request.ServerVariables("Authenticated Username")

IF EMPTY(lcUserName)
    *** Send Password Dialog
    Response.Authenticate(Request.GetServerName(), ;
                        "<h2>Get out and stay out!</h2>")
    RETURN
ENDIF

*** Go on processing - user has been authenticated
THIS.StandardPage("You're Authenticated", ;
                "Welcome <b>" + lcUsername + "</b>. You may proceed to " + ;
                "wreak havoc on the system now...")
ENDFUNC
```

The actual authentication request is implemented via a special HTTP request that is returned instead of an HTML document. The following code generates the actual password box popup when sent back to the Web server:

```
* Response::Authenticate
FUNCTION Authenticate
LPARAMETERS tcRealm, tcErrorText, tlNoOutput

tcRealm = IIF(TYPE("tcRealm") = "C", tcRealm, "/")
tcErrorText = IIF(type("tcErrorText") = "C", tcErrorText, "<h2>Access
Denied!</h2>")

RETURN THIS.Send([HTTP/1.0 401 Not Authorized] + CR + ;
                [WWW-Authenticate: basic realm="] + tcRealm + ["]+ CR + CR + ;
                [<HTML>] + tcErrorText + [</HTML>])
ENDFUNC
```

If you're using ASP, you can use the following code (this has to happen prior to sending any other output!):

```
<%
Response.Clear
Response.Buffer = True
Response.Status = "401 Not Authorized"
Response.AddHeader "WWW-Authenticate","basic"
Response.Write "<h1>Get out and stay out</h1>"
Response.End
%>
```

Authentication provides a built-in mechanism tied to the operating system that validates users through code. Once the user is authenticated, you can always check his Username, which is passed along with each subsequent request until the browser is shut down, using the

REMOTE_USER ASP variable or Authenticated Username for FoxISAPI and Web Connection.

Keep in mind that Basic Authentication sends a password over the wire! Therefore, login dialogs such as this are inherently insecure. If you're worried about security beyond password information, it's recommended that you also use an SSL/HTTPS request to force the password authentication. That way the request information will be encrypted on the way to the server.

Non-NT custom security

Of course you can implement your own security scheme, rather than relying on NT. If you have a lot of users that must be added manually or through the Web, it might be easier to store user names in a database and access the data through plain code. To do this, you'd use an HTML page to prompt for login information. On submission you'd capture the user name and password and validate it against your database. Once the user is logged in, you can use either an HTTP cookie or a "license plate" (an ID tracked on the URL through every link of the site) to track the user through the site. You'd have to check for the ID or cookie on each hit to make sure the user is logged in.

Do you need secure transactions via SSL?

By default, none of the information that travels over the Web is encrypted. This includes HTML form variables, server information and authentication information that is returned to your back-end programs from the Web browser. This means somebody with a protocol analyzer could potentially snatch passwords or IDs or credit card numbers while in transit.

Secure server transactions use certificate-based encryption, which use private and public keys to encrypt all content that flows between the Web server and browser. Keys are administered by a few third-party key authority companies and cost $250 for a year. You create a key request with the server's key-manager utility and fill out an online submission form for a key request. (See www.versign.com for more information on obtaining a key or getting a free temporary key.) The server sends the key request, which is used to generate your private key. This key is returned to you as a file and merged with your existing key to provide the secure certificate on your site. Once the certificate is installed, using secure transactions is as easy as using the HTTPS:// protocol instead of the HTTP:// protocol. Everything else works the same as before. On the server side you can check to see whether a request is secure by looking at the SERVER_PORT (Server Port for FoxISAPI) server variable. If this value is 443, the request is secure running in HTTPS; port 80 is the standard HTTP port.

Do you really need secure transactions? If your site captures sensitive information like credit cards— definitely. If you're using a custom password scheme with passwords entered on HTML pages—probably. For general applications? Probably not.

Secure transactions are easy enough to implement, and the price for a certificate is not inhibiting. But secure transactions are much, much slower than non-secure transactions. Therefore, it's a good idea to use secure transactions only when you need them. On a commerce site this might mean that the entire store runs in plain HTTP mode until the order form appears, at which time the browser is switched into secure mode.

Summary

Building large-scale applications of any kind is not a trivial task; Web applications are even more complex than most other server-type applications. Web applications mix many different technologies, and once you reach a level where a single box is no longer sufficient to do your processing, you encounter aspects that go beyond application development and delve into system architecture, network administration and distributed systems. Regardless of the complexity involved, keep in mind that Visual FoxPro can be a player in this arena—it has the strengths and capabilities to scale and provide a flexible development tool for building Web applications quickly and efficiently. From the developer's point of view, VFP is ready for the Web, without much change in the way you develop applications. Just make sure your apps are as efficient as possible. It's also important to have a good understanding of the COM threading model in order to understand how your servers are accessed by the system. This will help you fine-tune applications and know when it's time to scale to additional server resources and possibly other machines.

When faced with this alphabet soup of technologies, many people I've talked to in the Fox community are a little intimidated—that's normal. The technology is complex and it takes a while to grasp the breadth of what's involved to make it all work right. But also realize that this chapter deals with high-end applications. The vast majority of applications don't need multiple servers to service a single Web site.

To put it all in perspective, keep in mind what you can accomplish today! You can build wide audience applications that serve hundreds of thousands of people a day—and it's possible to do this with a development tool that costs under $500! Think about that for a minute... it's an exciting time to be a developer, don't you think?

Chapter 11
The Development Process

Just as scalability becomes an issue for large commercial Web sites, the development process tends to get more complex once a site starts seeing large numbers of users. As site development gets more complex, a number of different people with different skill sets become involved. Integrating these people into a single, cooperating unit is critical to the success of the Web site.

In this chapter I'll discuss some different roles and activities that I encountered in one of my Web applications, which is fairly typical for large commercial Web applications. I'll look at the development process as a whole and focus on individual tasks, and I'll discuss some FoxPro-specific issues of working in this team environment.

Web applications tend to require a number of skills in order to handle all aspects of an application's development and deployment. As programmers, we're familiar with writing code and business logic to customer specifications, but often we don't have specialized skills in other areas of Web development such as graphics, network administration or even HTML design. While I (and probably many other developers) often take over some of these other tasks and might even be proficient, it tends not to be the best use of my time or skills.

Building complex Web sites typically involves more people than just programmers. Although many projects are initially put together by coders, most of them are eventually separated into different tasks. Specialists who handle these tasks can bring together a variety of skills such as the following:

- **Programming and code/data design**
  This is us. Regardless of the type of application, you'll likely find at least one developer— a few of them, more likely—on every dynamic data-driven Web application. The application design group is responsible for providing the business logic and data access as well as some elements of overall application flow and design, which also impacts on the HTML design group.

- **HTML design**
  Web applications are invariably HTML-based and visually oriented (there are exceptions, though, such as distributed apps that send data). The visual aspect of commercial Web sites is very important because it presents the "corporate image" to the world. The HTML design team is responsible for creating site flow and the actual page layout. They work closely with the graphics design team. They also work to a degree with the programming group to integrate data-driven elements into their forms. This group probably has the most overlap with the coding and graphics groups.

- **Graphics design**
  Graphics design plays a large part, especially for e-commerce applications, because a site's "look" is determined mainly by images on pages. Images constantly change for special sales, promotions and giveaways, and are updated daily and weekly. In addition, the graphics group manages product photographs that appear on the Web site. Graphics of products are crucial to commerce sites and should be optimized for speed.

- **Network and security administration**
  From the previous discussion on scalability, it should be fairly obvious that network know-how is extremely important. It's good for developers to have a working knowledge of the network environment, but many issues such as router configuration, managing the DNS server, optimizing net throughput, dealing with multiple servers and the IP Monitoring software really should be handled by a dedicated network administrator or group. Security configuration is also a huge, time-consuming issue. It's important to have somebody well-versed in NT security issues when dealing with mysterious login dialogs and managing the various internal users who access the Web site and network. Network administration is an ongoing job for sites that change a lot or are accessed by large numbers of users internally (i.e. not anonymously) for maintenance purposes. I'd say that 80% of problems encountered by Web applications have to do with security issues.

- **Web design/site marketing**
  Finally, there are people who are on the business end of the Web site. Decisions made here deal with how to attract traffic to the site, what promotions to run, what products to feature on the site, and so on. In addition, this group tracks site statistics by analyzing data captured by the application and Web statistics tools, and uses this information for further decision making regarding promotions and so on.

The following is a team list for a large commercial Web site serving two distinct commerce sites with a combined average total of 500,000 database server hits a day. This should give you an idea of how a Web team might be constructed:

- 2 on-site programmers (full time)
- 2 off-site developer consultants
- 3 HTML designers
- 2 e-mail mailing list managers
- 2 graphic and animation artists
- 1 network administrator plus several support technicians
- 1 round-the-clock operator position to monitor the site at any given time (3 people total)
- 1 site manager

Source code integration

In this environment, where multiple people are involved in the development and graphics design process, source control is extremely important to ensure integrity of code and HTML documents. Source control is applied on the Visual FoxPro project and the custom ISAPI DLL extensions to the Web Connection framework, as well as the HTML pages. Graphics are not under source control because the huge volume of graphics can slow down Visual SourceSafe (VSS) beyond usability.

Visual FoxPro developers

The Visual FoxPro developers on the project can take advantage of Visual SourceSafe directly from their VFP projects (see **Figure 11.1**). Visual FoxPro has built-in support for VSS, and integration with the VFP environment is smooth through the Project Manager. While Project Manager access works fine, I often find myself using VSS directly because it tends to be quicker, especially when connecting over the Internet. Yes, you can use VSS directly over TCP/IP—performance is slow but usable, even over a slow dial-up connection.

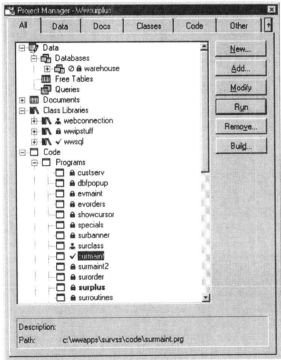

Figure 11.1. This FoxPro project is under source control with Visual SourceSafe, allowing users to check files in and out and locking simultaneous access.

Visual SourceSafe is a tremendous help for this project, since four developers—two of whom work off-site—are working on the application. Because many general-use files need to be frequently modified, source control is an absolute requirement to avoid code-update problems from different users.

Visual SourceSafe has the ability to store all Visual FoxPro code files, including PRGs, Classes, Forms, Menus, DBCs, and so on. In addition, it's possible to store support files and documentation as part of the project to keep everything in one place.

HTML designers

Because the HTML designers are working on HTML pages that also contain code snippets and data fields, HTML pages are especially vulnerable to overwriting updates from HTML designers as well as the code team. See **Figure 11.2**.

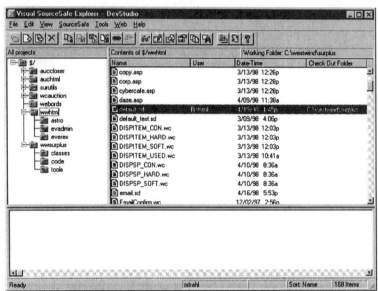

Figure 11.2. HTML files are managed directly through Visual SourceSafe using the Web Project option. The Web Deploy option makes it possible to deploy the HTML files directly to multiple servers simultaneously.

Visual SourceSafe is integrated into the HTML team's tools in two ways, depending on developer preferences: through Visual InterDev's built-in VSS or by using VSS directly for those using HomeSite.

The HTML designers don't like Visual InterDev's and FrontPage's HTML editors, so VID is only lightly used. The preferred method for the HTML designers is to use HomeSite (from Allaire) and then use VSS manually to check files in and out. The HTML project is also set up as a Web project that allows them to "Deploy" all changes made to the staging server, which is then used to distribute the final cut to multiple Web servers with a single 'deploy' operation. The Deploy option allows updating multiple servers simultaneously, which is crucial for the Web-farm scenario that runs up to eight simultaneous Web servers with identical HTML code. Web Deploy works through a list of IP addresses and paths that can be specified in the SrcSafe.ini file of the project's VSS server.

Consultants and staff

Using Visual SourceSafe provides an easy way to download an entire project to a local machine for local development. A consultant can be brought in and, within half an hour, can set up a local environment in which to develop against the staging server.

Because VSS can work over TCP/IP, it's also much easier for off-site developers to integrate into the VSS project remotely. For example, I can work out of my home office by connecting to the server on which I have an account. By telling SrcSafe.ini on my local machine to look at the on-site VSS project, I can access the project remotely:

```
; The two important paths used by SourceSafe.
Data_Path = \\206.111.111.111\DevShare \devstudio\vss\data
```

Note that connecting to the project can take a while, but once you're connected, working with the project is fairly quick, even over a slow dial-up connection.

If you log in remotely, you might want to consider creating multiple SrcSafe.ini files because VSS always tries to connect to the last project. If you're not online or you're trying to connect to a local VSS project, you'll be stuck waiting for VSS to access the remote server first, before allowing you even the chance to use the local process—or worse, timing out if you're not connected to the Internet. By keeping a local copy pointing to a local VSS server, Visual SourceSafe comes up immediately and you can change the path at a later time.

Separate staging test server

As Web applications grow and start receiving hits from large numbers of Web users, it's crucial that the site is tested on an independent server, which should *not* be the developer's machine.

All development and testing occurs on local machines, which are then "staged" on a separate test server that closely matches the configuration and setup of the online server. As such, it contains Internet Information Server (IIS), the dispatch manager client software (it can run as part of the Resonate pool), a local SQL Server database that matches the online server, a full copy of the VFP project, and all HTML and graphics. Product photos and graphics are uploaded here first and then transferred to the live site through the Visual SourceSafe Web Deploy option. The staging server serves both as a backup of the live sites (not so much an issue with multiple redundant Web servers) as well as a closely matched testing environment of the online site. It also serves as the main code-compilation location to provide consistent ClassIDs for COM objects by always using the same projects (which contain the same IDs every time). Finally, it serves as a depository of all code and content, from which new developers and workers can get working copies of their specific projects.

Everything is first tested on the staging server before moving things to the live site. HTML is moved by using the VSS Web Deploy option. The Web Deploy path points to multiple paths on the individual Web servers. Figure 11.3 shows how the staging server serves as the centerpiece between developers and the live site.

The final VFP servers bound for the online site are compiled and tested on the staging server. When everything has been extensively tested by developers and the HTML team (there is no official test team in this case) and everything runs okay, the data source is switched to the live SQL site and data changes are re-tested. Once this testing is complete, the compiled components are moved to the online site. In this case the applications are based on Web Connection, which means that the COM objects have only a single entry point. The COM interface never changes, so servers can simply be copied—they don't have to be reregistered to run on the server.

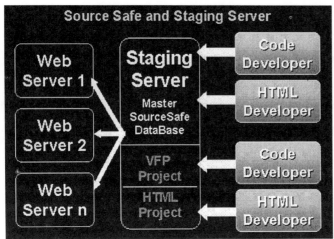

Figure 11.3. A separate staging server receives all file updates before changes go online. The staging server serves as a test bed that brings together the changes of all people involved in development and site content. The server also serves as the code depository from which new users can pull a working project.

It's very important to understand COM registration in this process. If the PUBLIC interface to your classes changes, you have to reregister your components on each server. If the interface doesn't change, the ClassIDs don't change, either, so no re-registration is required. In that case you can simply copy in a new EXE/DLL file, which is much more efficient, especially when you're dealing with eight machines that all need an update. It's clear that this can be a major issue if you have a lot of machines that require these components. Hence you'll want to minimize the amount of changes that occur to the PUBLIC interfaces of your servers. In Chapter 5 I gave an example of how to build servers with "central" entry-point methods such as Process(). This method can internally call other methods in a server. These central methods are the only PUBLIC interface methods, so adding methods to your server doesn't cause the COM interface to change and thus doesn't require re-registration.

It's important that the staging server is kept in sync with the online site. Data structures and actual physical data should be updated frequently to give a realistic snapshot of what will go on the server. HTML and images should be updated frequently. This is no small task, especially if your datasets are huge (accumulated logs, maybe?) and you have thousands of images and HTML pages on the site. But in order to provide a realistic test environment, synching is simply a requirement that must be figured into the business process.

Integrating HTML and code

HTML generation is probably the most "different" aspect of Web application development compared to traditional desktop applications. For most sites it's important to work closely with the HTML design team to create pages that can be visually maintained by the design staff. It's not sufficient to build a FoxPro back-end application that does *all* HTML generation internally. Instead, the tools need to provide a mechanism for mixing HTML with minimal code/expression syntax, so dynamic information from the database can be displayed in HTML.

Today you have many options for building HTML-based applications, whether you use a script-based engine like Active Server Pages or a code-based engine such as FoxISAPI or Web Connection. The key to successful integration is keeping code to a minimum within pages, which makes the HTML designers' job easier and avoids accidental changes to page logic.

I personally prefer to use binary code (VFP code in a class or PRG) in combination with scripting. At most of my sites, Web requests fire a method inside a VFP class that runs to process the mainline business logic for each request. When the code is complete, the code module "calls" an HTML page stored on disk that embeds FoxPro expressions into an HTML page. The Script page uses an Active Server-like scripting language (see Chapter 5 for the scripting engine examples and code) to allow embedding simple expressions like field names or PRIVATE/PUBLIC variables into a page. Any valid, string-based FoxPro expression can also be embedded—this includes FoxPro native functions as well as user-defined functions (UDF). In addition, blocks of code can be embedded in the page, but this should be left for short blocks of code because code-block performance is slow due to runtime interpretation.

If you use Active Server Pages instead, that scenario must be turned inside out, with the ASP HTML script driving component creation and returning information to be embedded into the HTML page. In either case, the goal should be to keep the HTML pages clear and simple so that the visual aspects don't trip over the code inside the page. For ASP this means moving much of the business logic into separate code pages that act as ASP function libraries or scriptlets, or by moving logic into COM components.

HTML is the front-end interface

For Web applications, HTML is the front end to the user. HTML usage can be as simple as using basic HTML at the lowest common denominator so all browsers can access pages, or as advanced as taking advantage of the most recent, proprietary DHTML browser enhancements, which embed advanced functionality in the HTML page on the client side.

For most commerce sites, the goal is to make the pages run on as many browsers as possible and to create pages that are quick to download. HTML extensions and scripting are kept to a minimum or at least are optional. The majority of script code tends to be for visual aspects such as button highlights and other special effects—effects that, if not supported by the browser, will still allow the user to continue viewing the site.

Understand the limitations of HTML

Even the newest HTML standards don't provide the same functionality you'd expect from a typical GUI development environment. DHTML, introduced in Internet Explorer 4.0, takes a huge step in the right direction, but building complex forms and user interfaces is currently a far cry from using tools such as the Form Designer in Visual FoxPro. The event model in the browser is also more limited, and trapping events and responding to them is a little more complex and can require a fair amount of code. The biggest problem with even the new DHTML support is its lack of development tool support. Most DHTML creation is non-visual, using nothing more than a fancy text editor. The few tools that do provide visual DHTML editing support are buggy or woefully incomplete (the VID editor is a good example).

If you check the Web for online stores, you won't find many that use anything but basic HTML 2.0 standard content. (The most "advanced" features in use are optional JavaScript and tables.) The reason is simple: A large chunk (20% or more) of the browsing public still uses ancient browsers, those that are stripped down or embedded, or browsers that come with other applications. This is a large percentage of customers for a mainstream site—imagine Sears turning down 20% of its customers with the message, "Sorry, you don't have the right (fill in the blank) to shop here."

Data connectivity
Pure HTML makes no provisions for data connectivity! If you're dealing with typical Web-server-based Web applications, you're really seeing apps that are all driven by the server. The server generates the HTML for a page and re-creates the entire page whenever the user makes new choices and updates.

There are many new technologies you can use to talk to the server: I discussed RDS a few chapters back, and you can also use ActiveX controls, Java, and even a Fat Client VFP application. But the reality is that most of those technologies are too advanced in client requirements. Very few (I've never actually seen one) mainstream commerce sites use these types of tools. They are great for intranet/extranet applications, but for general-public consumption the restrictions are too drastic. The majority of Microsoft's new technology that provides distributed connectivity over the Internet is very specific to Internet Explorer 4.0 and later, which further reduces the number of capable clients that can connect to a site. Be sure you understand your audience and the limitations your tools will impose on that audience.

Again, DHTML makes provisions for data connectivity, but at the cost of substantial installation on the client site, which is usually not an option for public commercial applications. No one wants to wait around for 20 minutes to download a set of ActiveX data controls and their client-side ADO engine at 28.8k. Most of these technologies also require IE 4.0 exclusively, which leaves out an even larger portion of the market.

The bottom line is that mainstream commercial sites will continue to be driven by heavy, server-side applications that rely on the server to access the data and generate HTML from it.

Keep HTML and code separate
When possible, try to build your application in such a way that business logic and HTML are clearly separated and don't reside in the same place. This should be easy if you're using a tool like Web Connection or FoxISAPI, because most of the code will sit in a VFP project and most of the HTML will sit in pages stored in a Web directory. If you're using Active Server Pages, it's easy to get pages that heavily mix HTML and code, which is a bear to maintain. With ASP it's a good idea to create "code modules" as ASP "include" files, or to use ASP pages that act as router pages containing code to perform logic and redirect to the actual display pages. You can also move logic to COM components to get code out of HTML pages, although there is a performance penalty and more complexity in development.

The reasons for all of this are twofold: First, it's easier to maintain code in a code environment! I don't care how much better Visual InterDev has gotten in the latest revision; it has nothing on the VFP or VB development environments in richness. Even with color syntax highlighting (which helps a lot), it's difficult to look through a huge HTML page just to find that two-line snippet of code that was embedded in the middle of the page. Second, it's important to keep code out of the way when passing pages to the HTML team. Most of the HTML team probably doesn't know how the database logic works—nor should they have to look at it and be tempted to mess with it, accidentally or otherwise. Some useful things should be accessible to HTML designers, but they should be kept to a minimum. Typical accessible items include database fields, known (and hopefully documented) variables that might be required, basic operations for handling HTTP headers (such as redirects and cookie read/write), and simple functions used for data formatting or conditional display of data. Other than that, treat HTML as the presentation layer and move code to other places.

Scripting and templates for data and display logic

I'm a little biased toward the development approach of code driving the HTML (Web Connection/FoxISAPI), which is the approach I've used in almost all sites I've worked on. Basically you have an application that handles each request and then branches off to a script page to handle the HTML display. This functionality is completely implemented at the Visual FoxPro code level within the Web Connection/FoxISAPI framework that handles the script parsing. However, to the developer, the details of the script parser are hidden so that, like ASP, scripting becomes just another aspect of the development environment.

Whether you use FoxISAPI/Web Connection or Active Server Pages, scripting is a necessary part of development. Scripting makes it possible to keep the display logic in an easily maintainable medium (a simple text file) that can be edited and updated simply by copying the file to the Web server. With scripting, you can build the user interface logic in such a way that you can change it without having to recompile the entire application. Imagine if you had to recompile the binary executable every time an image had to be changed! Scripting gets around that by storing the UI in a text document that can be easily changed with any editor.

Graphics and site design

A lot of times when taking on a new Web project, I'm blown away by how little thought goes into graphics design. This is especially true when pure development companies are leading the project, where the focus is on application logic and HTML, and graphics design is secondary.

While application logic is rightfully the most important part of a usable and stable application, don't underestimate the aesthetic value of a site. Graphics are extremely important to commerce sites, which use graphics to attract customers and get their attention with promotions and other eye-catching gimmicks. Most sites that start out without graphic designers end up adding them later at greater expense, because they have to overhaul everything at once. Doing it right from the start can save significant headaches and money later on.

Graphics design can add tremendously to the appeal of a site, but the layout of the site is just as important. Many sites are not very user friendly. Menus aren't clearly laid out, and it takes too many steps to get where you want to go. Not only is this a hassle to the user, but it can also cause unnecessary load on your site. As users click around to find what they want, they're using resources on your server. If looking up an item in the catalog takes five steps, drilling down through category lists, there will be a lot of overhead on that site for people wanting to look at items. Simplifying common operations and search operations to allow the user to go directly where he wants to go is an important aspect of a balanced server. Taking one superfluous link out of a process can reduce your server load by a large percentage!

When comparing two sites, you can usually tell which site's graphics and layout was designed by a graphic designer, and which site was designed by a programmer. The bottom line is that good graphic designers are a valuable asset to a successful Web project because it frees up a programmer's time from having to sit down in PaintShop or Image Composer to "quickly create a button."

Other frequent operations related to graphics are banners. Big-time commercial sites advertise heavily on other sites, and many sites run many different banners and buttons simultaneously. Formats and requirements for the advertising host sites are not all the same, so a lot of work goes into creating these banners.

If you're building an online store, you have additional tasks for managing product images: Taking photos, touching them up if necessary, naming and archiving them, and finally managing the images that go to the Web site. I've seen directories of 50,000 images that have only 1,000 active ones—don't let it get out of hand like that, or you'll seriously degrade your Web server performance.

You also might want to give some thought to how to store images—on disk or in a database. In general it's much more efficient to store images on the file system, rather than going through the database to retrieve the images. The Web server already knows how to get image content from files, so there's very little overhead with disk files. Windows NT also caches frequently accessed files, so access often ends up coming from memory, especially for small images. Dynamic access to image data can be handled with links based on IDs, such as Primary Keys or product SKUs. To access the image, create a matching file with the appropriate name and then embed links to the image into an HTML page (the Web server will do the rest):

```
<src img="/itemimages/SKU1234.GIF">
```

The only thing to be careful about with file-based access is to avoid letting your directories get too large. With too many files, directory lookup time can become a problem. Grouping image files into categories of a few hundred or so is key to maintaining good directory lookup performance.

If the image data comes out of a database, a dynamic request must pull the data out of the database, which is going to be much slower because a back-end application must fire up and retrieve the data. In order to display images from a database, you should store them as binary data that is copied directly from a file into the field:

```
replace Image with FileToStr("filename.gif"
```

To pull data out of the database, retrieve the entire binary image and then add the appropriate HTTP header:

```
HTTP/1.0 200 OK
Content-type: image/gif

...Binary image data here
```

If you're creating an HTML page that uses these images, keep in mind that each image will add an additional hit to the database for that page. A page with two dynamic images takes three back-end requests: One to create the HTML page and two for the images. The image links will look like this:

```
<src img="/webapp/GetImage.asp?Image=SKU1234">
<src img="/webapp/foxisapi/foxisapi.dll?Method=GetImage&Image=SKU1234">
```

In my opinion, there's not much reason to store data in a database unless it's stored that way already. Otherwise, take advantage of the Web server's capability and speed to load images from disk.

Network administrators

The logistics of Web servers are easy enough when you're dealing with them on a development machine. However, when you start dealing with a large Web site hosted in-house, there are a significant number of resources that need to be juggled. Here are just a few common tasks that fall under the Network Administrator's responsibilities:

- **Network infrastructure**
  Web servers are applications connected to complex networks. Creating the infrastructure to administer a network is very time consuming. On the physical end, here are four things that must be managed:

  - **Routers**
    Routers connect networks. You'll have to deal with at least one router for handling the incoming Internet connection and routing it onto your local network.

  - **Wiring**
    Physical wiring of machines is a drag. If you've ever dealt with bad cables or faulty hubs, you know how time-consuming it can be to troubleshoot wiring issues.

  - **Internet connection**
    The actual connection to the Internet comes from either an ISP or from a telephone company that provides the live connection plugged into your router. There are a number of things to continuously troubleshoot on these connections when dealing with the provider. You'll always be haggling about service rates as well.

  - **Physical server machines**
    The actual servers that run the Web software (as well as other servers such as SQL Server and application servers) must be installed with NT, and properly configured and tuned for their respective operations. A standard process should be in place here to make sure that machines are configured consistently. This is a time-consuming process, and it doesn't stop when the machines are up and running. Machines must be monitored for performance, upgraded to the latest patches, and so on.

- **Hardware security management**
  Most commercial Web sites are separated from the company network via a router or firewall. These routing issues require you to set up rules to allow access through the firewall from inside the local network to the outside. These connections also must be monitored for suspicious activity from people trying to break in.

- **System NT security**
  Windows NT servers make extensive use of user security for all services that run it. So the Web service uses NT user accounts for authenticating users, as does SQL Server (version 7.0), Microsoft Transaction Server, Message Queue, and so on. Properly configuring user rights for the internal network and the Web server is crucial in order to avoid exposing any weak links.

  The vast majority of serious problems I see in Web development are related to NT security. For example, misconfigured file access rights can cause havoc on a Web site. The wrong access permission for a DCOM object will cause the server to simply fail.

  This is one area that you should be familiar with from an application development perspective. The reason is that some of these security aspects are specially implemented for application development tools. It's important to understand how security is passed forward to your Web server component—whether you use ASP or FoxISAPI. Both Chapters 4 and 5 have discussed security issues and authentication as related to NT security to give you a good head start.

- **User/domain administration**
  Right along with setting the proper permissions goes administration of network users and groups. Many employees will access the Web server, whether to update HTML or data files or to access images on the Web site. Security for this access must be carefully configured in order to avoid exposing security holes that can cause Web users to access your network.

- **Web server configuration**
  Properly configuring the Web server involves a number of settings that should be consistently set. It goes beyond just setting the various IIS settings, but also includes installing any required add-on components and DLLs. You have to install secure certificates, place downloadable support files (ActiveX controls, Java Applets, COM components) on the site, and install any third-party DLLs for development tools. When installing Web components, you might have to deal with support files and registration.

  This is another one of those jobs to be familiar with, because many of the settings are specific to application development. If you're using ASP, there are an especially large number of settings that can adversely affect performance. It's crucial to keep a log of installed components along with reinstallation instructions. Storing the components on the staging server can be a big help in this process.

- **Middleware pieces (Resonate)**
With application servers, there's often a requirement for middleware software that manages server and network resources. The IP routing software in the previous chapter is a good example, as is MS Cluster Server and more closely system-related tools such as Microsoft Transaction Server and Message Queue Server. These tools must be administered with security and the server environment. You should be familiar with the more system-oriented tools, but the Network Administrator is likely to be in charge of the network tools.

- **Performance monitoring**
In order to keep NT running efficiently, performance monitoring is required. Running Performance Monitor to track server resource usage and access speed is important for figuring out server load boundaries. Also, resources like the hard disk system and the registry tend to fill up, causing performance to change as servers are up longer. Performance monitoring can capture these issues and make it possible to correct or otherwise address them before it's too late.

- **Security monitoring**
Sadly, many commercial sites are targeted by hackers. Any site that's sufficiently popular is likely to encounter some sort of attack, whether it's a usage blast trying to overload the site or an outright attack on site security. Monitoring audit logs and usage patterns on the Web site and network can help isolate these problems. It's a tricky job to track these kinds of things down, but a monitoring regime can help isolate patterns that stand out and cause alerts to be fired.

  Along those same lines, you should always think in terms of security as you add functionality to your site. Are there ways that outside users could access new functions to gain information they shouldn't be getting, or manipulate data in unintended ways? If people can guess operations or user IDs, it might be possible to hack into parts of the system that shouldn't be accessed.

  While many of you are proficient in the jobs associated with network administration, this is a full-time job for an administrator trained in these operations (with a group of techs for bigger organizations). It's also a good idea to learn as much as possible about these operations, especially as they relate to NT security and Web server configuration, without having it become a full-time job.

Site management

Finally there's the issue of site management in terms of the business. Think of this job as "upper management" specific to the Web site, but at a more involved, lower level that deals with some of the day-to-day tasks. Some responsibilities include:

- **Designing site layout**
  The overall site design and concepts tend to be planned at this level, including decisions about how the site should look and flow. These decisions are made in close cooperation with the design team, with input on efficiency from the code teams.

- **Dealing with advertisers**
  A large part of driving traffic to the site has to do with advertising on other sites. Advertising banners can run on multiple sites simultaneously, and these efforts should be coordinated closely with specials that run on the site.

- **Coming up with special promotions**
  This ties in closely with advertising, because special promotions are usually featured in advertising banners on other Web sites. You'll find that many commercial sites constantly run promotions to give away free stuff. As we all know, "Free" is the most clicked-on word on the Internet—even if your chance for the free item is one in 5 million.

- **Negotiating partnerships with other sites/advertisers**
  This falls somewhat into advertising. Working out arrangements with big gateway sites (like Netscape, Yahoo, and so on) to host your company's product does two things: It adds value to the gateway sites and at the same time drives traffic to your own Web site. This can be a beneficial arrangement for both parties. Negotiating these kinds of deals—and, more importantly, deciding which ones are worthwhile—falls into this category.

- **Analyzing statistics**
  In order to efficiently deal with advertisers, it's important to gather figures on the efficiency of advertising programs. This relates to evaluating how well the banners or other ads work, as well as providing information about how much traffic is generated from the banner-hosting site. Visitor information should always capture referring links or some sort of advertising code that can link a visitor back to a specific site and ad. Running statistical reports on this information can provide detailed feedback about what works where. Using these numbers, you can set reasonable budgets for further advertising.

Don't underestimate the value of these functions! Getting these kinds of programs and partnerships in place is extremely important for large commercial sites and for getting traffic to the site. Keep in mind that all of this takes time. Even an established retailer who moves to the Web isn't likely to see an immediate onslaught of traffic. Rather, traffic builds over time, and advertising helps fortify the image of a vendor dedicated to providing a solid Web presence. We'll see further commercialization of the Web, which surely will move into more traditional advertising media such as print and television. It's all a part of growing up for the Web...

Summary

This chapter is a good place to end this book because I believe it has a simple message: Don't try to do it all on your own! Realize that large Web applications will require a number of people with different skills to create a successful site. There is likely to be overlap in the skills, and as time goes on that overlap will only get bigger as different groups pick up skills from each other. This is a good thing, of course—it always helps to understand more of the pieces in the full solution. But full-scale Web apps are hideously complex beasts, so don't be afraid to offload to specialists those areas that are outside your own expertise.

Chapter 12
Loose Ends

I've covered a lot of ground in this book, but even so, there are a number of technologies I decided not to explain in detail. In this chapter I'll address using TCP/IP to access data directly over the Web, which is a simple option for Intranet applications to access data on a server. I'll also discuss Active Documents, which are not quite as useful as they might seem from a demo. XML was meant to have its own chapter in this book, but at the time of this writing the standard was still in flux and it was hard to pin down on paper the current state of the art. The XML section of this chapter gives an overview and some simple examples you can use today to get started with XML.

Finally, I wanted to point out some additional non-Microsoft Web development tools so you can decide what tools are best for you. The information isn't extensive, but it should provide enough information to go out and find more detail if you're interested. Because all these topics have very little in common, this chapter is laid out differently from the others in the book—the various sections are very distinct and don't relate as well to one another.

Data access over TCP/IP

I've discussed providing data to client applications in great detail in this book. I've shown pure server-side solutions that deliver content made up of data to the client in display form and I've shown how to transport data over HTTP using RDS and wwIPStuff. However, there is another, potentially easier way to access data over the Internet—using the TCP/IP protocol. TCP/IP is just another Windows-supported network protocol, so it's possible to use the Internet as a giant network to access data and resources directly.

Accessing VFP data directly over TCP/IP

For example, it's entirely possible for me to connect to my Web server in Oregon from my house in Hawaii using the following:

```
USE \\www.west-wind.com\d$\webapps\wwdemo\guest.dbf
```

 Using IP address and domain names in UNC resource references works only with WinNT (Windows 2000). For Win95/98 you have to set LMHOSTS entries to map IP addresses to Netbios names.

The above command will connect to my Web server and open the Guest.dbf file, which I can then peruse like any other VFP data table. Although this works just fine, the process is slow even on a small table. The problem is that it takes a while to make remote connections like this over the Internet. Using a 56K dialup connection it takes approximately one minute to connect to the above file, which contains about 200 records. In this case, the overhead is the connection time. If your files contain lots of data with index files, opening a file on the server will pull down the index information over the slow connection, further slowing down the connect time.

Once the initial connection has been made and the table is open, though, operation is reasonably fast—but it depends on the size of the data file. If the index is small and cached locally, lookups can be very fast. However, if the index is not all downloaded you can see long delays as VFP pulls down more index data to perform the lookup. On slow connections, VFP's indexing—and Rushmore optimization that requires it—actually can become a handicap, requiring more data than necessary to be downloaded initially.

Here you can see the problem with a file-based database tool like VFP: It does all of its processing on the client side, so while the data sits on the server with a slow connection, the client needs to pull all the necessary data to perform lookups and get the data itself. This can require significant amounts of local data, causing much traffic to occur over the network connection. In this scenario, a SQL Server that performs the processing on the server and then returns only the results is much more efficient. I'll look at this in the next section.

You should notice an important point now—if you tried to connect to my Web server using the USE and UNC syntax above, you'd fail. And that's a good thing—you obviously shouldn't have access to tables on my Web server because you don't have permissions on that machine. For applications that want to use TCP/IP file access, this means that you need to properly set up NT security using a specific NT account that has the required access rights. This username can either be a generic "application" account that's hidden in the binary executable of the application, or a particular user password that's provided by the user. Note that NT can validate security across the Internet connection automatically. If I'm logged on as *rstrahl* on my local machine and that same account exists on the server with the same password, passthrough validation allows me access on the server automatically without having to log on. If I try to connect with a different username, the NT password dialog will pop up, requiring me to enter a valid user account for the server. The behavior is identical to the way you'd use a LAN connection with Windows NT or Windows 95/98.

Another related issue is data security. Once you're connected and data is transferring over the Internet connection, that data isn't in any way encrypted. This means anyone with a protocol analyzer can grab the data off the wire.

Using a SQL server over TCP/IP

Just as you can access DBF files over the Internet, you can access a SQL server. If you're using Microsoft SQL Server, you can configure that server to run using TCP/IP as its network protocol (with SQL Server 7.0 this is the default protocol—SQL Server 6.5 uses Named Pipes by default and will carry forward that setting if upgraded to version 7.0). Once you've configured the server with TCP/IP, you could then connect to the server like this:

```
lnHandle = SQLSTRINGCONNECT("driver={SQL Server};server=www.west-wind.com;" + ;
                            "database=Pubs;uid=sa;pwd=;")
SQLEXEC(lnHandle,"SELECT * FROM Authors")
BROWSE
```

This also works as expected. However, just like with direct VFP table access, connecting can take a long time. Over the same dialup connection, connect time to the server is about one minute. Once a connection's been made, the remote SQL Server runs the query and then returns *only the results* back over the Internet. In this respect the access is very efficient and you should be able to run queries fairly efficiently—even over a slow dialup connection—assuming you return reasonable amounts of data. Because the slowness comes primarily from the connect time, you'll want to set up your applications so that you open a connection on startup and then keep that connection to the server alive for all future queries against the server. If you use persistent connections in your applications, performance over even a slow Internet connection can be very good, since only query strings to the servers and result sets from the server are sent over the wire.

There are a few problems with this approach, and they all have to do with security. In order to allow access to the SQL Server, you're essentially opening up that server to the Internet. Anybody can access that server and potentially let hackers at the server to break in. You are exposing at least one password as part of your application. If that password gets out, anybody can access the server and potentially delete or otherwise corrupt data. The other issue is lack of encryption. The data is sent in plain network packets, so the data can be plucked directly from the wire and hijacked by anybody listening with a protocol analyzer.

If you have a lot of SQL clients to the server, you'll also be using up connections for each user. This can be a problem because the license count might get so high as to overrun your existing number of licenses configured on the server. As such, a generic Web solution using SQL Server can get very expensive quickly. Using SQL Server in this fashion is not covered by Microsoft's generic SQL Web publishing license, so individual user licensing applies.

With any direct data access over TCP/IP, make sure you check out your security environment. Before rushing into direct data access, make sure you have a clear idea who will be accessing your server and whether the data traveling over the wire might be insecure.

For intranet applications you can look into Point to Point Tunneling Protocol (also known as Virtual Private Network), which allows you to set up a dedicated network segment that communicates securely with recognized TCP/IP clients. This solution requires client-side configuration and information about the client's machine, so this is not a generic access solution, but it should work fine for intranet and extranet applications of known and preconfigured clients where security is a requirement.

The Great Active Document Swindle

It might seem strange that I didn't dedicate a chapter of this book to Active Documents. Active Document support has been one of the most demonstrated features of Visual FoxPro. I'm sure you've seen an image of a Visual FoxPro application running inside Internet Explorer with all functionality preserved. It's a great demo feature, but unfortunately the functionality is only skin deep.

Active Documents are a special kind of object that can be hosted inside other applications. If you've ever used the Microsoft Office Binder to combine multiple documents into a compound document, you've seen Active Documents in action. Internet Explorer also acts as a host container for Active Documents—using this mechanism it's possible to view any Active Document application inside the browser. For example, all Office documents can be hosted this way. Active Documents become part of the browser, with the ability to modify the menus and display their own user interface features while preserving the browser frame, including the familiar browser bar.

When you view a Word document in IE you're actually using Word's Active Document container, which is hosted in IE. Visual Basic was the first tool to introduce Active Document support for applications in a generic way. Using the mechanism made it possible to run an application inside the browser using the Active Document container. With Visual FoxPro 6.0, Active Documents are also available to your FoxPro applications.

The problem with Active Docs is that they give the wrong initial impression to a first-time spectator. When you see a Visual FoxPro application running inside the browser, your first thought is likely to be, "Hey, that's an easy way to port my 100,000-line VFP application to the Web without modifications." If that's your goal you will be disappointed.

Treat Active Docs for what they are: browser-hosted standalone applications

The most important thing to understand about Active Documents is that they are just like an application that resides on the local machine. For example, when you view a Word document in the browser, you need to have Word installed. If you run a VB Active Doc application, the VB Runtime must be available. The same goes for Visual FoxPro. The application *executes on the local machine, not the server,* regardless of whether the Active Document was downloaded from the Web. For Visual FoxPro Active Docs, this means you still need to have the Visual FoxPro runtime available on the client machine. There's no *automatic* mechanism for downloading and installing the runtime. This likely means you'd have to have a separate link to download and install the application, or at least the runtime, prior to running the Active Document from the Web—which is going to be a sizable download (at least 3.5 megs plus your actual application's binary).

In addition to the fact that you have to have Visual FoxPro installed on the client, you also have to understand that data access over the Web is not automatically provided. An Active Document application is no different than a standalone application. In other words, you can access local database tables just fine, or use ODBC to access SQL Server or any other ODBC data source. However, you don't automagically get the ability to access and share data on the Web server from which you downloaded the Active Doc! When you USE a database it's going to be using local disk access.

Yes, with only a little bit of work wrapping an application, you can run that application inside the browser. But it won't be able to access data over the Web unless you use some of the features discussed elsewhere in this book: using TCP/IP to access data over the Internet, using HTTP to marshal data from client to server and back, or using Microsoft's RDS. If you use those mechanisms you can access data over the Web, but then again this isn't really transparent to an existing application. Using these data access mechanisms is likely to require major retooling to take advantage of this data.

Scenarios where Active Documents make sense

Getting the misconceptions about Active Documents out of the way first, you can now start to think about ways to use them. Frankly, I don't believe VFP Active Docs make much sense as a Web technology, but that shouldn't discourage you from using them as a local support interface for applications or for quick demonstrations that can be built as fully self-contained applications. I've used Active Docs for several Web applications that use Visual FoxPro servers. The Active Doc is used for the administration interface of the application. Users work mostly with the browser and HTML design tools to build their applications, and displaying the administration interface inside the browser makes sense because users are already familiar with the Web interface.

Active Docs also work reasonably well if you want to use remote data access using RDS or tools like wwIPStuff as demonstrated in Chapters 7 and 8. In fact, one of the examples in Chapter 7 that demonstrates using wwIPStuff to retrieve data over the Web is built as an Active Document.

A mini-tour of how Active Docs work

When you access an Active Doc through the browser using a local DOS path (such as d:\webbook\samples\activedoc\adoc.app) the browser loads the application from the specified directory. This is not much different from the way an application would start if you double-clicked the .APP file in Explorer. All data files and support files for that application will be easily found as the application starts in the specified directory.

When you download an Active Doc over the Web, however, things are very different. The browser downloads a copy of the .APP file from the Web server and copies it into the Temporary Files directory of your hard disk. This is important to understand: Any support files that might be needed at a later point must take this startup path into account. When the file is downloaded, only the .APP file is saved—none of the support or data files that might be required go with it.

> (i) *Installing files on the client*
> *If you want to include data files or other required support files as part of the application, store them in memo fields of a database. Each file gets its own record with a file name and the memo that contains the binary data for the file. You can load a file to string with FILETOSTR() and then use REPLACE to store the data into the memo field. When you run the application for the first time, you can then copy the files from the table into the temporary files location. To check for file existence, write out a dummy file once installation is complete and check for this file every time you start up. If the file exists, you know that it's installed. Note that you shouldn't rely on files being permanently available. Internet Explorer can clear its application cache and delete your application and data files that are stored locally!*

Once the file is downloaded, the browser looks up the extension (.APP) in the registry and finds the Run command instruction used to load the Active Doc. For VFP this means calling the VFP6RUN.exe file in your SYSTEM directory. VFP6RUN loads the Active Doc container into the browser, which essentially serves as the Visual FoxPro application frame. If you implement no code in the Active Doc class, you'll simply get a VFP window with a runtime toolbar and menu. To implement your own functionality, use the Run method of the Active Doc object to launch your application code.

Active Docs are surprisingly simple to implement, at least in their basic form. Visual FoxPro 6 includes a new base class called *ActiveDoc*. This class provides a handful of methods that are specific to Active Document operation. The class can also be used inside standalone applications—when the Active Document is marked as the main program in a project it can start your application and serve as a main entry point into your application, doing away with a procedural Main.prg or similar programs to start the application. *ActiveDoc* can be used as a fully self-contained application object that acts as a wrapper for an application.

The only required method that needs to be implemented by an Active Doc application is the Run method. Run is called when the Active Doc is loaded from a Web page (or if the Active Doc is marked as the main program). By default, when Run is called, the VFP frame comes up. One of the things you'll likely want to do right away is hide that frame and bring up your own form.

Getting your application to run as an Active Doc

For a sample, I took one of my applications—the West Wind Message Reader—and converted it to run as an Active Document. I'll use this as an example to demonstrate what changes are required for a typical application to run inside the browser. **Figure 12.1** shows what the application looks like running in Internet Explorer. Note that I didn't go all the way in cleaning up this app—in particular there are a few inconsistencies, like a status bar used by the application inside the browser frame. There are also two menus, which probably isn't a smart way to display a user interface in the browser. However, the application is fully functional inside the browser.

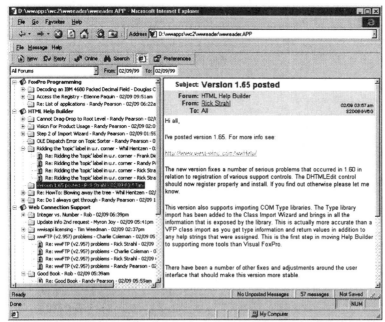

Figure 12.1. *This application was converted to run inside the browser. Only a handful of changes were required to make it work in the browser. However, note the inconsistencies: two menus, two status bars and two toolbars. These types of issues need to be addressed when doing a full-blown conversion.*

Here are the steps I took to make this application work in the browser:

Step 1—Create the Active Document class
I created a new class for my application called *wwReader6* and added *wwRead_Adoc* as the class to hold the Active Document. I also marked this class with "Set as Main" so this class would load at startup.

Step 2—Implement the Run method
The Run method is the heart of the *ActiveDoc* class. In its most basic form, Run() should contain the code to bring up your main form and enter a READ EVENTS loop:

```
*** Any set up code here
SET EXCLUSIVE OFF
SET TALK OFF
SET CLASSLIB TO …

…
*** Bring up my form in the browser
DO FORM wwreader


*** Make sure you have a READ EVENTS to keep things running
READ EVENTS
```

Step 3—Modify the form to run properly in an Active Document
In order to display properly in the browser it's probably a good idea to have your form display inside the browser. That may sound obvious, but the Message Reader application originally used a top-level form. Running the form from ActiveDoc as a top-level form causes the form to pop up on top of the browser, rather than running inside of it. To avoid this behavior I change the ShowWindow property to 2–In Screen or 1–In Desktop. The form should be maximized (Windowstate=2) and have no title bar (Titlebar=.F.) inside the browser. If you're like me and build mostly SDI-based applications that never show the VFP desktop, you'll have to modify forms to run inside the VFP desktop—this can be a problem if you plan to run your app both as a standalone and as an Active Document, since the ShowWindow property cannot be manipulated at runtime. You might have to build multiple versions or live with running inside the VFP frame.

If you're building multiple window applications, I suggest that you use the Visual FoxPro frame and maintain your child windows inside that frame, rather than popping up top-level forms. A VFP top-level form (ShowWindow = 2) will pop up on top of the browser, which is considered bad form.

Step 4—Handle shutdown situations
If you don't write a little code to handle shutdown scenarios from the browser, your application will pop out of the browser when the browser navigates off the page or is shut down. This is definitely not the effect you want to display. Use the CommandTargetExec method to trap for unload events:

```
*** ActiveDoc::CommandTargetExec
LPARAMETERS nCommandID, nExecOption, eArgIn, eArgOut

DO CASE
  CASE nCommandId = 37
     oReader.QueryUnload()
     oReader = .F.
     CLEAR EVENTS
ENDCASE
```

A command ID of 37 indicates that the browser either tried to navigate off the page or that the browser was shut down. In this situation, you want to tell your application to unload. In the example of the message reader, I can simply call my main form's QueryUnload method to simulate a user clicking the Close box, which effectively shuts down the application. Because the entire application is help up by a READ EVENTS, it's also necessary to call CLEAR EVENTS.

If you fail to call CLEAR EVENTS—either because your application crashed or exited with the call to CLEAR EVENTS—the Visual FoxPro frame along with any existing forms inside of it will pop out of the browser when the user navigates off the page. A good error handler is required to make sure that all errors either recycle the application or else shut down the application properly.

A number of other command IDs are available to notify you of requested operations that occur in the browser. CommandTargetExec exists to forward events from the browser to you. For example, when the user clicks the Print button in the browser, you get a command ID value of 6, which gives your application a chance to print from the application. Take a look at the ExecCommandTarget help topic for other operations that you can handle with Fox code.

Step 5—Run it in the browser
If you're working with a full-blown application that has local files, load the application into the browser using its full DOS path, such as "d:\wwapps\wc2\wwreader\wwreader.app". Then the app will start out of the directory where the APP file lives and should have no problems finding any support and data files.

To load the same thing over the Web, use syntax like http://localhost/wwreader/wwreader.app. Actually, in the case of the Message Reader there's no chance that this app will run properly over the Web, at least not without creating a complex install program that holds and copies all of the support files required by this application. In addition, because there is no guarantee that the application won't be wiped out, the data files cannot be loaded into the Temporary Files directory, but would have to be installed somewhere separately on the hard disk via install. In this case, this effort would not be worth it, just to have the app run in Internet Explorer!

You'll face the same issues with any application that is not fully self-contained in a single .APP file, including data. However, if you have applications that don't have any (or very few) support files, you can probably migrate the app so that it can run over the Web.

Getting an existing full-blown application to run over the Web as an Active Document is highly unlikely.

Limited menu options

Figure 12.1 shows two menus and toolbars. One belongs to IE and one belongs to my application. Unfortunately, there is no good way to merge the two into one menu. Although you have a little control over the IE menu by adding a couple of application-specific stock menu options (like Help), you cannot add a full menu's worth of application-specific menu pads to the IE menu. So, if you need to have menu options or toolbars, you'll end up with a second set inside your application inside the browser frame—far from professional.

Active Document Summary

I can't say that I'm excited about Active Documents. They provide only limited new functionality for browser hosting in Internet Explorer. While the process for creating an application that runs in the browser is easy enough, the functionality it provides is truly limited. When loading documents off the Web, the lack of an auto-installer really limits their usability, because any support files now become the responsibility of your application rather than an install utility. Finally, running out of the Temporary Files directory, which is temporary, can be a real problem for applications that have local data persistence. By the time it's all said and done, it might be much easier to have a setup program and install a standalone EXE. Running Active Documents as local files works well enough, but be prepared to spend some time for proper installation from a Web-installed Active Doc.

Active Document Pros

- Runs VFP apps in the browser.
- Allows automatic download of the application file (but only the .APP!). IE performs a timestamp check when accessing the file, so repeated access will not force another download and a changed version will prompt a new download.

Active Document Cons

- Requires full VFP runtime (3.5 megs) on client. Runtime is not downloaded automatically.
- Doesn't download support files.
- Runs out of Temporary Files directory when accessing ActiveDoc over the Web.
- Tight menu integration not possible.
- Data access is local only. Web data access must be implemented using RDS or wwIPStuff.
- There's no Web-specific functionality other than the browser hosting.

XML—The new data messaging standard

XML has been around for quite a while now, but until recently, when the XML 1.0 standard was finalized, XML has been more hype than reality. Even now XML is suffering from lack of tools. The XML 1.0 standard has recently been completed, which was the primary reason that this topic didn't get its own chapter. With Internet Explorer 5.0 (and Netscape 5.0 as well), XML support will be integrated into the popular browsers, which will likely result in XML being integrated into more applications.

What is XML?

When I first heard about XML, I have to admit I was very ho-hum about the topic. After all, XML doesn't provide anything radically new, and using XML is simply an alternative way to handle data. The real value of XML didn't hit me until I had the opportunity to integrate XML data output into some applications I've been working on. One of the problems with understanding XML is that it's not easily defined. Several articles and books I looked at in particular didn't do a good job of describing how XML can be applied. Let me try to summarize how I see XML's usefulness in relation to typical data-driven applications.

Think of XML as a mechanism to *transfer* data, but not as a replacement for a database. XML should be used in environments where data and information need to be shared across multiple applications or even objects internally. Using XML for *messaging* provides a standard mechanism that every client receiving the data can understand and work with.

XML's promise lies in its standardized definition as a text format that can be easily created and read via a common parsing interface. If the standard takes off, we no longer will have to face the hairy conversion problems that we often run into when data needs to be shared between disparate sources. XML's power lies in its flexibility to allow the designer to present either a very fixed, structured interface with a definition header, or a completely loose interface that can exist on its own. In either case, standard XML parsers can parse the document and retrieve the data—and if they follow the Document Object Model (DOM) standards, the parser will even use a standard property and method interface across different platforms and tools.

XML is text based, which means it's easy to create XML output, and it's very portable across operating systems. Text is also easily viewable, and XML's tag-based structure makes data easily readable and identifiable by any user of the data, even in its raw form. If a translation mechanism doesn't exist for the data form, it's relatively easy to create one.

XML and the Web

Currently the majority of information served on the Web is based on HTML, but HTML is an extremely poor mechanism to hold structured data that needs to be retrieved independently of its display structure. HTML is a display-based markup language. XML, on the other hand, is a *data-based* markup language and when returned can be easily parsed by using a standard XML parser. Two disparate applications, both using their own data access formats (say a DBF format on one end and a SQL back end on the other) don't have to go through a translation process or invent a common format. XML provides a vendor-independent baseline data format. By using XML as the data format, you're using a standard format that any client will be able to work with—XML support is surely going to be standard in all development tools in the next revision, and tools already exist to use XML in your own applications. The basic XML format is simple enough to implement using any application development language. Later I'll show examples of XML output creation with VFP. Parsing is more tricky, and you should definitely rely on a parser rather than building your own. The latest parsers support both read and write access to XML documents. The latest parsers from Microsoft ship with IE 5 and are compliant with the XML 1.0 standard, using a common object model. Regardless of whether you use the ActiveX or Java parsers, or even a parser from another company, the object model of these parsers is defined by the XML standard, which should simplify using XML on different development platforms. The version 5.0 browsers are not here yet, and IE 4 ships with the older MSXML parser, which is not XML 1.0 compliant, but will let you parse XML today prior to IE 5's release and acceptance.

In a Web environment XML especially makes sense. XML can be used as a standard format to transfer data between a client and server. Take some of the examples in Chapter 8, where I sent data back and forth between the wwIPStuff client and the Web server. The data was in a format I came up with on my own, thought up for the application. The format is simple enough, but rather than coming up with new and incompatible transfer mechanisms all the time, it's a good idea to use a standard mechanism and a standard format—XML. If the client application wasn't my own and didn't use Visual FoxPro, the data transfers I made over HTTP would be useless because DBF file access is required to make that work. Now imagine I'd sent XML data instead of the DBF file. The client app now no longer requires VFP on the client side—any language that can deal with the XML data set would be able to access that data instead. In the case of the VFP client, it would simply unpackage the XML back into a DBF file and continue on as before. The client end could then do the same thing when sending data back up to the server using XML. Other applications could do the same with their own internal data formats.

Furthermore, you could also create a simple protocol using XML and its document definition formats. The data could be wrapped into several XML-based objects that are all contained in the single-result XML document. One of the objects in this context could be a standard error object that contains error information, such as an error flag and description. The client app could check for this object in the XML document and, based on its existence, handle the error condition. No more loosely describing the format with a string like "Error: Error x occurred." Furthermore, it's possible to string multiple errors together if multiple successive errors occur.

In this scenario, XML defines a messaging protocol that's clearly defined and relatively easy to document. If you were to look at the XML content, you'd also understand easily what's going on—because XML is tag based, like HTML, it's easy to see the data structure even if no *Document Type Definition (DTD)* header is provided. XML's format is said to be self describing, and it's very powerful when dealing with foreign data structures that you might have to import, because both a key (or tag) and values are represented for each element in the document (`<key>value</key>`).

XML and data
The thing that makes XML different from other data technologies and formats is that it is becoming a standard, and we can expect just about any tool to be able to work with data in XML format, rather than dealing with a plethora of different file formats. No, XML won't replace a database—it's too inefficient for that. But XML is sophisticated enough to support all sorts of data types, and it also has the ability to contain hierarchical relationships within a single document, which is something that you can't do with any other text-based data format today. A single text file can hold information about customers, orders and line items, and allow easy retrieval of data in the properly related context of the data relationships.

XML holds data in text format using a markup format very similar to HTML. The format can include fully self-describing information that describes the data contained in the XML document in a special XML header, which is optional. The data itself is embedded inside a pair of tags like `<field>value</field>`.

A complete XML document, or a *valid document* as it's called in XML terms, must include a Data Type Definition, which is a header that describes the structure of the document. An analogy to a DTD is the table header in a DBF file that describes all of the fields available and the records of the table. XML represents the actual data in a hierarchical tree format where every element is a child of another. In the database analogy, a record is a child of the table and a field is a child of a record. Displaying this kind of format as XML (without the DTD) would look like this:

```
<?xml version="1.0"?>

<MyTable>
   <record>
      <field1>Your data for field1</field1>
      <field2>Your data for field2</field2>
   </record>
   <record>
      <field1>Your data for field1</field1>
      <field2>Your data for field2</field2>
   </record>
</MyTable>
```

Documents displayed without a DTD are considered *well formed* (assuming the XML is valid). Documents are considered *valid* if they also contain a matching DTD and the XML conforms to the rules in the DTD. The DTD, however, is optional, and so a well-formed document is all you need in most cases. DTDs serve mainly to define specific data formats that may be shared industry-wide for specific industries or applications. The valid document adds the ability for the parser to make sure that all tags are properly used in the XML document, allowing the parser to fully validate the document as it's building its internal structure. Parsers that report on the validity of the document are called *validating parsers,* and most new XML parsers support this functionality. To create a valid document for the above, I need to add a DTD to the XML document's header:

```
<?xml version="1.0"?>

<!-- Document DTD -->
<!DOCTYPE Mytable[

<!ELEMENT MyTable (record+)>
<!ELEMENT record (field1?,field2?)>
<!ELEMENT field1 (#PCDATA)>
<!ELEMENT field2 (#PCDATA)>

]>

<!-- Document data starts here -->
<MyTable>
...
</MyTable>
```

In this case, the DTD describes the relationship between the various element types of the document. It shows which tag contains what other tag and whether elements are optional (?) or required (+). The rules for a DTD can be fairly complex and can be extended to include detailed information about the formatting of each element. For simple tasks, such as transferring a flat object like a table or object, the DTD is optional and probably not necessary.

Generating XML

 In the course of applications that you build, you'll undoubtedly want to create XML output. With the Developer's Download Files at www.hentzenwerke.com you'll find the wwXML class, which is a small tool that can convert objects and table data into XML. The ObjToXML method allows you to create an XML object from any Visual FoxPro object. All object properties will be included in the XML string. Unfortunately, because of the way the VFP AMEMBERS() function works, all properties (including protected and VFP stock properties) are available. It's simple to use this object:

```
*** Run a query
SELECT * FROM Guest WHERE CustId = "N404WQYT"

*** Create an object from the result record
SCATTER NAME loGuest MEMO

*** Now create the XML
oXML = CREATEOBJECT("wwXML")
lcXMLString = oXML.ObjToXML(loGuest, "Guest")

*** If you're using FoxISAPI/Web Connection
Response.Write(lcXMLString)

*** With ASP you'd return the result to the ASP page
* RETURN lcXMLString
```

The result from this operation is:

```
<?xml version="1.0"?>
<Guest>
  <company>123  Systems</company>
  <custid>N404WQYT</custid>
  <email>bbob@test.com</email>
  <entered>05/21/97 02:30:05 AM</entered>
  <location>Home</location>
  <message>Hello World</message>
  <name>Billy Bob</name>
  <password>billy</password>
  <phone></phone>
</Guest>
```

Objects that are created with SCATTER NAME are special in VFP because they don't include any stock properties or methods. If you tried this with a Custom object you'd get stock properties like Left, Height, Tag, and so on, in addition to your custom properties.

Furthermore, Protected and Hidden properties also are exposed—a small tradeoff for the utility of this method.

Using objects for maintaining data and then using XML to send it back to a client application is a great way to transfer data over the Internet. The client application can take the object data contained in the XML and restore it back into an object so that, in effect, you've transferred an object's content over the Internet. ObjToXML also allows you to recurse through all embedded objects so you can nest objects into a single XML document. You can also add multiple objects one after the other into the XML document to send very complex data structures down to the client or back in one pass.

Another useful method in wwXML is CursorToXML(), which works in a similar fashion:

```
SELECT Guest
LcXMLString = oXML.CursorToXML()
```

which produces:

```
<?xml version="1.0"?>
<guest>
  <Row>
        <custid>N404WQYS</custid>
        <name>Rick Strahl</name>
        <company>West Wind Technologies</company>
        <email>rstrahl@west-wind.com</email>
        <entered>05/15/96 03:44:21 PM</entered>
        <message>Save the Planet - KILL YOURSELF</message>
        <location>Maui, Hawaii, USA</location>
        <password>Rick</password>
        <phone>(541) 386-2087</phone>
  </Row>
  <Row>
        <custid>N404WQYT</custid>
        <name>Billy Bob</name>
        <company>123  Systems</company>
        <email>bbob@test.com</email>
        <entered>05/21/97 02:30:05 AM</entered>
        <message>This is as neat as it gets!</message>
        <location>Home</location>
        <password>billy</password>
        <phone/>
  </Row>
  ...
</guest>
```

CursorToXML() takes the data from the currently selected work area and generically generates an XML document from it. Looking at this data, you'll probably notice that XML is not a very efficient data format. There's a lot of wasted space that's related to the start and end tags—unfortunately, this is part of the data format and a price you pay for the flexibility of XML. The tags are what makes XML work with any kind of data.

However, XML data elements (field values above) cannot contain certain characters. In particular, the markup tags <, >, and & are not allowed. Linefeeds are stripped and converted into spaces. In strict parsers, " and ' are not allowed, although the Internet Explorer XML parser doesn't care about these. In order to allow these special characters to be embedded into an element, you have to *escape* the data using the CDATA structure:

```
<Document>
       <data><![CDATA[This text contains markup
<Markup>Text</Markup>]]></browser>
</Document>
```

Failing to embed data in this fashion when illegal characters are embedded will cause XML parsers to fail parsing the document—it will be neither well-formed nor valid and the object collections won't be available.

Besides these simple methods to create XML, you can also create your own XML via code. You can simply scan through your tables and build up the XML as a string. This gives you the most flexibility and is the fastest way to generate XML.

Nested XML
One of the nice things you can do with XML is to embed data in hierarchical layouts that include master and detail relationships. You can nest these as deeply as you see fit. Consider the following example of an order described as an XML document:

```
<?xml version="1.0"?>
<Orders>
  <Order>
        <OrderDate>12/01/98</OrderDate>
        <OrderTotal>123.40</OrderTotal>
        <Customer>
            <name>Rick Strahl</name>
            <company>West Wind</company>
            <address>32 Kaiea</address>
        </Customer>
         <Detail>
            <item>
                <sku>LABOR</sku>
                <desc>Labor moving stuff</desc>
                <qty>1</qty>
                <price>50.00</price>
            </item>
            <item>
                <sku>SALESITEM</sku>
                <desc>New Toilet Seat Covers for Gov't</desc>
                <qty>10000</qty>
                <price>2000.00</price>
            </item>
        </Detail>
  </Order>
  <Order>
  ... another order could go here
  </Order>
</Orders>
```

If you had to download this data to a user using tables—even a fully denormalized one—it would be a drag. With XML the data is contained in a single text document that can be downloaded over the Internet. Also, most people can look at this XML document and figure out what the data means and how it's laid out. I hope you can see how XML can simplify moving data around from different applications and over the confines of an Internet connection. Just keep thinking along the lines of *data transfer mechanism*, not a replacement for existing database technology!

XML parsing

So far I've discussed creating XML, which is straightforward as long as you understand the basics. For most applications, creating your own XML is probably OK, but ideally you'll want to make sure your XML is fully compliant with the XML standard. In order to do so, you should use an XML parser to create and read your XML data.

The latest XML initiative calls for XML parsers to also follow a strict standard—the XML Document Object Model. The latest set of parsers all use the same object interface, so regardless of whether you use a Java, C++ or ActiveX parser they all support the same object names and methods. For Microsoft applications, a compliant parser will become available with Internet Explorer 5.0.

The MSXML parser—ready now, but it's not compliant

Internet Explorer 4.0 ships with an early XML parser that is not DOM compliant, but provides much of the same functionality. The IE 4 parser is not a validating parser, which means it can't read and validate a DTD. You might want to use the IE 4 parser for current applications until IE 5 gets more prevalent. Using the IE 4 MSXML parser (which is also available in IE 5) on the document above looks something like this:

```
oXML=create("msxml")
oXML.url = "c:\temp\test2.xml"

*** Check for a well-formed document
IF TYPE("oXML.root") # "O"
    RETURN .F.
ENDIF

*** Root Node - table level
oRoot = oXML.root

? oRoot.tagname     && Orders
? oRoot.Children.item(0).TagName    && Order - Note 0 based!!!
? oRoot.Children.item(0).Children.Item("OrderDate").text   && 12/01/98 as string
?
oRoot.Children.item(0).Children.item("Customer").Children.item("Address").text

FOR EACH order IN oRoot.Children
    ? "Order #:",Order.Children.Item("OrderDate").Text
    ? "Ordered by:
```

```
",Order.Children.item("Customer").Children.item("Name").Text
      FOR EACH item IN Order.Children.Item("Detail").Children
            ? Item.Text
      ENDFOR
ENDFOR

RETURN .T.
```

As you can see from the code, the document is abstracted into a hierarchical layout that starts with a root object. Each object has a zero-based *Children* collection, which can be used to iterate through the next lower-level items. Elements are accessed through the Item method, which can either take a numeric index value or a key name. These collections always start at element zero; you can check the size of each collection by looking at the Length property. To iterate through a collection use the FOR EACH construct.

The above demonstrates that anything but a flat structure gets a little confusing to write quickly. But while the syntax may be lengthy, it really takes very little code to drill down to the appropriate level if you know which element to access.

(i)   ***Tagnames that make sense***
       The generic routines in the wwXML class create records with a Record or Row tagname, which is not optimal for searching. Ideally you'd want to use a primary key for the record-level tag names, so each row's key would be easily accessed by its primary key value through the collection:

```
<?xml version="1.0"?>
<guest>
    <N404WQYS>
        <custid>N404WQYS</custid>
        <name>Rick Strahl</name>
    </N404WQYS>
    <Q404WQYS>
        <custid>Q404WQYS</custid>
        <name>Billy Bopp</name>
    </Q404WQYS>
</guest>
```

You can then access the individual records with:

```
oRecord = oRoot.Children.Item("Q404WQYS")
```

Using the final parameter of wwXML::CursorToXML you can specify a key expression that can automatically create keyed records for generic cursor conversion as well.

The IE 5 DOM parser

Why am I telling you about the MSXML parser if it's likely to become obsolete? Most people currently have MSXML on their machines, but it will take awhile for the IE 5 version with full DOM support to be available on all desktops. If you need to build applications with XML now, use MSXML, but make sure you wrap the code so that in the future you can easily switch to the DOM model. The new parser is faster and much more sophisticated in addition to being compliant with the DOM standard. The MSXML functionality is still available in IE 5 as well, so if you use it your code will be forward-compatible.

Using the IE 5 DOM is conceptually similar to using the MSXML parser—the biggest difference you'll see is in the syntax. Personally, I think MSXML has a much cleaner interface, but that's what you get from a standards body.

The IE 5 DOM is implemented via the Microsoft.xmlDOM ActiveX component. The DOM is a bit more complex than the MSXML control, but it also provides a lot of additional functionality that is required for DOM compliance. I suggest you look at MSXML.dll with the Visual Basic Class Browser (or the Vstudio OLEViewer utility) to check out the full object model.

Using the same Orders data set shown above, you can parse a document as follows:

```
CLEAR
oXML = CREATEOBJECT("Microsoft.xmlDom")
oXML.Async = .F.

oXML.Load(FULLPATH(CURDIR()) + "msxml.xml")
IF !EMPTY(oXML.ParseError.reason)
    RETURN .F.
ENDIF

*** Root element - Note 1 = first document entry
oOrders = oXML.ChildNodes(1)
? oOrders.NodeName

*** Elements are 0 based - get first order
oOrder = oOrders.ChildNodes(0)
? oOrder.NodeName

*** Select the order total
oOrderTotal = oOrder.SelectSingleNode("OrderTotal")
? "Order Total: " + oOrderTotal.Text
? "Order Date: " + oOrder.SelectSingleNode("OrderDate").Text

? "Customer: " + oOrder.SelectSingleNode("Customer").;
                      SelectSingleNode("name").Text

*** Get the Detail record
oDetailRec = oOrder.SelectSingleNode("Detail")
* ? oDetailRec.Text

*** Select the selection of Items
oItems = oDetailRec.SelectNodes("item")

*** Print all of the descriptions
FOR EACH oItem IN oItems
   ? "    " + oItem.SelectSingleNode("desc").text
ENDFOR

RETURN
```

One of the things you need to watch out for with the DOM version is that nodes are always treated as individual objects even if those objects have subnodes. This is in contrast to typical behavior of Collection objects in the MSXML control, so it's easy to get tripped up. You can use the ChildNodes collection to step into the lower branch, but unlike a collection, ChildNodes supports only a numeric index. In order to use named index keys into the child nodes, you need to select the node in question and then use its SelectSingleNode or SelectNodes with a character value to get a reference to either a single node or a collection of nodes if more than one is available.

This is legal:

```
oOrders.ChildNodes(0).SelectSingleNode("OrderDate")
```

This is not:

```
oOrders.ChildNodes.SelectSingleNode("OrderDate")
```

Although the syntax is a little more complex and you'll typically end up creating all the node objects along the way to drill down, you'll get used to this syntax. It turns out that it's more flexible in getting exactly what you need from an XML document.

Direct object access is very nice, and you can loop through the collections as well. To loop through the Guest XML with the unique row keys shown above, use the following code:

```
CLEAR
oXML = CREATEOBJECT("Microsoft.xmlDom")
oXML.Async = .F.

oXML.Load(FULLPATH(CURDIR()) + "CursorToXML.xml")
IF !EMPTY(oXML.ParseError.reason)
    RETURN .F.
ENDIF

*** Root element - Note 1 = first document entry
oGuests = oXML.ChildNodes(1)
? oGuests.NodeName

*** Look for an individual row by the PK written
oGuest = oGuests.SelectSingleNode("N404WQYS")
? oGuest.SelectSingleNode("name").Text
? oGuest.SelectSingleNode("message").Text

oGuest = .F.

*** Now display all of them in a loop
FOR EACH oGuest IN oGuests.ChildNodes
    ? oGuest.SelectSingleNode("name").Text
    ? oGuest.SelectSingleNode("message").Text
    ?
ENDFOR

RETURN
```

I've only scratched the surface of what you can do with the XML parser, though I suspect the majority of its functionality is covered here—namely it's used to parse output. You can also use the object model to create XML documents. Frankly, I haven't had a chance to use this because in most scenarios my data is stored in objects or flat file layouts where it's easy enough and faster to generate the XML directly from code or using some of the wwXML object methods. But if you're building complex documents that are deeply hierarchical or that require complex DTD and attribute values, it might make good sense to use the parser to build your XML document.

Once loaded, the parser maintains its own XML document, so any files or URLs that the document loaded from can be deleted or released. When you're building a document or manipulating it via the parser, you can retrieve the entire document XML with the following code:

```
oXML = CREATEOBJECT("Microsoft.XMLDOM")
… Create or manipulate your document
lcXML = oXML.XML
```

XML can be loaded either from a local file or a URL on the Internet with the Load method:

```
oXML.Load(FULLPATH(CURDIR()) + "msxml.xml")
oXML.Load("http://www.west-wind.com/somepage.xml")
```

You can also use the LoadXML method, which can accept XML as string into the document:

```
lcXML = FILETOSTR("SomeFile.xml")
oXML.LoadXML(lcXML)
```

XML summary
XML is promising technology for Web applications and standalone applications alike. Think of XML as a data transfer mechanism rather than as a database or even a storage mechanism. XML has many uses, but for Web applications the primary use will likely be to provide data-driven content to non-browser applications, where XML is used as the messaging protocol to transfer data over the wire. XML can also be used in HTML documents with the latest version 5.0 browsers, which feature built-in XML support. This will only further facilitate the process of separating the HTML display mechanism from the content in the future, and simplify the process of retrieving data from the Web in a more meaningful manner.

We're at the very beginning of the XML standard process, but don't be surprised to see many new industry-specific XML formats springing up that will facilitate the process of sharing data in the near future. There's been a lot of hype about XML recently, and it's a little difficult to see the true value of this technology above all the banter. Whenever you think about providing data to other applications, or even your own application, whether it's over the Web or in one object calling another in your own application, give some thought to whether a standard message format in XML wouldn't make your application more flexible and extensible in the future.

XML Pros
- XML is becoming a widely used standard.
- It's text based and it's easy to create XML markup.
- It has a self-describing data format.
- It's great for metadata as well as a common shared data exchange format.
- 5.0 browsers will support XML natively.

XML Cons
- Tag-based format makes document size much bigger than data alone.
- XML standards are just now complete—tools are not yet officially available but will be shortly (IE 5 timeframe).

Other Web Application Tools

This book has discussed Web development technologies that are provided by Microsoft. But realize that third-party products and tools are available that provide similar functionality—and sometimes provide functionality not available in Microsoft products. For FoxPro development I want to mention two popular tools that you might want to take a look at, along with some links to a couple of other Fox-based tools that I have no experience with.

Cold Fusion

Cold Fusion is one of the oldest players in the Web development tools arena. These guys were around from the very beginning and were one of the first to provide database functionality in Web applications. Cold Fusion is now owned by Allaire, which is a company dedicated to providing quality tools that compete very closely with Microsoft's. I personally have not worked much with Cold Fusion; however, I have heard many positive comments from those who have used it. In particular, Allaire is very customer oriented, so unlike Microsoft, problems are examined and responded to in a timely manner. The result of this customer service has also been a very stable product, again in sharp contrast with many of the Microsoft tools, which often get released too early with buggy versions that are updated only in slipstream updates that you might not even know about.

The following review of features was kindly provided by Rod Paddock of Dashpoint Software. Rod has used Cold Fusion on several sizable projects.

Cold Fusion is a Web development tool that works and behaves in a manner similar to Active Server Pages from Microsoft. Cold Fusion consists of two different products: Cold Fusion Studio and Cold Fusion Server. Cold Fusion Server is an Integrated Development Environment (see **Figure 12.2**) used to develop and manage Web sites. Cold Fusion Server is a set of server-side applications. Some of the features of each product are as follows:

Cold Fusion Studio
- HTML shortcuts and wizards
- IntelliSense
- HTML validation

- Server-side debugging
- Color codes syntax highlighting
- Web project management
- Integration with version control

Cold Fusion Server
- Server-side processing of Web code
- Support for POP, SMTP and LDAP
- Integration with ODBC and OLE DB
- Automatic load balancing and server clustering
- Support for Windows NT and Sun-OS (Linux coming soon)

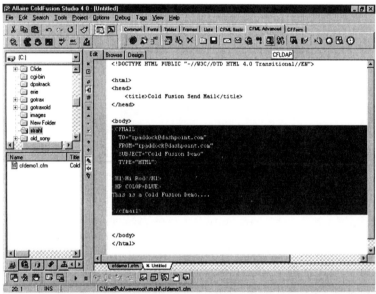

Figure 12.2. *Cold Fusion Studio consists of what was formerly the HomeSite editor with some integration into the Cold Fusion server environment. This is similar to the way Visual InterDev is tied to Active Server Pages, but unlike VID, Cold Fusion Studio is actually fast enough to use efficiently.*

How does it work?

Much like Active Server Pages (ASP) from Microsoft, Cold Fusion processes code on a Web server and returns regular HTML to a Web browser. This application differs from ASP in that ASP is a purely script-based coding metaphor, where Cold Fusion is a TAG-based metaphor. Cold Fusion utilizes a set of custom tags known as the Cold Fusion Markup Language (CFML). CFML consists of tags that can be used to add programming logic to your Web applications. The CFML code that you add to your pages is processed on the Web server and returns HTML to the client's browser. To better understand Cold Fusion, let's take a look at how it works.

Using Cold Fusion to access data

One of Cold Fusion's primary capabilities is data access. Cold Fusion provides a set of tags that can be used to run queries against databases found on your Web server. The following example demonstrates using Cold Fusion to query the Authors table from the SQL Server Pubs database:

```
<CFQUERY DATASOURCE="pubs" NAME="get_authors" username="sa" password="">
  SELECT *
    FROM Authors
    ORDER BY au_lname, au_fname
</cfquery>

<TABLE BORDER="2">
<TR><TH COLSPAN="2">Cold Fusion Demo</th></tr>
<CFOUTPUT QUERY="get_authors">
  <TR>
       <TD>#au_lname#</td>
       <TD>#au_lname#</td>
  </tr>
</cfoutput>
</table>
```

 To run this example you will need an ODBC System DSN configured for the Pubs database.

The above example uses a number of CFML tags and constructs. The first encountered tag is CFQUERY, which is used to send a query to an ODBC data source. The above example specifies four parameters:

- DATASOURCE—the System ODBC data source set up on the Web server
- NAME—represents the name of the result set returned
- USERNAME—the user name to use when logging into a database (optional)
- PASSWORD—the password to use when logging into a database

The second CFML tag is CFOUTPUT, which is used to scan through result sets returned by a CFQUERY tag (like the SCAN/ENDSCAN construct of VFP). To specify a result set to scan, use the QUERY parameter. This parameter corresponds to the NAME parameter specified in the CFQUERY tag.

The last CFML construct utilized is ##. You use the ## delimiters to output data into the CFML stream. In the above example, the *au_lname* and *au_fname* columns are returned into the HTML document.

Using Cold Fusion to send e-mail

One of the other benefits of Cold Fusion is its simple integration with e-mail. You can send e-mail from Cold Fusion Server using the CFMAIL tag. You need to first configure your server application to point at an e-mail server. Do this in the Cold Fusion Administrator program, where you specify the SMTP server IP address or domain name, port, and timeout. After configuring your server, you can use the CFMAIL tag to send e-mail. The following example shows how to send e-mail formatted as HTML:

```
<CFMAIL
  TO="rpaddock@dashpoint.com"
  FROM="rpaddock@dashpoint.com"
  SUBJECT="Cold Fusion Demo"
  TYPE="HTML">

<H1>Hi Rod</H1>
<HR COLOR=BLUE>
This is a Cold Fusion Demo....

</cfmail>
```

Cold Fusion Summary
Hopefully from the brief examples above, you can see that Cold Fusion's tag-based metaphor makes data access fairly simple without a lot of code. For more information about Cold Fusion, take a look at www.allaire.com. There are a number of resources available and demos that you can download.

West Wind Web Connection
Web Connection was created by my company, West Wind Technologies, before Microsoft came out with a real Web development strategy. This tool's focus has been to use Visual FoxPro for developing Web applications from start to finish. Over the years the tool has updated its technology from its CGI origins to embrace ISAPI, COM and the Microsoft Enterprise Platform, all the while maintaining the Fox-centric focus—this is a tool geared squarely to those who are more comfortable with Visual FoxPro and want to take advantage of its functionality in its fullest.

Web Connection is a complete Web solution that includes just about everything a developer needs for building Web apps with Visual FoxPro. It starts with a fully automated installation that properly configures your Web server for operation of the product, so no manual configuration is required to get started. Tools allow you to add more configurations programmatically, so applications you build can include their own configuration code.

Architecturally, Web Connection is fairly similar to FoxISAPI, which means it uses an ISAPI extension communicating over COM with a Visual FoxPro server. The difference between it and FoxISAPI is that Web Connection provides a solid framework on the Web Connection end to simplify processing incoming requests and handle the HTML generation. The framework extends from the ISAPI extension's administration features, which include full control over all servers loaded, unloading and reloading servers, automatic crash recovery if a VFP server GPFs or hangs, hot swapping of executable code, error logging, request logging and summaries. On the FoxPro end, server operation is encapsulated into four easy-to-use objects that manage the server, the incoming request, the outgoing response and the currently running request process. I introduced the very basics of this functionality in Chapter 5, but Web Connection goes far beyond the basic functionality in providing a full server environment for managing the actual Web communications between the Fox app and the Web server, and supplying numerous tools to facilitate the process of creating Web output quickly.

One of the major strengths of Web Connection is its ability to run in a non-COM environment while debugging applications. Unlike FoxISAPI, which works only with COM objects called from the Web server, Web Connection can run as a standalone application that is started from the command window. This makes for much easier debugging of applications because you can interactively run live Web requests right inside Visual FoxPro. You can even debug Web Connection scripts interactively with Visual FoxPro. Typically, you'll develop applications right inside Visual FoxPro—coding, testing and debugging there—and then recompile the application into a COM object that actually runs on the server. A single switch in a header file and a recompile takes care of switching the server into the appropriate runtime mode.

Web Connection also provides support for templates, scripting, PDF reports, DHTML form rendering, basic charting, SMTP e-mail support, FTP support, support for building distributed applications over HTTP, XML output and much more. If all this sounds familiar from this book, you're right—I've shared a good chunk of the basic technology in this book generically. Web Connection includes this same technology and wraps it tightly into a full Web application framework for Visual FoxPro.

For more information, visit www.west-wind.com/WebConnection.asp.

Other FoxPro tools

A couple of other tools are available that work directly with Visual FoxPro as well. I have no experience with these products so I'm not going to discuss their feature sets. Many applications run FoxPro code with these tools as well. Visit the links to the respective Web sites to decide for yourself whether these tools have features that you need.

FoxWeb

CGI-based Web interface for Visual FoxPro: www.FoxWeb.com

X-Works

CGI-based Web interface for Visual FoxPro and FoxPro 2.x and Visual Basic: www.x-works.com

How to Download Source Code, Sample Files, And .CHM files

Several additional resources are available to you from Hentzenwerke Publishing's website. They include: source code referred to in the book, sample data sets, and the .CHM file of the entire book.

To download the files:

1. Go to our website:

   www.hentzenwerke.com

2. Click on **Books by Hentzenwerke Publishing**

3. Click on
   Download Pre-release Versions or Source Code and Final .CHM File

4. Follow the prompts on the screen.

As a protection to your investment (and ours!), there is a password scheme in place to prevent the downloading of these files without purchasing the book.

**You will need to have the book with you
in order to download the files!**

Note: the .CHM file is covered by the same copyright laws as the printed book. Reproduction and/or distribution of the .CHM file is prohibited.

About the Author

Rick Strahl is well known for his Internet and component development expertise with Microsoft technologies, and Visual FoxPro in particular. He is the owner of West Wind Technologies in Maui, Hawaii, and is the author of several popular Visual FoxPro Web development tools including West Wind Web Connection, West Wind Internet Protocols and West Wind HTML Help Builder. He also co-authored Visual WebBuilder with Markus Egger of EPS Software.

Rick is actively involved in the FoxPro community and frequently publishes articles for *FoxPro Advisor* and *FoxTalk*. His West Wind Web site also contains a number of frequently updated development white papers on cutting-edge Web and COM technologies. He's been a featured speaker at many recent FoxPro developer conferences, including the last three years at Microsoft Visual FoxPro DevCon, and at a number of user groups throughout the United States. Rick has been a Microsoft MVP for the last five years.

Rick has been involved with Internet development for the last four years and has built a number of very visible, high-volume Internet applications, including the much publicized Surplus Direct (now Egghead) commerce and auction sites. He has acted as an advisor for the Microsoft Visual FoxPro development team on issues related to building large-scale applications, both for the Web and the Enterprise.